FRE

vol. 1

KHAN Original

Yi DongEun ·Yu Chung

ice
Kunion

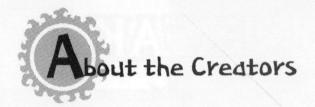

About the Creators

Writer : Dong-Eun Yi
- Debuted with <Freak> in year 2004.
- Birth sign : Aquarius
- Wish : World Peace!

Artist : Chung Yu
- Debuted with <Leagueveda> in year 2002.
- Birth sign : Libra
- Wish : To Conquer the World!

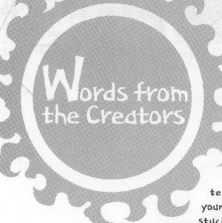

Words from the Creators

Thanks to my parents, who took me in, fed me, and gave me a room to sleep in despite my long-term unemployment; to my younger sibling, who continually stuck knives in my back; to my friends, who bought me food and drinks when I was jobless; to my girlfriend, who cheered me on from the sidelines with her endless compliments for my style and ability; to my editor, who gave both compliments (about a nano-particle's worth) and whippings; and to all my fellow sopsn colleagues, whom I've known for the last 10 years, I thank you all. (I think everyone would agree this is a pretty good book when you consider that it's merely the first steps of a toddler!)

- Dong-Eun Yi

I want to thank everyone for their help during my work on <Freak>.
My family deserves the biggest thanks. I am so, so grateful to you all, to the point of tears—thank you. Someday I will repay you for everything.
I also want to thank Soo-Young Park and Mir Choi, as well as Honey, our editor and team leader.
And thanks to Dong-Eun for writing a fun story.

- Chung Yu

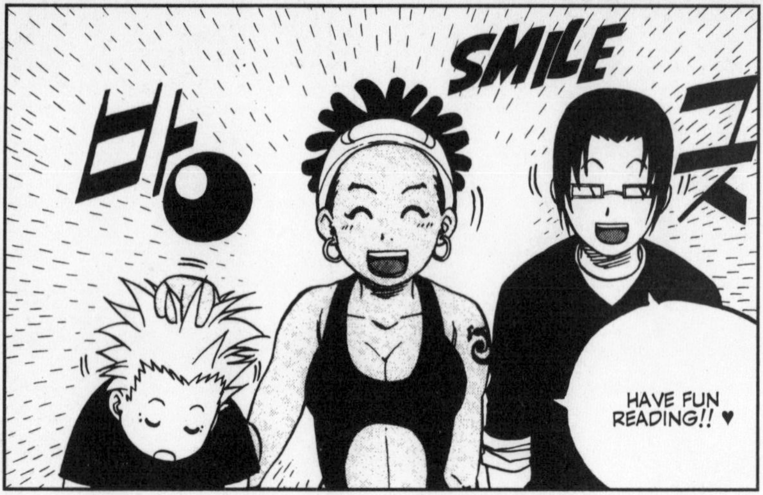
SMILE
HAVE FUN READING!! ♥

CONTENTS

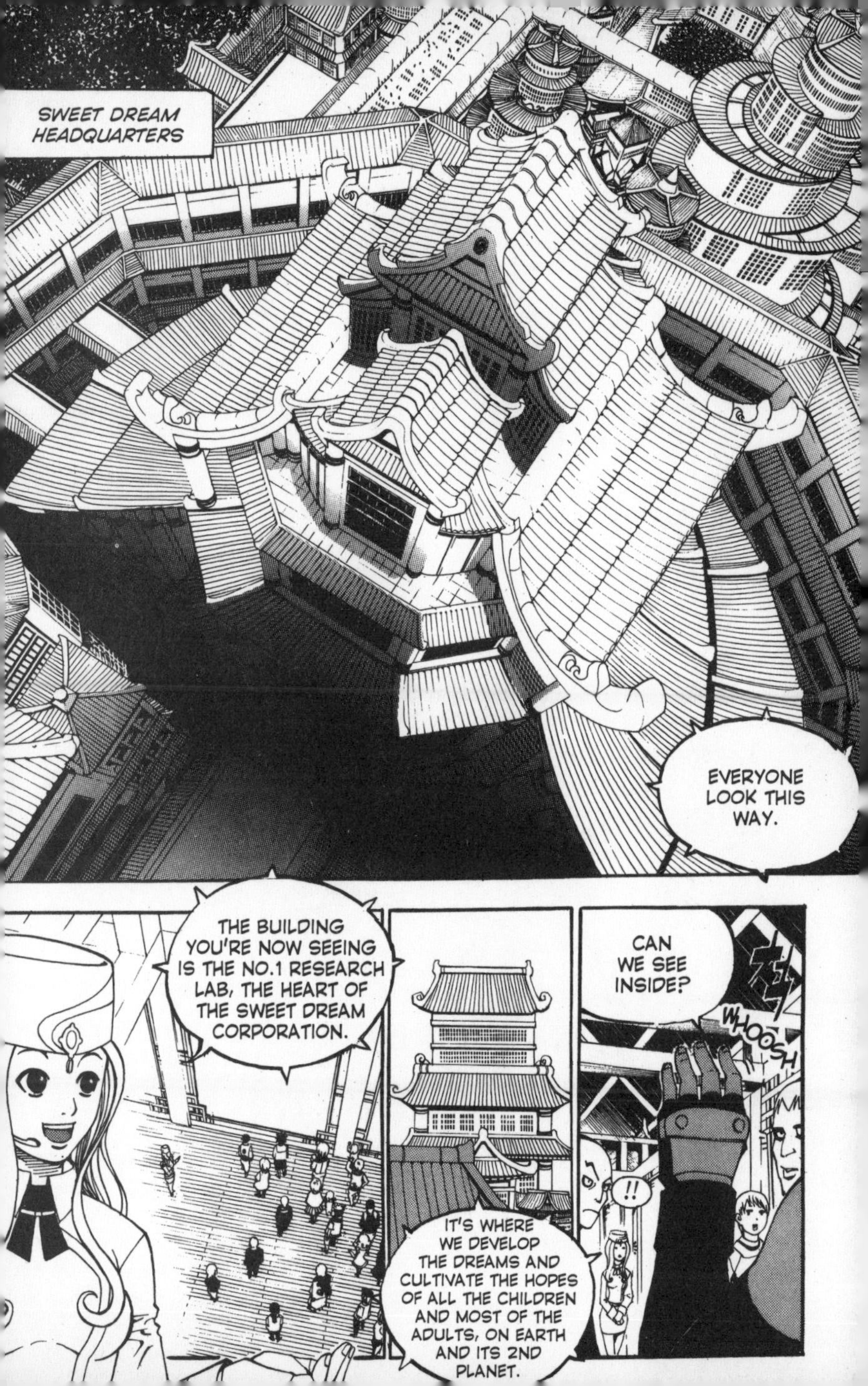
SWEET DREAM HEADQUARTERS
EVERYONE LOOK THIS WAY.
THE BUILDING YOU'RE NOW SEEING IS THE NO.1 RESEARCH LAB, THE HEART OF THE SWEET DREAM CORPORATION.
IT'S WHERE WE DEVELOP THE DREAMS AND CULTIVATE THE HOPES OF ALL THE CHILDREN AND MOST OF THE ADULTS, ON EARTH AND ITS 2ND PLANET.
CAN WE SEE INSIDE?
WHOOSH
!!

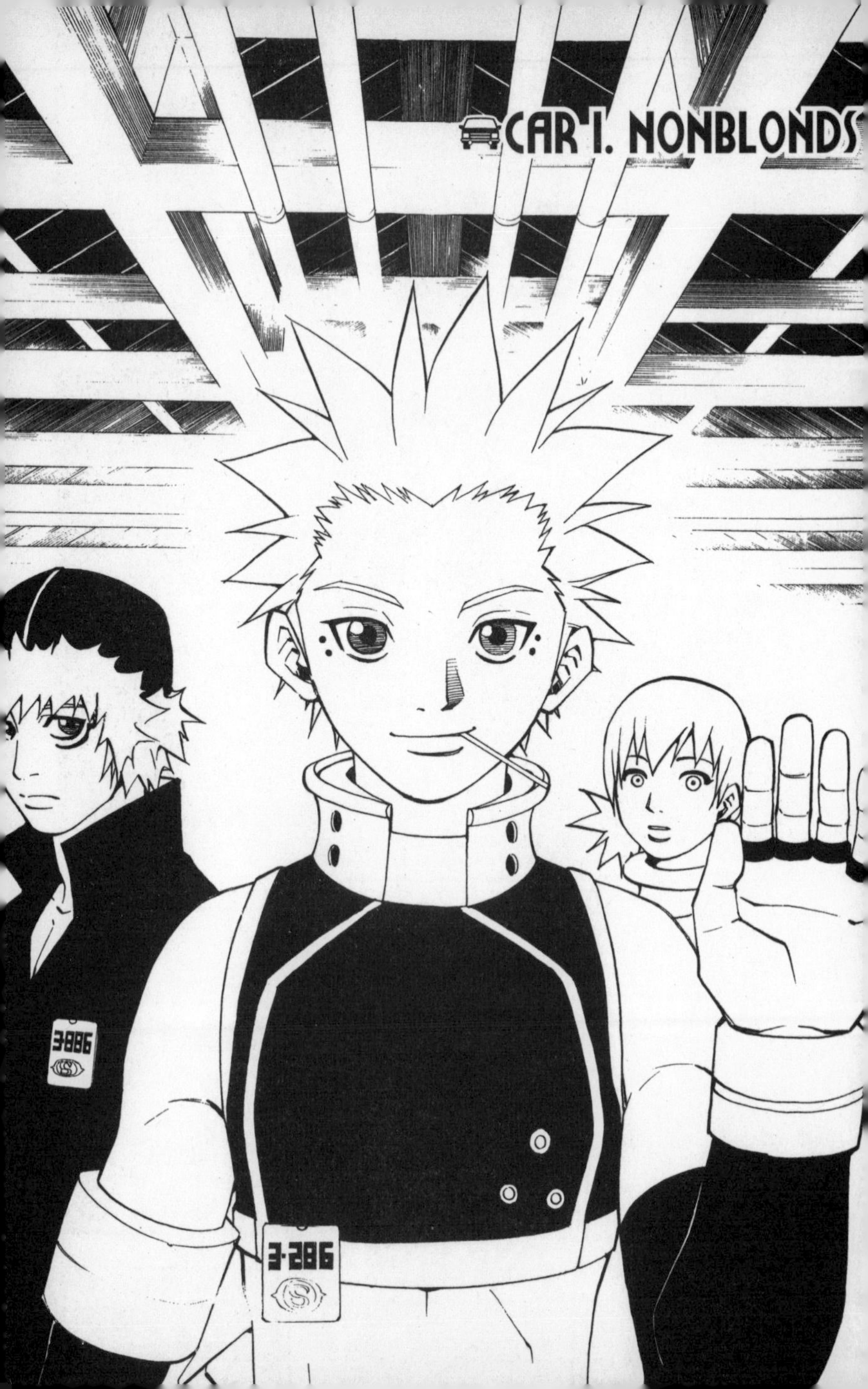
CAR 1. NONBLONDS
3-886
3-286

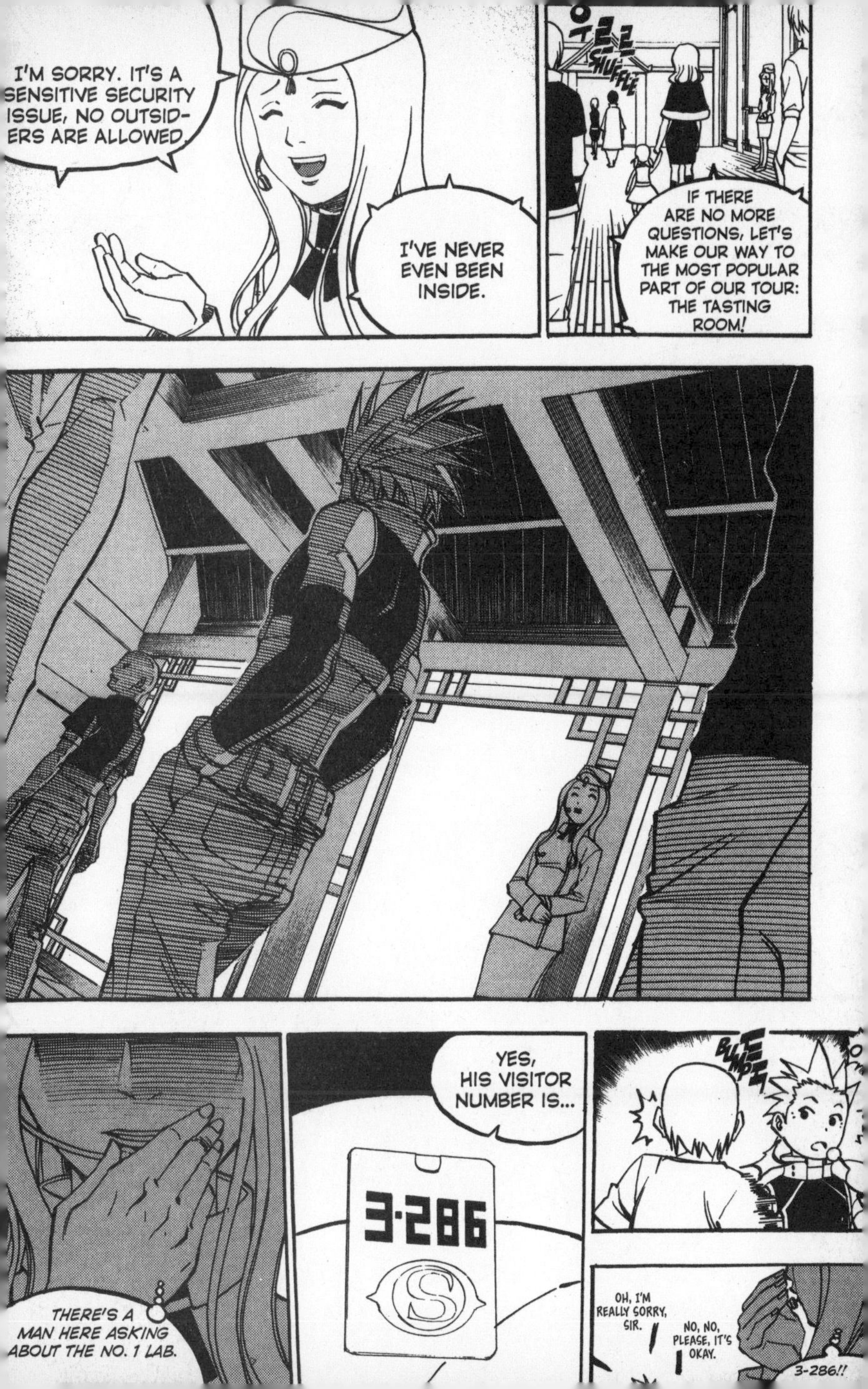
I'M SORRY. IT'S A SENSITIVE SECURITY ISSUE, NO OUTSIDERS ARE ALLOWED.
I'VE NEVER EVEN BEEN INSIDE.
SHUFFLE
IF THERE ARE NO MORE QUESTIONS, LET'S MAKE OUR WAY TO THE MOST POPULAR PART OF OUR TOUR: THE TASTING ROOM!
THERE'S A MAN HERE ASKING ABOUT THE NO. 1 LAB.
YES, HIS VISITOR NUMBER IS...
3·286
BUMP
OH, I'M REALLY SORRY, SIR.
NO, NO, PLEASE, IT'S OKAY.
3-286!!

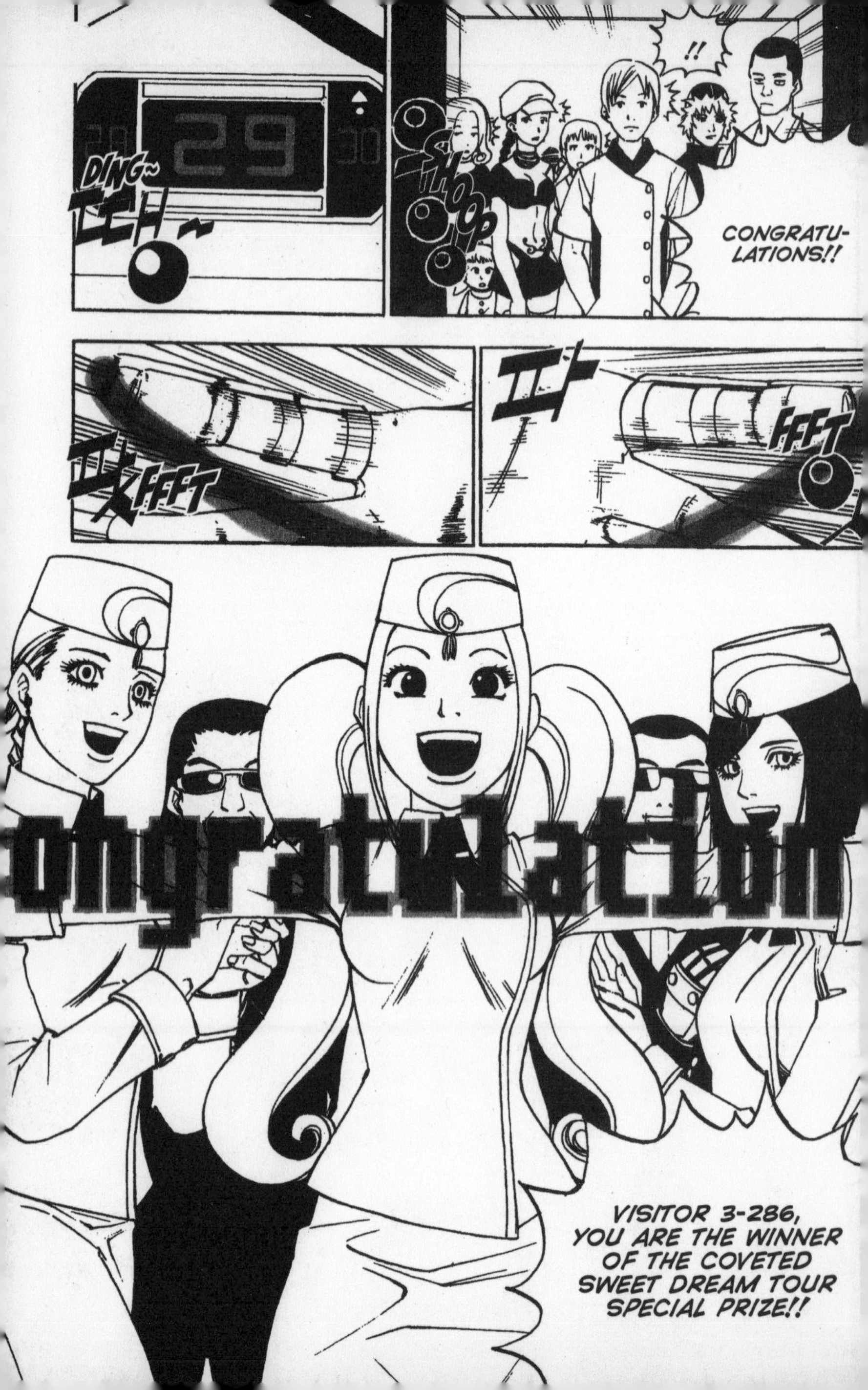
DING~
SHOOOP
!!
CONGRATU-
LATIONS!!
FFFT
FFFT
VISITOR 3-286,
YOU ARE THE WINNER
OF THE COVETED
SWEET DREAM TOUR
SPECIAL PRIZE!!

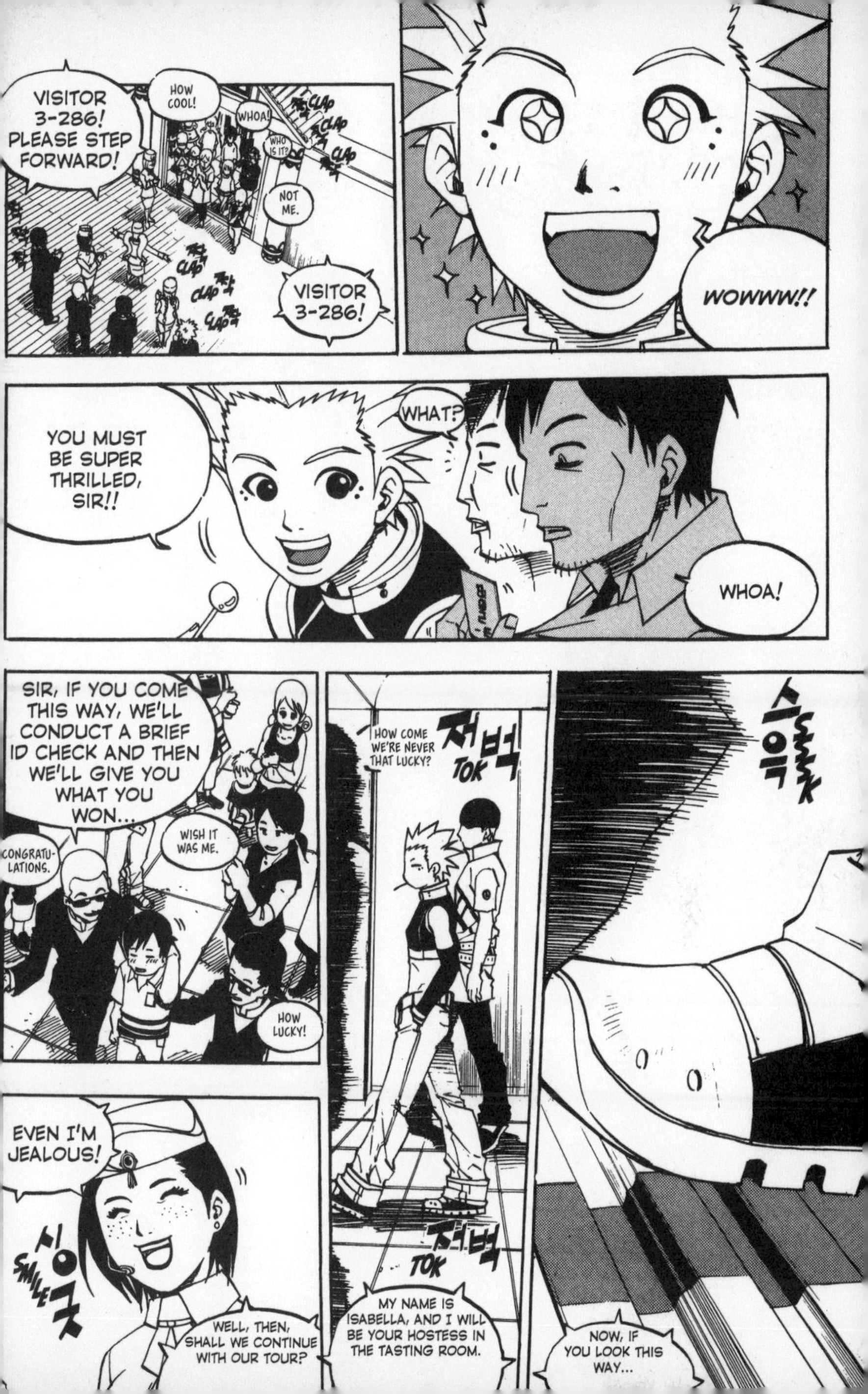
VISITOR 3-286! PLEASE STEP FORWARD!
HOW COOL!
CLAP CLAP CLAP
WHOA!
WHO IS IT?
NOT ME.
CLAP CLAP CLAP
VISITOR 3-286!
WOWWW!!
YOU MUST BE SUPER THRILLED, SIR!!
WHAT?
WHOA!
SIR, IF YOU COME THIS WAY, WE'LL CONDUCT A BRIEF ID CHECK AND THEN WE'LL GIVE YOU WHAT YOU WON...
CONGRATULATIONS.
WISH IT WAS ME.
HOW LUCKY!
EVEN I'M JEALOUS!
SMILE
WELL, THEN, SHALL WE CONTINUE WITH OUR TOUR?
HOW COME WE'RE NEVER THAT LUCKY?
TOK
TOK
MY NAME IS ISABELLA, AND I WILL BE YOUR HOSTESS IN THE TASTING ROOM.
NOW, IF YOU LOOK THIS WAY...

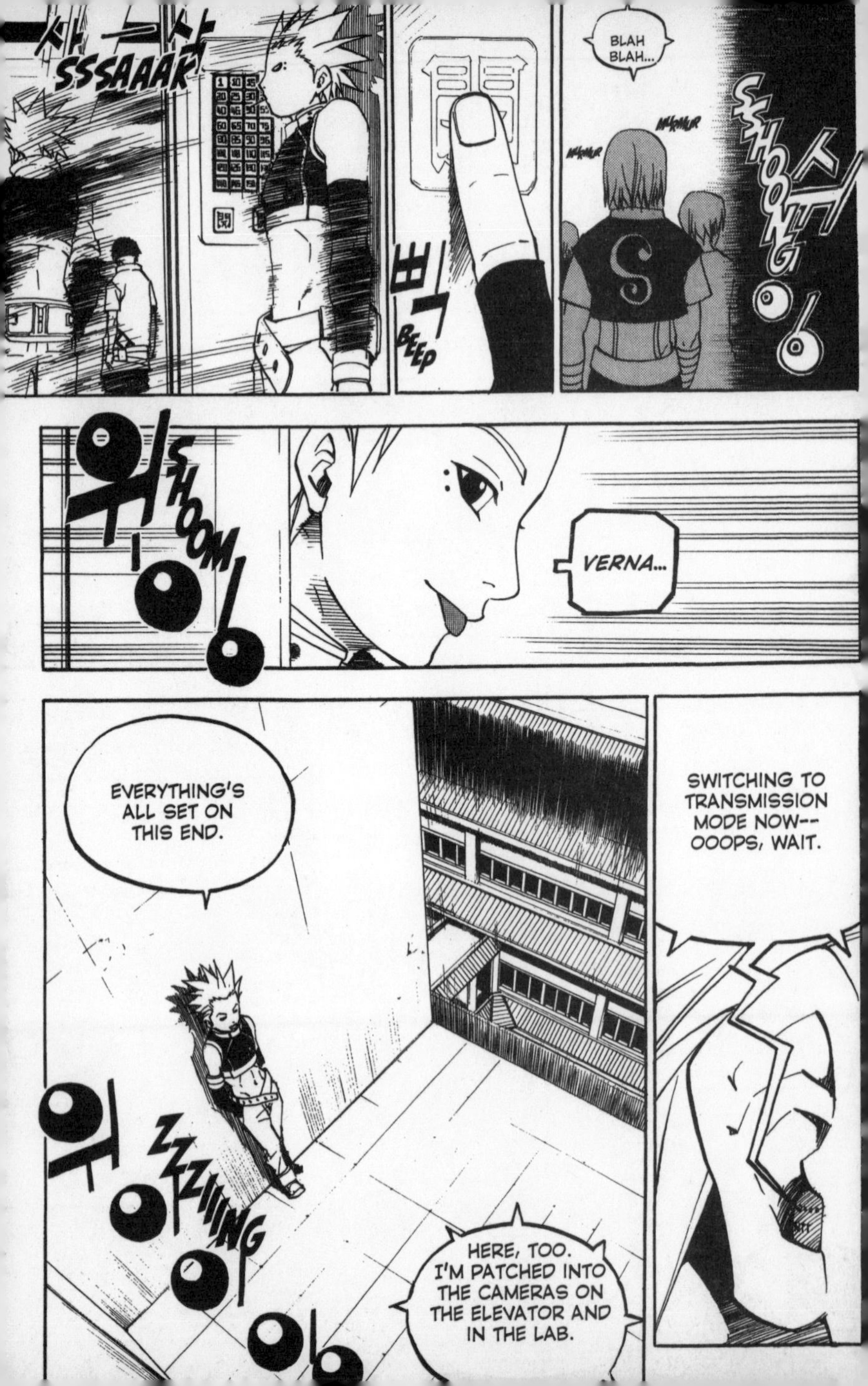

SSSAAAK!
BEEP
BLAH BLAH...
SHOONG
SHOOM
VERNA...
EVERYTHING'S ALL SET ON THIS END.
ZZZIIING
HERE, TOO. I'M PATCHED INTO THE CAMERAS ON THE ELEVATOR AND IN THE LAB.
SWITCHING TO TRANSMISSION MODE NOW-- OOOPS, WAIT.

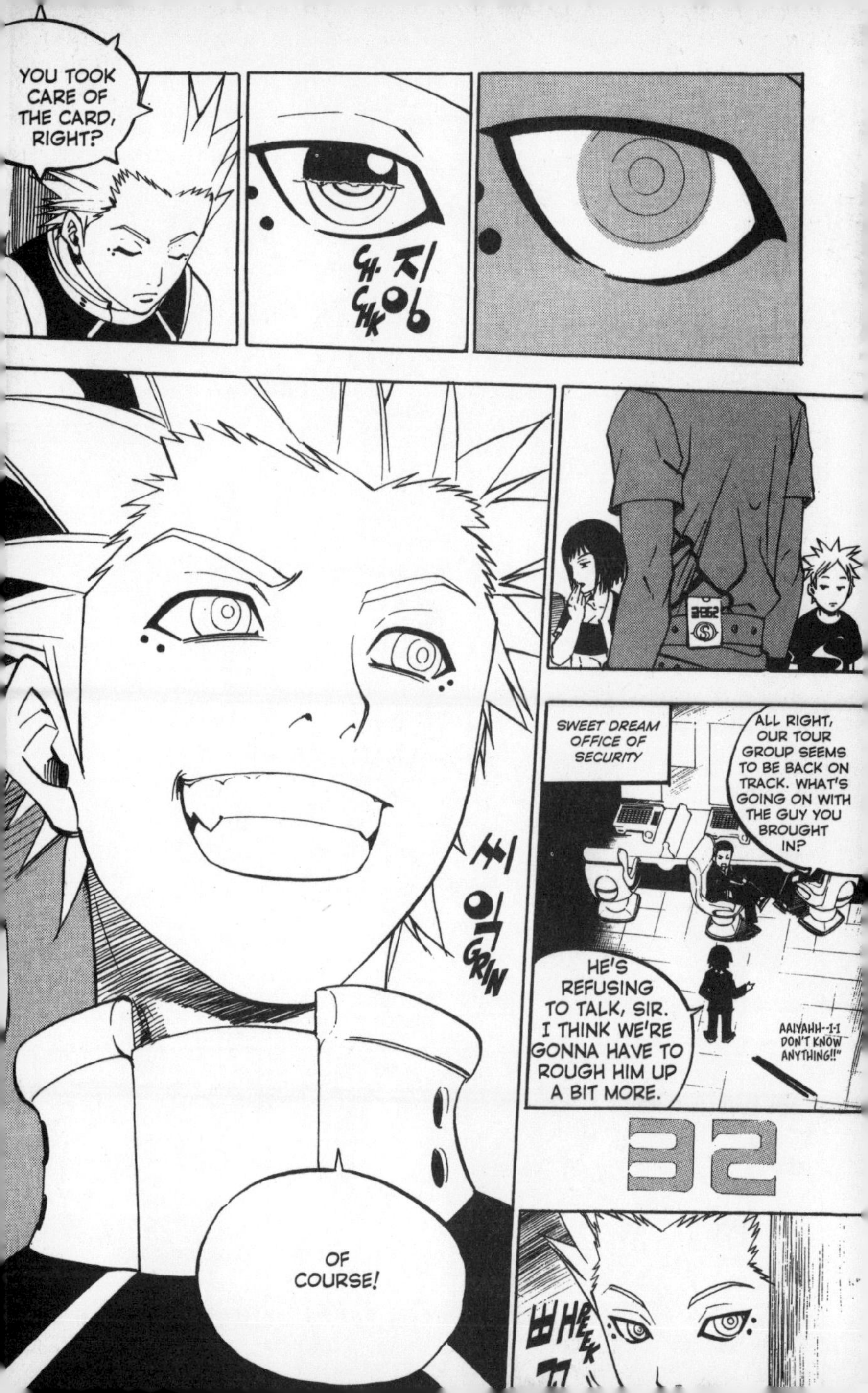
YOU TOOK CARE OF THE CARD, RIGHT?
CH-CHK
GRIN
OF COURSE!
SWEET DREAM OFFICE OF SECURITY
ALL RIGHT, OUR TOUR GROUP SEEMS TO BE BACK ON TRACK. WHAT'S GOING ON WITH THE GUY YOU BROUGHT IN?
HE'S REFUSING TO TALK, SIR. I THINK WE'RE GONNA HAVE TO ROUGH HIM UP A BIT MORE.
AAIYAHH--I-I DON'T KNOW ANYTHING!!"
32
HEEK

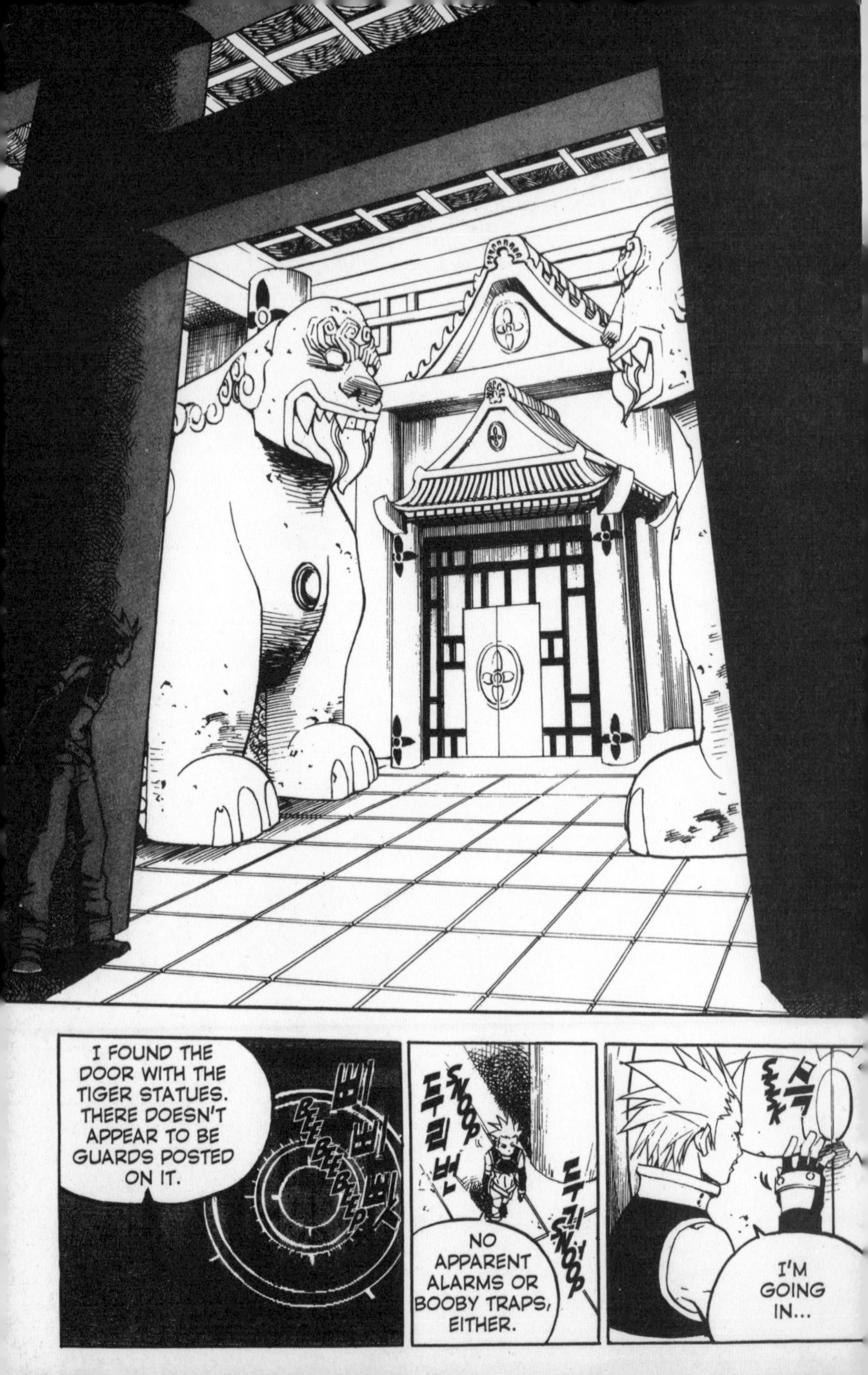
I FOUND THE DOOR WITH THE TIGER STATUES. THERE DOESN'T APPEAR TO BE GUARDS POSTED ON IT.
삐삐삑
BEEBEEBEEP
두리번
SNOOP
NO APPARENT ALARMS OR BOOBY TRAPS, EITHER.
두리
SNOOP
I'M GOING IN...

YAAHH...!

COME IN! THE SWEET DREAM CORPORATION WELCOMES YOU TO THE NO. 1 RESEARCH LAB!

!!

CREEEAAAKK

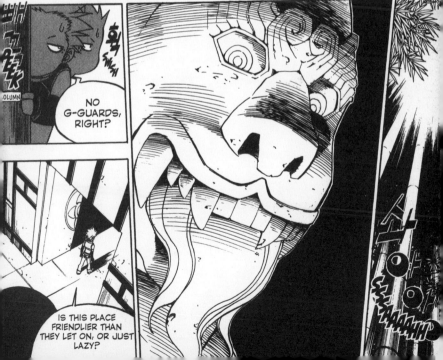

NO G-GUARDS, RIGHT?

IS THIS PLACE FRIENDLIER THAN THEY LET ON, OR JUST LAZY?

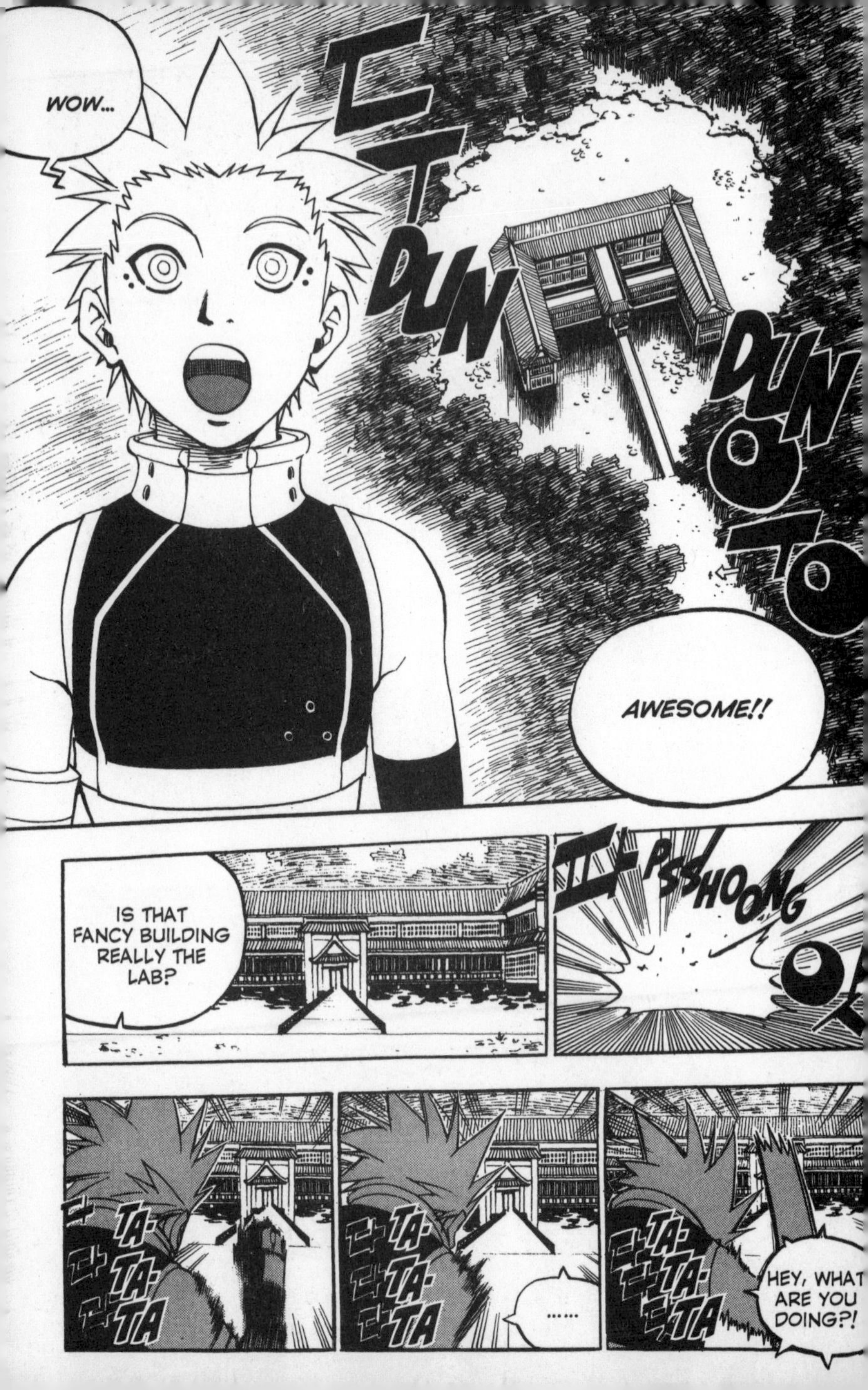
WOW...
DUN
DUN
AWESOME!!
IS THAT FANCY BUILDING REALLY THE LAB?
PSSHOONG
TA-TA-TA
TA-TA-TA
......
TA-TA-TA
HEY, WHAT ARE YOU DOING?!

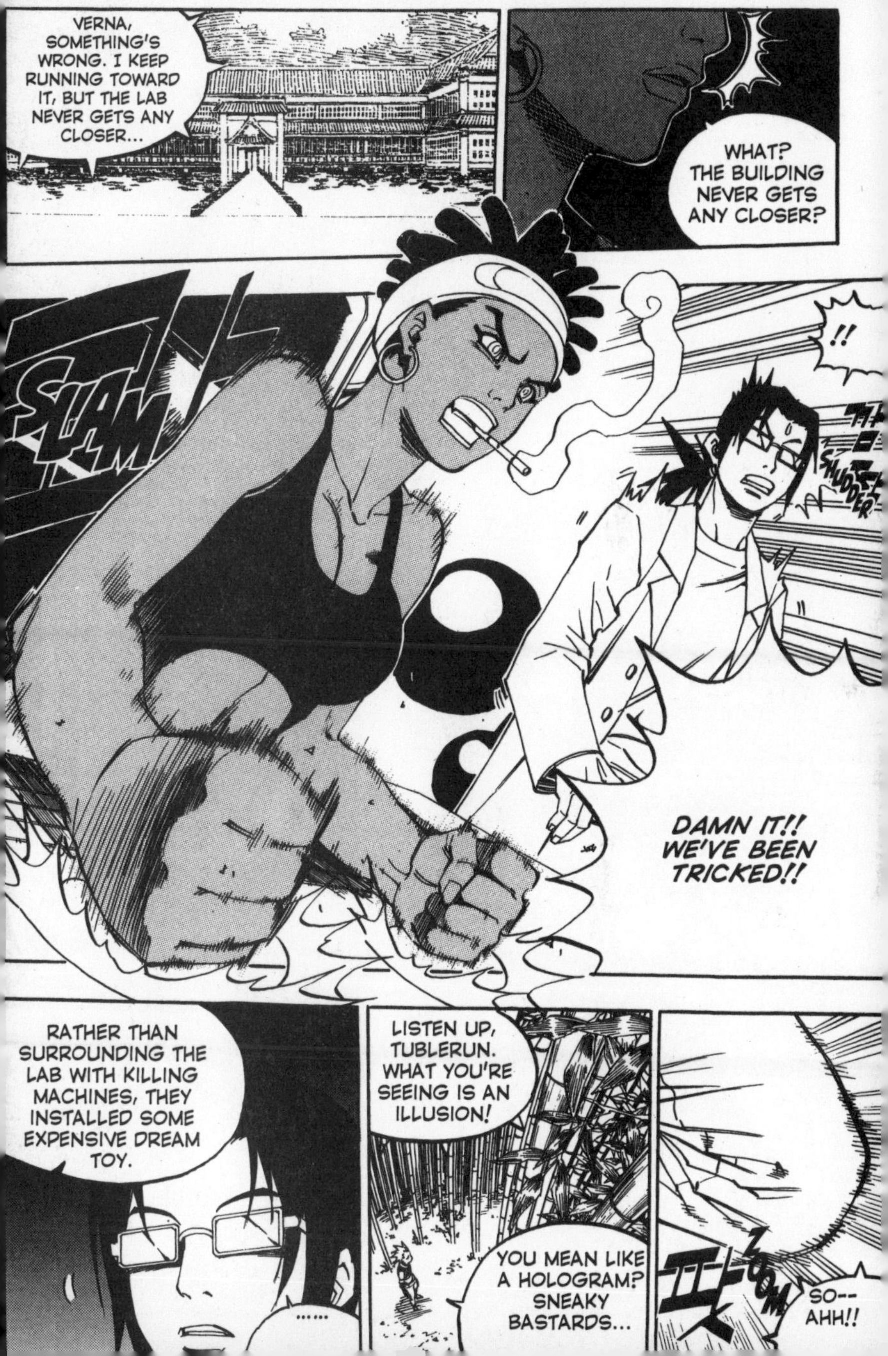

VERNA, SOMETHING'S WRONG. I KEEP RUNNING TOWARD IT, BUT THE LAB NEVER GETS ANY CLOSER...
WHAT? THE BUILDING NEVER GETS ANY CLOSER?
SLAM
!!
SHUDDER
DAMN IT!! WE'VE BEEN TRICKED!!
RATHER THAN SURROUNDING THE LAB WITH KILLING MACHINES, THEY INSTALLED SOME EXPENSIVE DREAM TOY.
......
LISTEN UP, TUBLERUN. WHAT YOU'RE SEEING IS AN ILLUSION!
YOU MEAN LIKE A HOLOGRAM? SNEAKY BASTARDS...
ZOOM
SO-- AHH!!

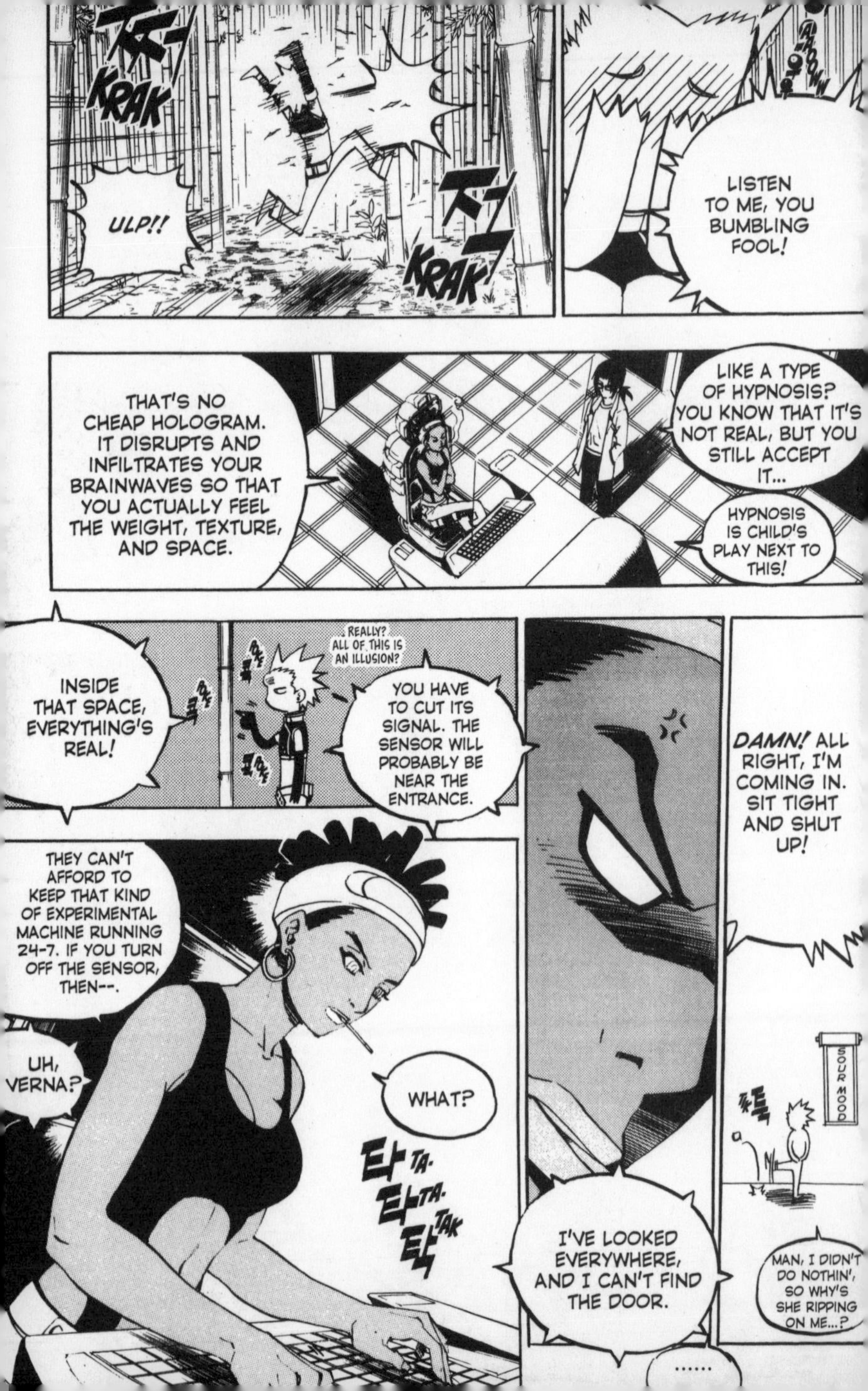
KRAK
ULP!!
KRAK
AAOOWW
LISTEN TO ME, YOU BUMBLING FOOL!
THAT'S NO CHEAP HOLOGRAM. IT DISRUPTS AND INFILTRATES YOUR BRAINWAVES SO THAT YOU ACTUALLY FEEL THE WEIGHT, TEXTURE, AND SPACE.
LIKE A TYPE OF HYPNOSIS? YOU KNOW THAT IT'S NOT REAL, BUT YOU STILL ACCEPT IT...
HYPNOSIS IS CHILD'S PLAY NEXT TO THIS!
INSIDE THAT SPACE, EVERYTHING'S REAL!
POKE
POKE
POKE
REALLY? ALL OF THIS IS AN ILLUSION?
YOU HAVE TO CUT ITS SIGNAL. THE SENSOR WILL PROBABLY BE NEAR THE ENTRANCE.
THEY CAN'T AFFORD TO KEEP THAT KIND OF EXPERIMENTAL MACHINE RUNNING 24-7. IF YOU TURN OFF THE SENSOR, THEN--.
UH, VERNA?
WHAT?
TA-TA-TAK
I'VE LOOKED EVERYWHERE, AND I CAN'T FIND THE DOOR.
......
DAMN! ALL RIGHT, I'M COMING IN. SIT TIGHT AND SHUT UP!
SOUR MOOD
MAN, I DIDN'T DO NOTHIN', SO WHY'S SHE RIPPING ON ME...?

WAIT THERE FOR 1 MINUTE, 30 SECONDS.

WIINNGG

CHCHK CHCHK

HOLD ON...

SHNNK

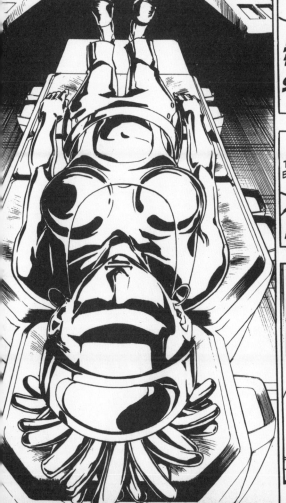

......

STARE

THAT GIRL JUMPS INTO THAT MACHINE EVERY CHANCE SHE GETS.

THERE'S NO USE PICKING A FIGHT WITH HER WHEN SHE'S ALREADY IN CYBER-CEREBRO...

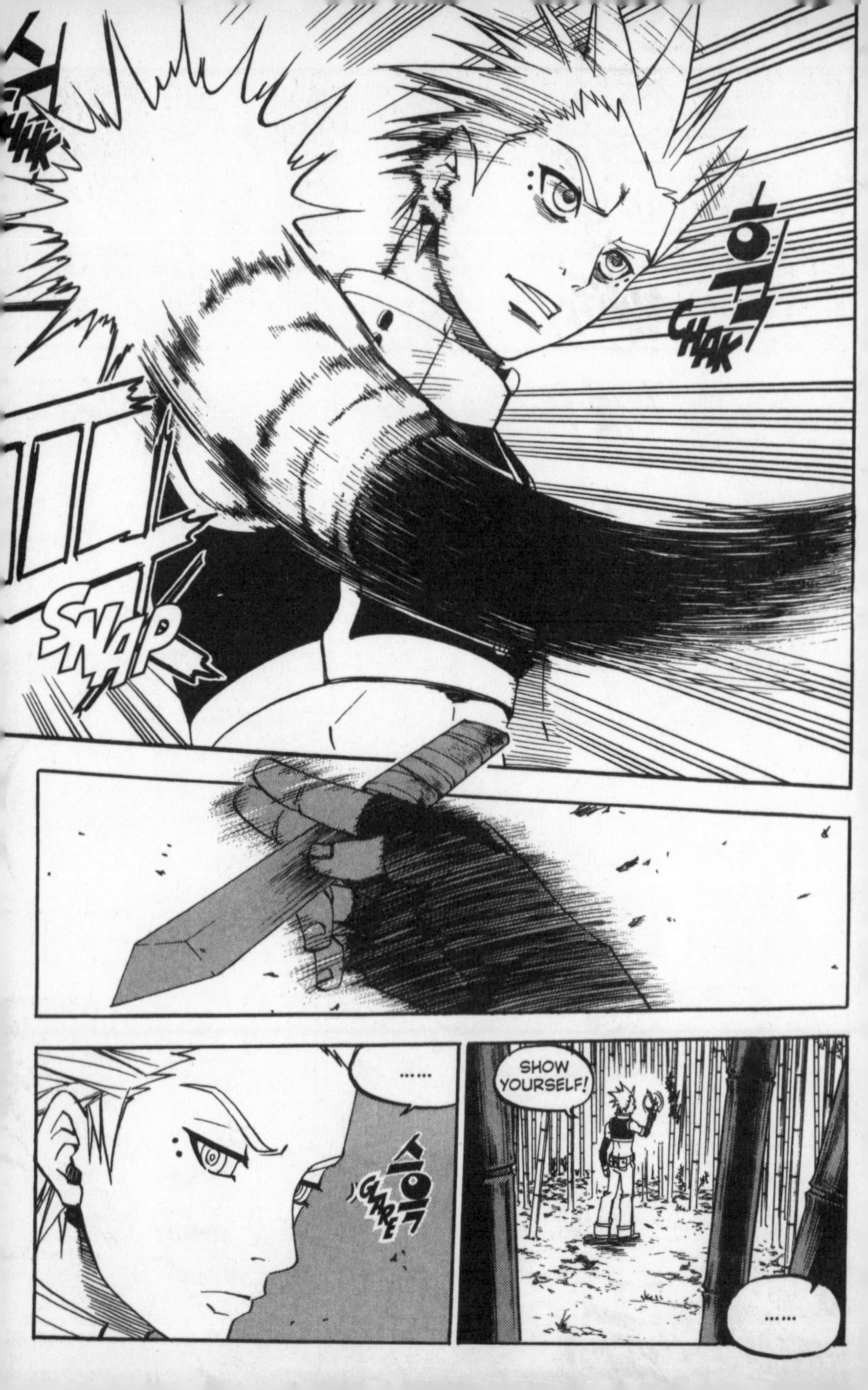
CHAK
CHAK
SNAP
......
GLARE
SHOW YOURSELF!
......

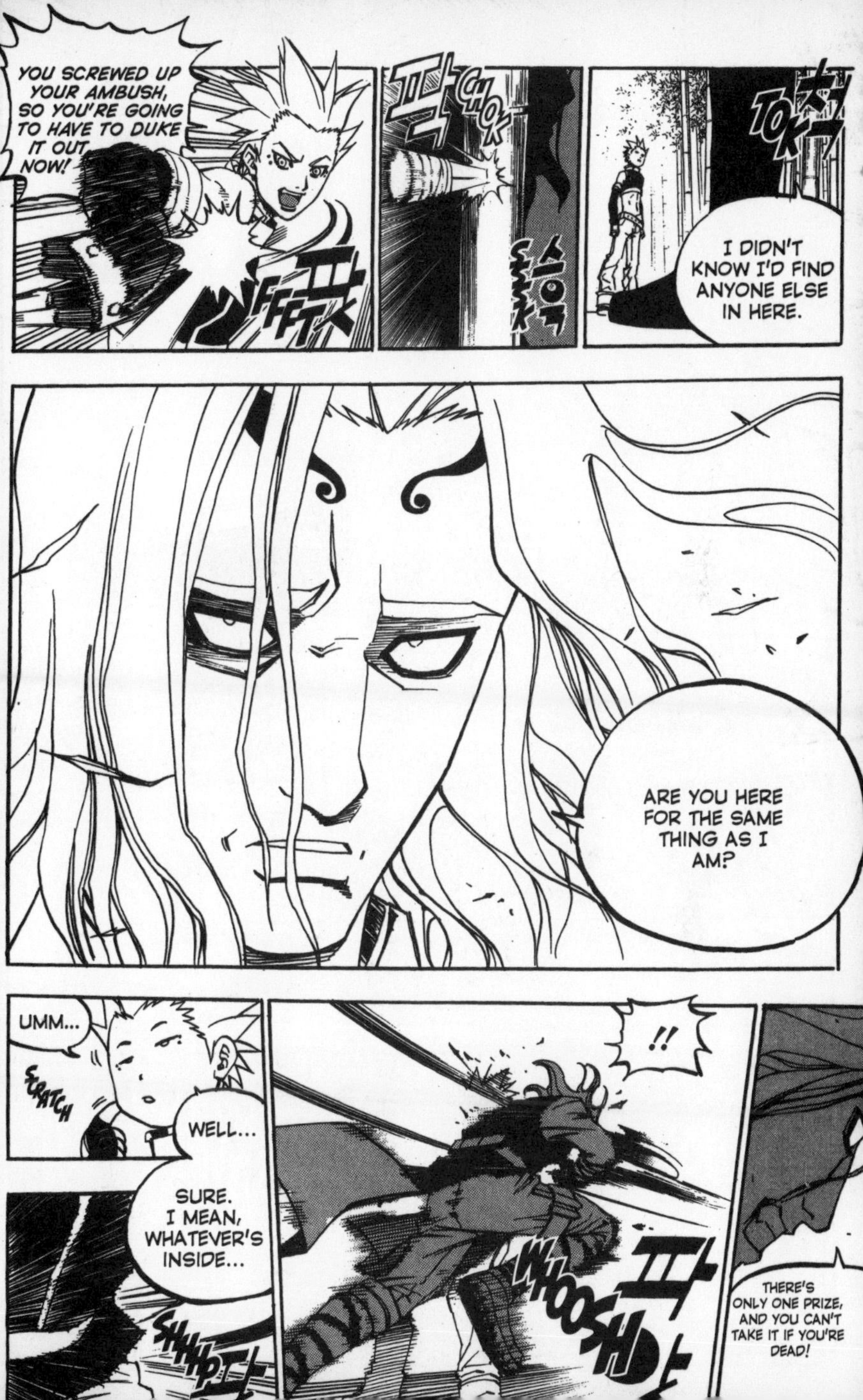
YOU SCREWED UP YOUR AMBUSH, SO YOU'RE GOING TO HAVE TO DUKE IT OUT NOW!
FFFT
CHOK
TOK
I DIDN'T KNOW I'D FIND ANYONE ELSE IN HERE.
ARE YOU HERE FOR THE SAME THING AS I AM?
UMM...
SCRATCH
WELL...
SURE. I MEAN, WHATEVER'S INSIDE...
!!
WHOOSH
THERE'S ONLY ONE PRIZE, AND YOU CAN'T TAKE IT IF YOU'RE DEAD!

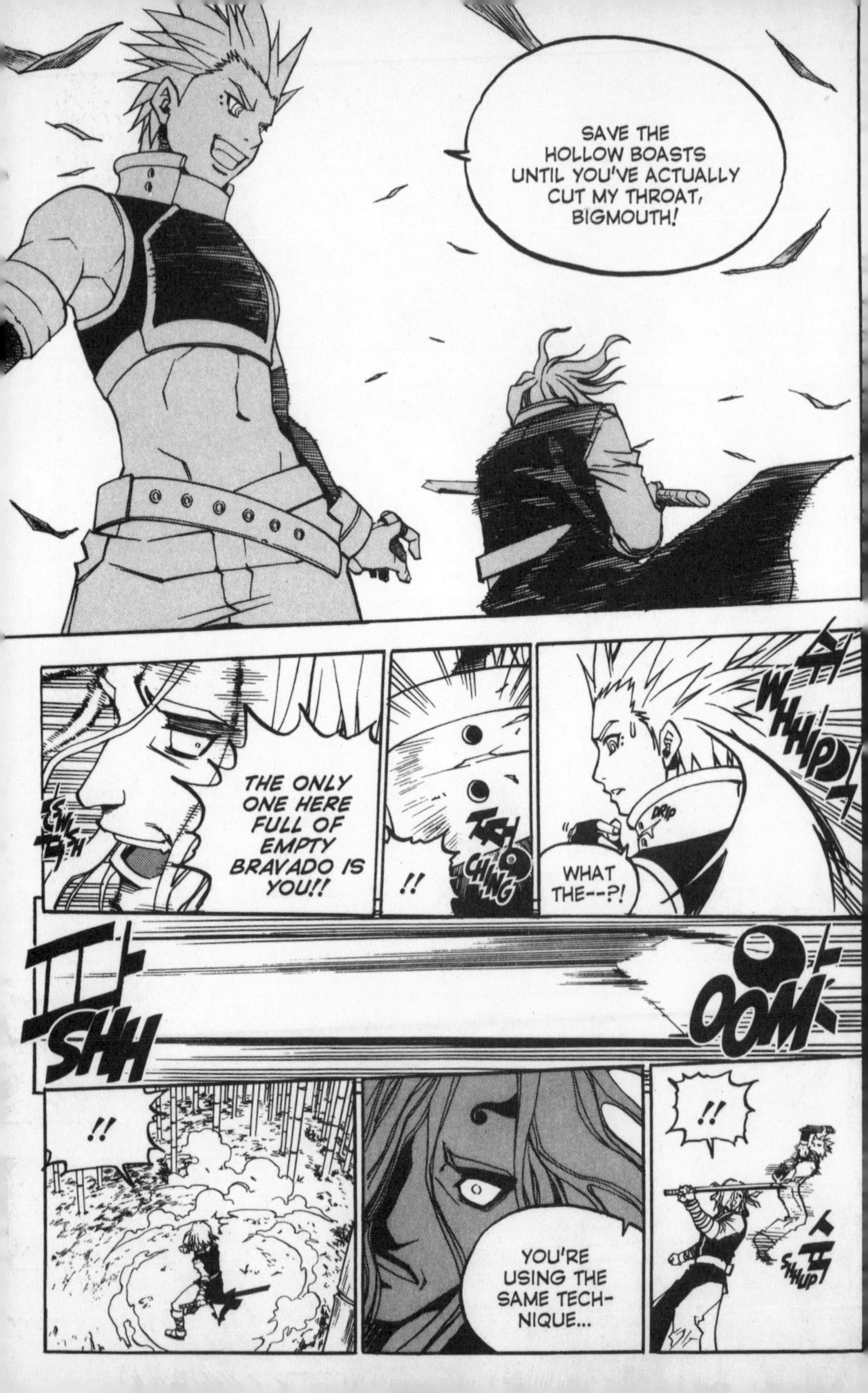
SAVE THE HOLLOW BOASTS UNTIL YOU'VE ACTUALLY CUT MY THROAT, BIGMOUTH!
THE ONLY ONE HERE FULL OF EMPTY BRAVADO IS YOU!!
!!
CHING
WHAT THE--?!
DRIP
WHHIP
SHH
OOM
!!
YOU'RE USING THE SAME TECH-NIQUE...
!!
SHHUP

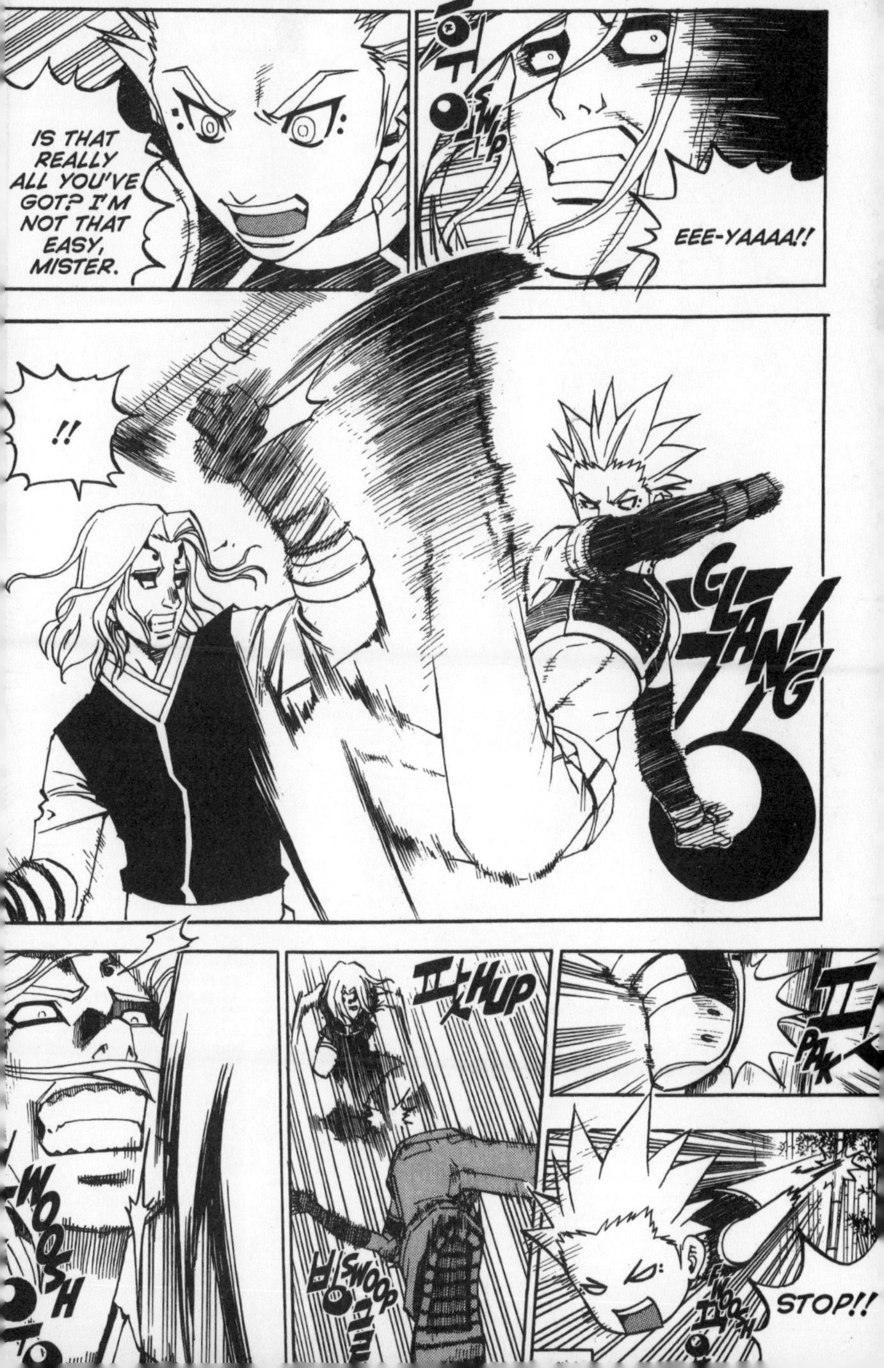
IS THAT REALLY ALL YOU'VE GOT? I'M NOT THAT EASY, MISTER.
SWIP
EEE-YAAAA!!
!!
CLANG!
WOOSH
HUP
SWOOP
PAK
WHOOSH
STOP!!

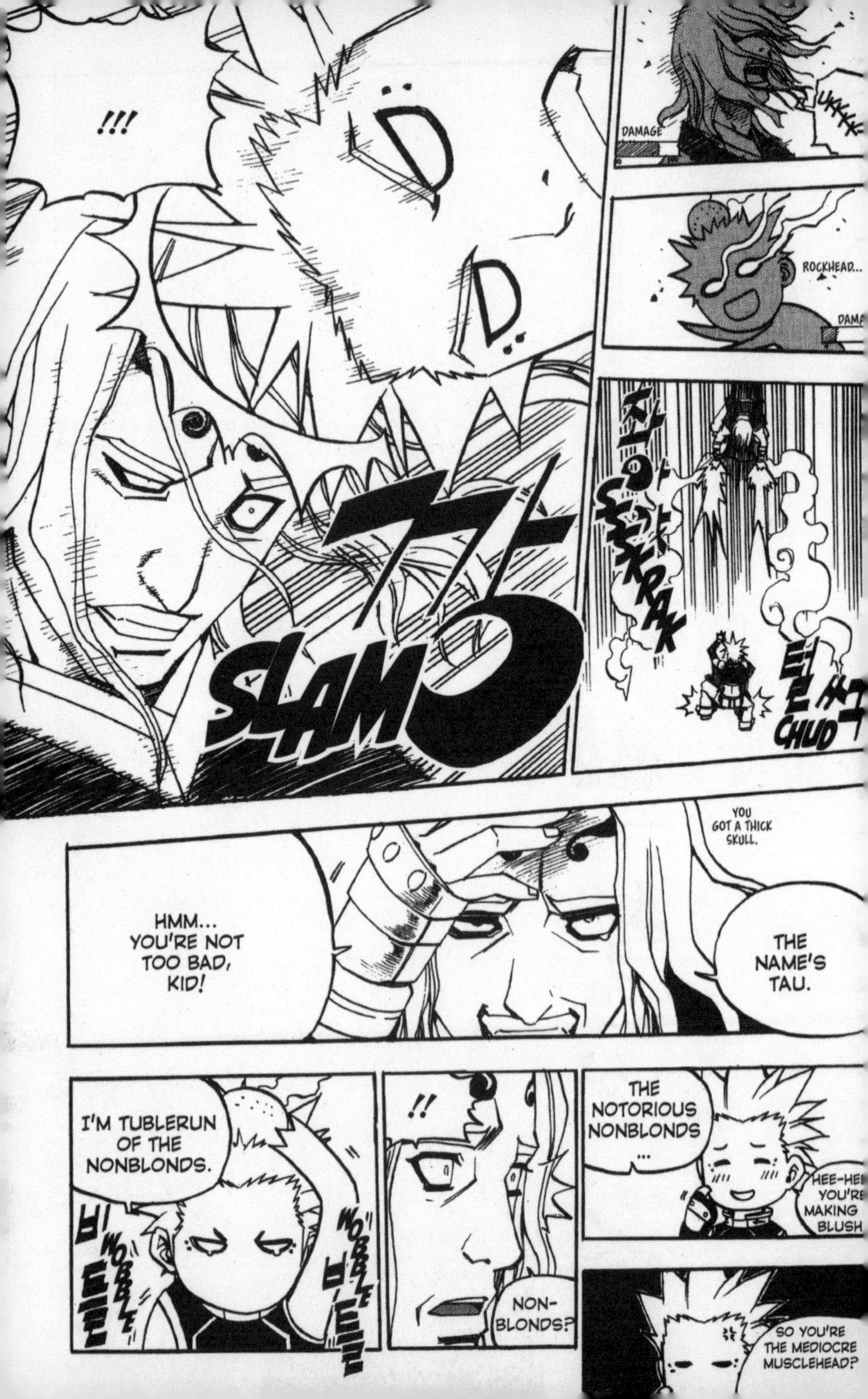
!!!
SLAM
DAMAGE
UKKKK
ROCKHEAD...
SSSKRAK
CHUD
HMM... YOU'RE NOT TOO BAD, KID!
YOU GOT A THICK SKULL.
THE NAME'S TAU.
I'M TUBLERUN OF THE NONBLONDS.
WOBBLE
WOBBLE
!!
NON-BLONDS?
THE NOTORIOUS NONBLONDS ...
HEE-HEE YOU'RE MAKING BLUSH
SO YOU'RE THE MEDIOCRE MUSCLEHEAD?

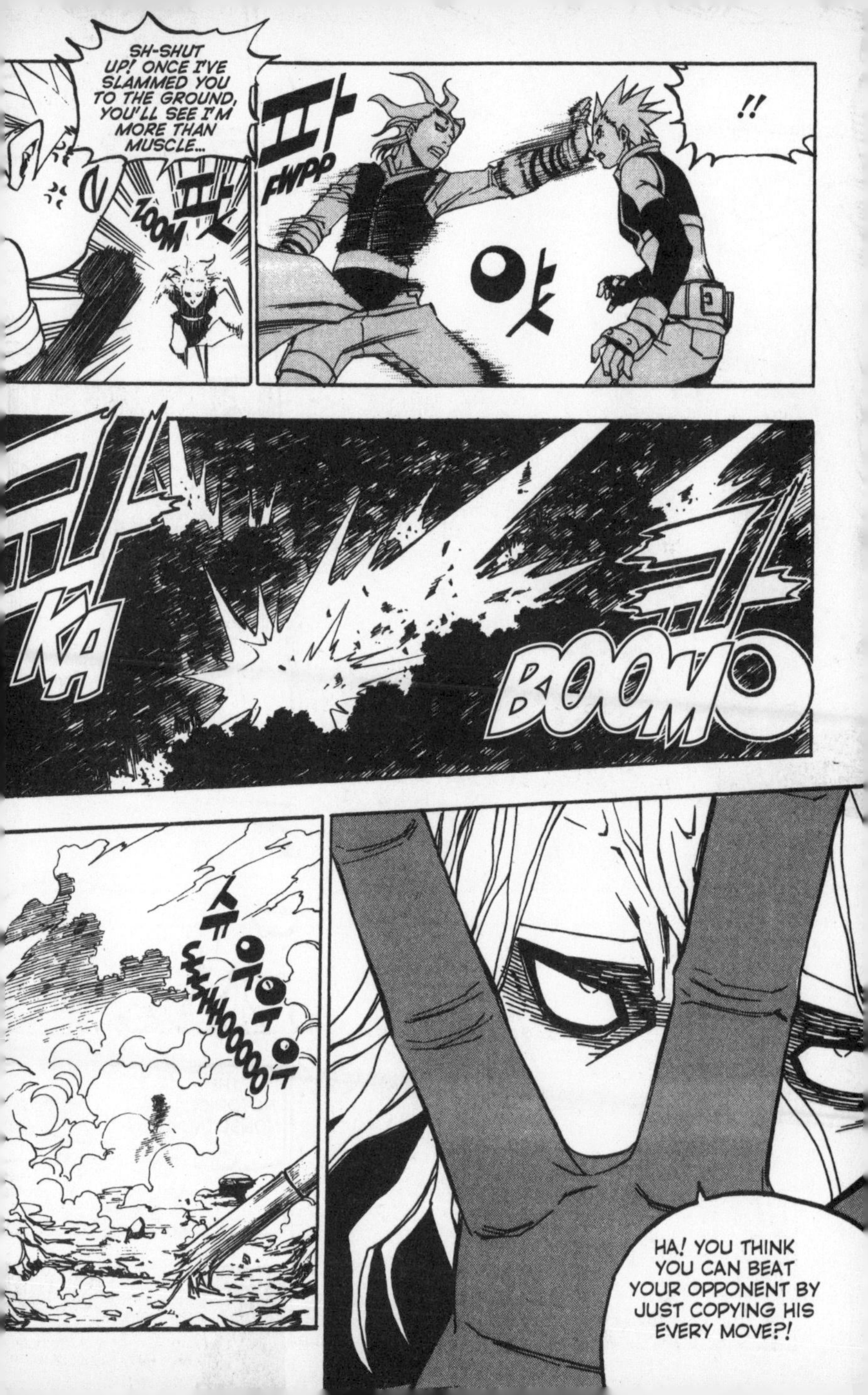
SH-SHUT UP! ONCE I'VE SLAMMED YOU TO THE GROUND, YOU'LL SEE I'M MORE THAN MUSCLE...
ZOOM
FWPP
!!
KA
BOOM
WHHOOOOO
HA! YOU THINK YOU CAN BEAT YOUR OPPONENT BY JUST COPYING HIS EVERY MOVE?!

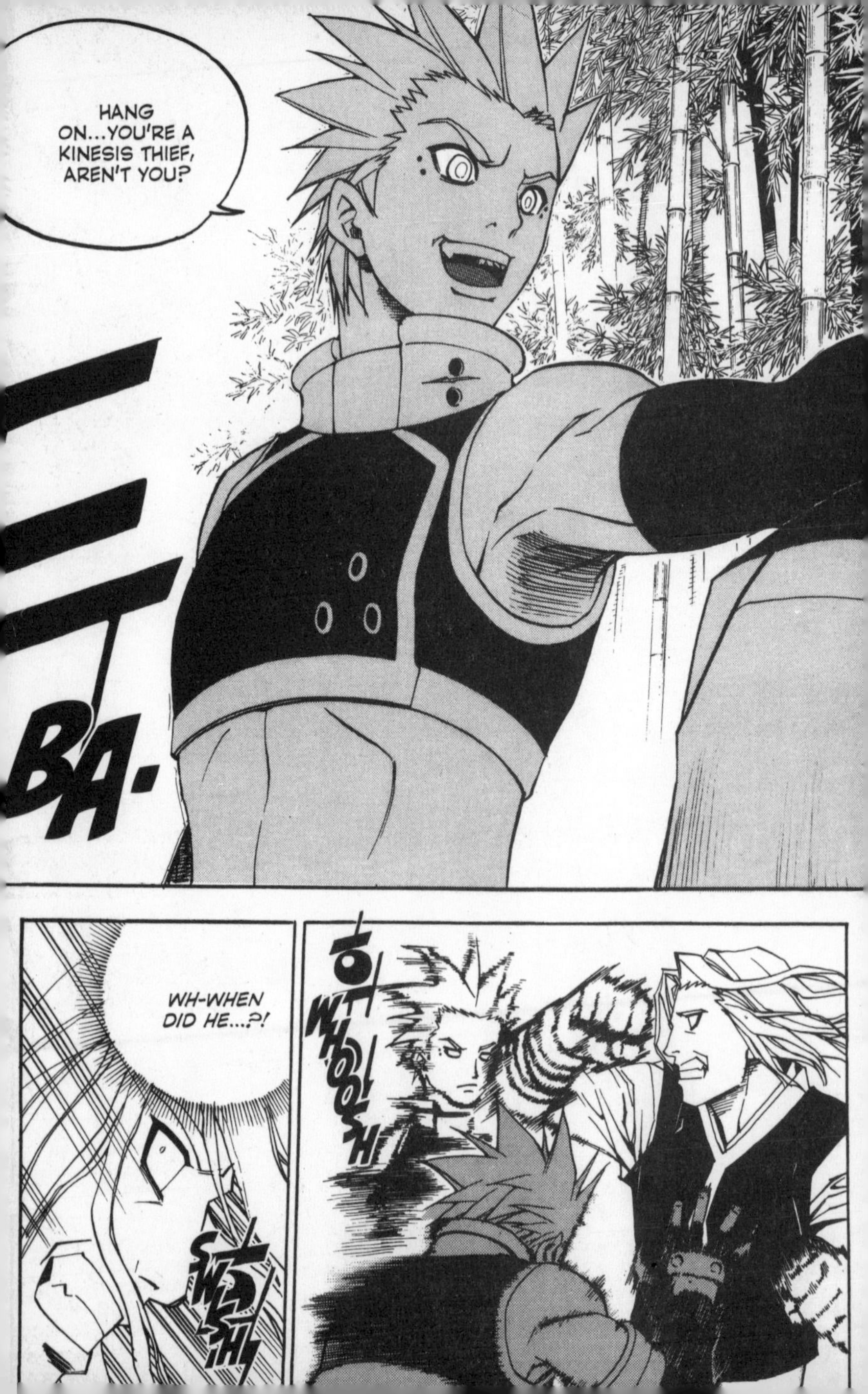
HANG ON...YOU'RE A KINESIS THIEF, AREN'T YOU?
BA-
WH-WHEN DID HE...?!
SWISH
WHOOSH

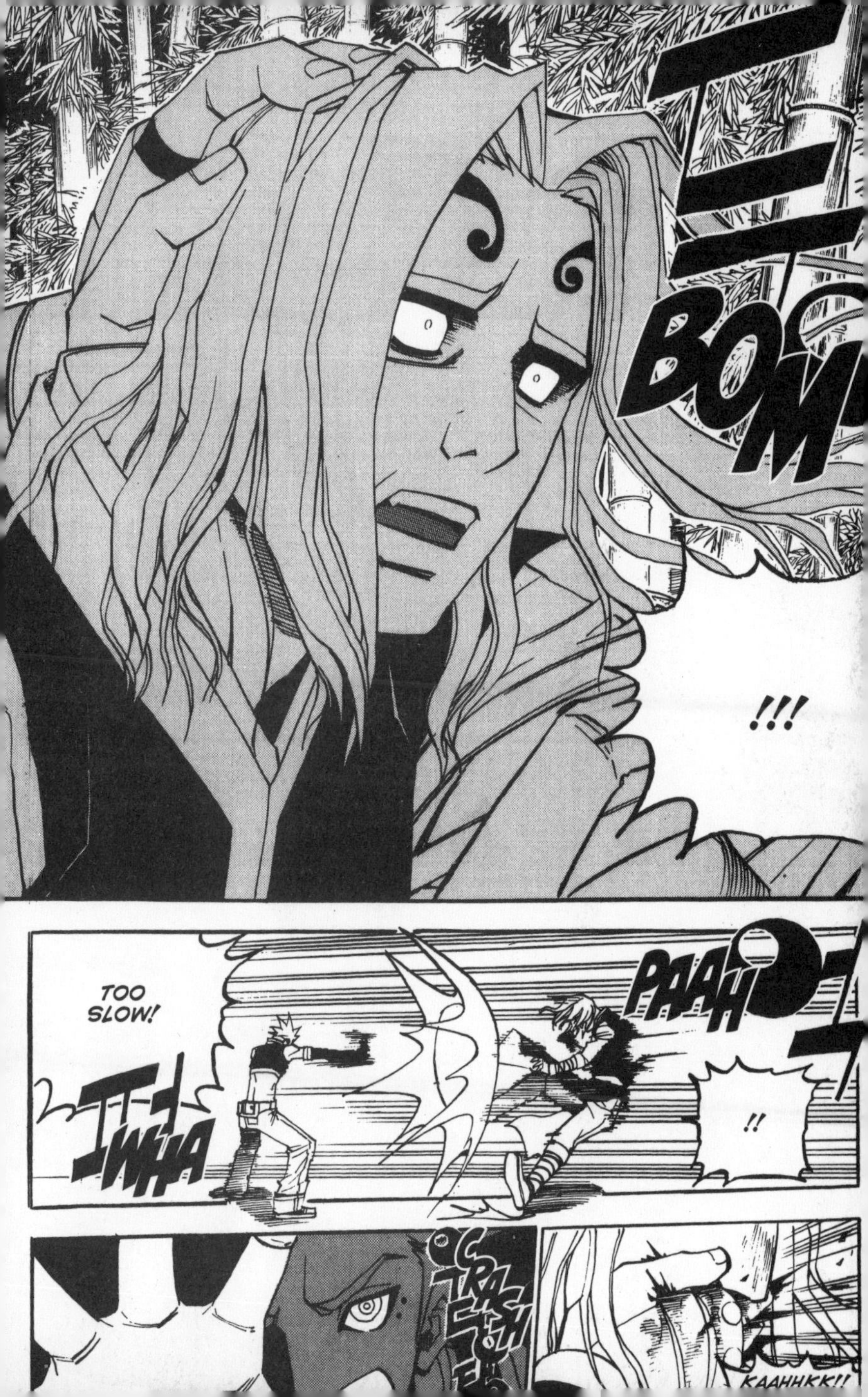
BOOM
!!!
TOO SLOW!
I-I-I-WHA
PAAH
!!
CRASH
KAAHHKK!!

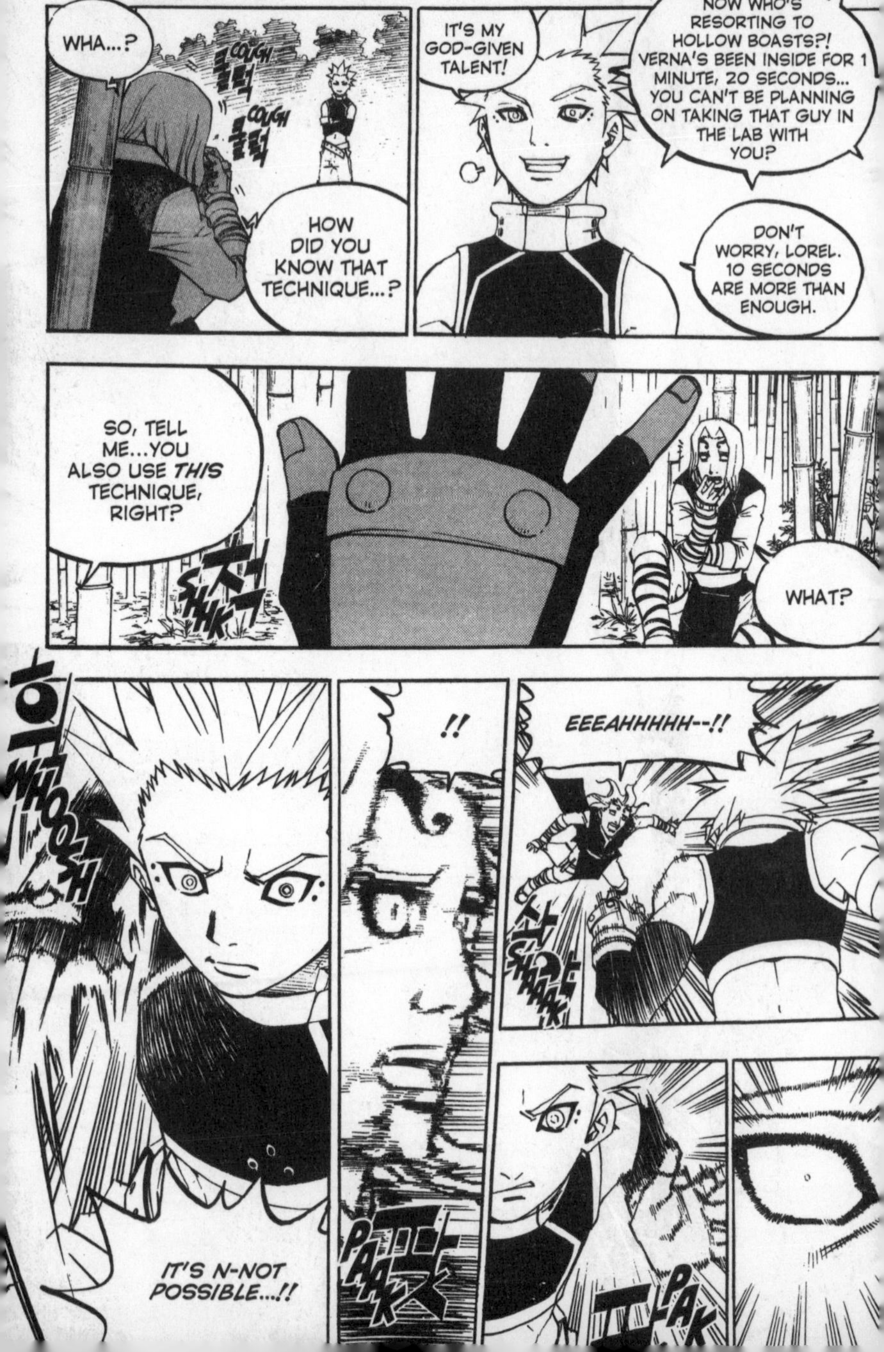
WHA...?
COUGH
COUGH
HOW DID YOU KNOW THAT TECHNIQUE...?
IT'S MY GOD-GIVEN TALENT!
NOW WHO'S RESORTING TO HOLLOW BOASTS?! VERNA'S BEEN INSIDE FOR 1 MINUTE, 20 SECONDS... YOU CAN'T BE PLANNING ON TAKING THAT GUY IN THE LAB WITH YOU?
DON'T WORRY, LOREL. 10 SECONDS ARE MORE THAN ENOUGH.
SO, TELL ME...YOU ALSO USE THIS TECHNIQUE, RIGHT?
SHHK
WHAT?
WHOOOSH
IT'S N-NOT POSSIBLE...!!
!!
PAAAK
EEEAHHHHH--!!
SHAAAK
PAK

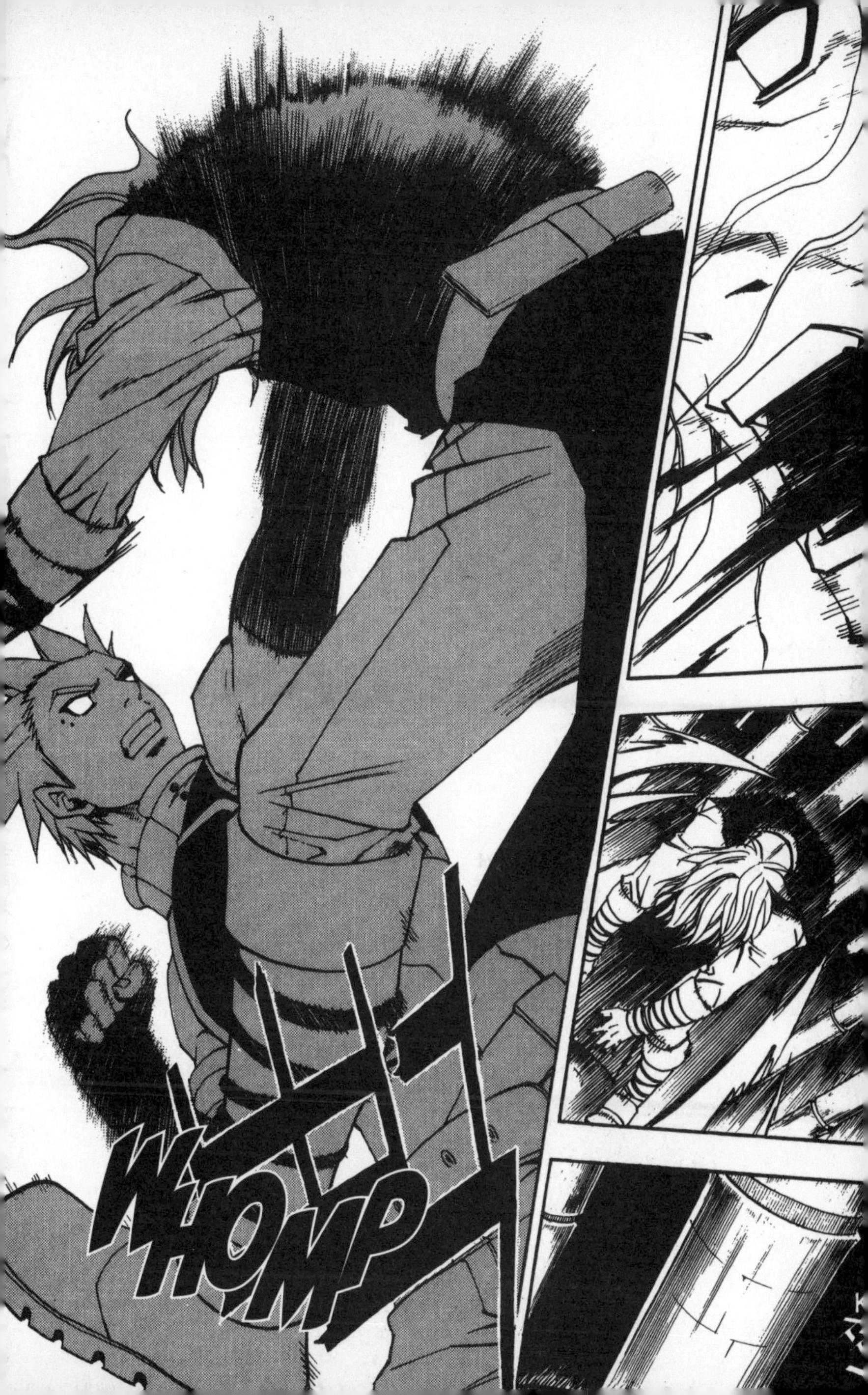
WHOMP

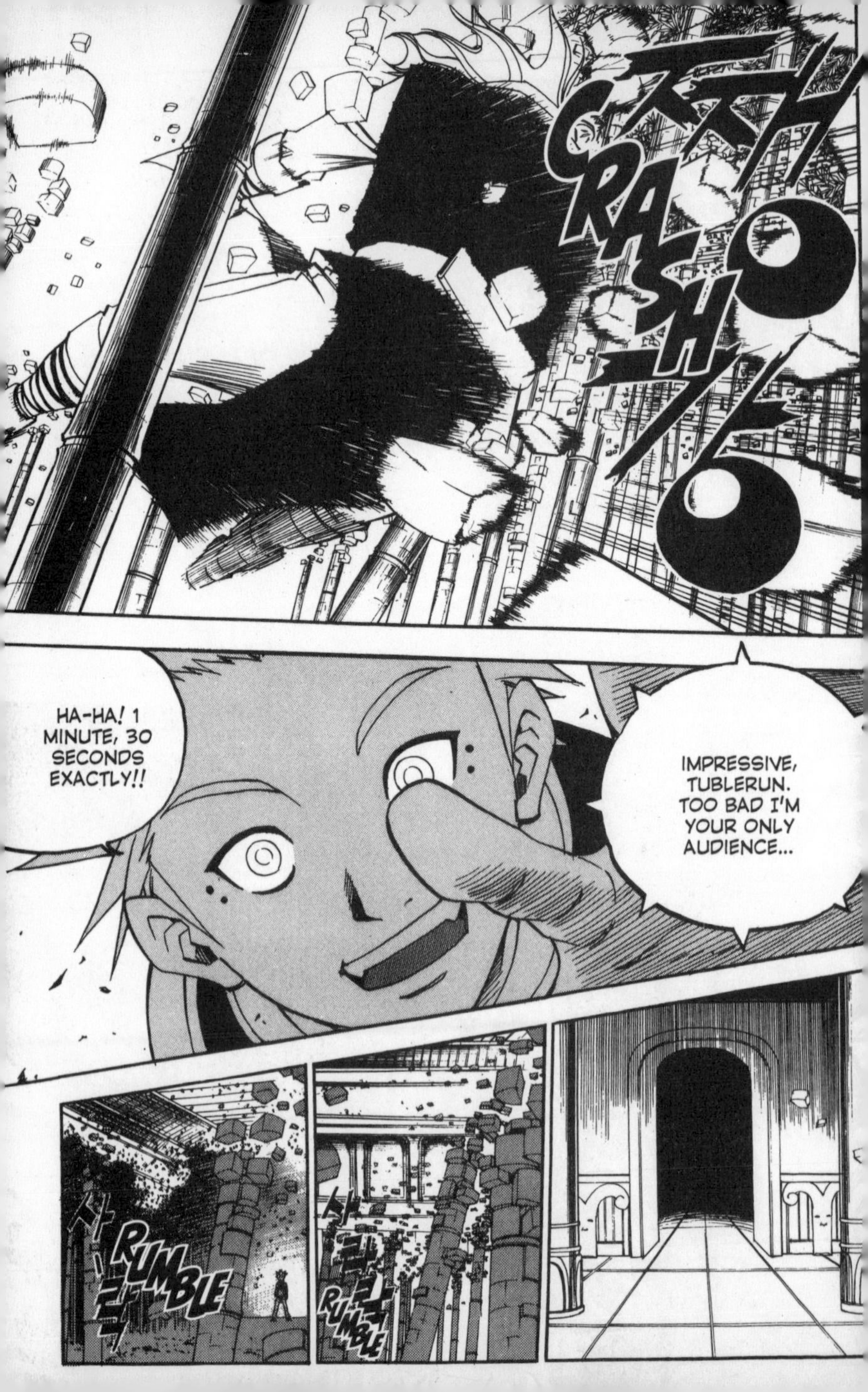
CRASH
HA-HA! 1 MINUTE, 30 SECONDS EXACTLY!!
IMPRESSIVE, TUBLERUN. TOO BAD I'M YOUR ONLY AUDIENCE...
RUMBLE
RUMBLE

COUGH
COUGH

BE SURE TO TELL ALL YOUR FRIENDS HOW THIS MEDIOCRE MUSCLEHEAD TOOK YOU DOWN...OKAY?

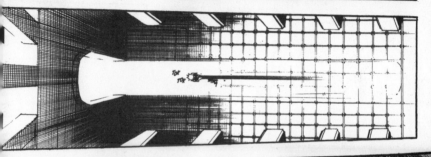

TOK
TOK

SNOOP

GLOM

SHHHHM

SHHHHM

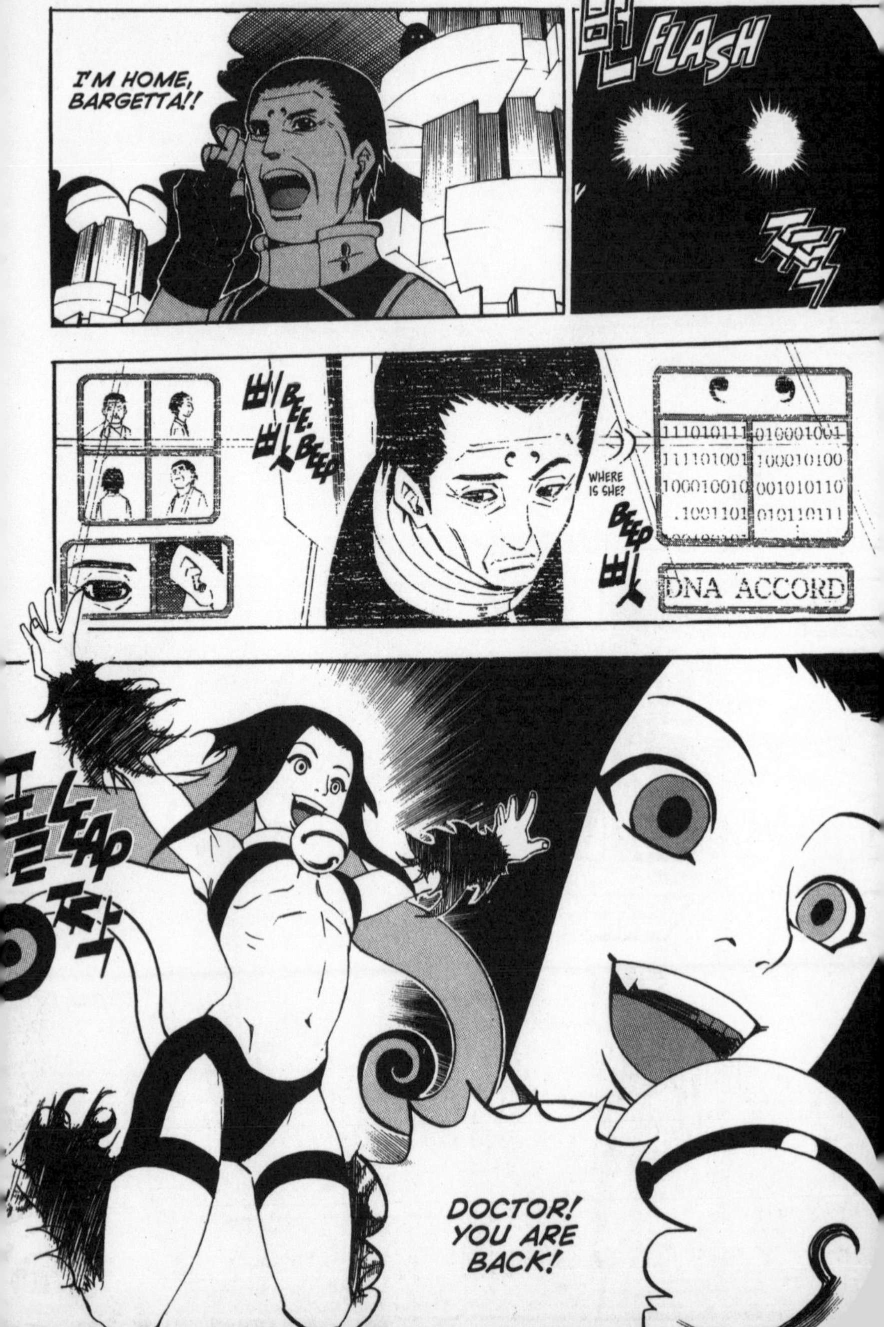

I'M HOME, BARGETTA!!
FLASH
BEE. BEEP
WHERE IS SHE?
BEEP
111010111 010001001
111101001 100010100
100010010 001010110
.1001101 010110111
DNA ACCORD
LEAP
DOCTOR! YOU ARE BACK!

BARGIE MISS DOCTOR SOOOO MUCH...

YES, YES, MY PRETTY PET.

THAT'S VERY SWEET.

DOCTOR, YOUR CLOTHES SOOO SEXY TODAY.

P- PERVERT...THIS DOCTOR'S A PERVERT!!

DRIP
DRIP
DRIP

INSIDE

DID DOCTOR COME TO CHECK UP? I OPEN THE DOOR?

Y-YES...

I WORK HARD TO GUARD PLACE LIKE DOCTOR SAYS.

THREE PEOPLE CAME TODAY, BUT BARGIE STOPPED THEM ALL!

......

HA! THIS ONE'S OURS! I'M THE ONLY ONE WHO KNOWS THE LOCATION OF THIS LAB.

WHO'S HE KIDDING?!

WHAT MAKES HIM SO SURE? WE GOT HERE DEAD LAST.

UM... BARGETTA, TODAY...

HMM?

SHLOOP

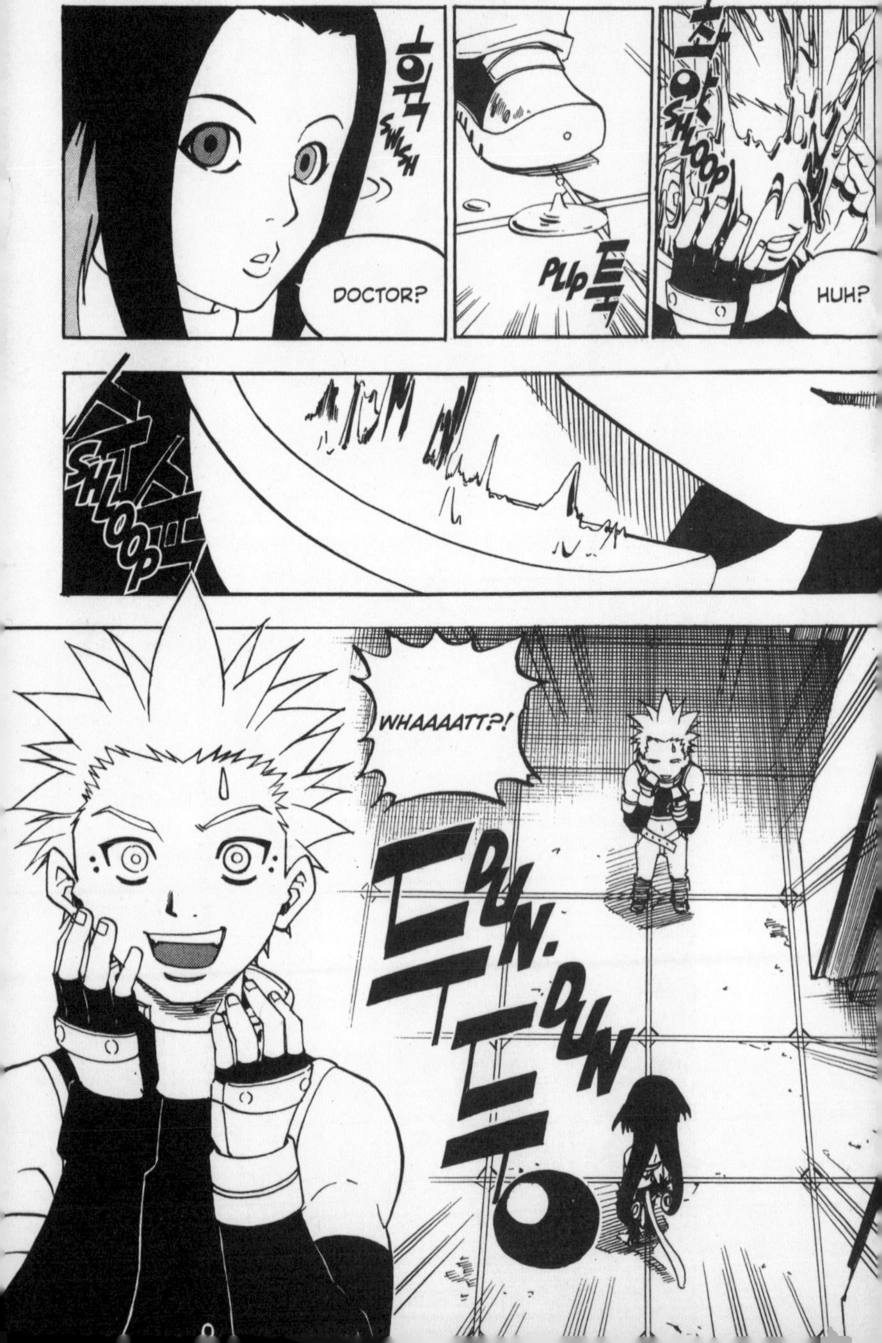

휘익
SWISH
DOCTOR?
PLIP
톡
츠르륵
SHLOOP
HUH?
SHLOOP
WHAAAATT?!
DUN.
DUN

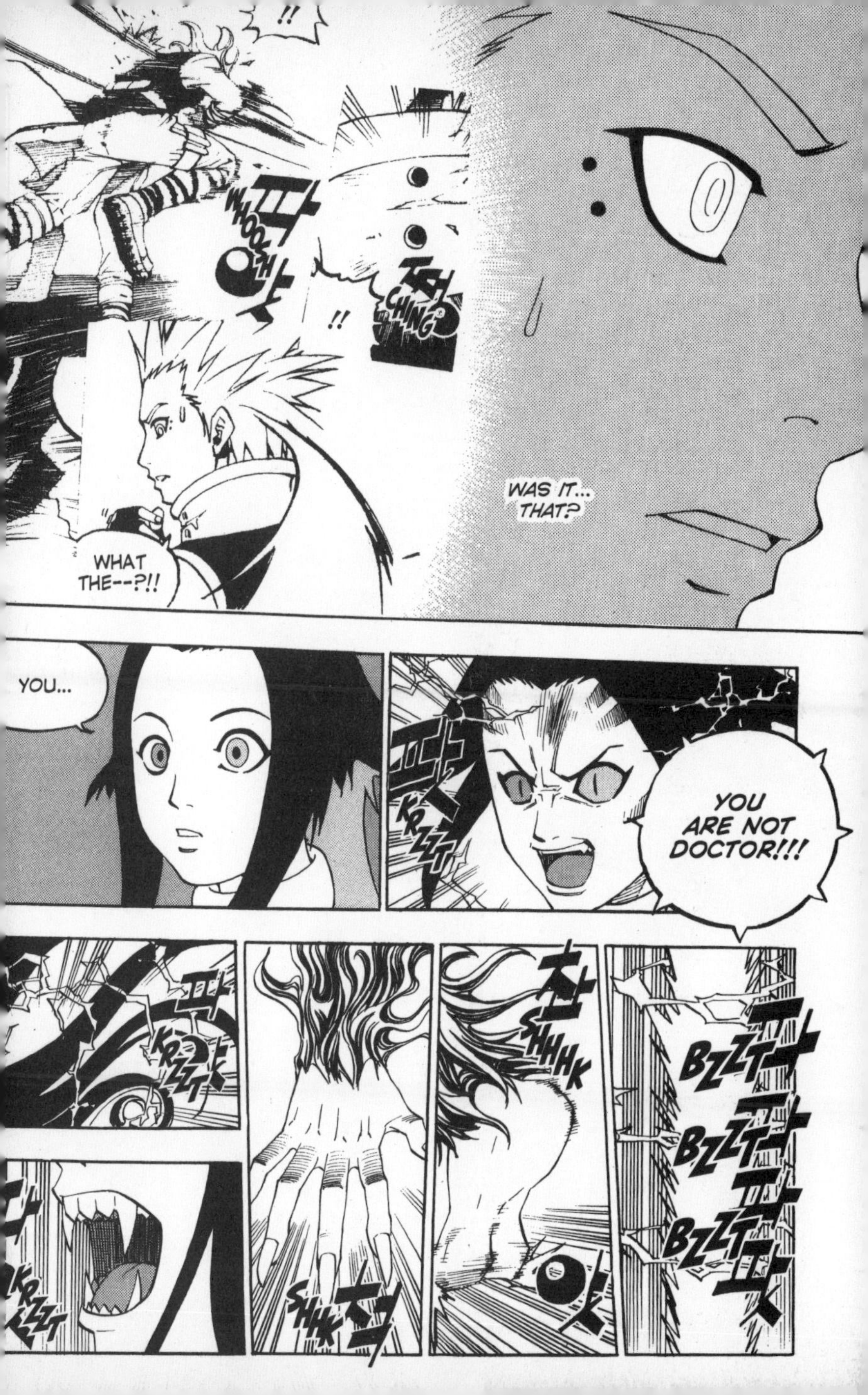
!!
WHOOSH
CHING
!!
WHAT THE--?!!
WAS IT... THAT?
YOU...
KRZZT
YOU ARE NOT DOCTOR!!!
KRZZT
KRZZT
SHHK
SHHHK
BZZT
BZZT
BZZT

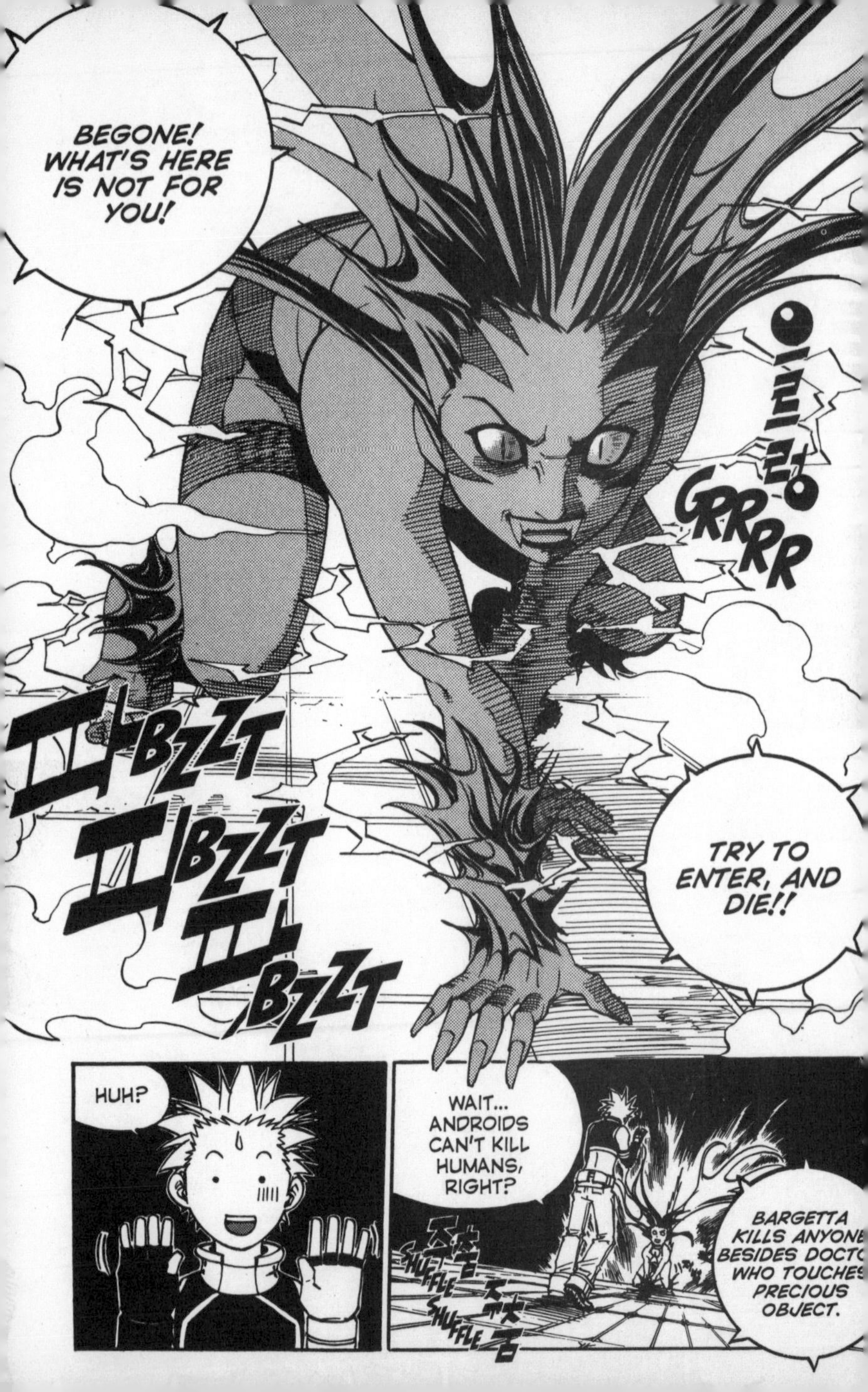
BEGONE! WHAT'S HERE IS NOT FOR YOU!
으르렁
GRRRR
BZZT
BZZT
BZZT
TRY TO ENTER, AND DIE!!
HUH?
WAIT... ANDROIDS CAN'T KILL HUMANS, RIGHT?
SHUFFLE
SHUFFLE
BARGETTA KILLS ANYONE BESIDES DOCTO WHO TOUCHES PRECIOUS OBJECT.

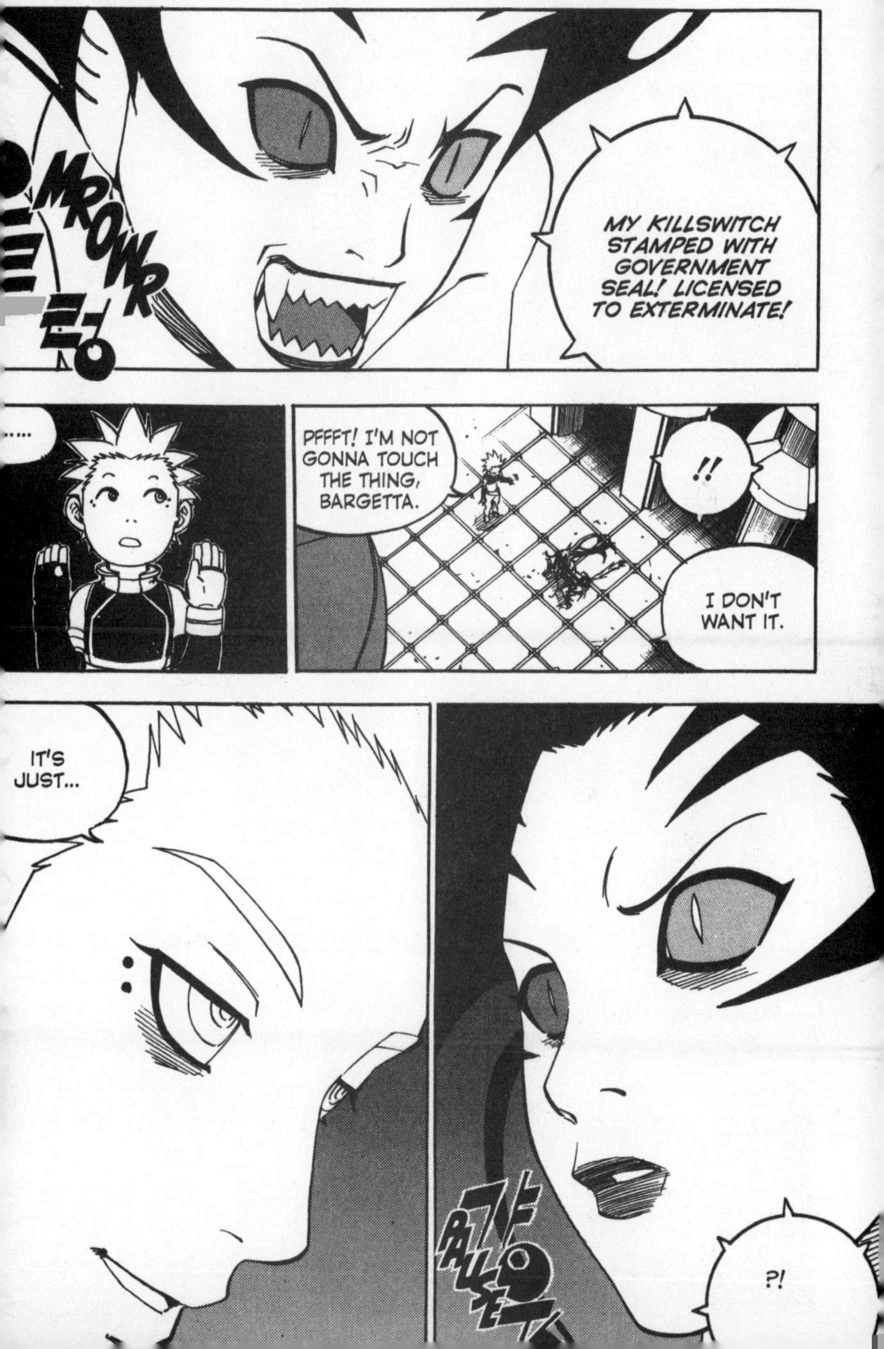
MROWR
MY KILLSWITCH STAMPED WITH GOVERNMENT SEAL! LICENSED TO EXTERMINATE!
.....
PFFFT! I'M NOT GONNA TOUCH THE THING, BARGETTA.
!!
I DON'T WANT IT.
IT'S JUST...
PAUSE
?!

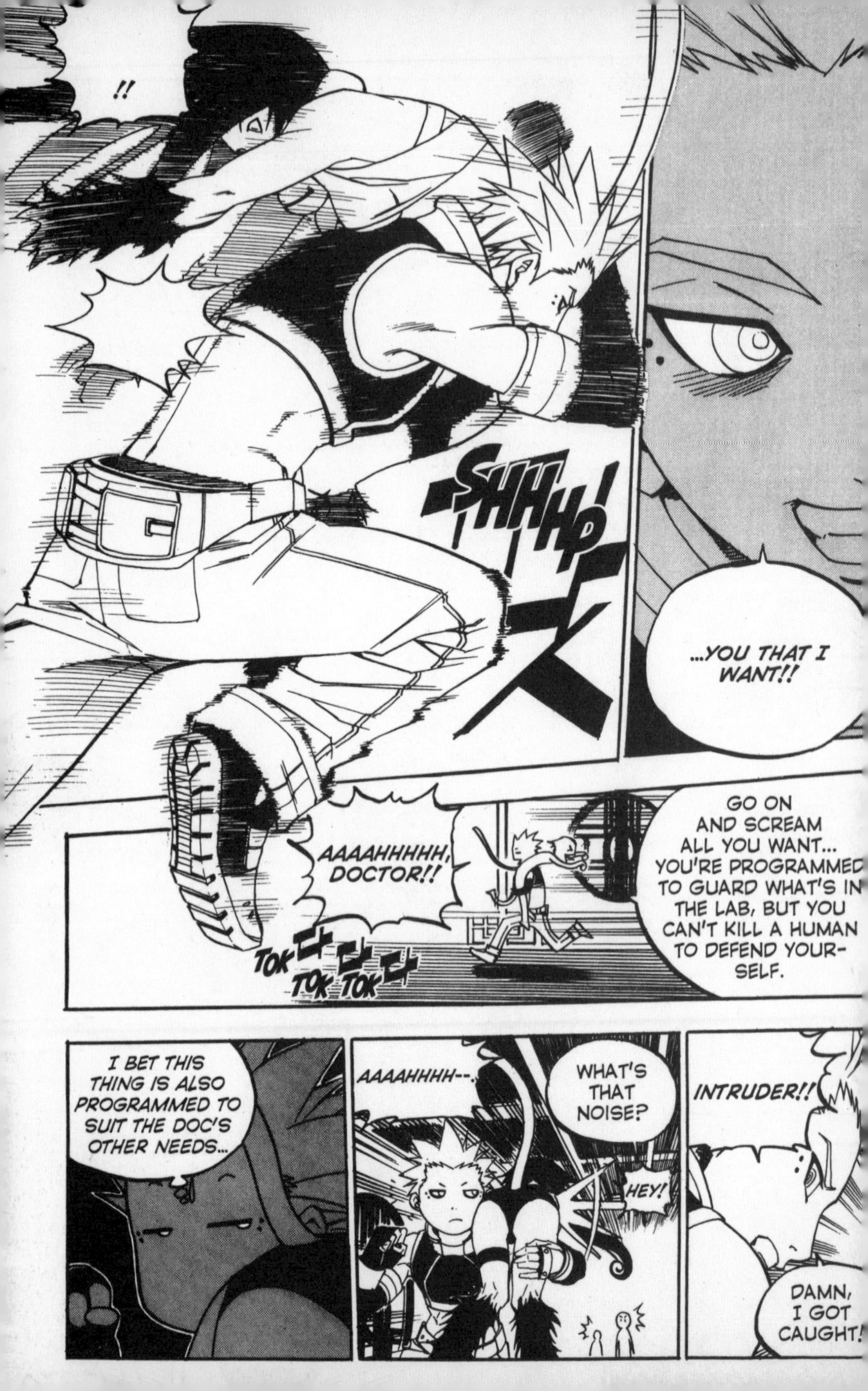
!!
SHHHP!
...YOU THAT I WANT!!
AAAAHHHHH, DOCTOR!!
TOK TOK TOK
GO ON AND SCREAM ALL YOU WANT... YOU'RE PROGRAMMED TO GUARD WHAT'S IN THE LAB, BUT YOU CAN'T KILL A HUMAN TO DEFEND YOUR-SELF.
I BET THIS THING IS ALSO PROGRAMMED TO SUIT THE DOC'S OTHER NEEDS...
AAAAHHHH--.
WHAT'S THAT NOISE?
HEY!
INTRUDER!!
DAMN, I GOT CAUGHT!

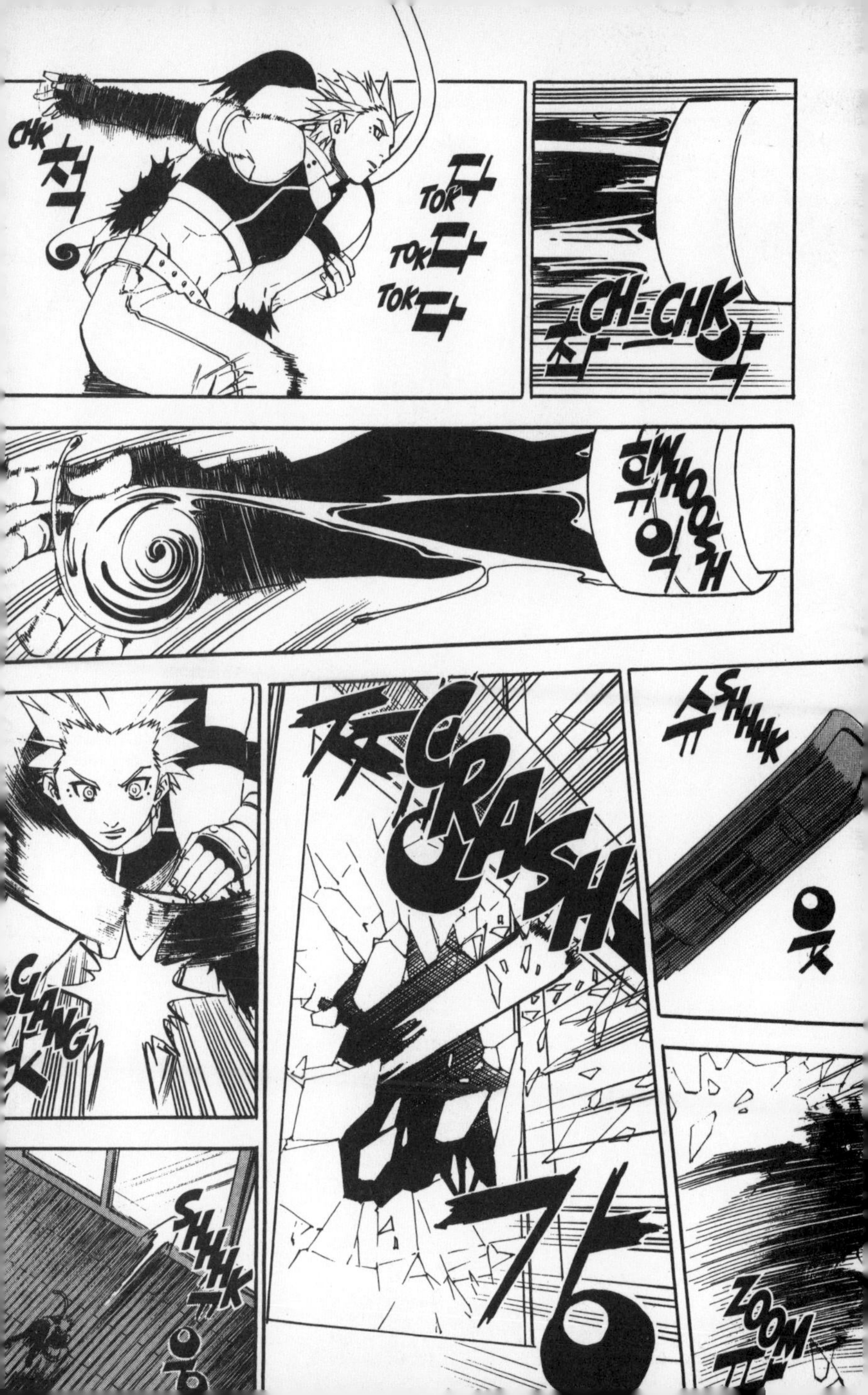

CHK 척
TOK
TOK
TOK
CH-CHK
WHOOOSH
CLANG
CRASH
SHHHK
SHHHK
ZOOM

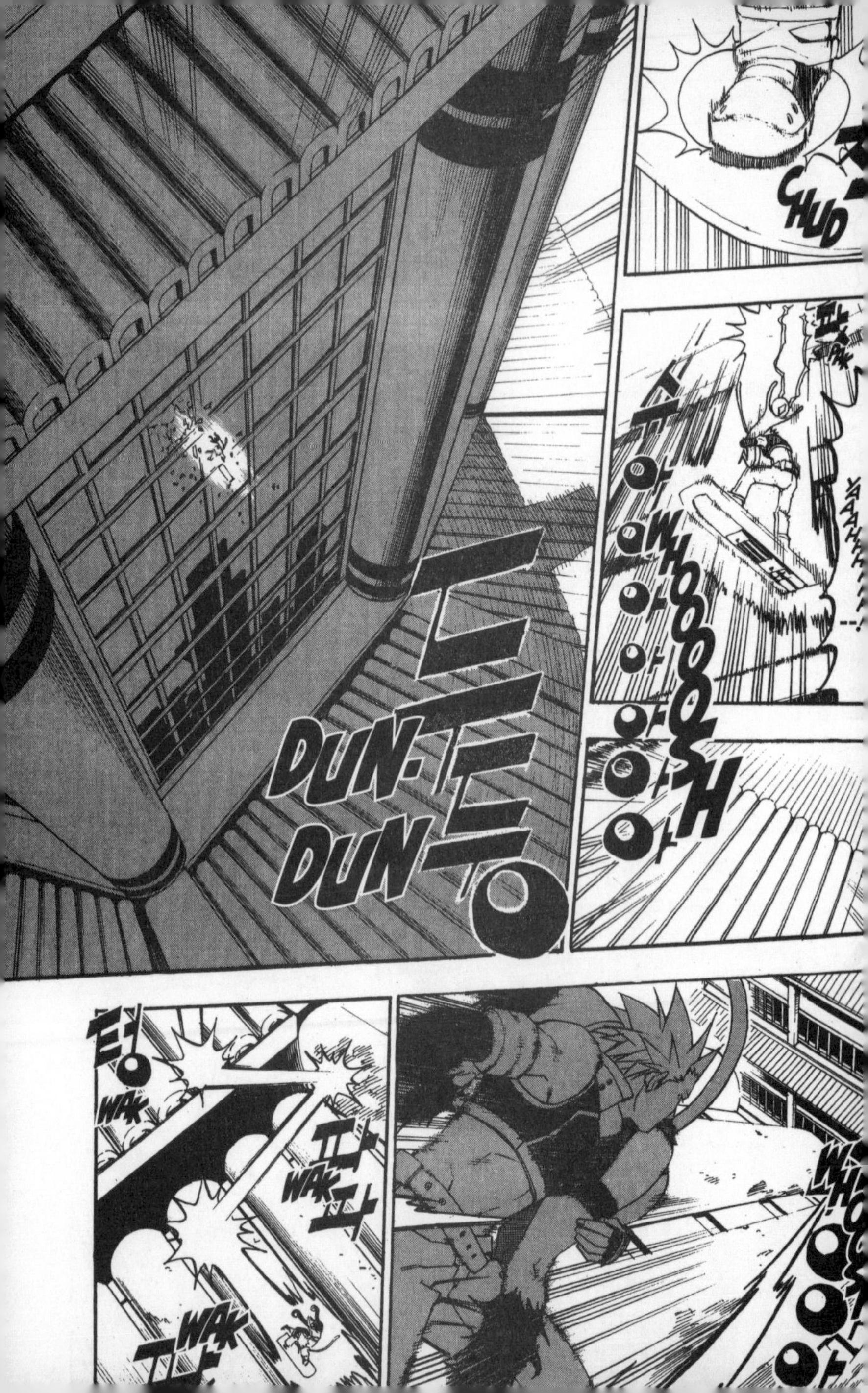
CHUD
팍
PAK
YAAAHH--!
WHOOOOOOOSH
DUN-
DUN-
WAK
WAK
WAK

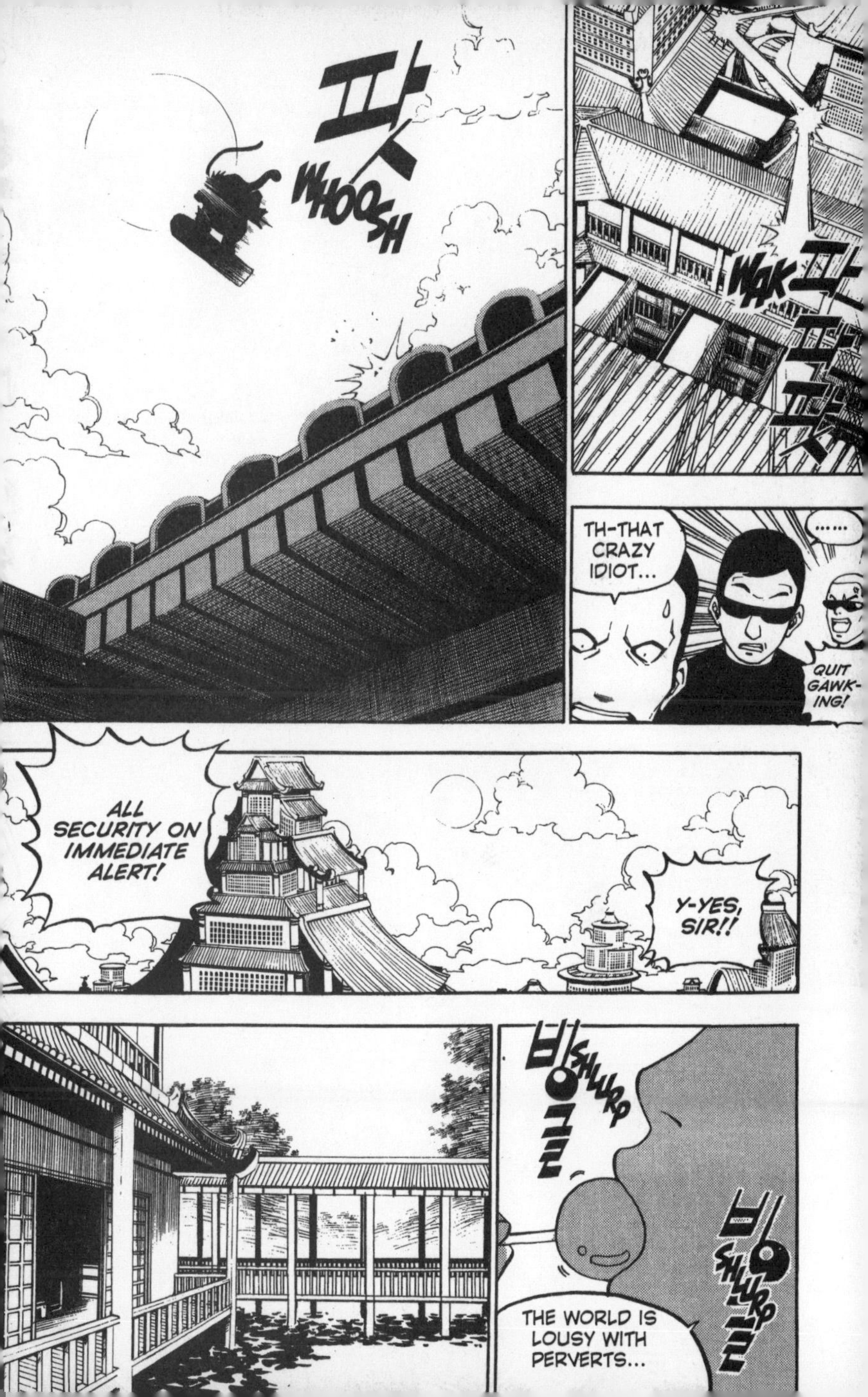
WHOOSH
WAK
TH-THAT CRAZY IDIOT...
......
QUIT GAWK-ING!
ALL SECURITY ON IMMEDIATE ALERT!
Y-YES, SIR!!
SHLURP
SHLURP
THE WORLD IS LOUSY WITH PERVERTS...

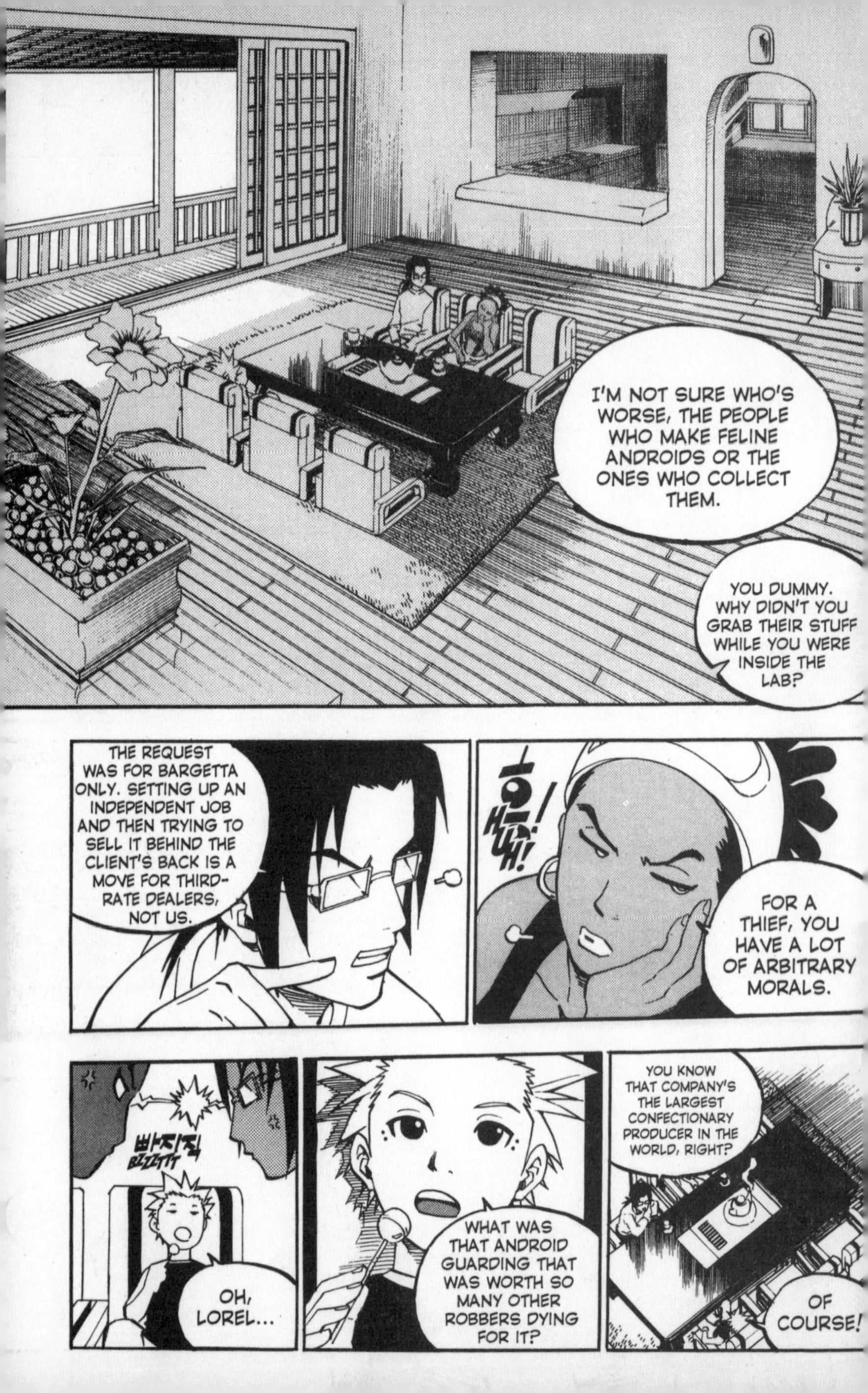
I'M NOT SURE WHO'S WORSE, THE PEOPLE WHO MAKE FELINE ANDROIDS OR THE ONES WHO COLLECT THEM.
YOU DUMMY. WHY DIDN'T YOU GRAB THEIR STUFF WHILE YOU WERE INSIDE THE LAB?
THE REQUEST WAS FOR BARGETTA ONLY. SETTING UP AN INDEPENDENT JOB AND THEN TRYING TO SELL IT BEHIND THE CLIENT'S BACK IS A MOVE FOR THIRD-RATE DEALERS, NOT US.
흥! HUH!
FOR A THIEF, YOU HAVE A LOT OF ARBITRARY MORALS.
빠지직 BZZTTT
OH, LOREL...
WHAT WAS THAT ANDROID GUARDING THAT WAS WORTH SO MANY OTHER ROBBERS DYING FOR IT?
YOU KNOW THAT COMPANY'S THE LARGEST CONFECTIONARY PRODUCER IN THE WORLD, RIGHT?
OF COURSE!

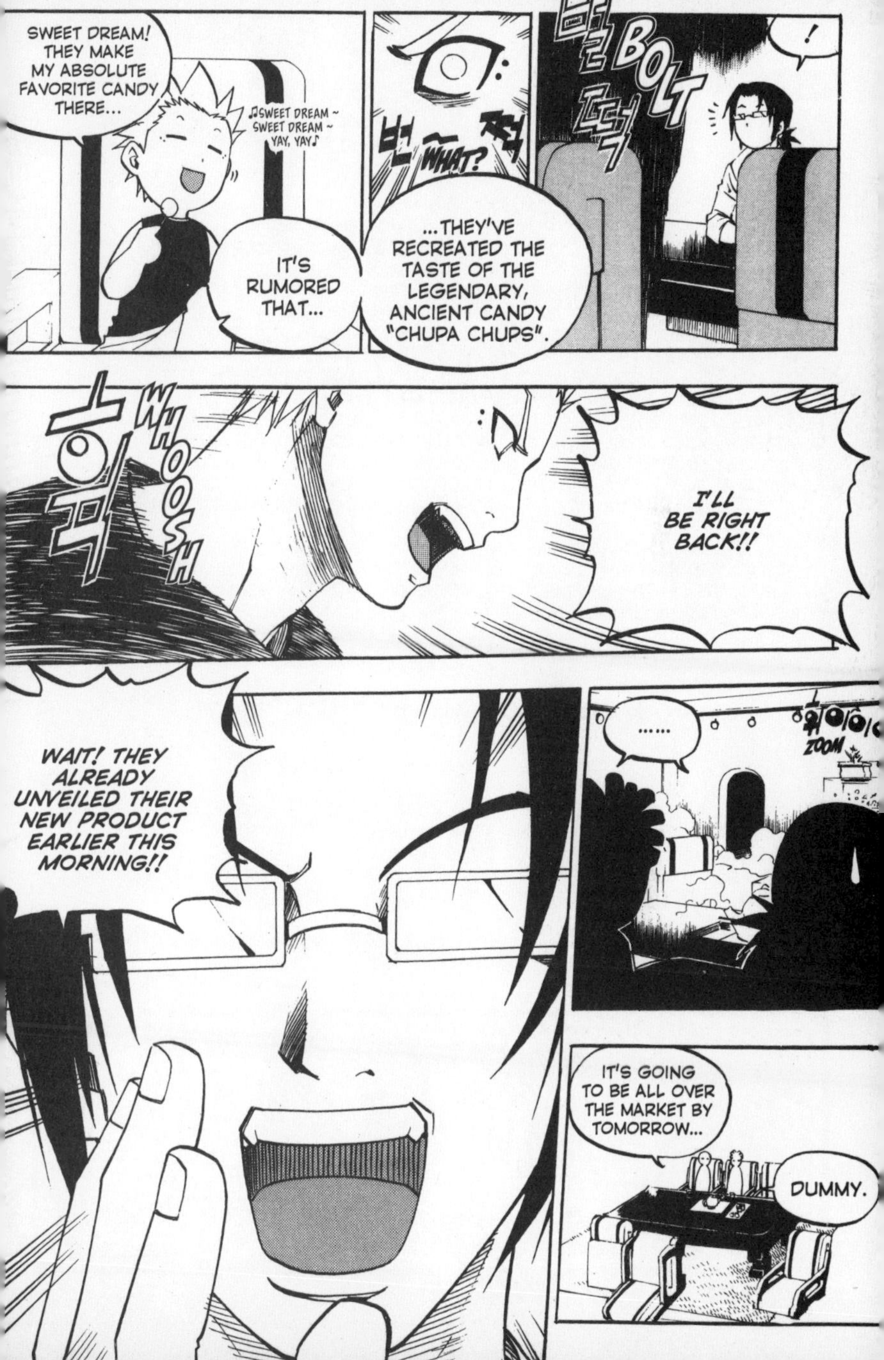
SWEET DREAM! THEY MAKE MY ABSOLUTE FAVORITE CANDY THERE...
♫SWEET DREAM ~ SWEET DREAM ~ YAY, YAY♪
IT'S RUMORED THAT...
WHAT?
...THEY'VE RECREATED THE TASTE OF THE LEGENDARY, ANCIENT CANDY "CHUPA CHUPS".
BOLT
!
WHOOSH
I'LL BE RIGHT BACK!!
WAIT! THEY ALREADY UNVEILED THEIR NEW PRODUCT EARLIER THIS MORNING!!
......
ZOOM
IT'S GOING TO BE ALL OVER THE MARKET BY TOMORROW...
DUMMY.

BACK TALK... NO, NO...AFTER WORD?!

MAYBE IT'S BECAUSE THIS IS MY FIRST MANUSCRIPT IN A LONG TIME, BUT I CERTAINLY HAD A HARD GO WITH IT (AND STILL DO, REALLY). IT TOOK THREE REVISIONS TO FINALLY GET TO THE FINAL DRAFT.
I THOUGHT OF SEVERAL THINGS WHILE I WAS WRITING UP THE FIRST CHAPTER. FIRST WAS THE GADGET WORN BY THE SWEET DREAM TOUR GUIDE ON HER FINGER. I HAVE A TENDENCY TO WANDER OFF WHEN I HAVE TIME TO SPEND WITH MY THOUGHTS...I'M PRETTY GOOD AT KEEPING MYSELF COMPANY.
WHAT IF YOU COULD CONVENIENTLY WRITE IN THE AIR, THE WAY A JET PLANE WRITES ACROSS THE SKY WITH EXHAUST FUMES? AS I THOUGHT ABOUT THIS (WISP-WISP, TALK TALK), I REALIZED IT WOULD HAVE MANY USES. IMAGINE...PRETTY LADIES IN PARADES MAKING DRAWINGS OR WRITING MESSAGES IN THE AIR AS THEY MARCH AND DANCE! UNFORTUNATELY, I COULD ONLY SQUEEZE IT ONTO ONE PAGE, BUT IT WAS SUCH A GOOD IDEA, I HAD TO USE IT RIGHT AWAY. HOW FUN WOULD IT BE IF IT WERE REAL? (SHOULD I APPLY FOR A PATENT? I COULD MAKE A BUNDLE...)

ANOTHER IDEA WAS TUBLERUN'S LENS CAMERA.
INITIALLY, I WAS SET ON GOGGLES FOR TUBLERUN. THE EYES THAT APPEAR ON THE GOGGLES THEMSELVES WOULD BE SIMILAR TO A HOLOGRAM. THESE EYES WOULD NATURALLY CHANGE APPEARANCES DEPENDING ON THE PERSON'S EMOTION OR DIRECTION OF GAZE.

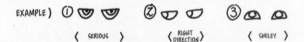

EXAMPLE)
①
②
③
SERIOUS
RIGHT DIRECTION
SMILEY

HA...I USED SIMPLE EXAMPLES, ONES THAT ARE EASY TO DRAW.
I WORRIED A LOT ABOUT CHANGING THE GOGGLES TO LENSES. THE FOUR-WHEEL EYE IN <NARUTO> WORRIED ME, BUT THE FUNCTIONS ARE COMPLETELY DIFFERENT. DON'T YOU THINK? HA-HA, AND IT'S NOT LIKE IT CONSTANTLY APPEARS, SO I DECIDED TO GO WITH THE LENSED CAMERA ANYWAY.

THIS IS ALL THE EXTRA SPACE I HAVE FOR CHAPTER 1, SO I'LL SEE YOU AFTER CHAPTER 2.

HE RECEIVES HIS DRIVER'S LICENSE AT 17.
I'M AN ADULT NOW.
SEOUL, KOR 5668
NEW CAR PURCHASES
SIR, MADAME... THIS WAY PLEASE.
SALES+ PARTS DISPOSAL
USED CARS
FREE STUFF
AUCTION
ARE YOU KIDDING ME?
WHAT DO YOU MEAN "TO BE CONTINUED"?!

CAR 2. WONDER DIAMOND

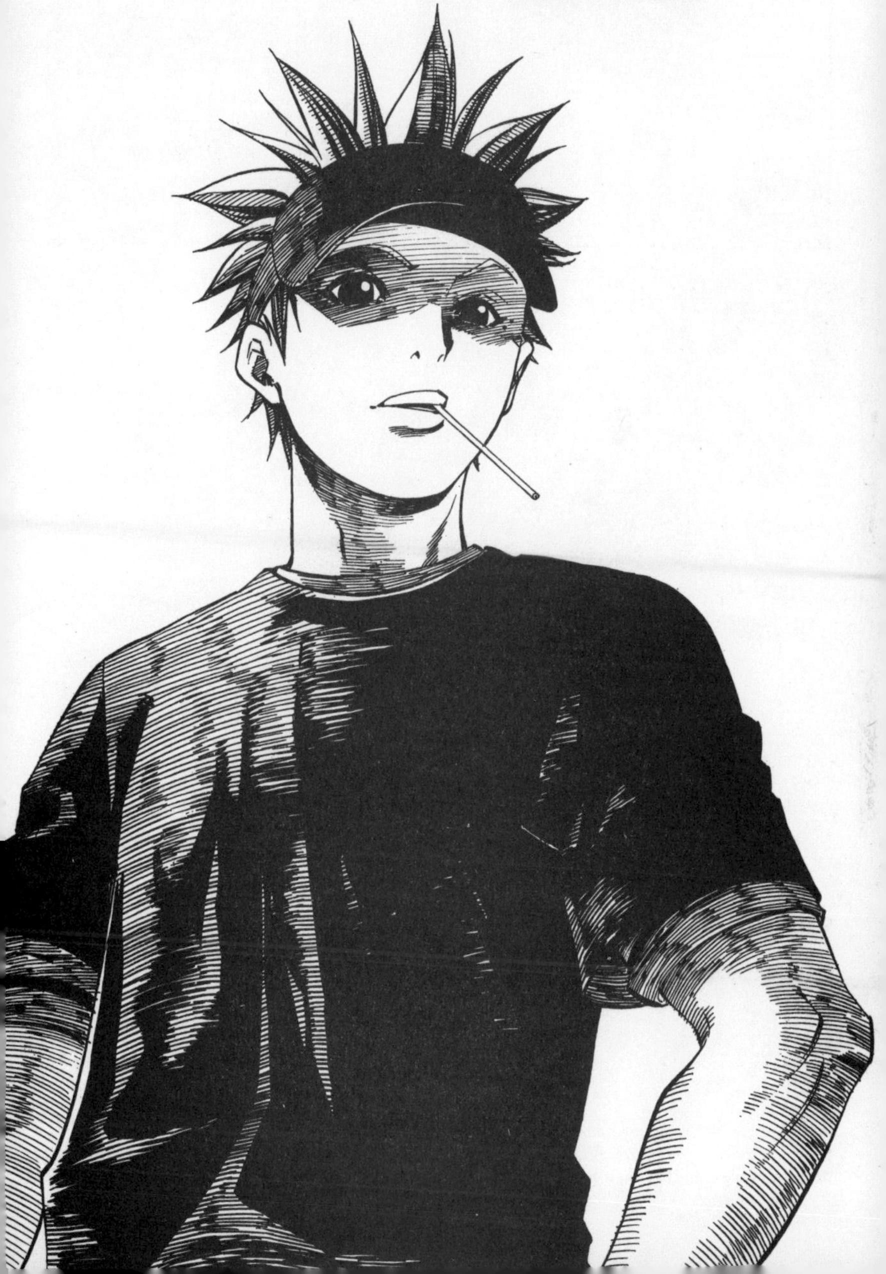

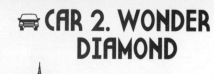

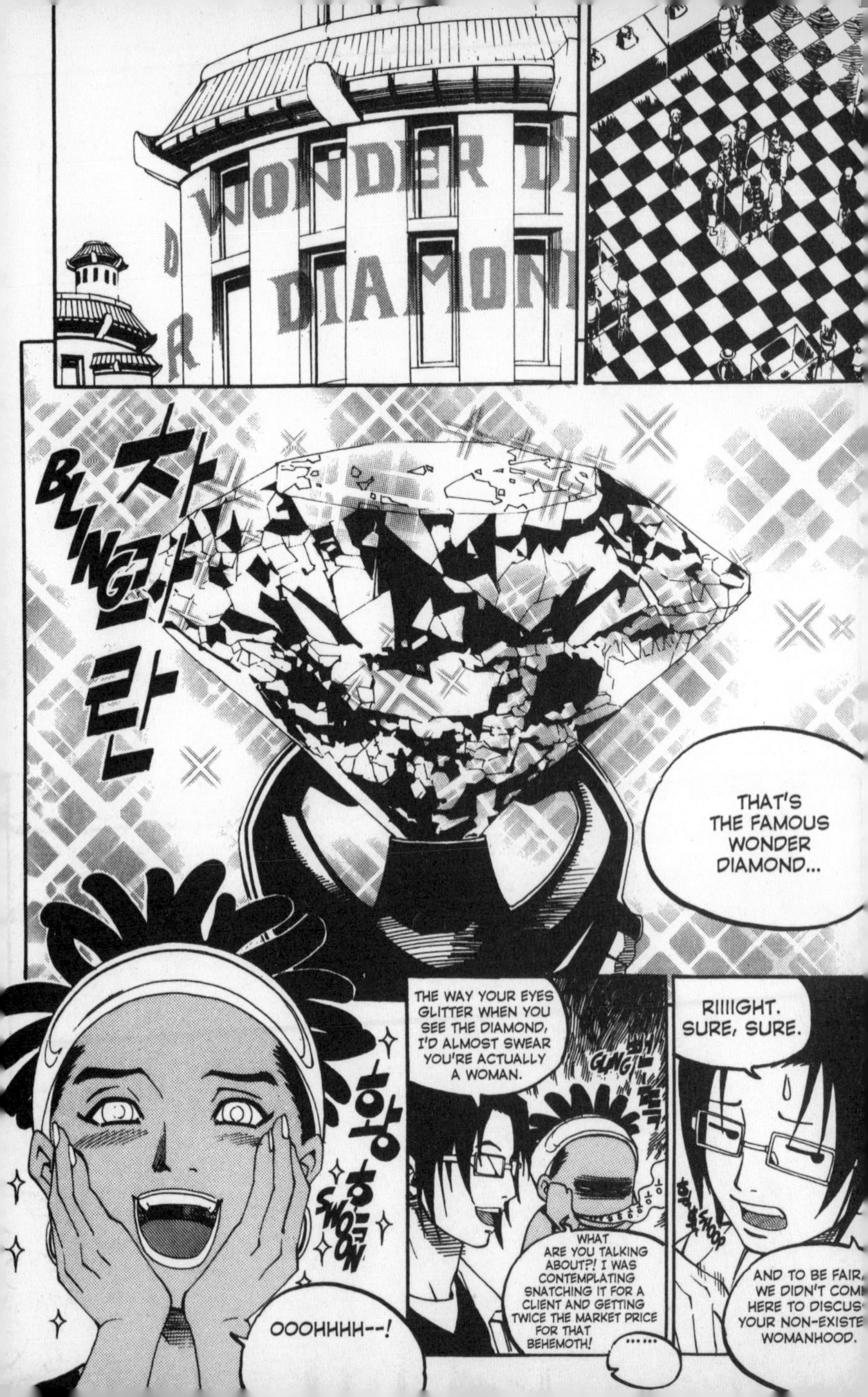
WONDER DI
DIAMON
BLING
THAT'S THE FAMOUS WONDER DIAMOND...
SWOON
OOOHHHH--!
THE WAY YOUR EYES GLITTER WHEN YOU SEE THE DIAMOND, I'D ALMOST SWEAR YOU'RE ACTUALLY A WOMAN.
GLING
WHAT ARE YOU TALKING ABOUT?! I WAS CONTEMPLATING SNATCHING IT FOR A CLIENT AND GETTING TWICE THE MARKET PRICE FOR THAT BEHEMOTH!
......
RIIIIGHT. SURE, SURE.
SNOOP
AND TO BE FAIR, WE DIDN'T COM HERE TO DISCUS YOUR NON-EXISTE WOMANHOOD.

WHEN THE DISPLAY STAND DETECTS ANY SHIFT IN WEIGHT...

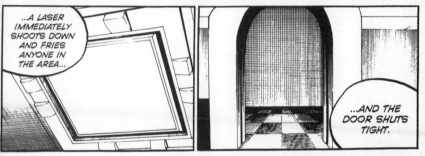

...A LASER IMMEDIATELY SHOOTS DOWN AND FRIES ANYONE IN THE AREA...

...AND THE DOOR SHUTS TIGHT.

THIS SHOULD BE A WALK IN THE--.

RA-TA-TA-TA-TAT-

EVERYONE GET DOWN!!

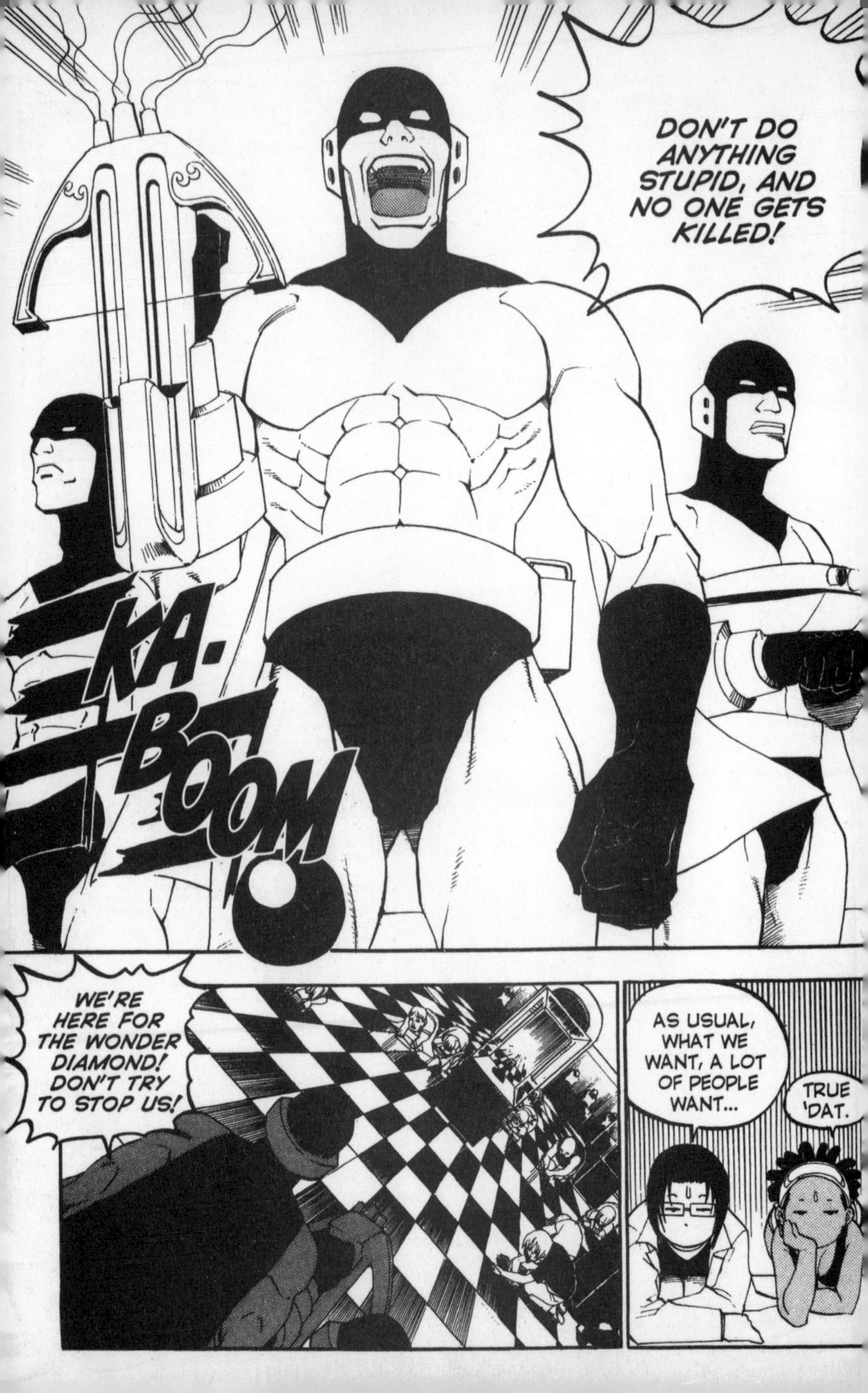
DON'T DO ANYTHING STUPID, AND NO ONE GETS KILLED!
KA-BOOM
WE'RE HERE FOR THE WONDER DIAMOND! DON'T TRY TO STOP US!
AS USUAL, WHAT WE WANT, A LOT OF PEOPLE WANT...
TRUE 'DAT.

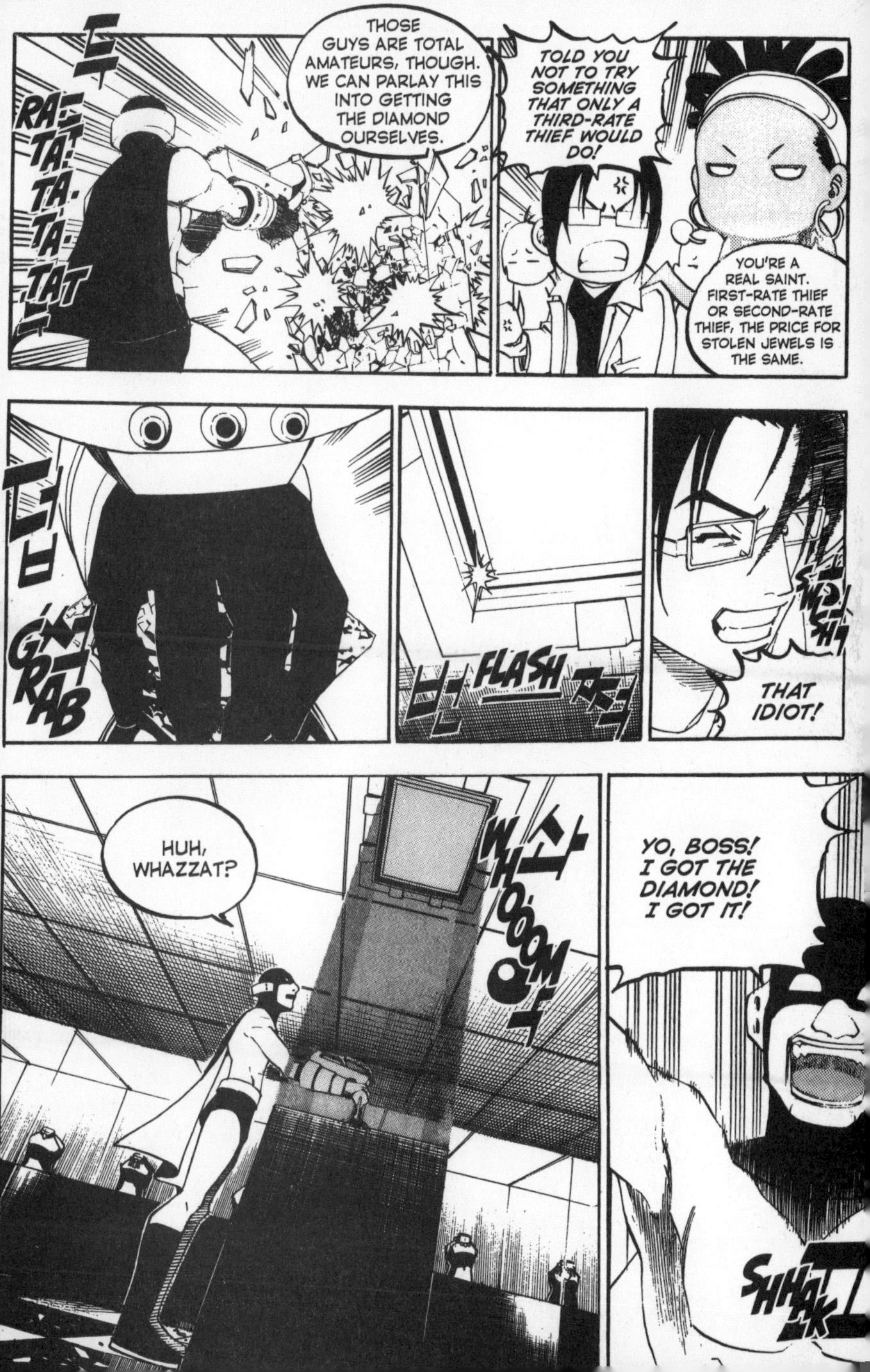
RA-TA-TA-TA-TA-TAT
THOSE GUYS ARE TOTAL AMATEURS, THOUGH. WE CAN PARLAY THIS INTO GETTING THE DIAMOND OURSELVES.
TOLD YOU NOT TO TRY SOMETHING THAT ONLY A THIRD-RATE THIEF WOULD DO!
YOU'RE A REAL SAINT. FIRST-RATE THIEF OR SECOND-RATE THIEF, THE PRICE FOR STOLEN JEWELS IS THE SAME.
GRAB
FLASH
SWISH
THAT IDIOT!
HUH, WHAZZAT?
WHOOOM
YO, BOSS! I GOT THE DIAMOND! I GOT IT!
SHHAK

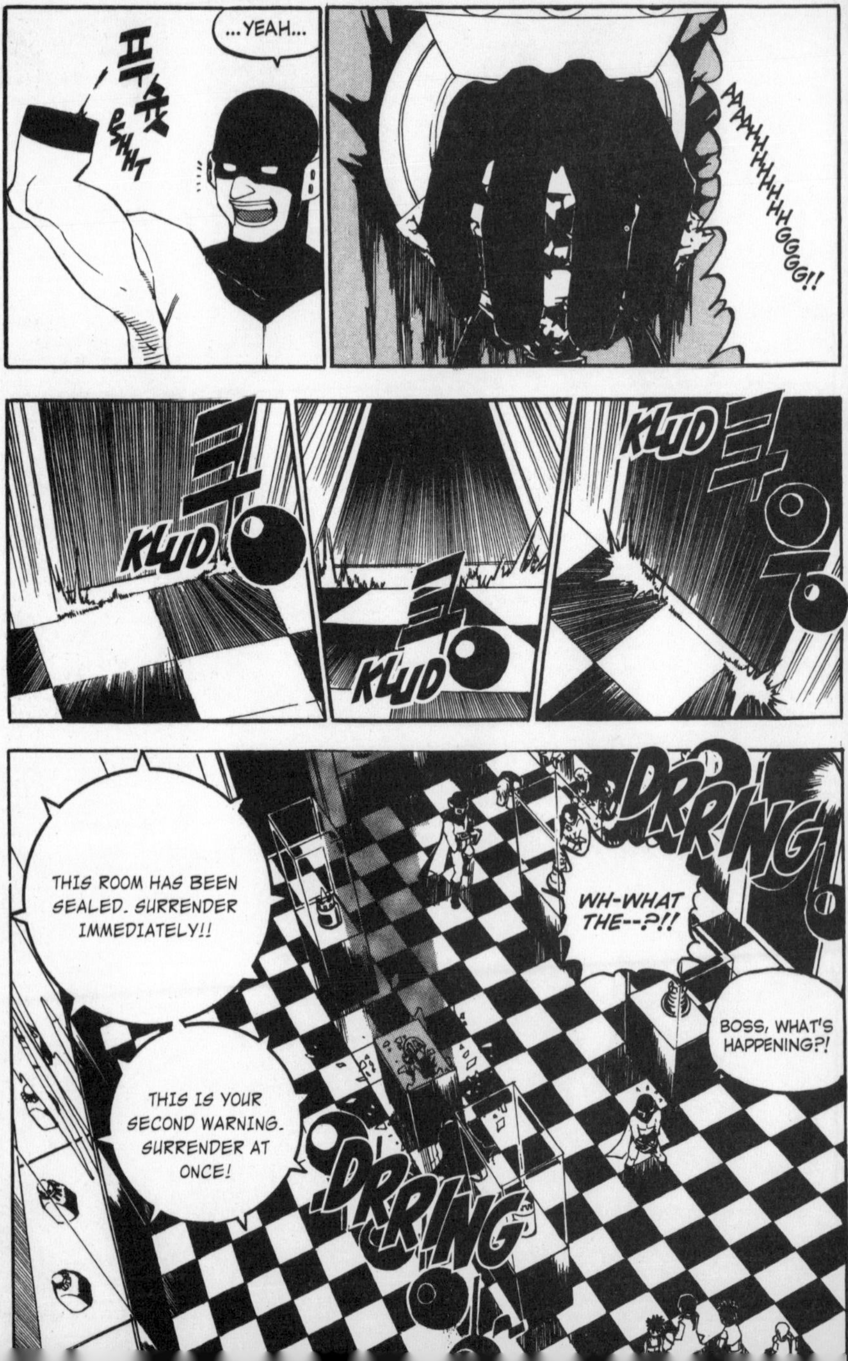

...YEAH...
프슛
PSHHT
AAAAHHHHHGGG!!
크앙
KLUD
크앙
KLUD
KLUD
크앙
THIS ROOM HAS BEEN SEALED. SURRENDER IMMEDIATELY!!
DRRING!
WH-WHAT THE--?!!
BOSS, WHAT'S HAPPENING?!
THIS IS YOUR SECOND WARNING. SURRENDER AT ONCE!
DRRING

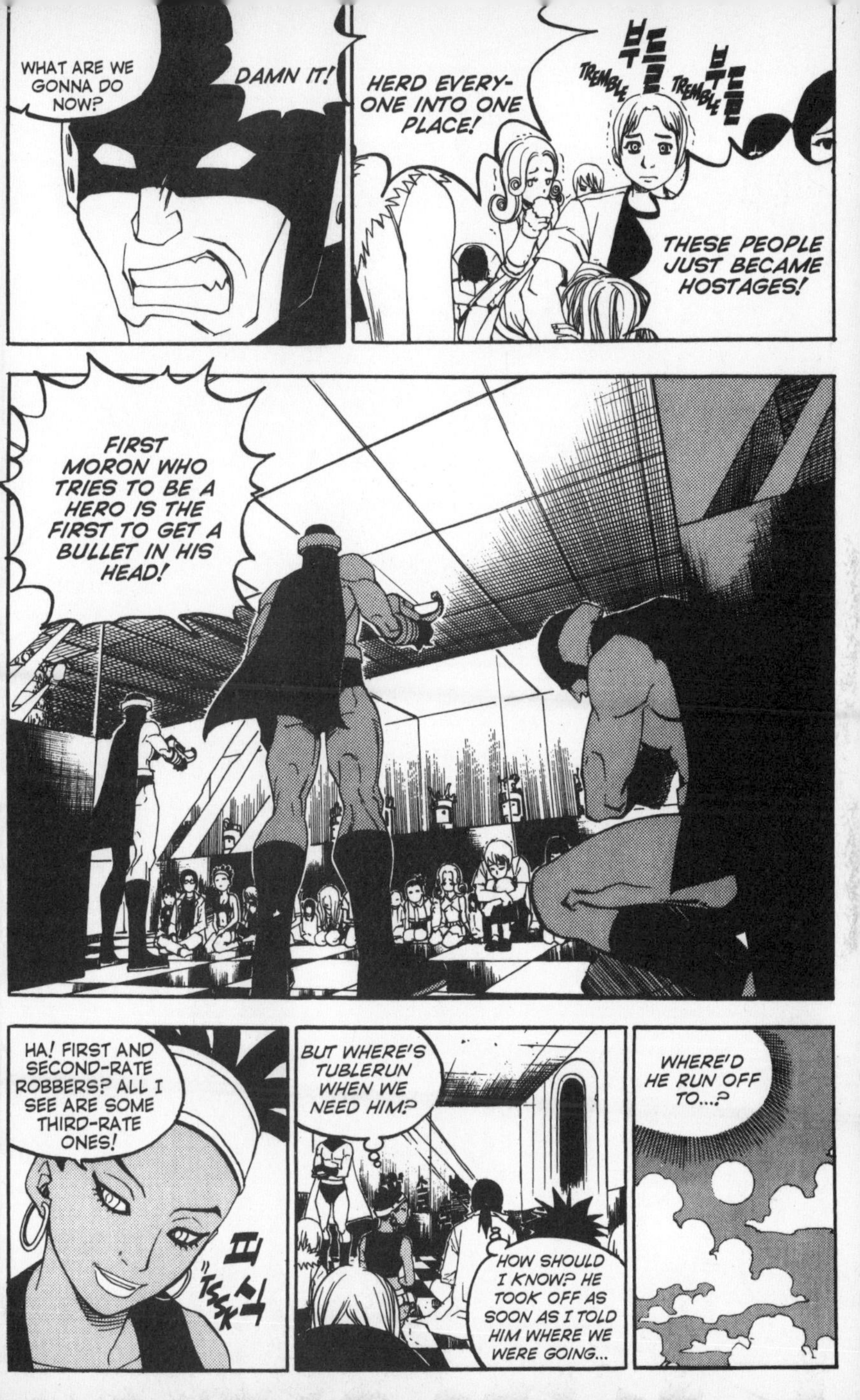

WHAT ARE WE GONNA DO NOW?
DAMN IT!
HERD EVERY-ONE INTO ONE PLACE!
TREMBLE TREMBLE
THESE PEOPLE JUST BECAME HOSTAGES!
FIRST MORON WHO TRIES TO BE A HERO IS THE FIRST TO GET A BULLET IN HIS HEAD!
HA! FIRST AND SECOND-RATE ROBBERS? ALL I SEE ARE SOME THIRD-RATE ONES!
TSSK
BUT WHERE'S TUBLERUN WHEN WE NEED HIM?
HOW SHOULD I KNOW? HE TOOK OFF AS SOON AS I TOLD HIM WHERE WE WERE GOING...
WHERE'D HE RUN OFF TO...?

HERE!

IS THERE ACTUALLY A CREAMY STRAWBERRY IN THERE OR ARE YOU PRANKING ME...?!!

DOONG

HOW SHOULD I KNOW? ACCORDING TO SWEET DREAM, THERE'S ONE CREAMY STRAWBERRY PER ONE THOUSAND CANDIES. YOU NEED A LOT OF LUCK...OR A LOT OF MONEY.

A LOT OF MONEY?

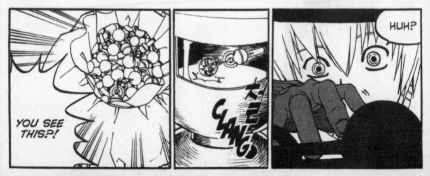

YOU SEE THIS?!

CLANG

HUH?

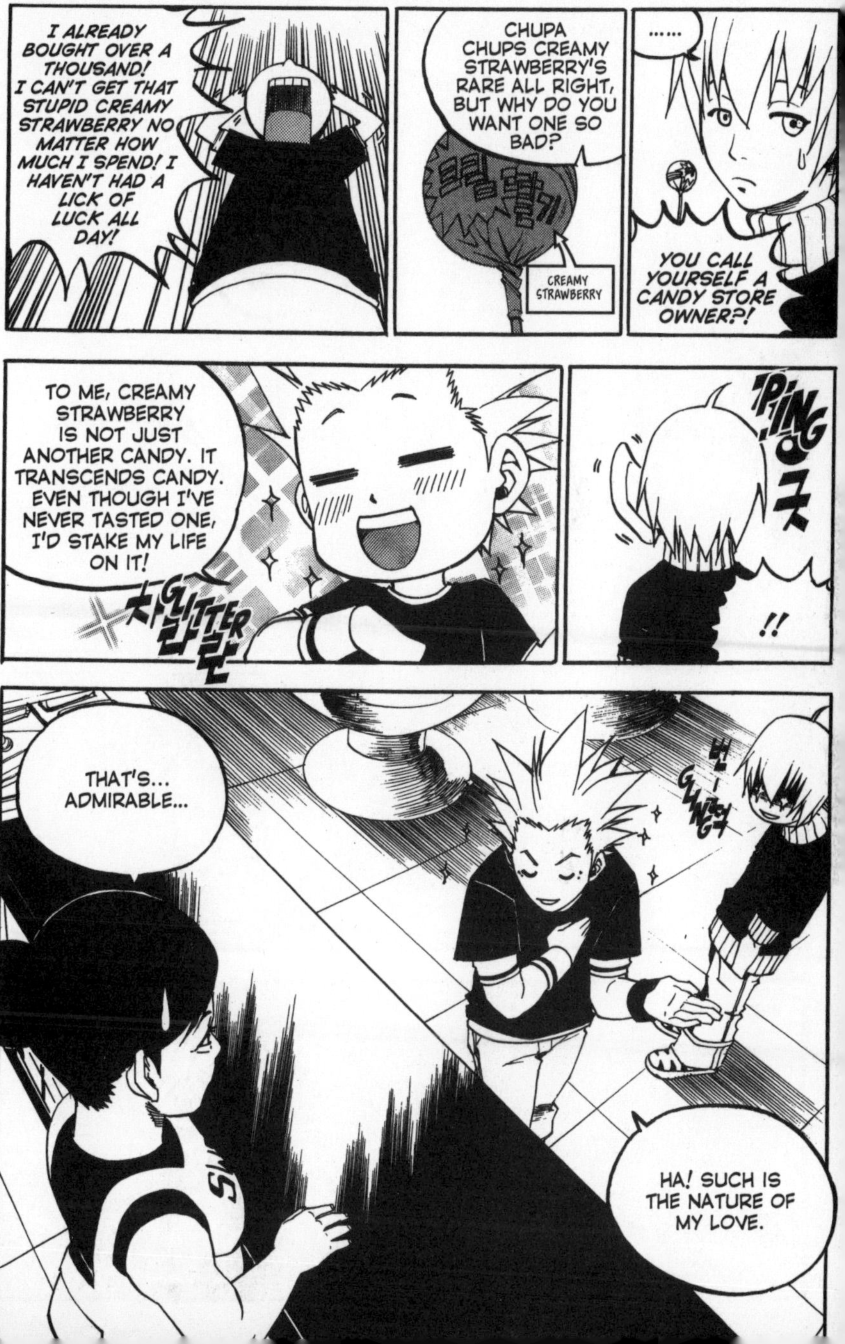
I ALREADY BOUGHT OVER A THOUSAND! I CAN'T GET THAT STUPID CREAMY STRAWBERRY NO MATTER HOW MUCH I SPEND! I HAVEN'T HAD A LICK OF LUCK ALL DAY!
CHUPA CHUPS CREAMY STRAWBERRY'S RARE ALL RIGHT, BUT WHY DO YOU WANT ONE SO BAD?
CREAMY STRAWBERRY
......
YOU CALL YOURSELF A CANDY STORE OWNER?!
TO ME, CREAMY STRAWBERRY IS NOT JUST ANOTHER CANDY. IT TRANSCENDS CANDY. EVEN THOUGH I'VE NEVER TASTED ONE, I'D STAKE MY LIFE ON IT!
GLITTER
PING
!!
THAT'S... ADMIRABLE...
GLING
HA! SUCH IS THE NATURE OF MY LOVE.

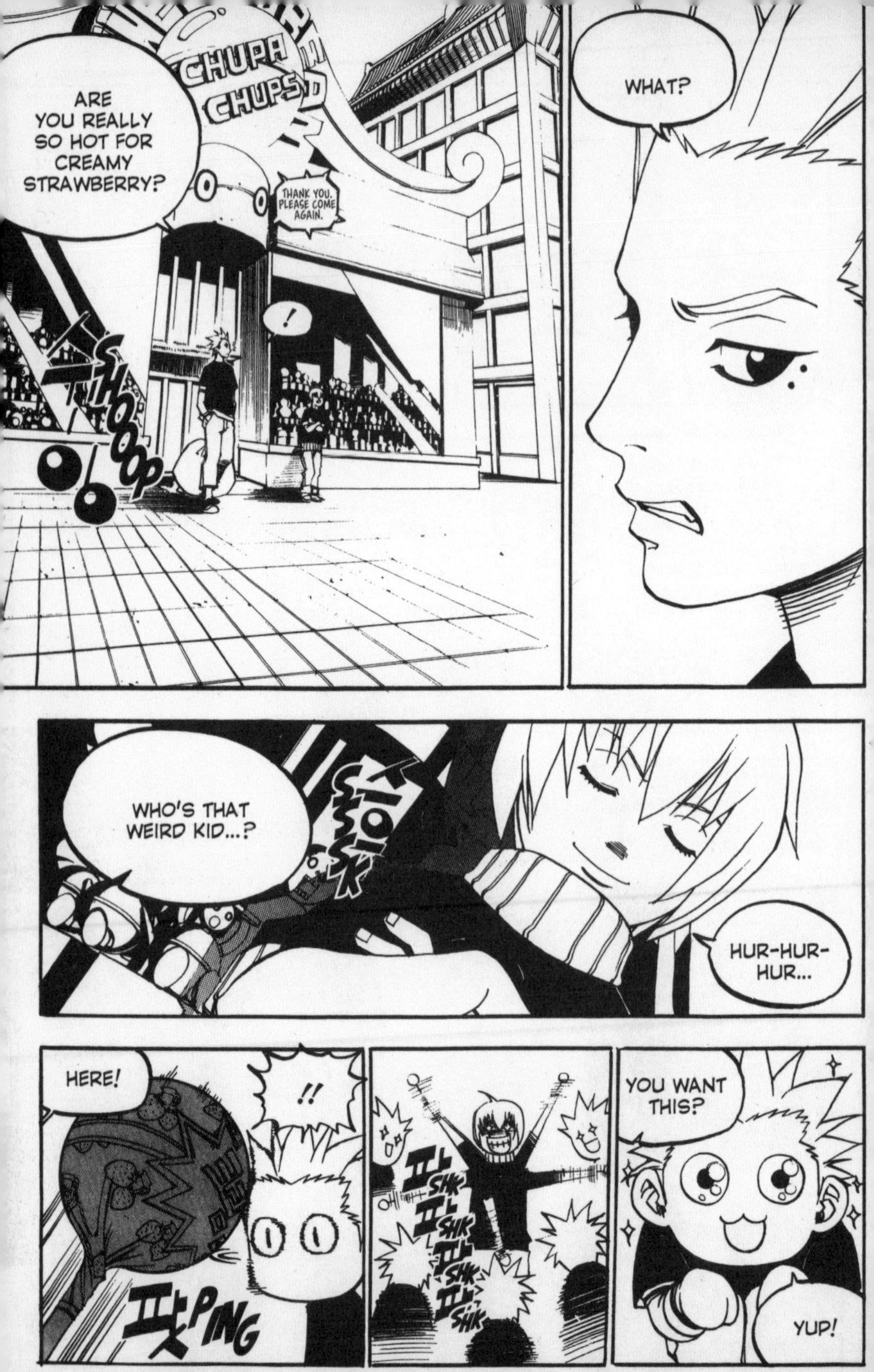
ARE YOU REALLY SO HOT FOR CREAMY STRAWBERRY?
CHUPA CHUPS
THANK YOU. PLEASE COME AGAIN.
!
SHOOOP
WHAT?
WHO'S THAT WEIRD KID...?
HUR-HUR-HUR...
HERE!
!!
PING
SHK SHK SHK SHK
YOU WANT THIS?
YUP!

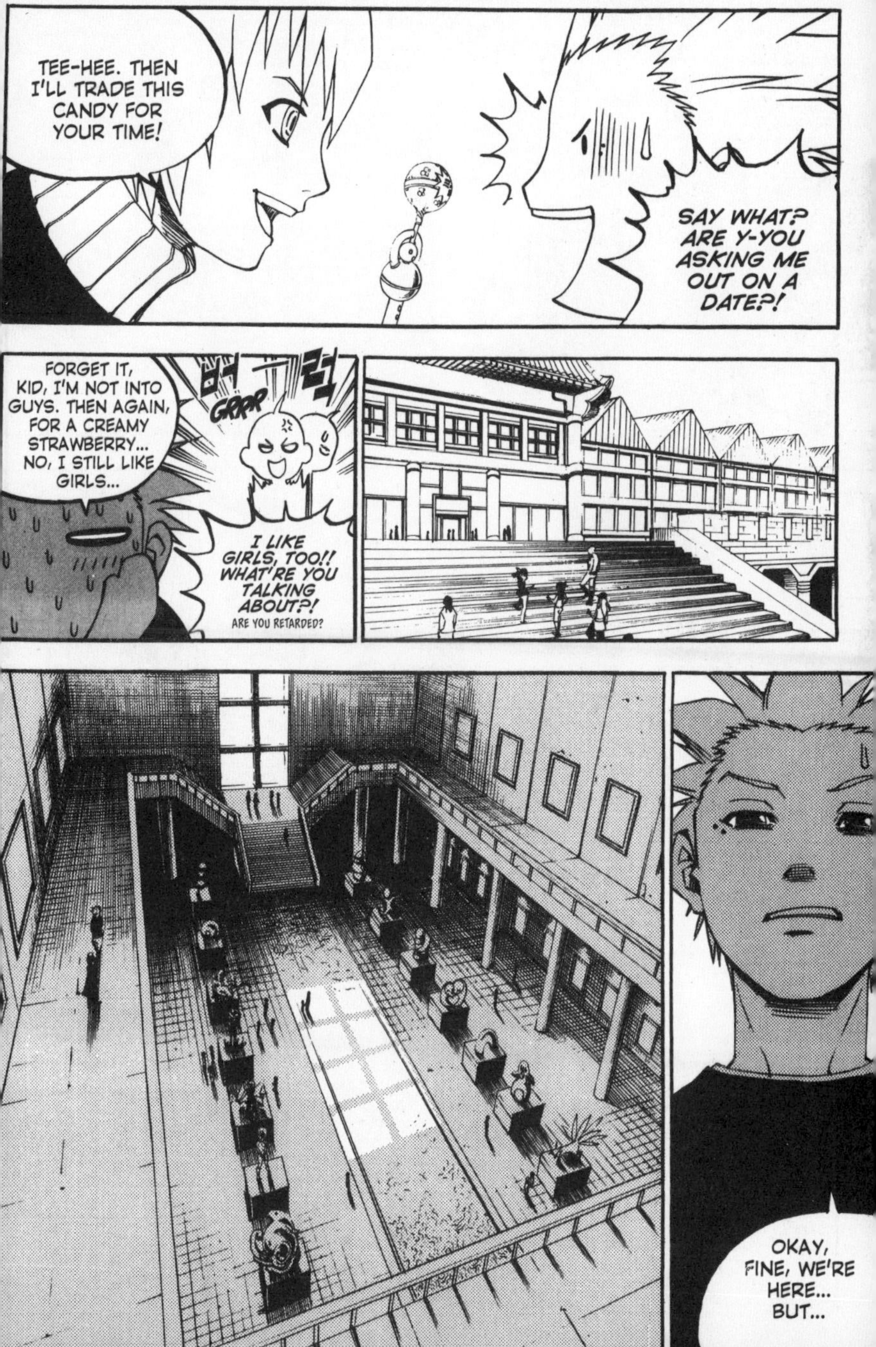
TEE-HEE. THEN I'LL TRADE THIS CANDY FOR YOUR TIME!
SAY WHAT? ARE Y-YOU ASKING ME OUT ON A DATE?!
FORGET IT, KID, I'M NOT INTO GUYS. THEN AGAIN, FOR A CREAMY STRAWBERRY... NO, I STILL LIKE GIRLS...
GRRR
I LIKE GIRLS, TOO!! WHAT'RE YOU TALKING ABOUT?!
ARE YOU RETARDED?
OKAY, FINE, WE'RE HERE... BUT...

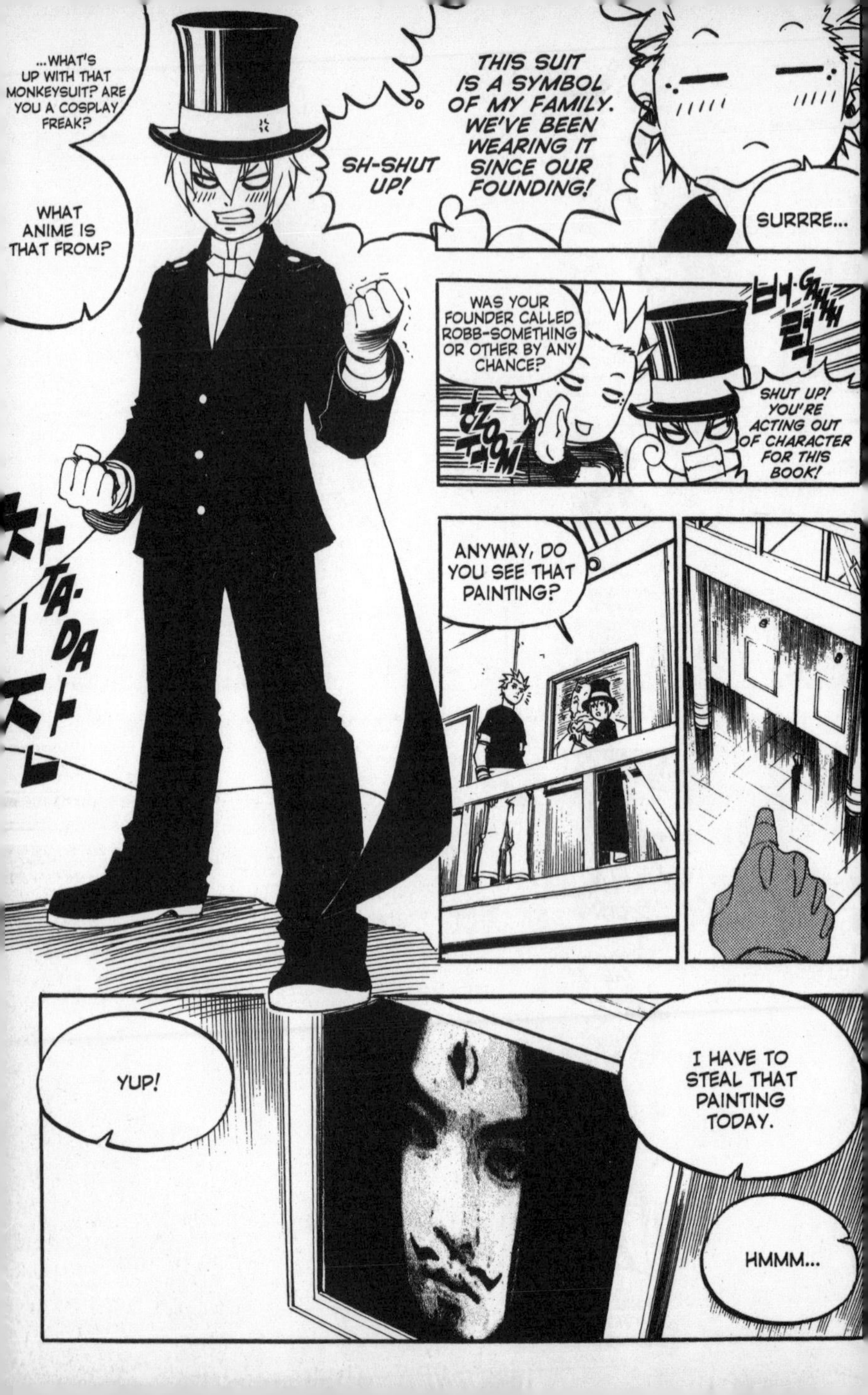
...WHAT'S UP WITH THAT MONKEYSUIT? ARE YOU A COSPLAY FREAK?
WHAT ANIME IS THAT FROM?
SH-SHUT UP!
TA-DA
THIS SUIT IS A SYMBOL OF MY FAMILY. WE'VE BEEN WEARING IT SINCE OUR FOUNDING!
SURRRE...
WAS YOUR FOUNDER CALLED ROBB-SOMETHING OR OTHER BY ANY CHANCE?
ZOOM
SHUT UP! YOU'RE ACTING OUT OF CHARACTER FOR THIS BOOK!
ANYWAY, DO YOU SEE THAT PAINTING?
YUP!
I HAVE TO STEAL THAT PAINTING TODAY.
HMMM...

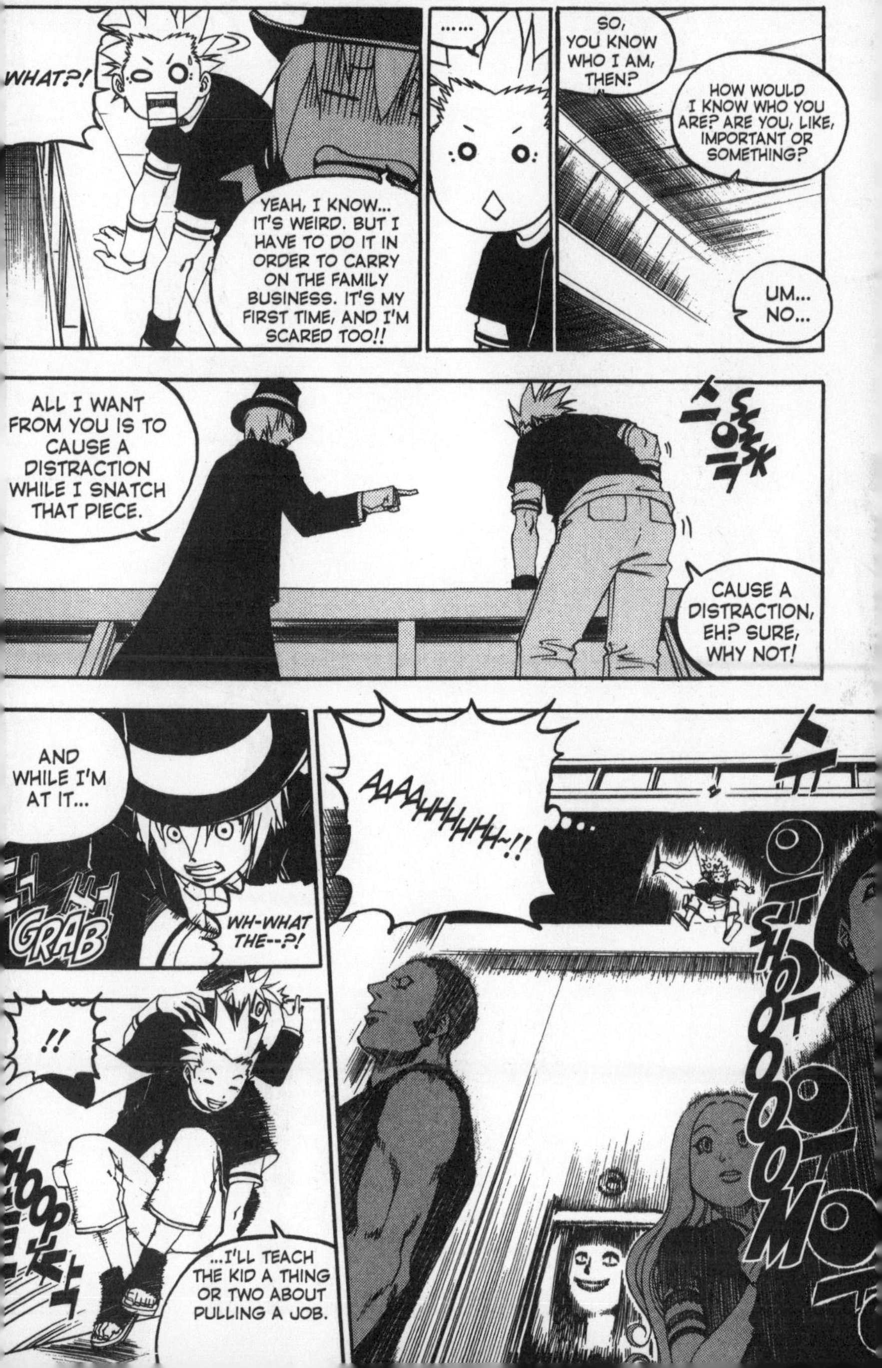
WHAT?!
YEAH, I KNOW... IT'S WEIRD. BUT I HAVE TO DO IT IN ORDER TO CARRY ON THE FAMILY BUSINESS. IT'S MY FIRST TIME, AND I'M SCARED TOO!!
......
SO, YOU KNOW WHO I AM, THEN?
HOW WOULD I KNOW WHO YOU ARE? ARE YOU, LIKE, IMPORTANT OR SOMETHING?
UM... NO...
ALL I WANT FROM YOU IS TO CAUSE A DISTRACTION WHILE I SNATCH THAT PIECE.
CAUSE A DISTRACTION, EH? SURE, WHY NOT!
AND WHILE I'M AT IT...
GRAB
WH-WHAT THE--?!
!!
...I'LL TEACH THE KID A THING OR TWO ABOUT PULLING A JOB.
AAAAHHHHHH~!!

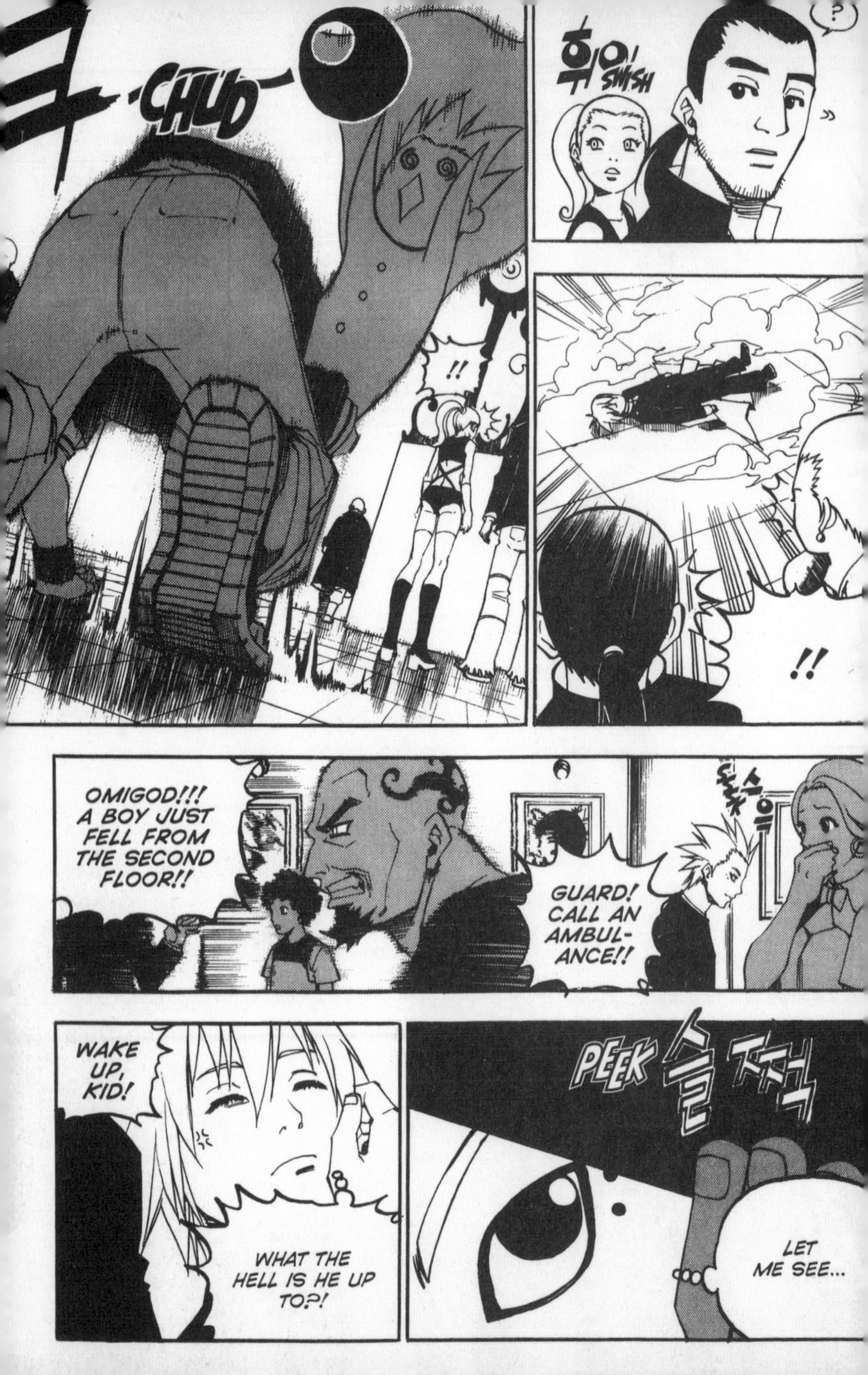
CHUD
!!
SWISH
?
!!
OMIGOD!!! A BOY JUST FELL FROM THE SECOND FLOOR!!
GUARD! CALL AN AMBUL-ANCE!!
WAKE UP, KID!
WHAT THE HELL IS HE UP TO?!
PEEK
LET ME SEE...

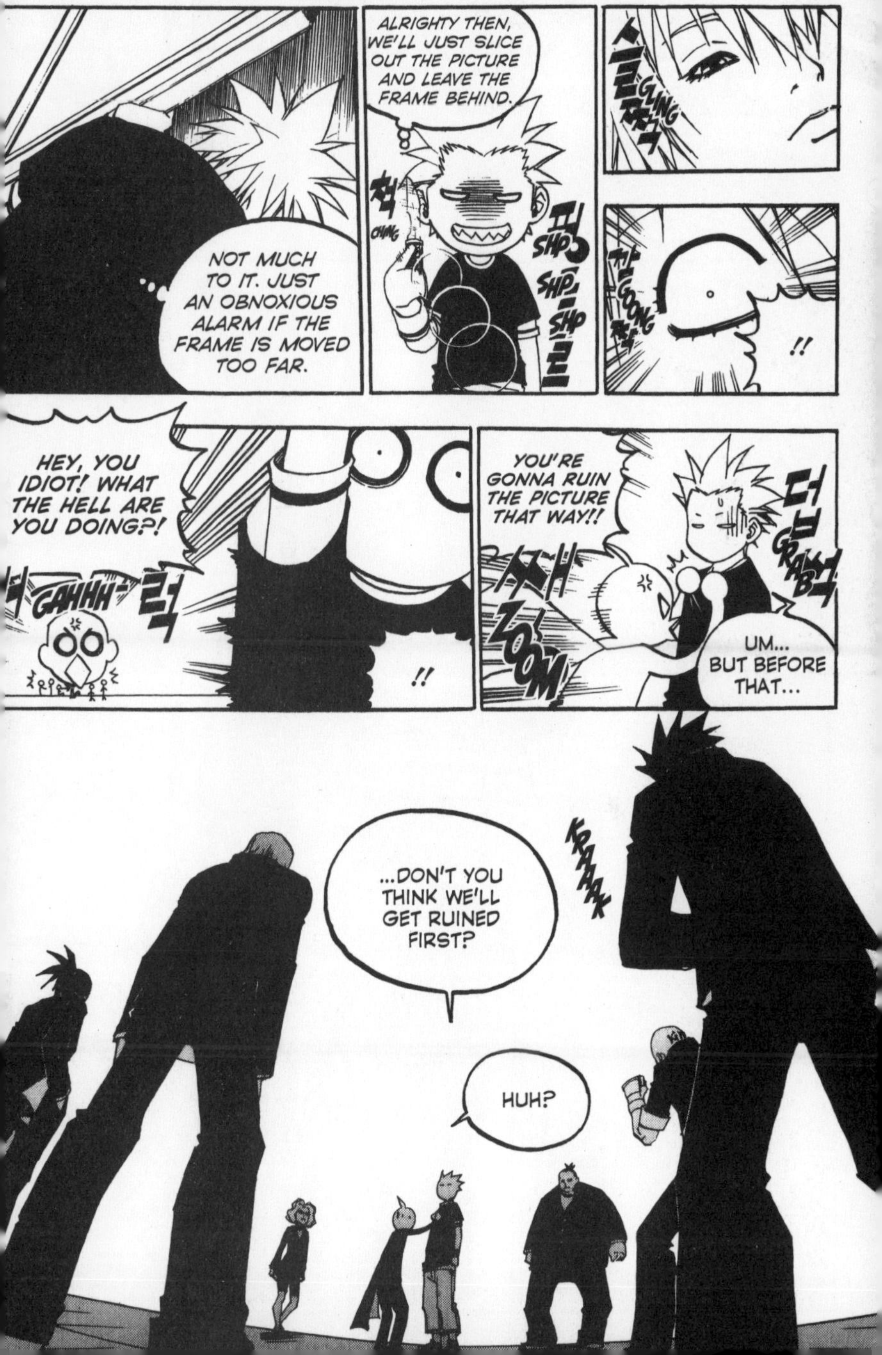
NOT MUCH TO IT. JUST AN OBNOXIOUS ALARM IF THE FRAME IS MOVED TOO FAR.
ALRIGHTY THEN, WE'LL JUST SLICE OUT THE PICTURE AND LEAVE THE FRAME BEHIND.
척
CHING
SHP
SHP
SHP
GLING
GOONG
!!
HEY, YOU IDIOT! WHAT THE HELL ARE YOU DOING?!
GAHHH
!!
YOU'RE GONNA RUIN THE PICTURE THAT WAY!!
ZOOM
GRAB
UM... BUT BEFORE THAT...
...DON'T YOU THINK WE'LL GET RUINED FIRST?
KRAAAK
HUH?

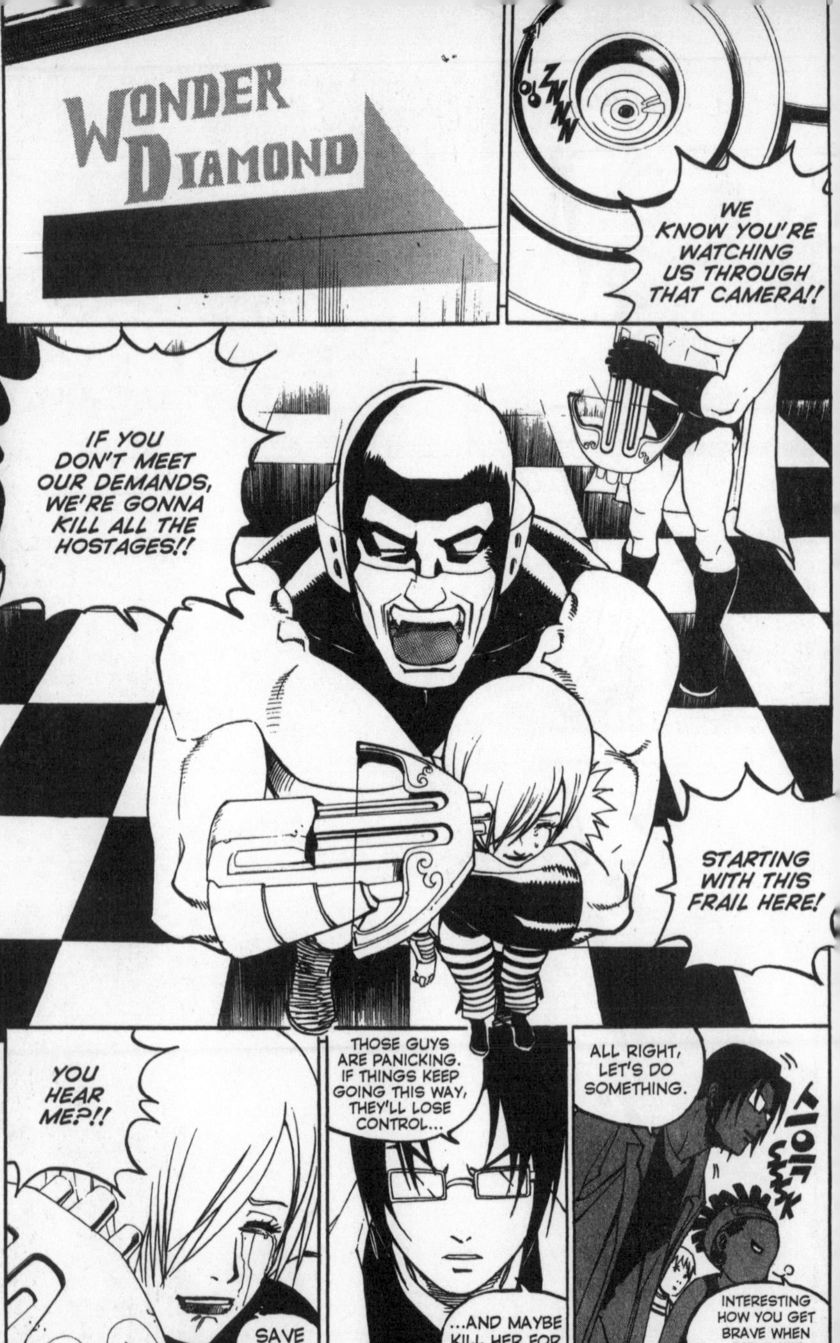
WONDER DIAMOND
WE KNOW YOU'RE WATCHING US THROUGH THAT CAMERA!!
IF YOU DON'T MEET OUR DEMANDS, WE'RE GONNA KILL ALL THE HOSTAGES!!
STARTING WITH THIS FRAIL HERE!
YOU HEAR ME?!!
SAVE ME...
THOSE GUYS ARE PANICKING. IF THINGS KEEP GOING THIS WAY, THEY'LL LOSE CONTROL...
...AND MAYBE KILL HER FOR REAL.
ALL RIGHT, LET'S DO SOMETHING.
INTERESTING HOW YOU GET BRAVE WHEN GIRLS ARE INVOLVED.

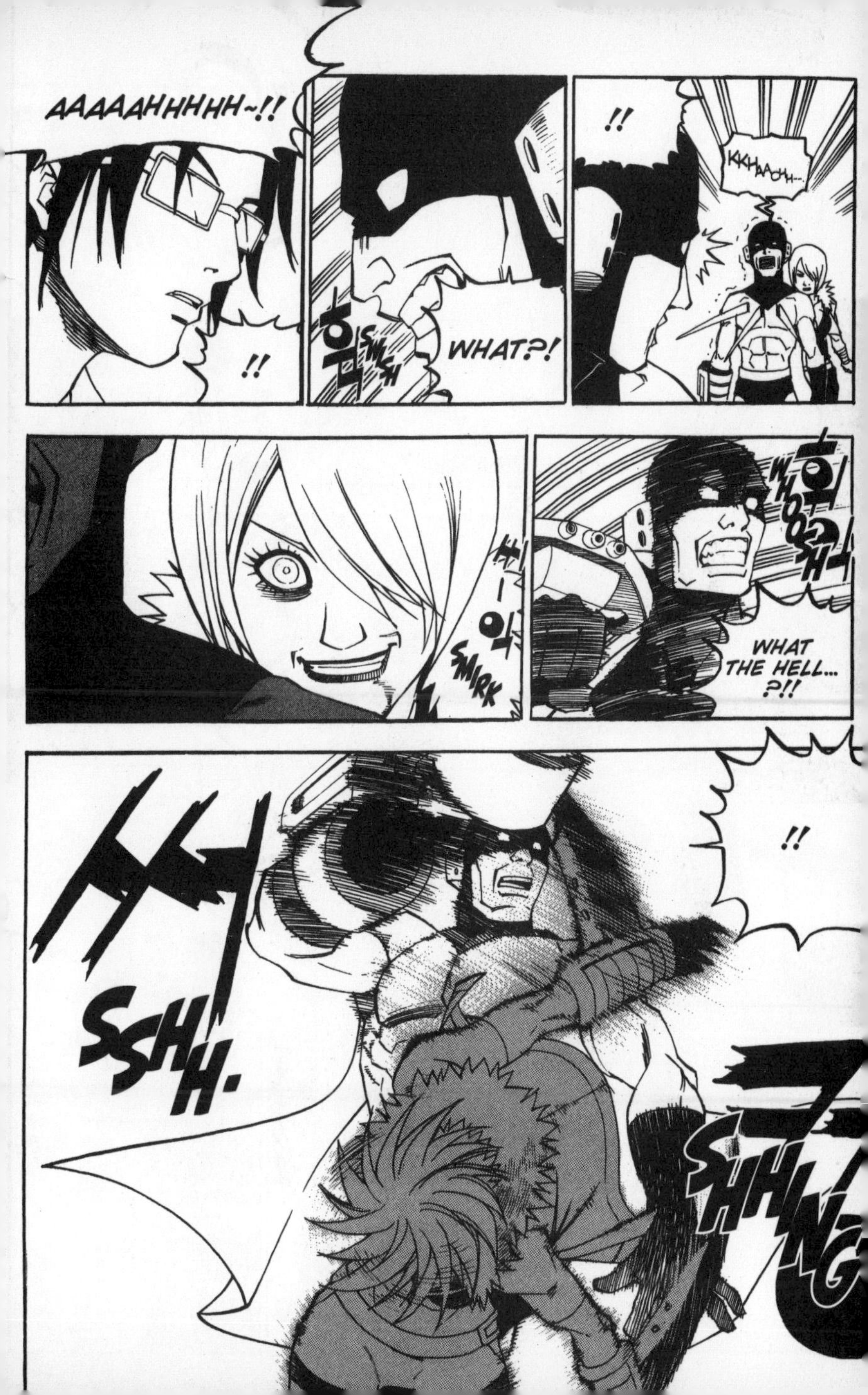
AAAAAHHHH~!!
!!
SWISH
WHAT?!
!!
KKHAACHH...
SMIRK
WHOOSH
WHAT THE HELL...?!!
!!
SSHH.
SHHING

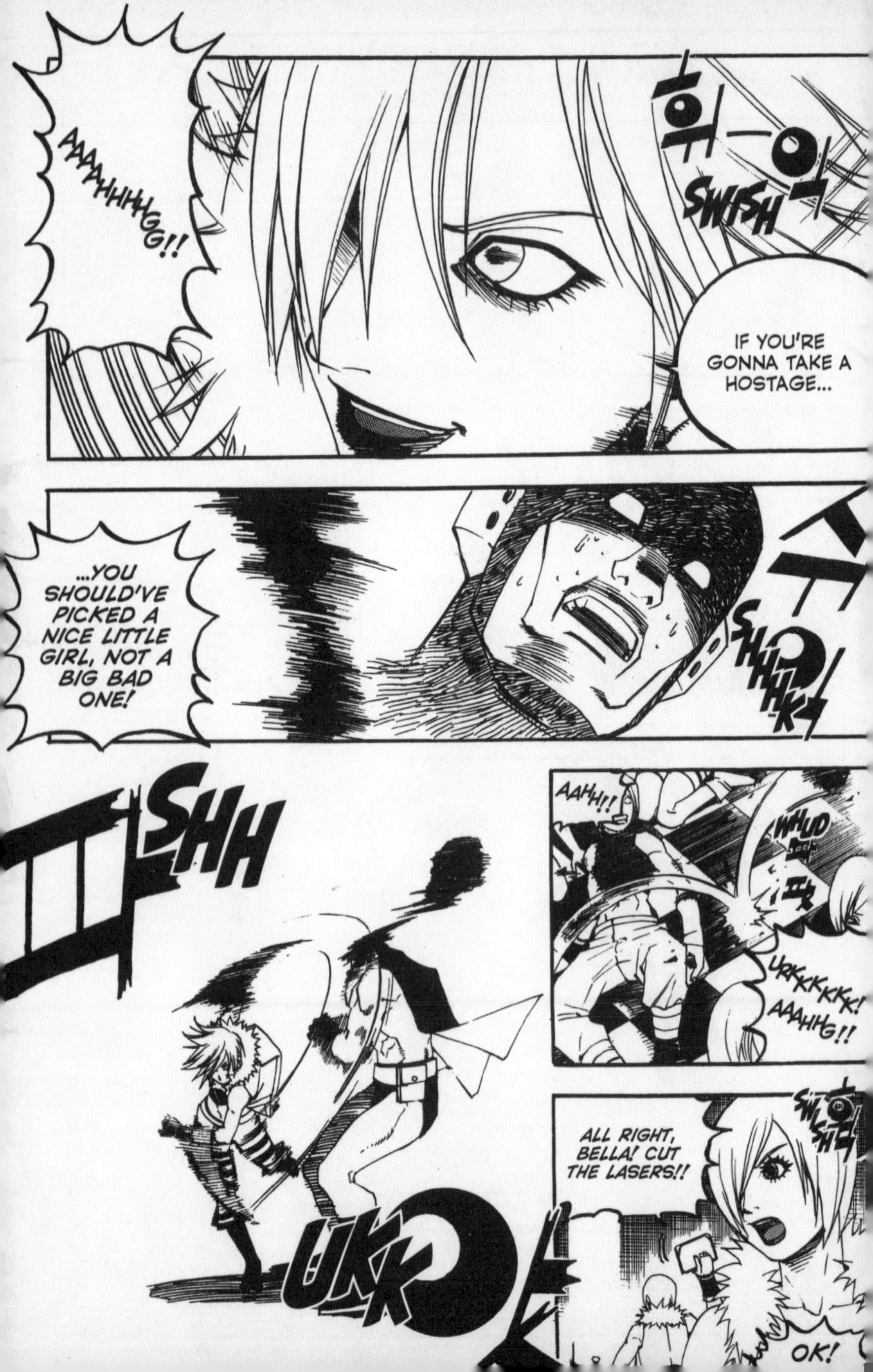
AAAAAHHHHGG!!
SWISH
IF YOU'RE GONNA TAKE A HOSTAGE...
...YOU SHOULD'VE PICKED A NICE LITTLE GIRL, NOT A BIG BAD ONE!
SHHHHK
SHH
UKK
AAHH!!
WHUD
URKKKKKK! AAAHHG!!
ALL RIGHT, BELLA! CUT THE LASERS!!
SWISH
OK!

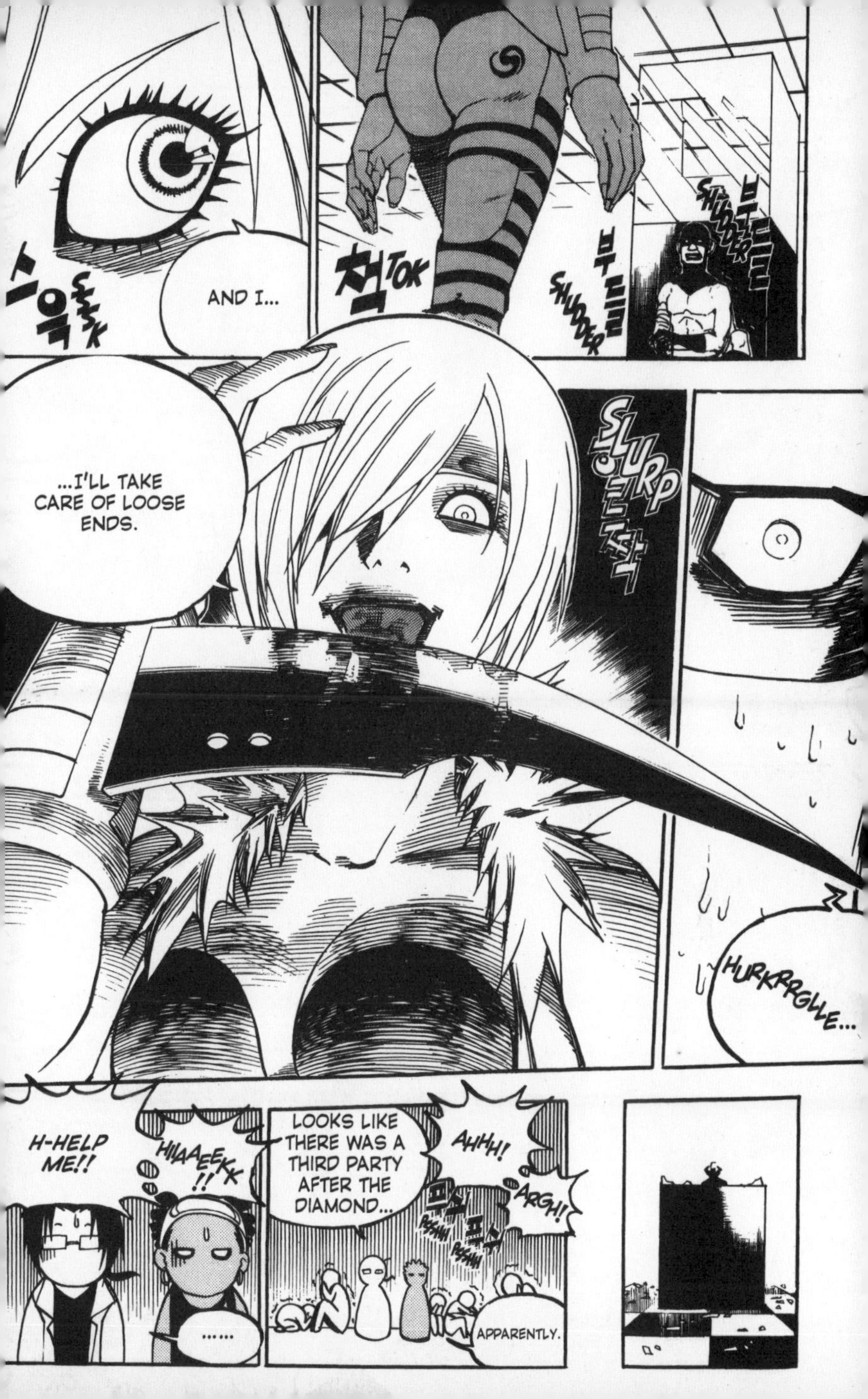
스윽
SEEK
AND I...
척 TOK
부르르
SHUDDER
부르르
SHUDDER
...I'LL TAKE CARE OF LOOSE ENDS.
SLURP
할짝
HURKRRGLLE...
H-HELP ME!!
HIIAAEEKK!!
......
LOOKS LIKE THERE WAS A THIRD PARTY AFTER THE DIAMOND...
AHHH!
ARGH!
PSSHH
PSSHH
APPARENTLY.

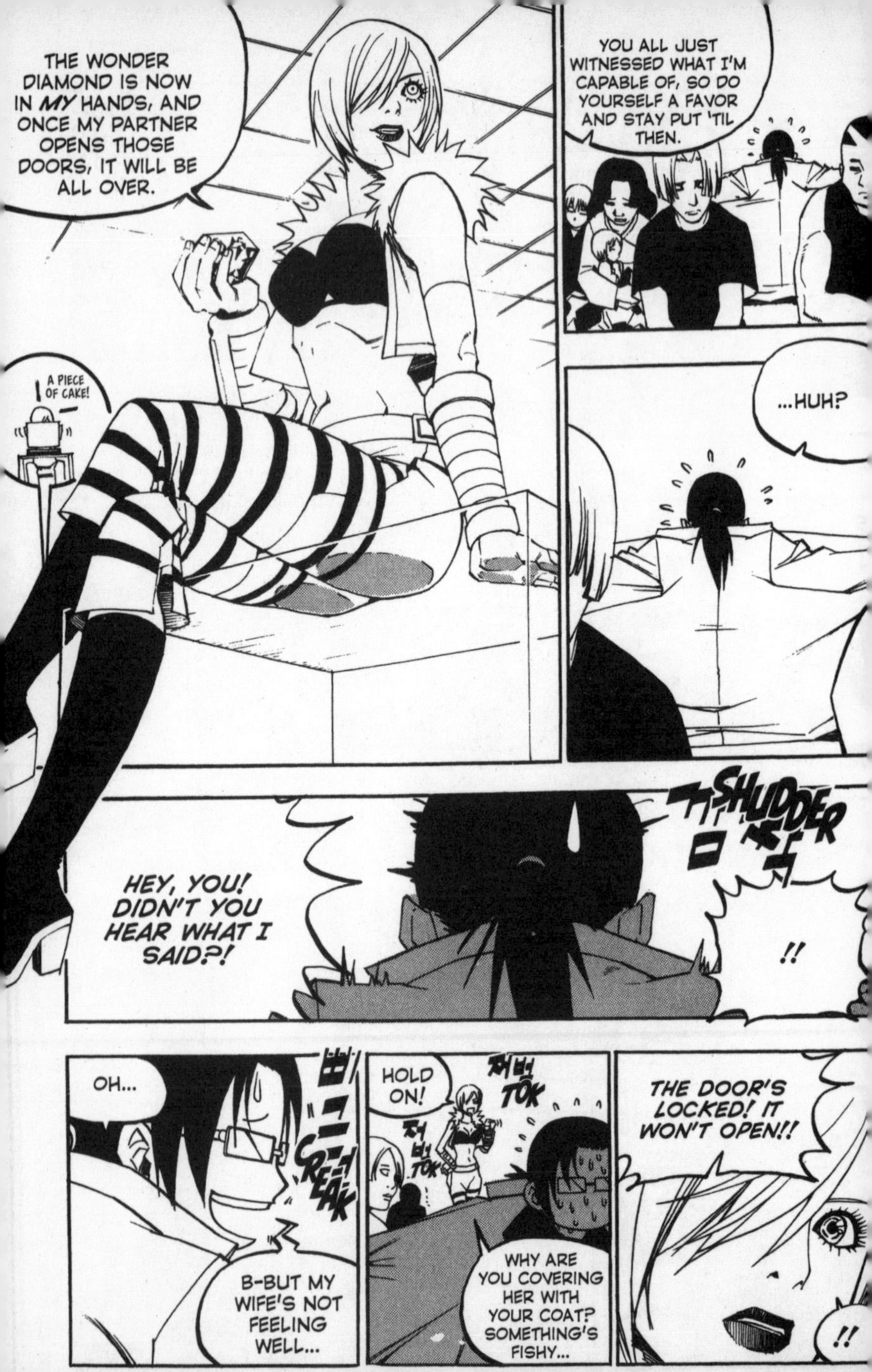
THE WONDER DIAMOND IS NOW IN *MY* HANDS, AND ONCE MY PARTNER OPENS THOSE DOORS, IT WILL BE ALL OVER.
A PIECE OF CAKE!
YOU ALL JUST WITNESSED WHAT I'M CAPABLE OF, SO DO YOURSELF A FAVOR AND STAY PUT 'TIL THEN.
...HUH?
HEY, YOU! DIDN'T YOU HEAR WHAT I SAID?!
SHUDDER
!!
OH...
CREAK
B-BUT MY WIFE'S NOT FEELING WELL...
HOLD ON!
저벅 TOK
저벅 TOK
WHY ARE YOU COVERING HER WITH YOUR COAT? SOMETHING'S FISHY...
THE DOOR'S LOCKED! IT WON'T OPEN!!
!!

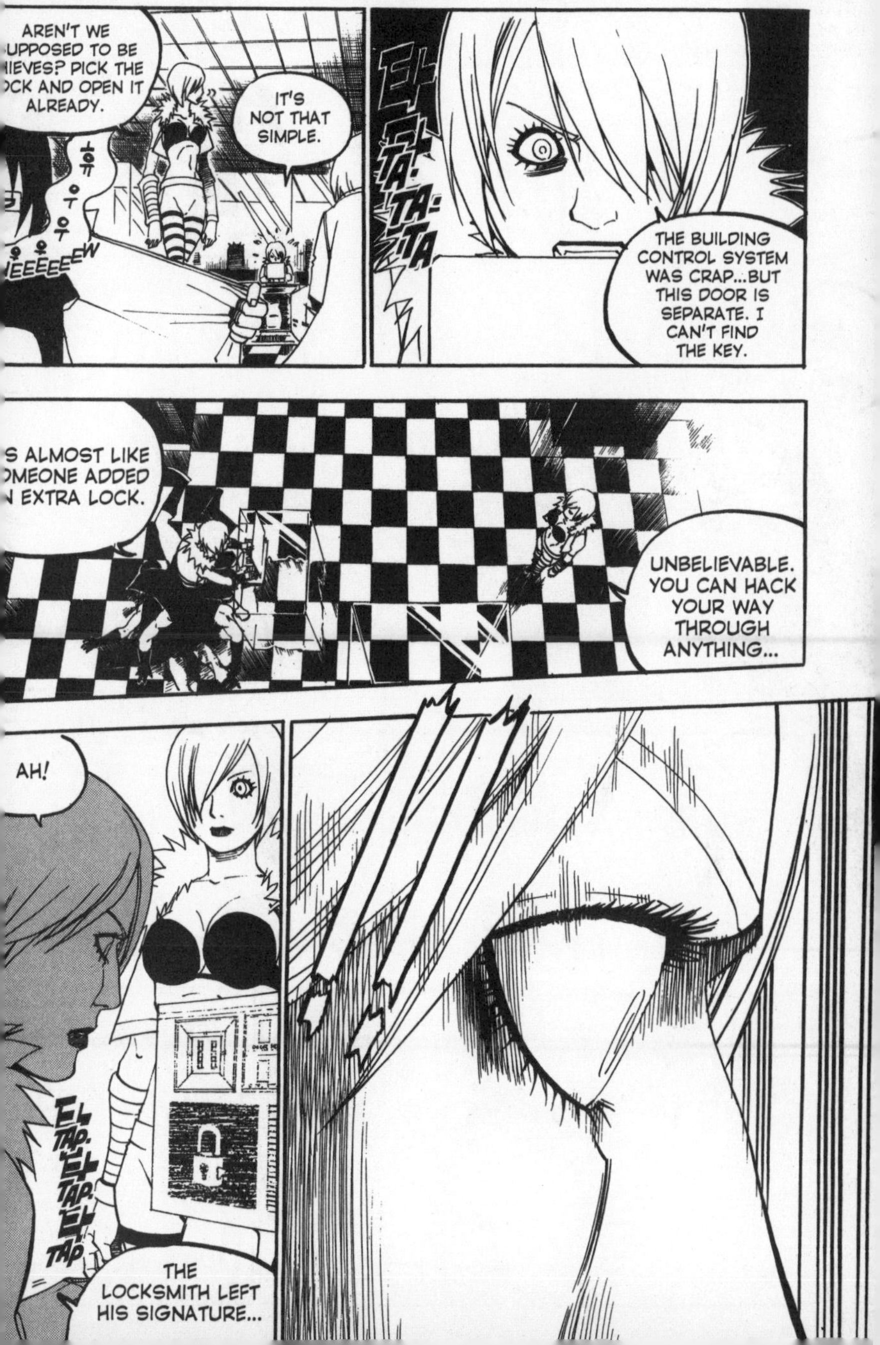

AREN'T WE UPPOSED TO BE HIEVES? PICK THE OCK AND OPEN IT ALREADY.
EEEEEEW
IT'S NOT THAT SIMPLE.
TA-TA-TA
THE BUILDING CONTROL SYSTEM WAS CRAP...BUT THIS DOOR IS SEPARATE. I CAN'T FIND THE KEY.
S ALMOST LIKE OMEONE ADDED N EXTRA LOCK.
UNBELIEVABLE. YOU CAN HACK YOUR WAY THROUGH ANYTHING...
AH!
TAP. TAP. TAP
THE LOCKSMITH LEFT HIS SIGNATURE...

THE
INVISIBLE
MAN?!!!

WHO'S THAT?

BF BF BF
WANGA WANGA

IT...IT MAKES NO SENSE! WHY WOULD HE EVEN BE HERE...?

KRA-
KOOM

SHOOM

HOOO...

GEEZ! IT TAKES YOU THE WHOLE DAY TO CLOSE A DOOR NOW? YOU GET SO TOTALLY LOST WHEN YOU GO ALL CYBER CEREBRO!!

......

YOU GOT SOME SECRET BOYFRIEND STASHED IN THERE?

STOP WHINING. IT'S UP TO YOU NOW.

TSSK!!

WE'VE GOT THREE MINUTES BEFORE THOSE LAZY COPS SHOW UP! I GOTTA BREAK THE LOCK BEFORE THAT! HOW CAN I BEAT THE INVISIBLE MAN IN THREE MINUTES?

THIS IS MAKING MY HACKER BLOOD BOIL.

FWOOM
FWOOM

SHE'S GONE OFF THE DEEP END...

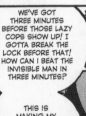

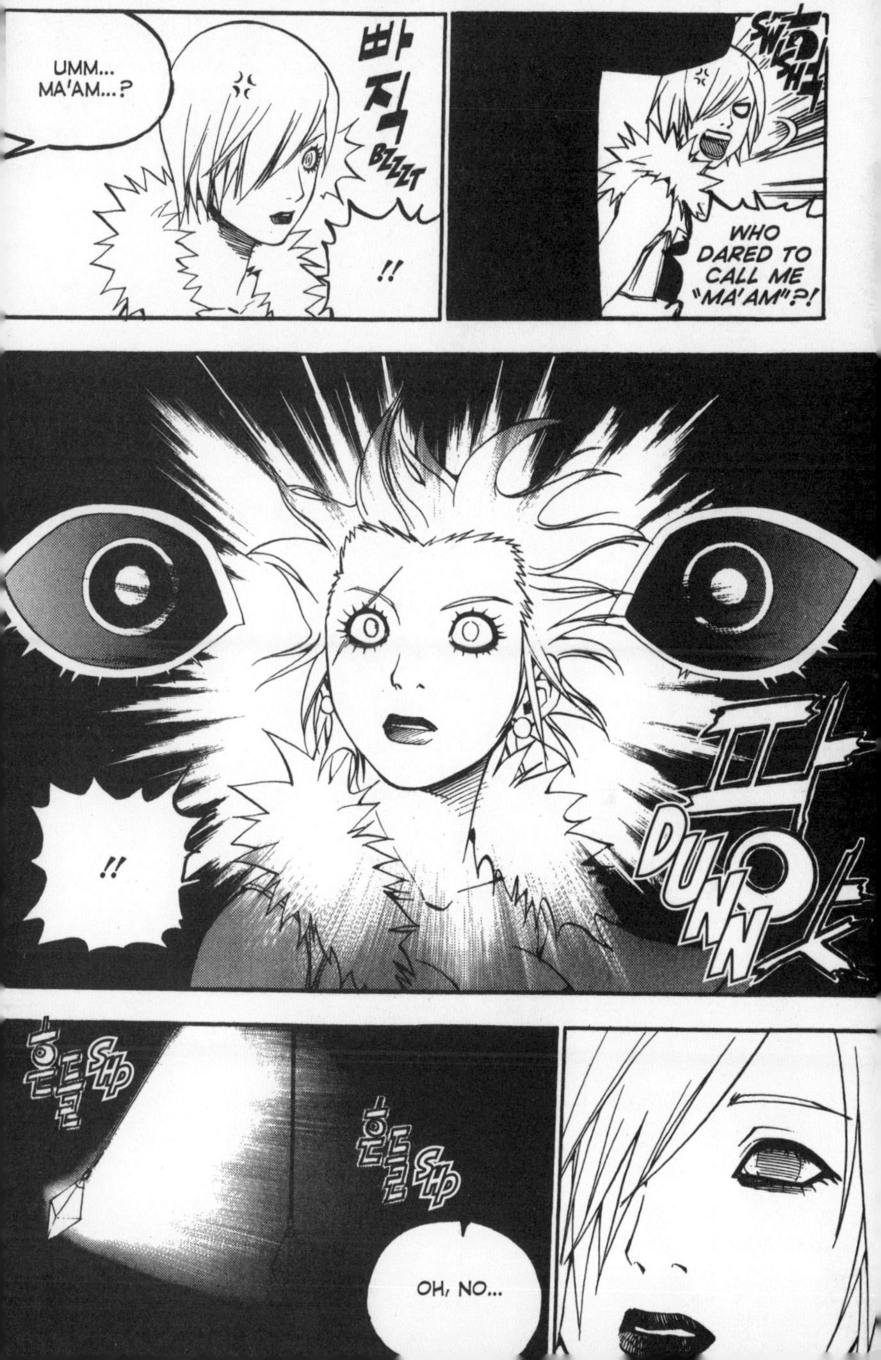
UMM... MA'AM...?
빠직
BZZZT
!!
SWISH
WHO DARED TO CALL ME "MA'AM"?!
!!
DUNN
SHP
SHP
OH, NO...

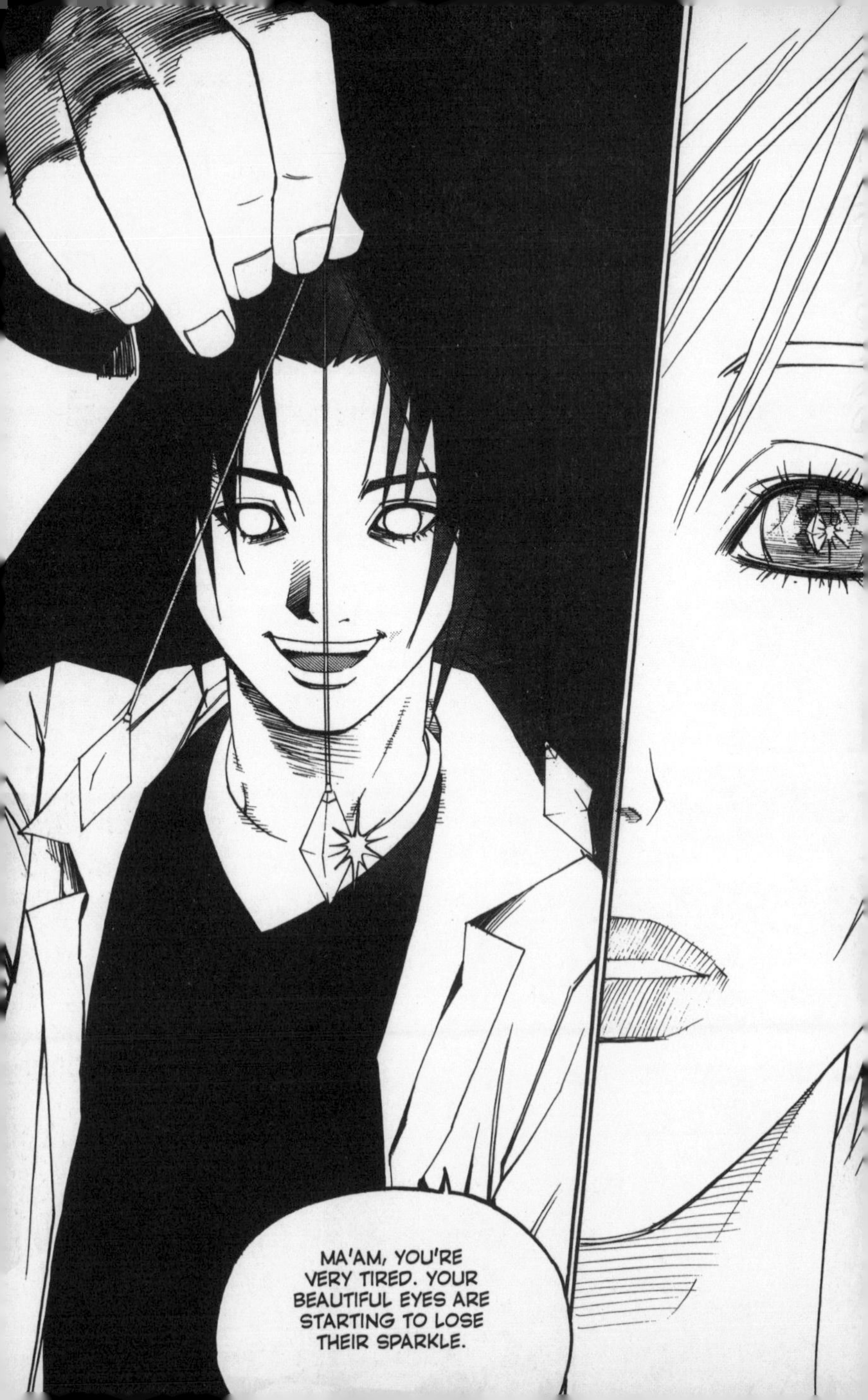
MA'AM, YOU'RE VERY TIRED. YOUR BEAUTIFUL EYES ARE STARTING TO LOSE THEIR SPARKLE.

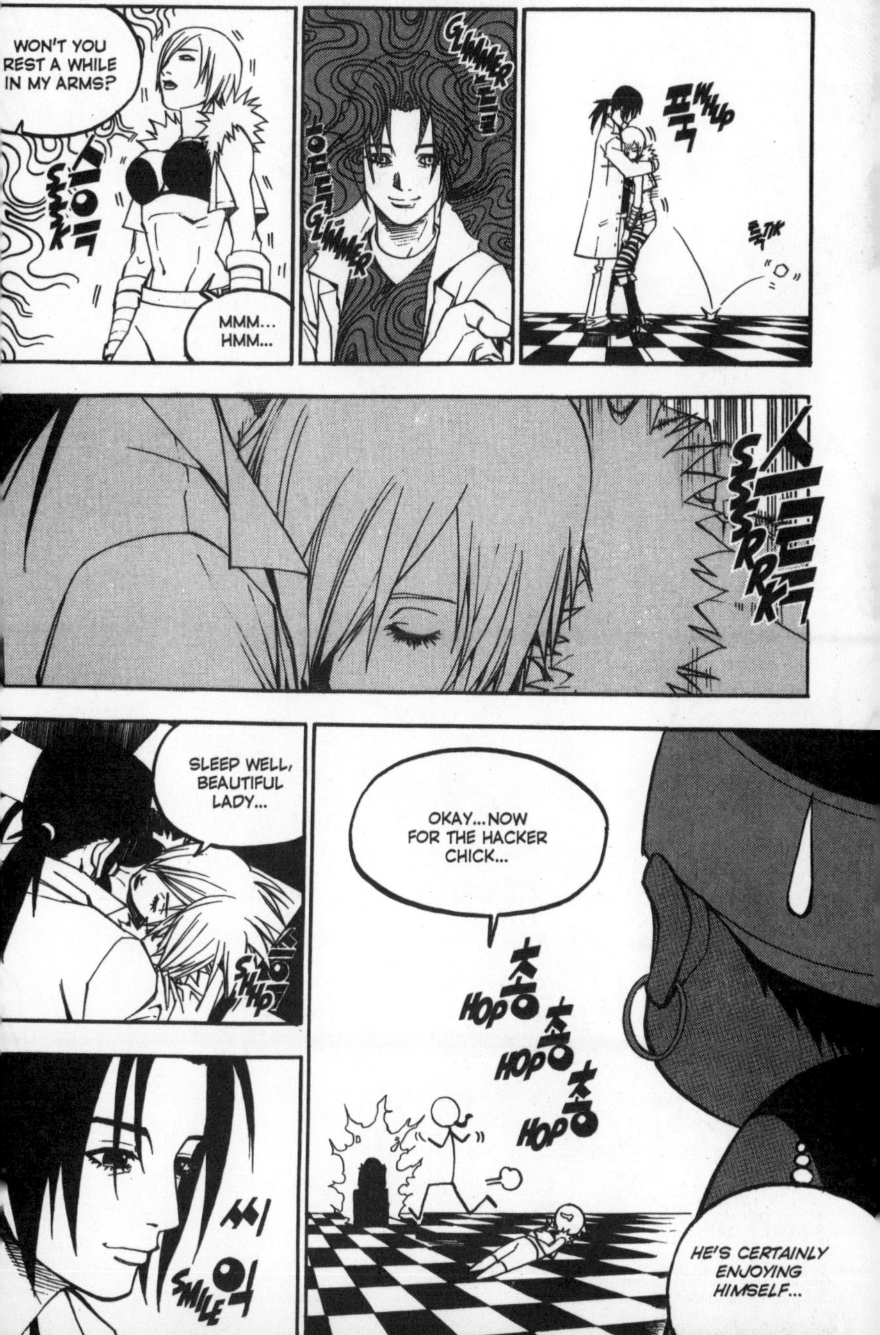

WON'T YOU REST A WHILE IN MY ARMS?
SMACK
MMM... HMM...
GLIMMER
GLIMMER
WHUP
TIK
SSSRRK
SLEEP WELL, BEAUTIFUL LADY...
SHHP
SMILE
OKAY...NOW FOR THE HACKER CHICK...
HOP
HOP
HOP
HE'S CERTAINLY ENJOYING HIMSELF...

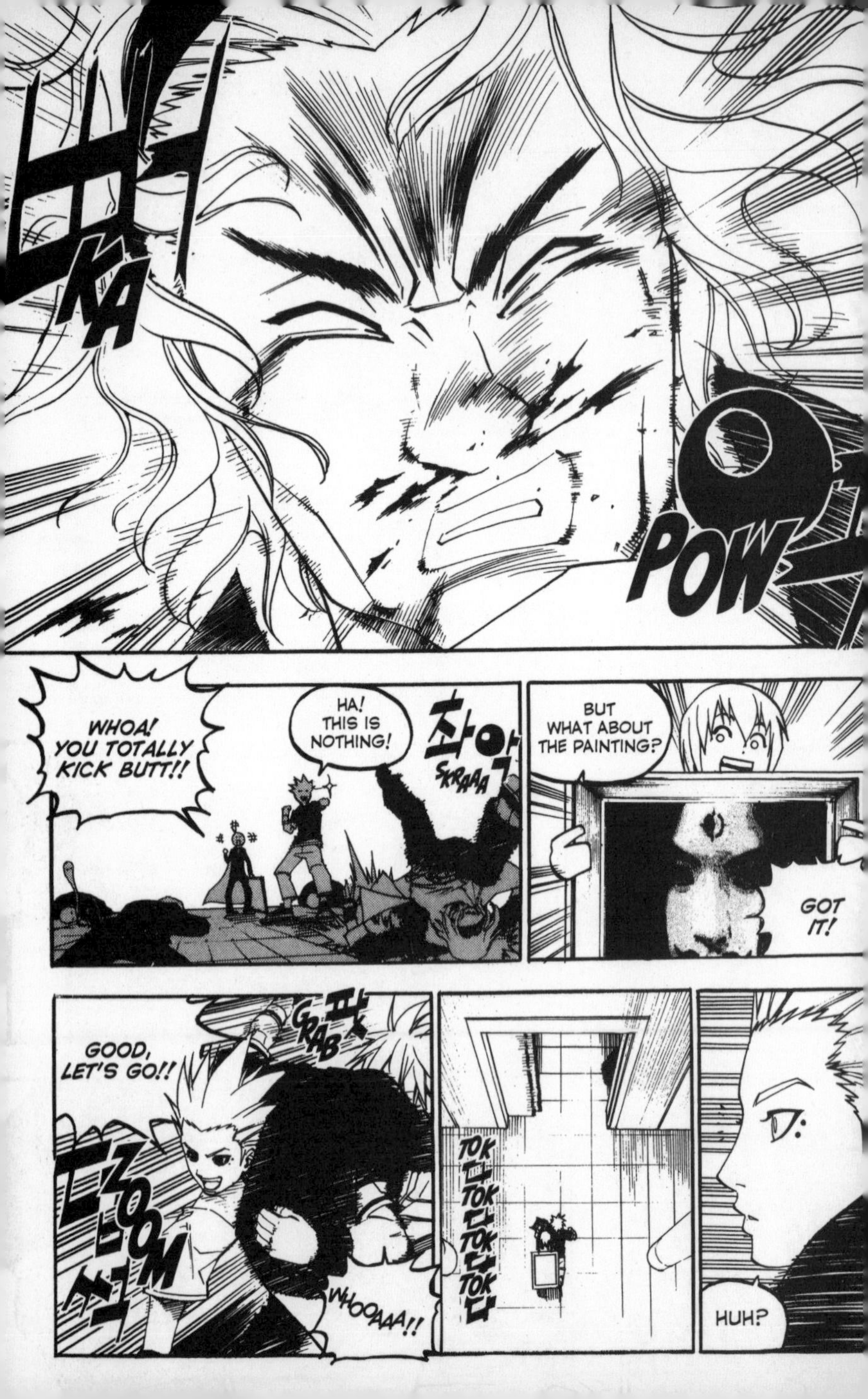
KA
POW
WHOA! YOU TOTALLY KICK BUTT!!
HA! THIS IS NOTHING!
SKRAAA
BUT WHAT ABOUT THE PAINTING?
GOT IT!
GOOD, LET'S GO!!
GRAB
ZOOM
WHOOAAA!!
TOK TOK TOK TOK
HUH?

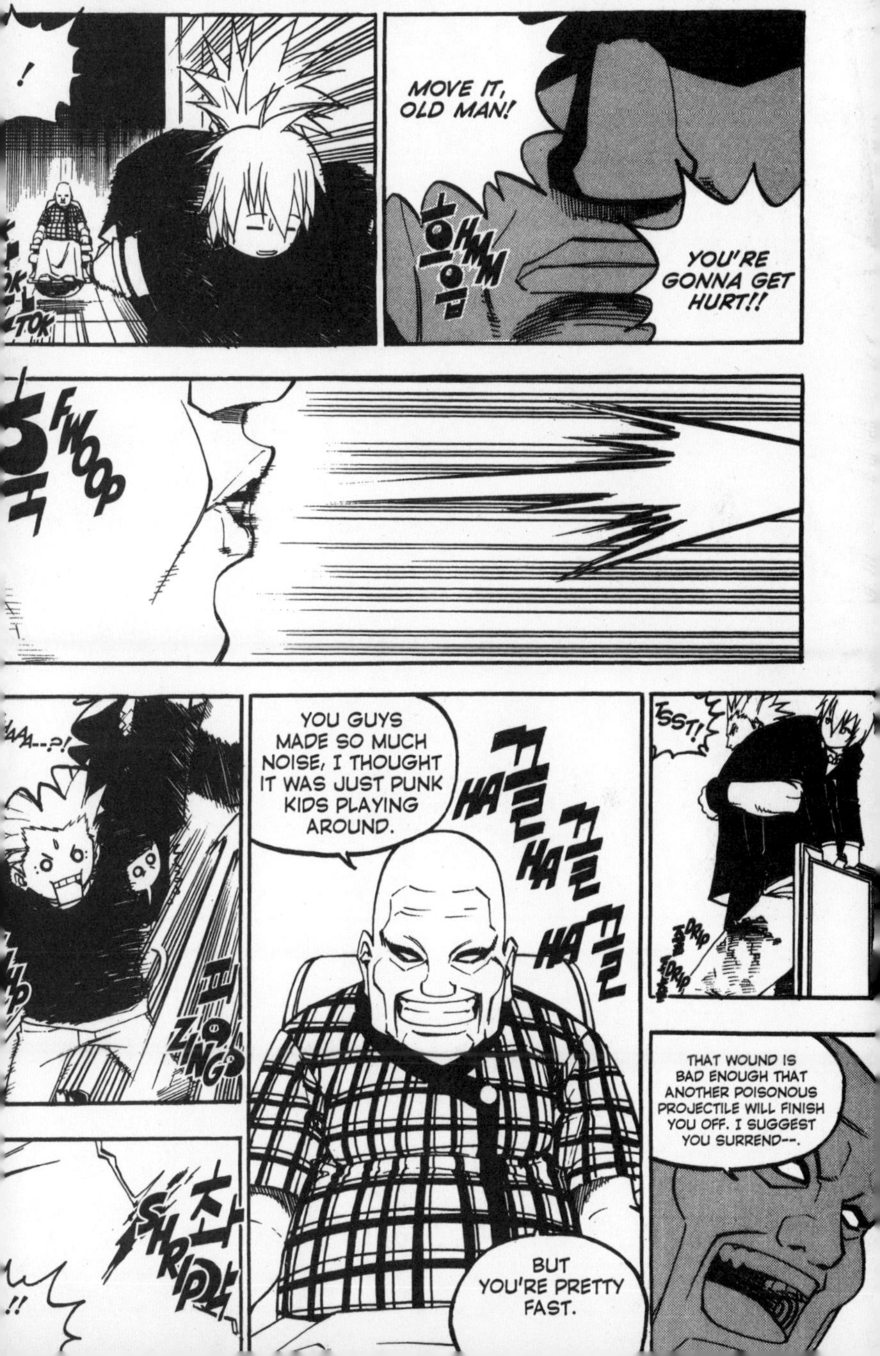
!
TOK
TOK
MOVE IT, OLD MAN!
HMM
YOU'RE GONNA GET HURT!!
FWOOP
AAAA--?!
ZING
YOU GUYS MADE SO MUCH NOISE, I THOUGHT IT WAS JUST PUNK KIDS PLAYING AROUND.
HA HA HA
TSST!
DRIP DRIP
THAT WOUND IS BAD ENOUGH THAT ANOTHER POISONOUS PROJECTILE WILL FINISH YOU OFF. I SUGGEST YOU SURREND--.
SHRIP
!!
BUT YOU'RE PRETTY FAST.

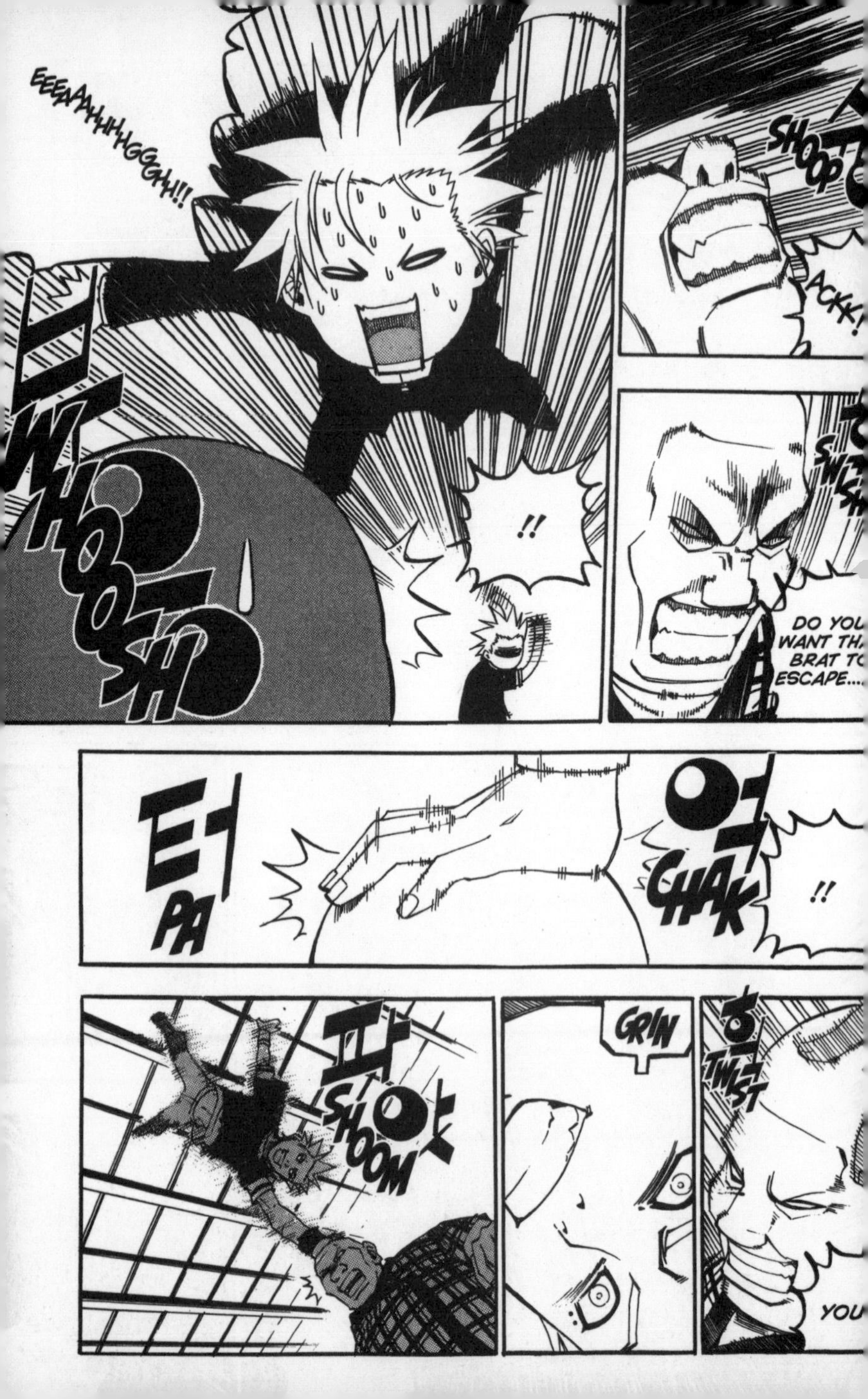
EEEAAAHHHGGGHH!!
WHOOSH
!!
SHOOP
ACKK!
SWISH
DO YOU WANT THA BRAT TO ESCAPE....
PA
CHAK
!!
SHOOM
GRIN
TWIST
YOU

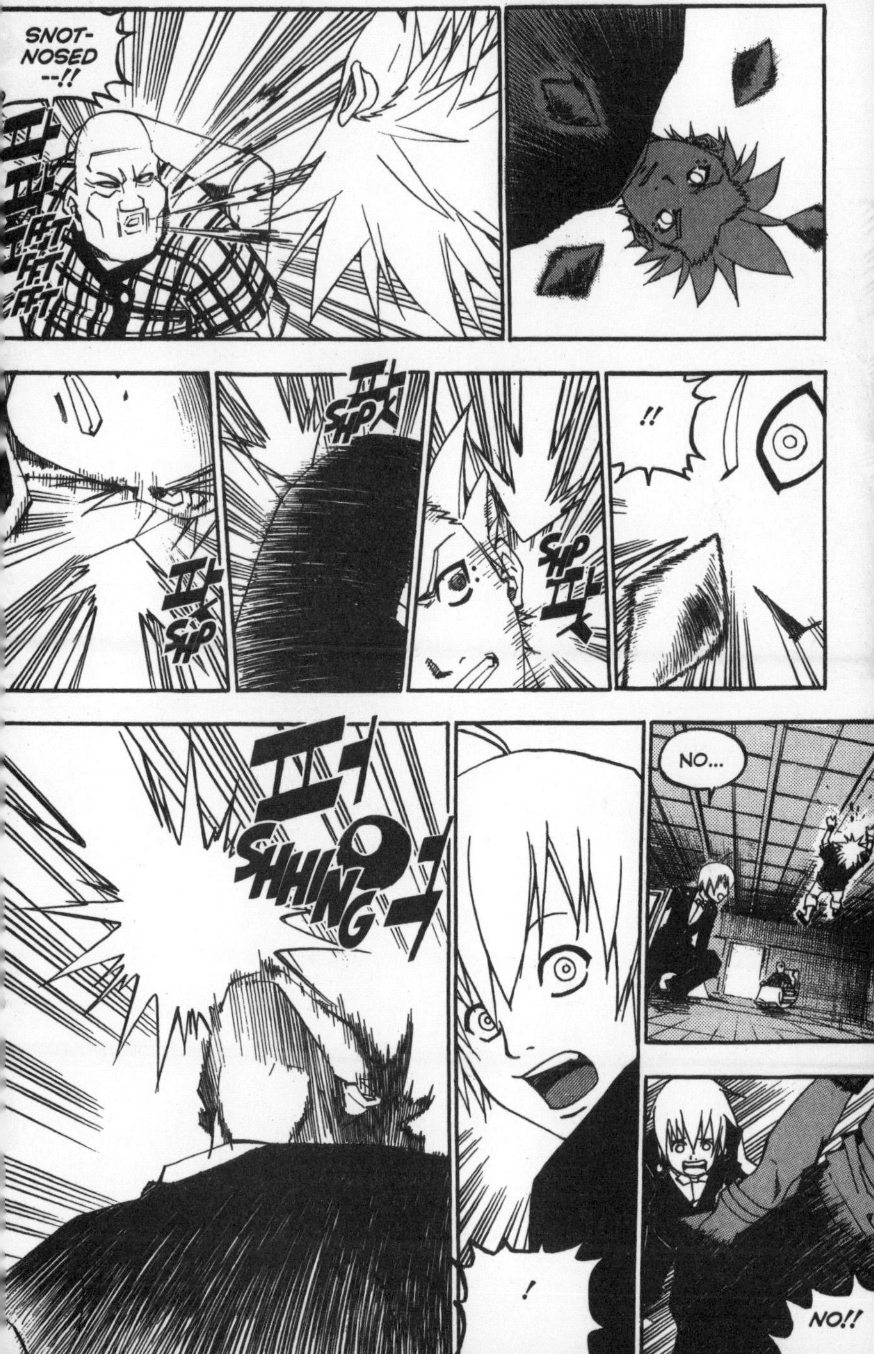
SNOT-NOSED --!!
FFT FFT FFT
SHP
SHP
SHP
!!
SHHING
!
NO...
NO!!

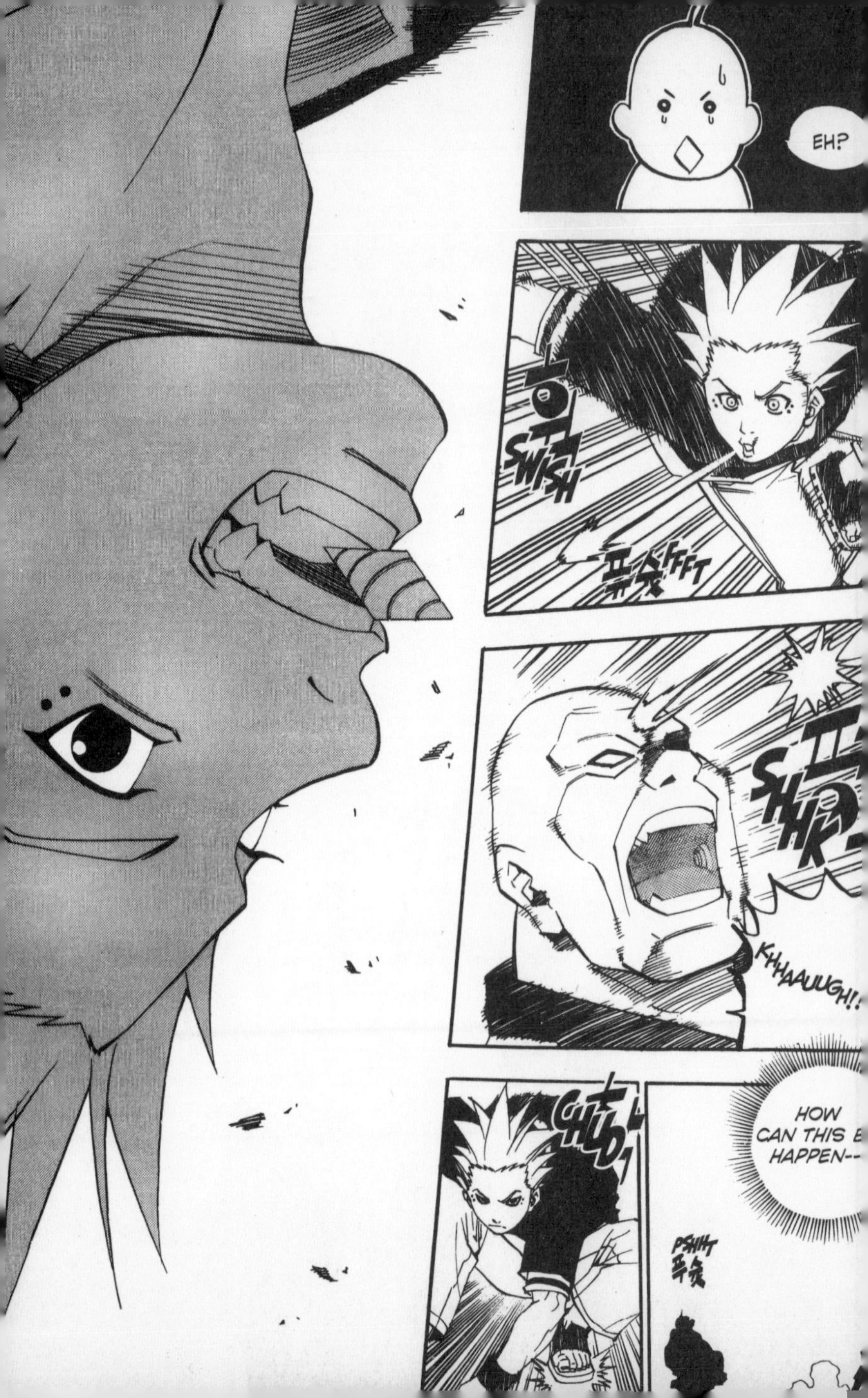

EH?
SWISH
퓨슉 FFFT
SHHR
KHHAAUUGH!!
CHUD
HOW CAN THIS B HAPPEN--
PSHHT

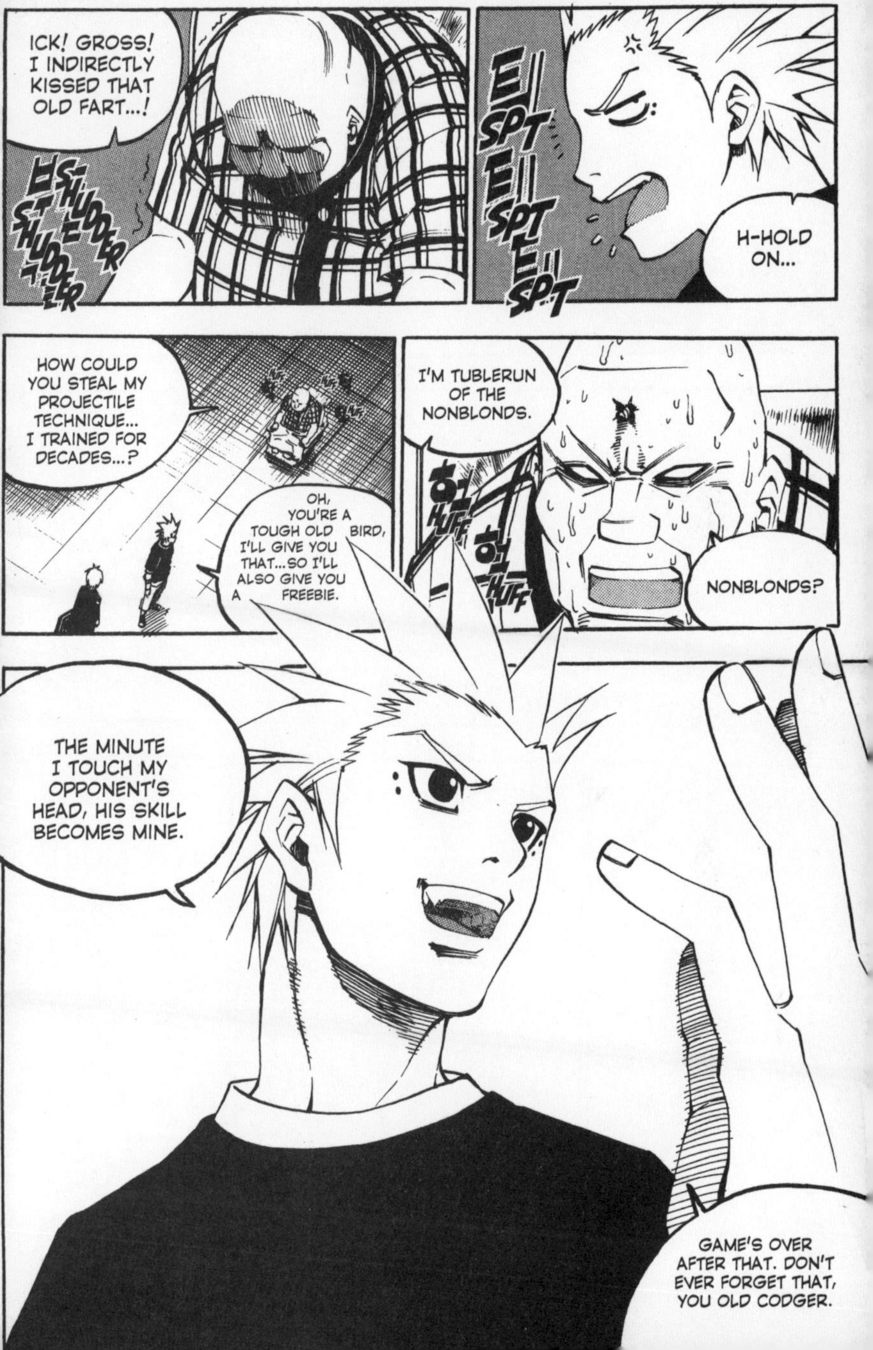
ICK! GROSS! I INDIRECTLY KISSED THAT OLD FART...!
S-SHUDDER
SHUDDER
SPT
SPT
SPT
H-HOLD ON...
HOW COULD YOU STEAL MY PROJECTILE TECHNIQUE... I TRAINED FOR DECADES...?
HUFF
HUFF
HUFF
OH, YOU'RE A TOUGH OLD BIRD, I'LL GIVE YOU THAT...SO I'LL ALSO GIVE YOU A FREEBIE.
I'M TUBLERUN OF THE NONBLONDS.
HUFF
HUFF
NONBLONDS?
THE MINUTE I TOUCH MY OPPONENT'S HEAD, HIS SKILL BECOMES MINE.
GAME'S OVER AFTER THAT. DON'T EVER FORGET THAT, YOU OLD CODGER.

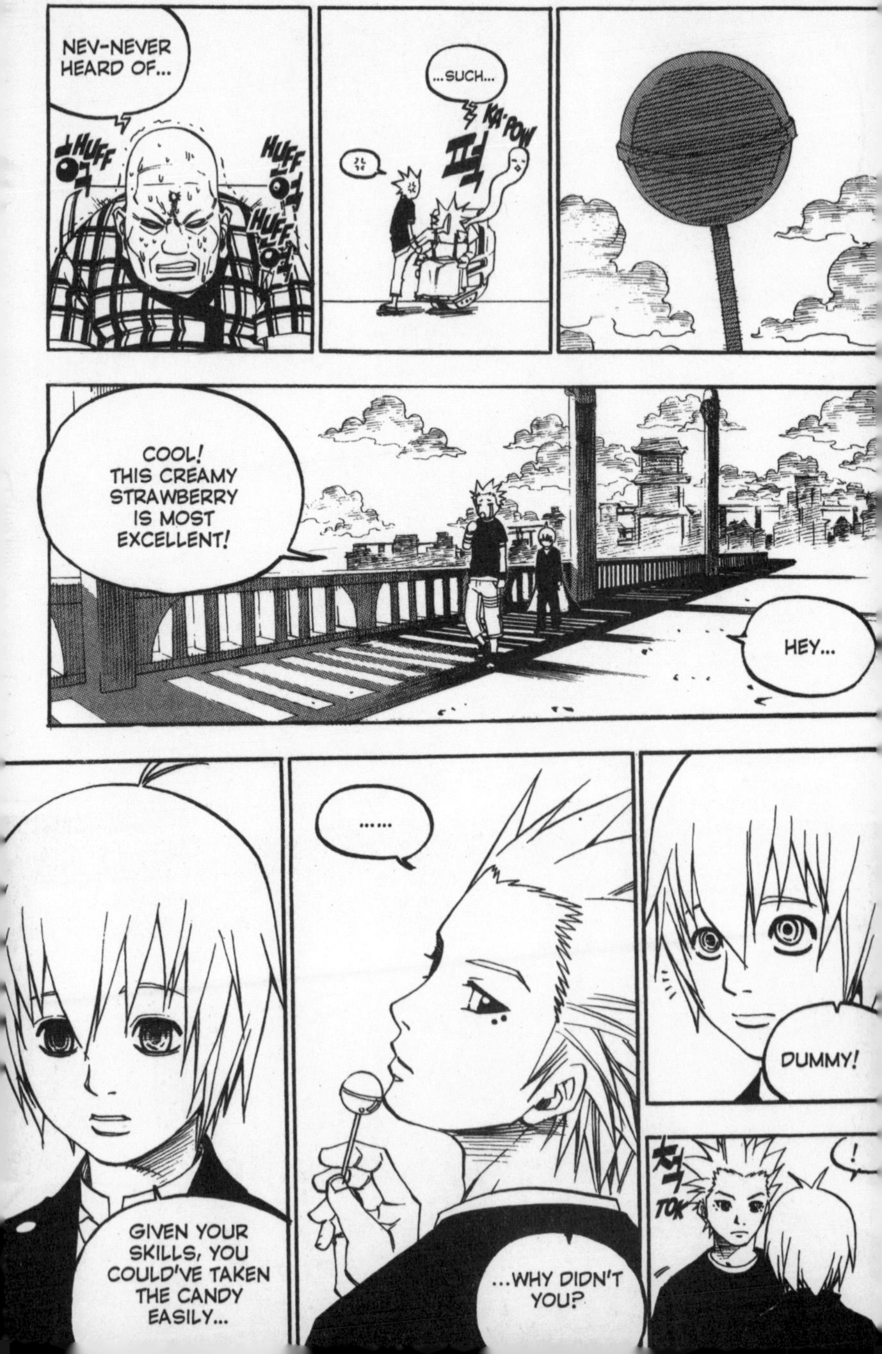
NEV-NEVER HEARD OF...
HUFF
HUFF
HUFF
...SUCH...
KA-POW
COOL! THIS CREAMY STRAWBERRY IS MOST EXCELLENT!
HEY...
GIVEN YOUR SKILLS, YOU COULD'VE TAKEN THE CANDY EASILY...
......
...WHY DIDN'T YOU?
DUMMY!
TOK
!

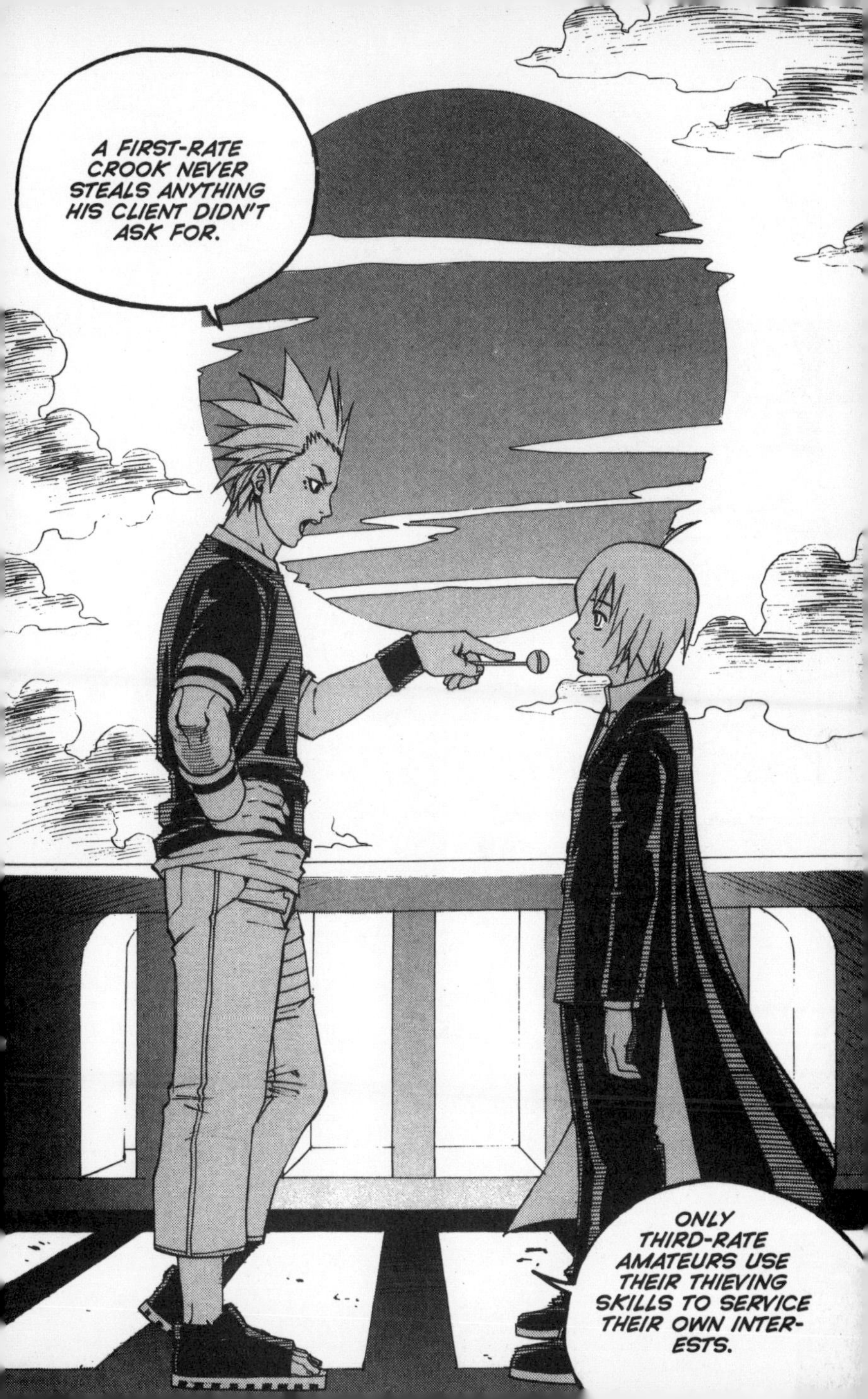
A FIRST-RATE CROOK NEVER STEALS ANYTHING HIS CLIENT DIDN'T ASK FOR.
ONLY THIRD-RATE AMATEURS USE THEIR THIEVING SKILLS TO SERVICE THEIR OWN INTER-ESTS.

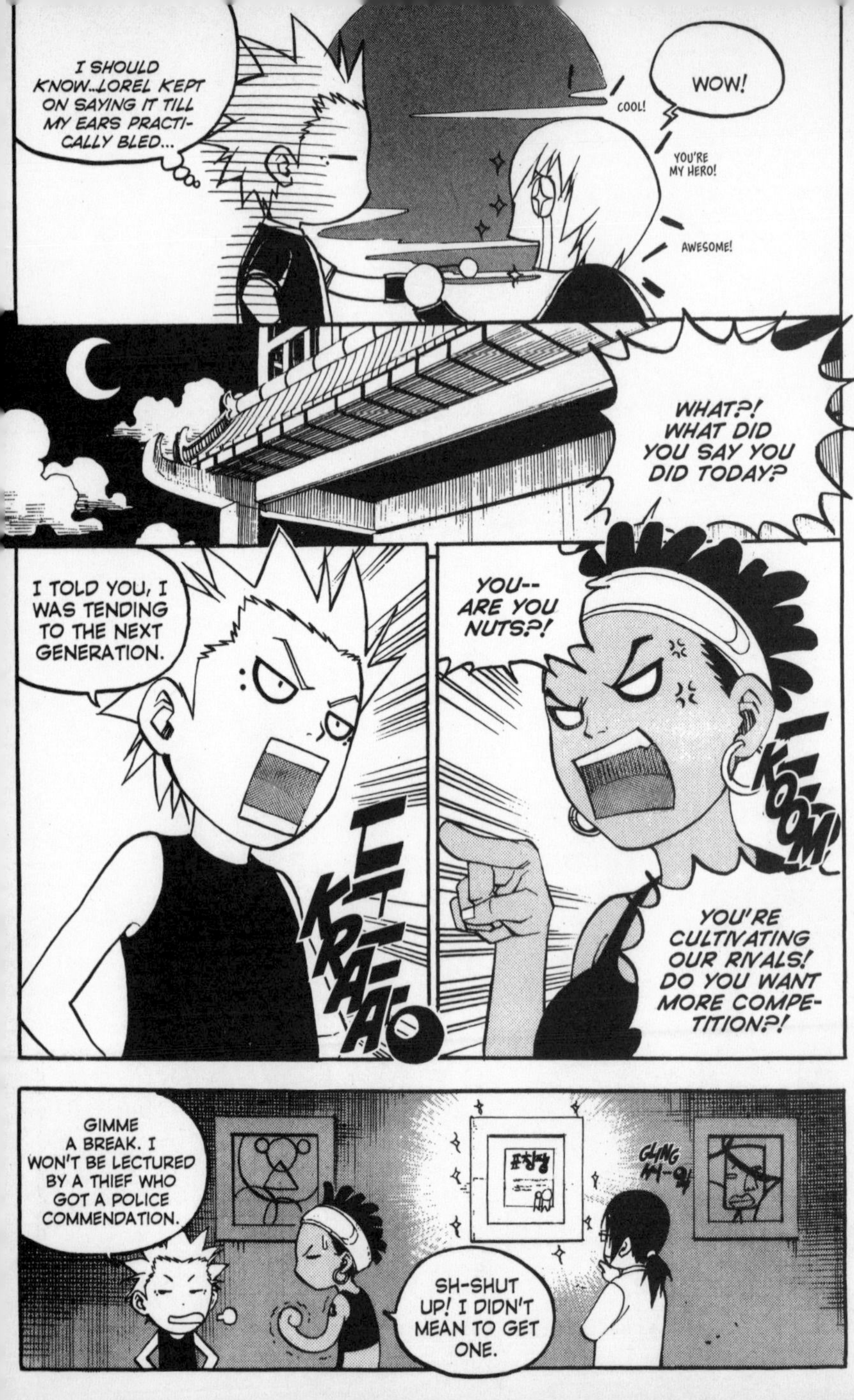
I SHOULD KNOW...LOREL KEPT ON SAYING IT TILL MY EARS PRACTI-CALLY BLED...
WOW!
COOL!
YOU'RE MY HERO!
AWESOME!
WHAT?! WHAT DID YOU SAY YOU DID TODAY?
I TOLD YOU, I WAS TENDING TO THE NEXT GENERATION.
YOU-- ARE YOU NUTS?!
KOOM!
YOU'RE CULTIVATING OUR RIVALS! DO YOU WANT MORE COMPE-TITION?!
GIMME A BREAK. I WON'T BE LECTURED BY A THIEF WHO GOT A POLICE COMMENDATION.
SH-SHUT UP! I DIDN'T MEAN TO GET ONE.

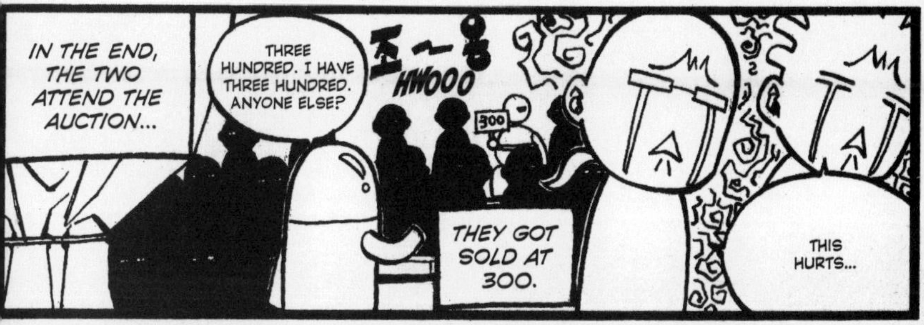
IN THE END, THE TWO ATTEND THE AUCTION...
THREE HUNDRED. I HAVE THREE HUNDRED. ANYONE ELSE?
HWOOO
300
THEY GOT SOLD AT 300.
THIS HURTS...

BACK TALK...
NO, NO...AFTER WORD?!

I DIDN'T HAVE ENOUGH SPACE IN THE AFTER WORD FOLLOWING CHAPTER 1, SO LET ME SAY A BIT MORE ABOUT IT BEFORE GOING ON TO CHAPTER 2. I THREW IN A CONCEPT CALLED "INVISIBLE MAN" AT THE BEGINNING. IT'S A SYSTEM THAT TRICKS SECURITY CAMERAS. TO MAKE AN ANALOGY TO THE HUMAN BODY, IT RECONFIGURES THE VISUAL NERVES TO PREVENT THEM FROM TRANSMITTING SIGNALS TO THE BRAIN, THUS KEEPING IT FROM RECOGNIZING OUTSIDE OBJECTS. FROM WHAT I HEAR, THE FAMOUS INVISIBLE MAN INCIDENT ACTUALLY OCCURRED IN THIS WAY. BECAUSE THE SIGNALS DON'T REACH THE BRAIN, YOU SEE FOOTPRINTS OR HEAR SOMEONE'S VOICE BUT YOU CAN'T SEE ANYONE THERE. I THOUGHT IT'D BE GREAT TO USE THAT WITH A BATTLE ROBOT OR IN TRICKING A SECURITY CAMERA, BUT SADLY THIS WAS REJECTED ;(

I'LL STOP THERE. LET'S GO ON TO CHAPTER 2.

CHAPTER 2 IS...WELL...NOT MUCH. A THREE-MAN THEFT RING USES AN AUTOMATIC RIFLE SHAPED LIKE A CROSSBOW (IS THAT RIGHT?). THE BULLETS ARE LIQUID METAL AND EASY TO CARRY. WHAT'S LIQUID METAL? YOU'LL FIND OUT MORE IN THE CHAPTER 3 AFTER WORD. AND THE THINGS THAT SHOOT OUT OF THE OLD MAN'S MOUTH, IT WOULDN'T BE VERY CONVENIENT FOR HIM TO LOAD UP HIS WHOLE MOUTH WITH THEM--I MEAN, REALISTICALLY, HE WOULD SOUND VERY STRANGE. SO, I CAME UP WITH THE IDEA OF A LIQUID METAL DEVICE INSIDE THE STOMACH, CONNECTED TO THE INSIDES OF HIS CHEEKS, AND THE LIQUID METAL TAKES THE FORM OF SCREWS OR DARTS THAT HE CAN SHOOT FROM HIS MOUTH.

EXAMPLE)

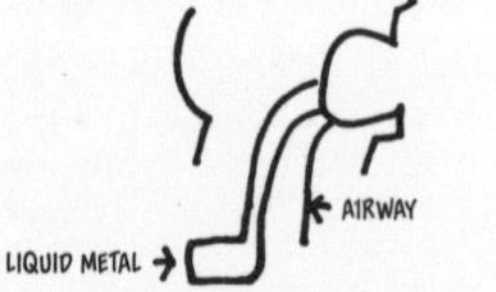
AIRWAY
LIQUID METAL

CONNECTED BY A THIN TUBE. HMM...
I IMAGINE IT IMPLANTED LIKE A BLOOD VESSEL.

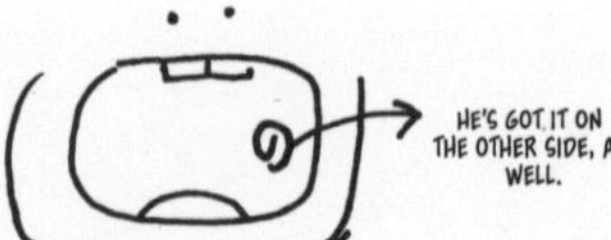
HE'S GOT IT ON THE OTHER SIDE, AS WELL.

IT LOOKS LIKE THIS BEFORE THE LIQUID METAL CHANGES INTO A PROJECTILE. THIS IS A DIGRESSION, BUT THERE'S A SURPRISE GUEST FOLLOWING IN THE FOOTSTEPS OF THE ONE IN CHAPTER 1. TRY LOOKING AND SEE IF YOU CAN SPOT THIS ONE. OH, THE GUEST IN CHAPTER 1 IS VERY DIFFICULT TO FIND, HEE-HEE-HEE. IF YOU UNCOVER THE CHAPTER 1 GUEST, SEND ME A POSTCARD. WE'LL DRAW A LOTTERY AND OUR EDITOR HERE WILL GIVE AN AWARD OF--OUCH!!

CAR 3. VALENTINE'S BRAIN, PART I

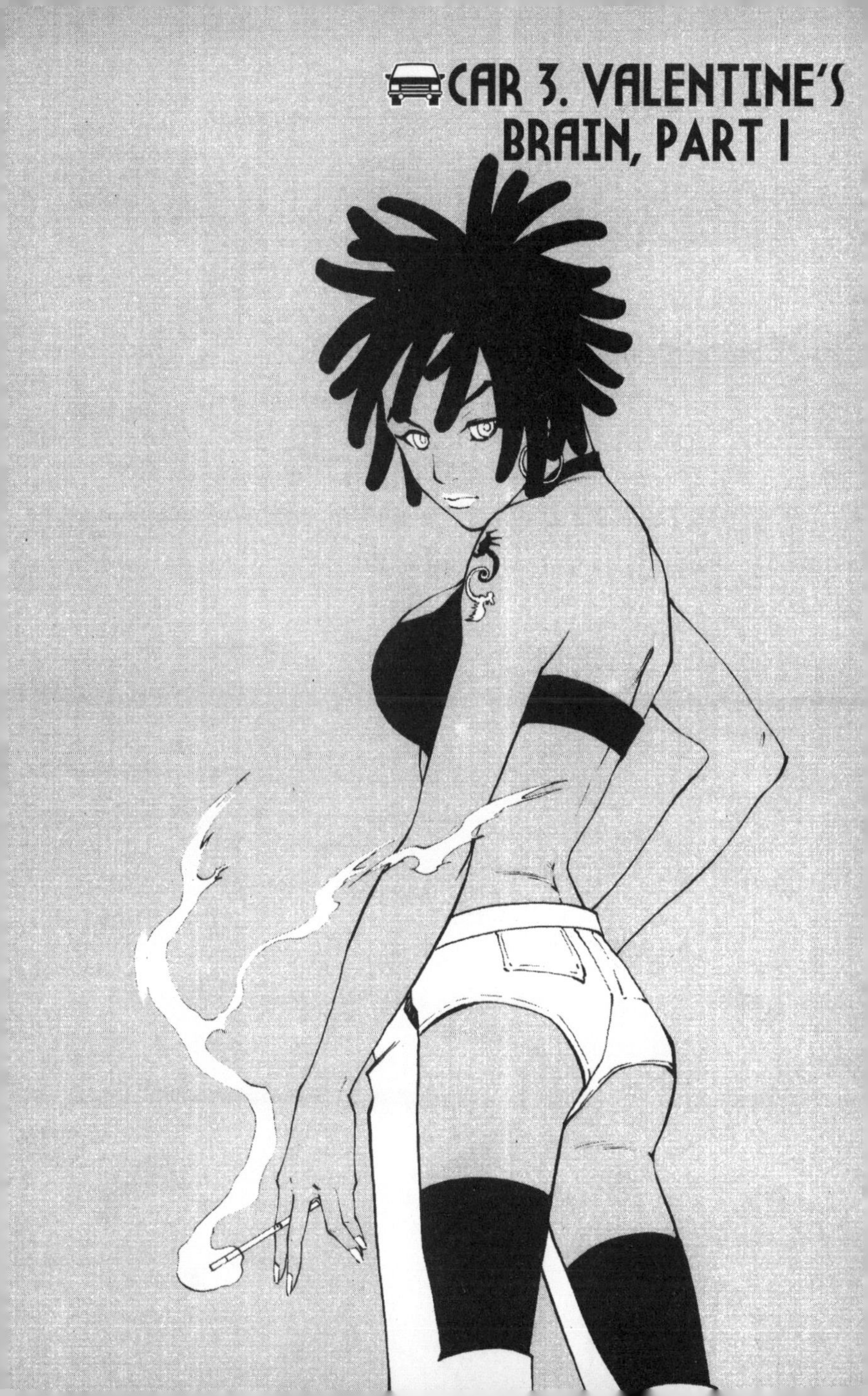

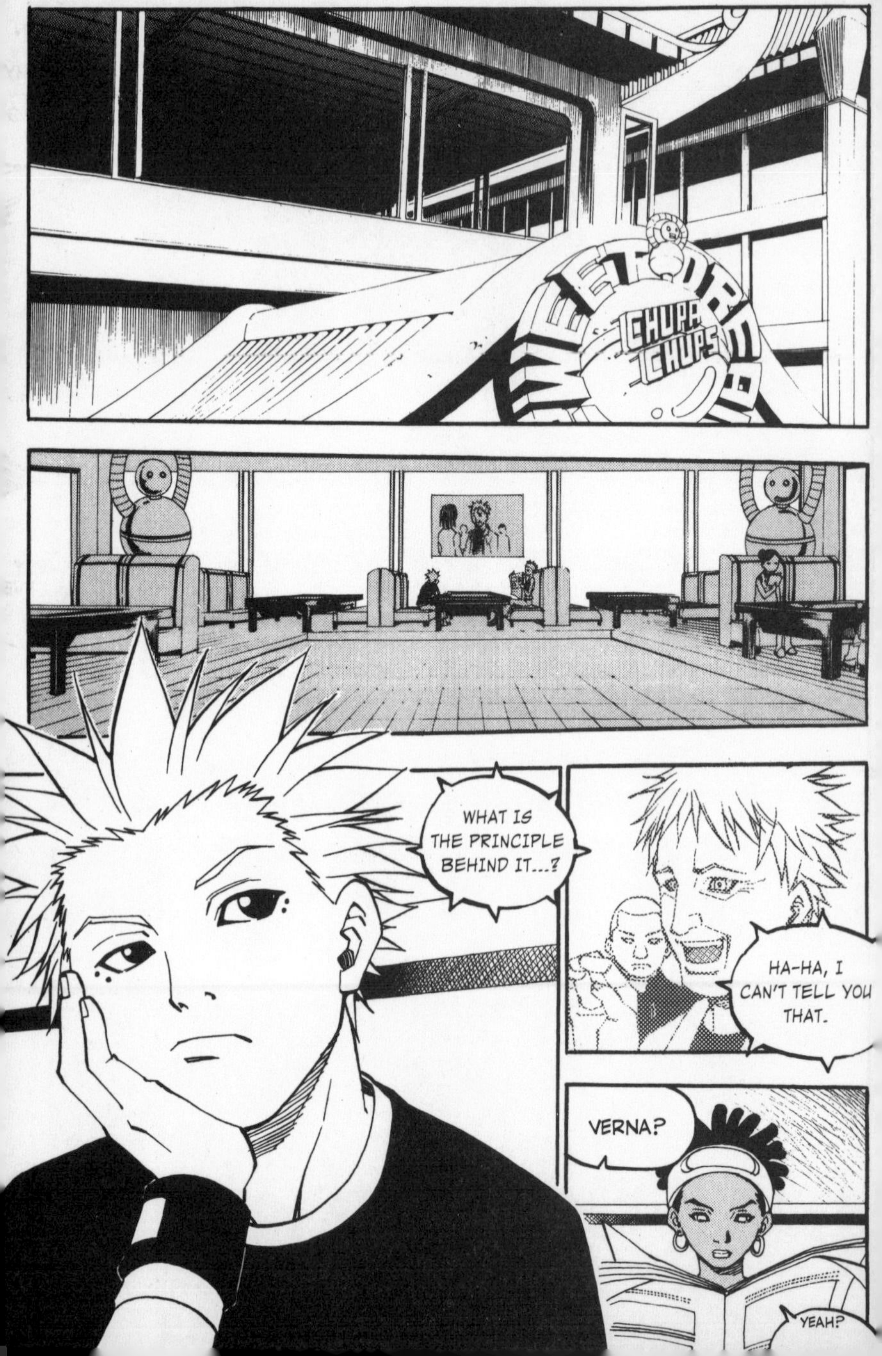
WEE TOR
CHUPA CHUPS
WHAT IS THE PRINCIPLE BEHIND IT...?
HA-HA, I CAN'T TELL YOU THAT.
VERNA?
YEAH?

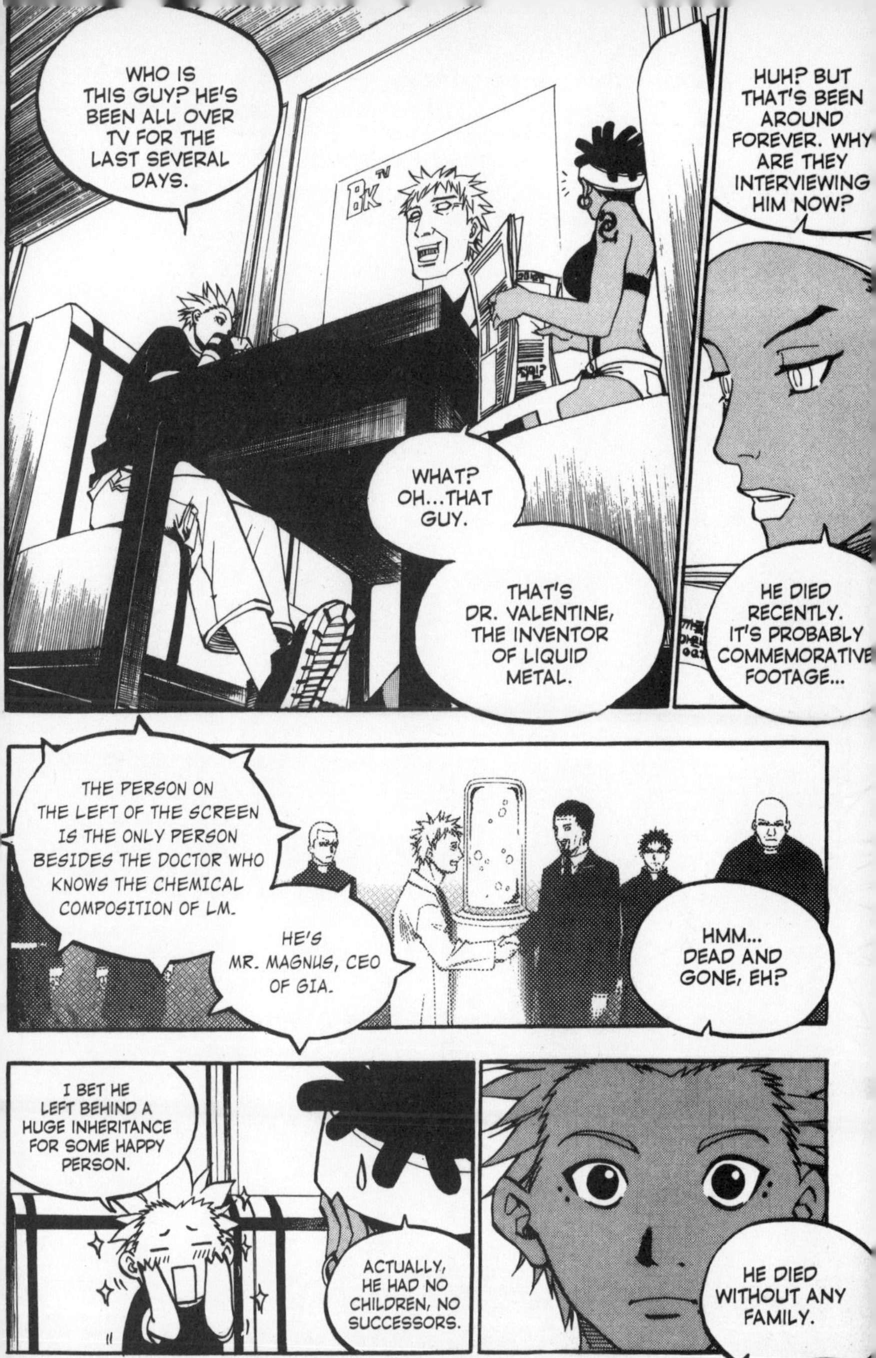
WHO IS THIS GUY? HE'S BEEN ALL OVER TV FOR THE LAST SEVERAL DAYS.
WHAT? OH...THAT GUY.
THAT'S DR. VALENTINE, THE INVENTOR OF LIQUID METAL.
HUH? BUT THAT'S BEEN AROUND FOREVER. WHY ARE THEY INTERVIEWING HIM NOW?
HE DIED RECENTLY. IT'S PROBABLY COMMEMORATIVE FOOTAGE...
THE PERSON ON THE LEFT OF THE SCREEN IS THE ONLY PERSON BESIDES THE DOCTOR WHO KNOWS THE CHEMICAL COMPOSITION OF LM.
HE'S MR. MAGNUS, CEO OF GIA.
HMM... DEAD AND GONE, EH?
I BET HE LEFT BEHIND A HUGE INHERITANCE FOR SOME HAPPY PERSON.
ACTUALLY, HE HAD NO CHILDREN, NO SUCCESSORS.
HE DIED WITHOUT ANY FAMILY.
...!

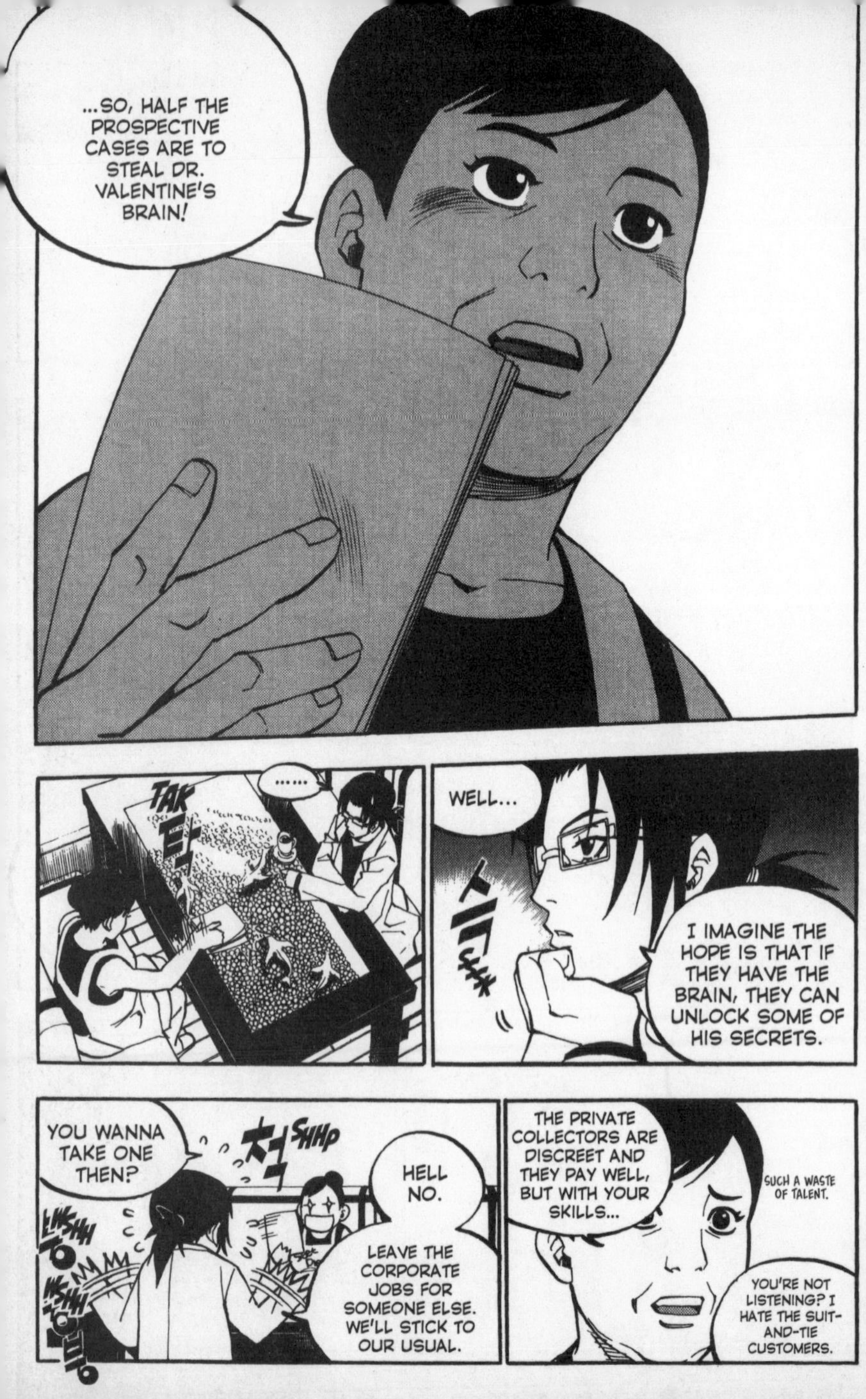
...SO, HALF THE PROSPECTIVE CASES ARE TO STEAL DR. VALENTINE'S BRAIN!
TAK
......
WELL...
I IMAGINE THE HOPE IS THAT IF THEY HAVE THE BRAIN, THEY CAN UNLOCK SOME OF HIS SECRETS.
YOU WANNA TAKE ONE THEN?
SHHP
HELL NO.
LEAVE THE CORPORATE JOBS FOR SOMEONE ELSE. WE'LL STICK TO OUR USUAL.
THE PRIVATE COLLECTORS ARE DISCREET AND THEY PAY WELL, BUT WITH YOUR SKILLS...
SUCH A WASTE OF TALENT.
YOU'RE NOT LISTENING? I HATE THE SUIT-AND-TIE CUSTOMERS.

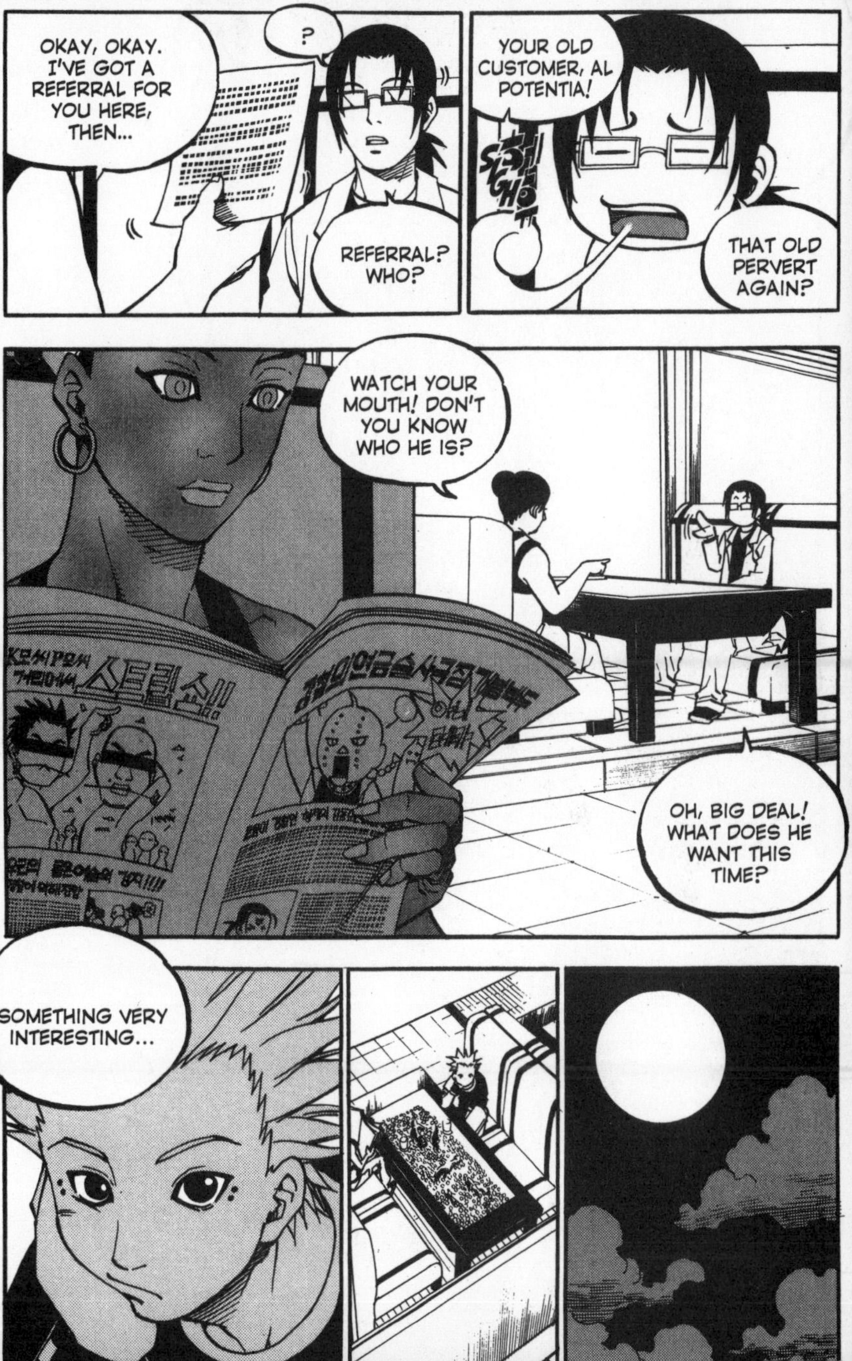
OKAY, OKAY. I'VE GOT A REFERRAL FOR YOU HERE, THEN...
?
REFERRAL? WHO?
YOUR OLD CUSTOMER, AL POTENTIA!
THAT OLD PERVERT AGAIN?
WATCH YOUR MOUTH! DON'T YOU KNOW WHO HE IS?
OH, BIG DEAL! WHAT DOES HE WANT THIS TIME?
SOMETHING VERY INTERESTING...

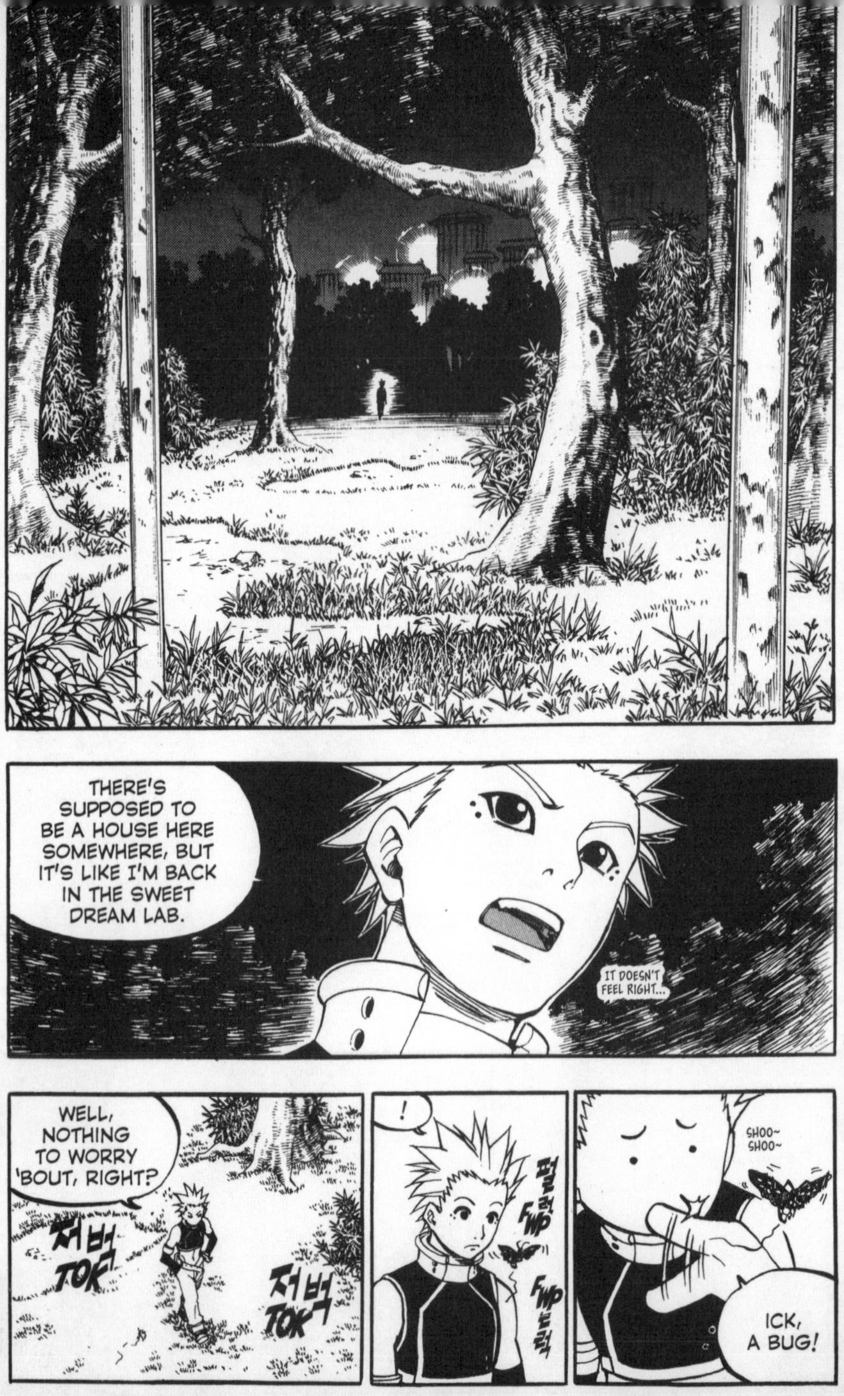
THERE'S SUPPOSED TO BE A HOUSE HERE SOMEWHERE, BUT IT'S LIKE I'M BACK IN THE SWEET DREAM LAB.
IT DOESN'T FEEL RIGHT...
WELL, NOTHING TO WORRY 'BOUT, RIGHT?
저벅 TOK
저벅 TOK
!
펄럭 FWP
FWP 펄럭
SHOO~ SHOO~
ICK, A BUG!

FWP

FWP

ㅉㅈ
BZZZT 짐

......

FWT
FWT
FWT

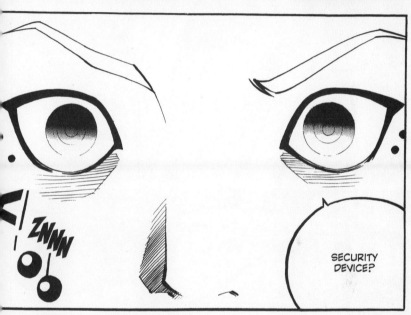

ZNNN

SECURITY DEVICE?

BEE
BEE
BEEP

!!

HA-HA-HA, THEY G-GOT ALL THE BASICS IN PLACE...

CUT THE CURRENT?

NO, NEVER MIND!

HMM, ABOUT 6 METERS.

CHK!

A BIT STRONGER...

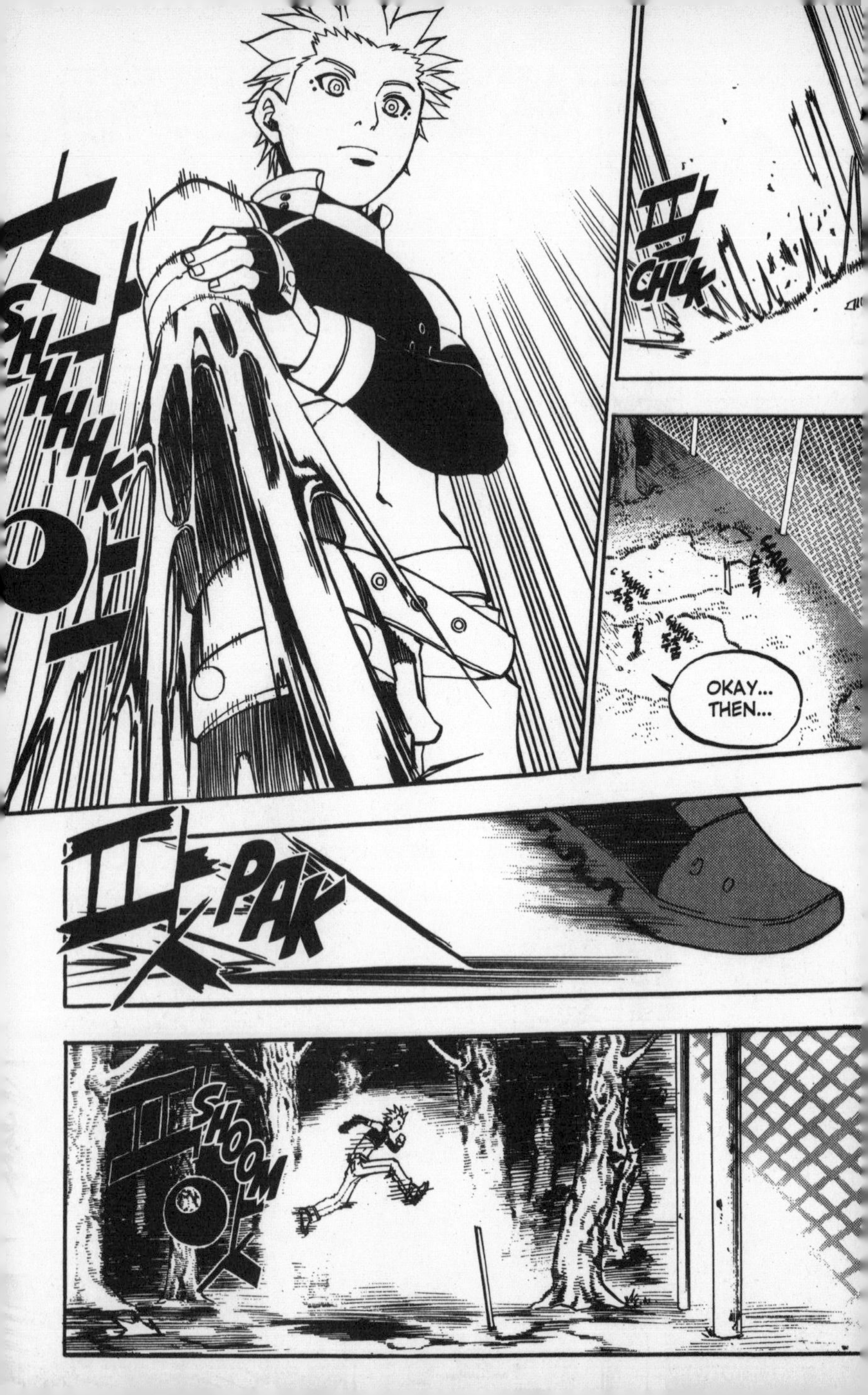
SHHHHK
CHUK
OKAY... THEN...
PAK
SHOOM

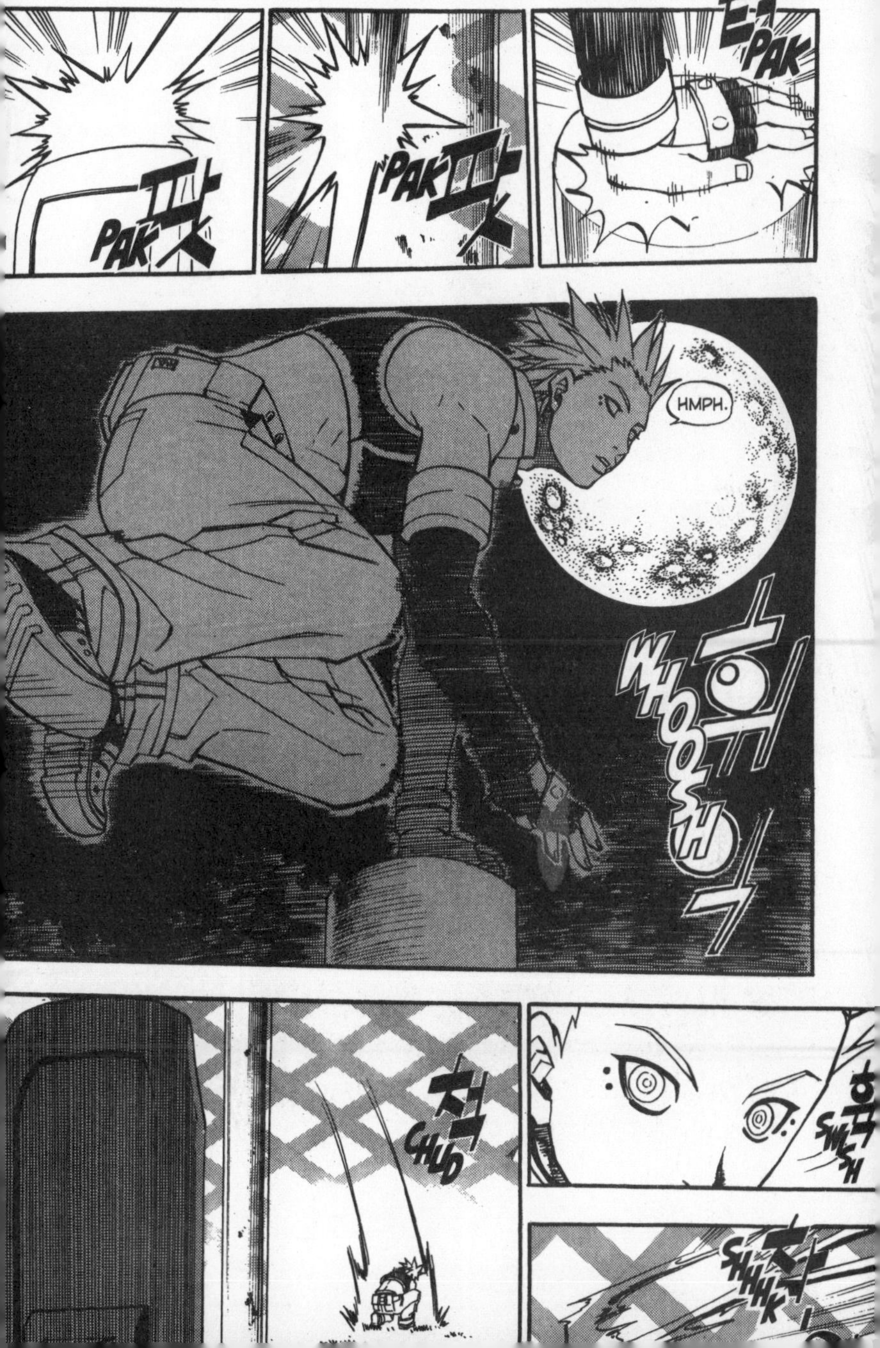
PAK
PAK
PAK
HMPH.
WHOOSH
CHUD
SWISH
SHHHK

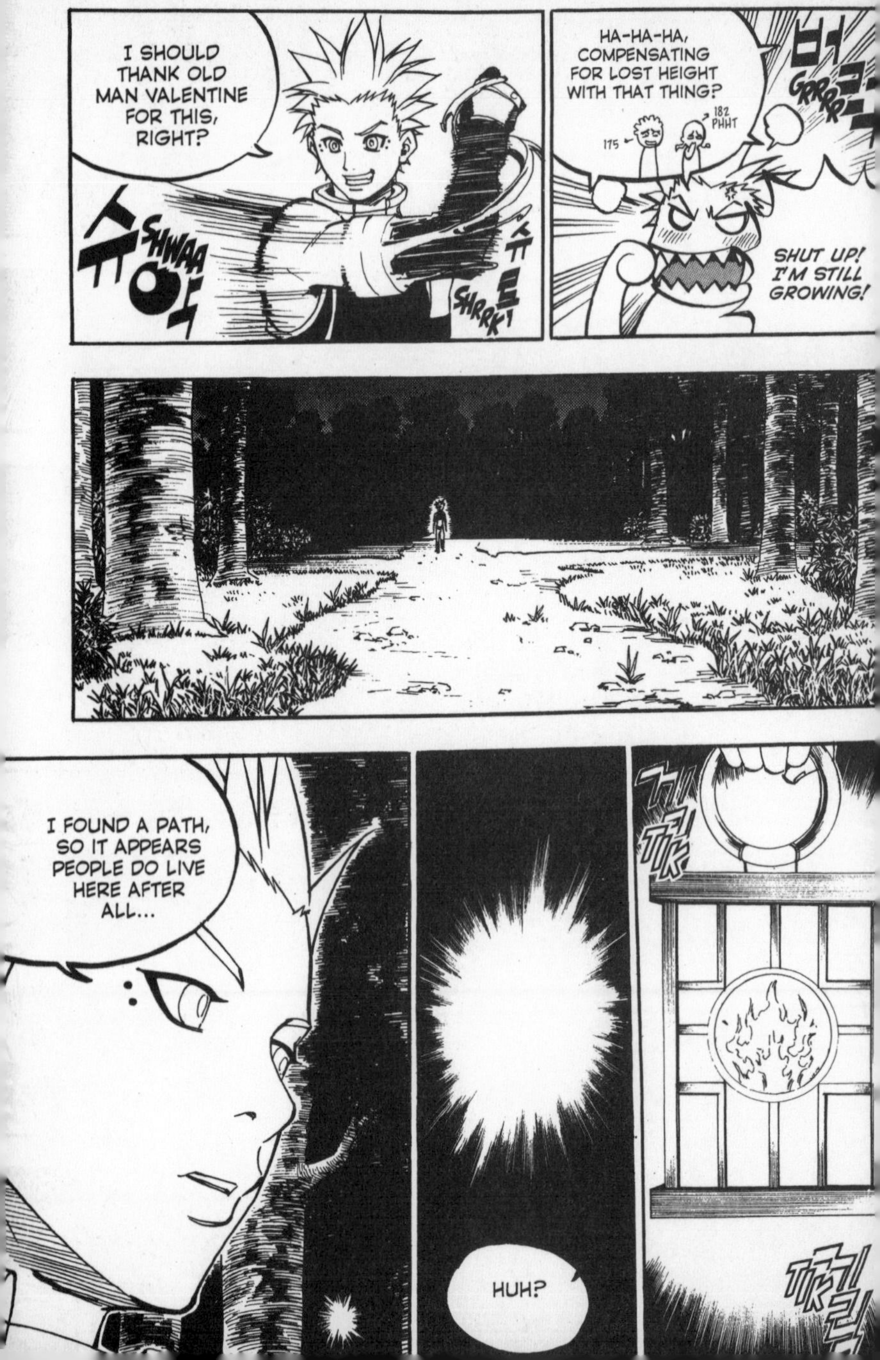
I SHOULD THANK OLD MAN VALENTINE FOR THIS, RIGHT?
SHWAA
SHRRK
HA-HA-HA, COMPENSATING FOR LOST HEIGHT WITH THAT THING?
175
182
PHHT
GRRRR
SHUT UP! I'M STILL GROWING!
I FOUND A PATH, SO IT APPEARS PEOPLE DO LIVE HERE AFTER ALL...
HUH?
TIK
TIK

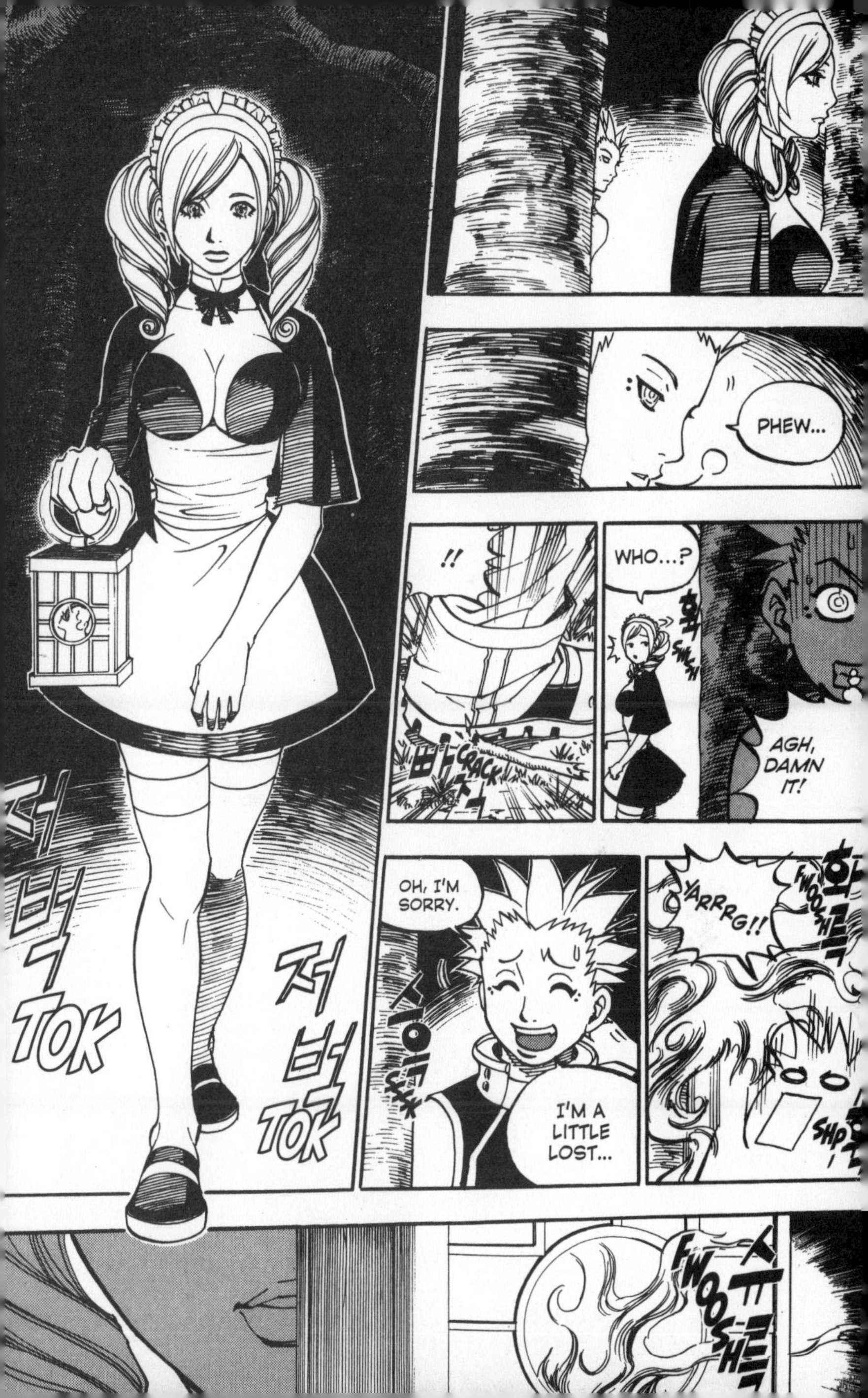

저벅
TOK
저벅
TOK
PHEW...
!!
CRACK
WHO...?
SWISH
AGH, DAMN IT!
OH, I'M SORRY.
I'M A LITTLE LOST...
YARRRG!!
FWOOSH
SHP
FWOOSH

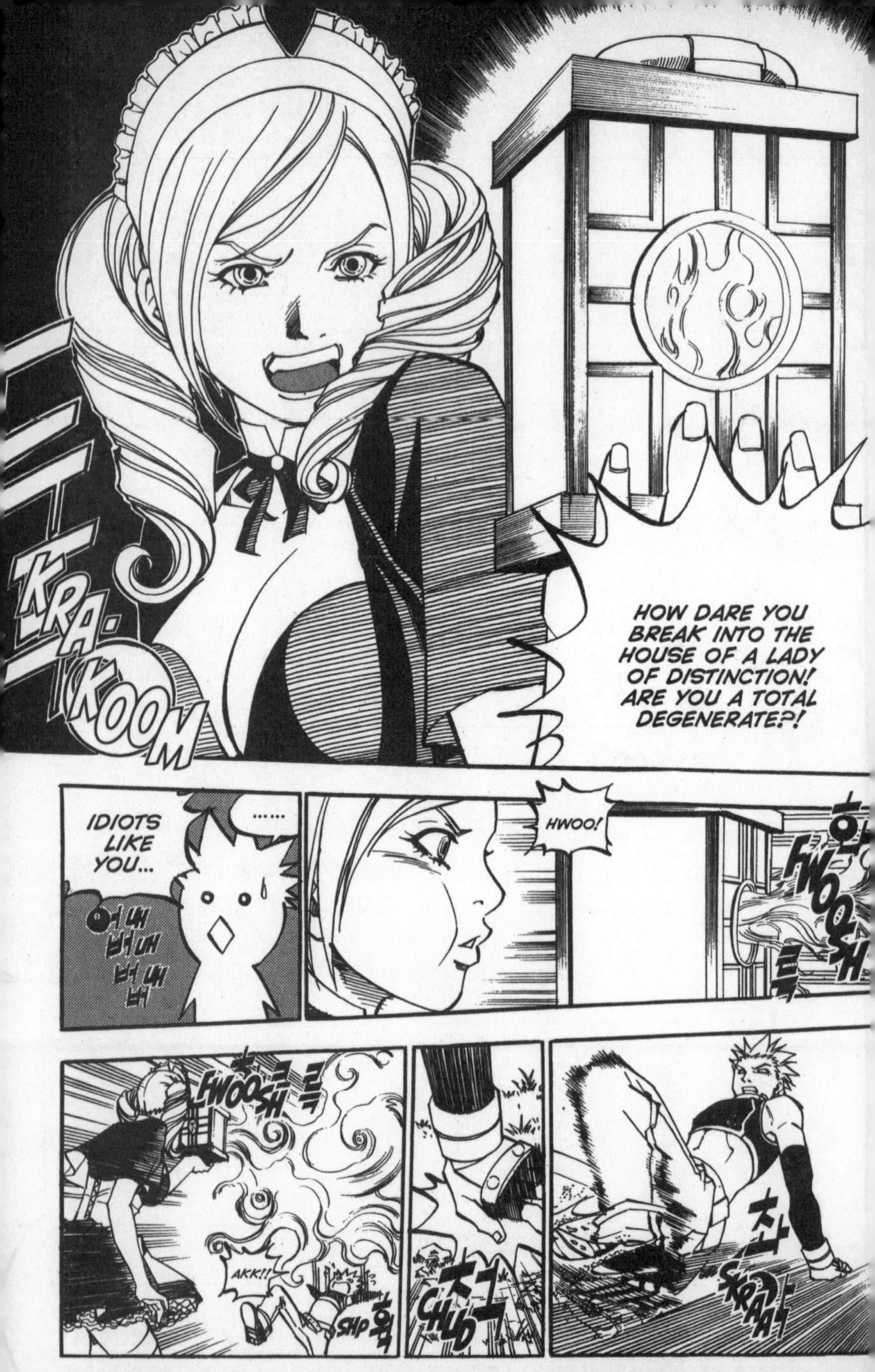
KRA-KOOM
HOW DARE YOU BREAK INTO THE HOUSE OF A LADY OF DISTINCTION! ARE YOU A TOTAL DEGENERATE?!
IDIOTS LIKE YOU...
......
HWOO!
FWOOSH
FWOOSH
AKK!!
SHP
CHUD
SKRAAA

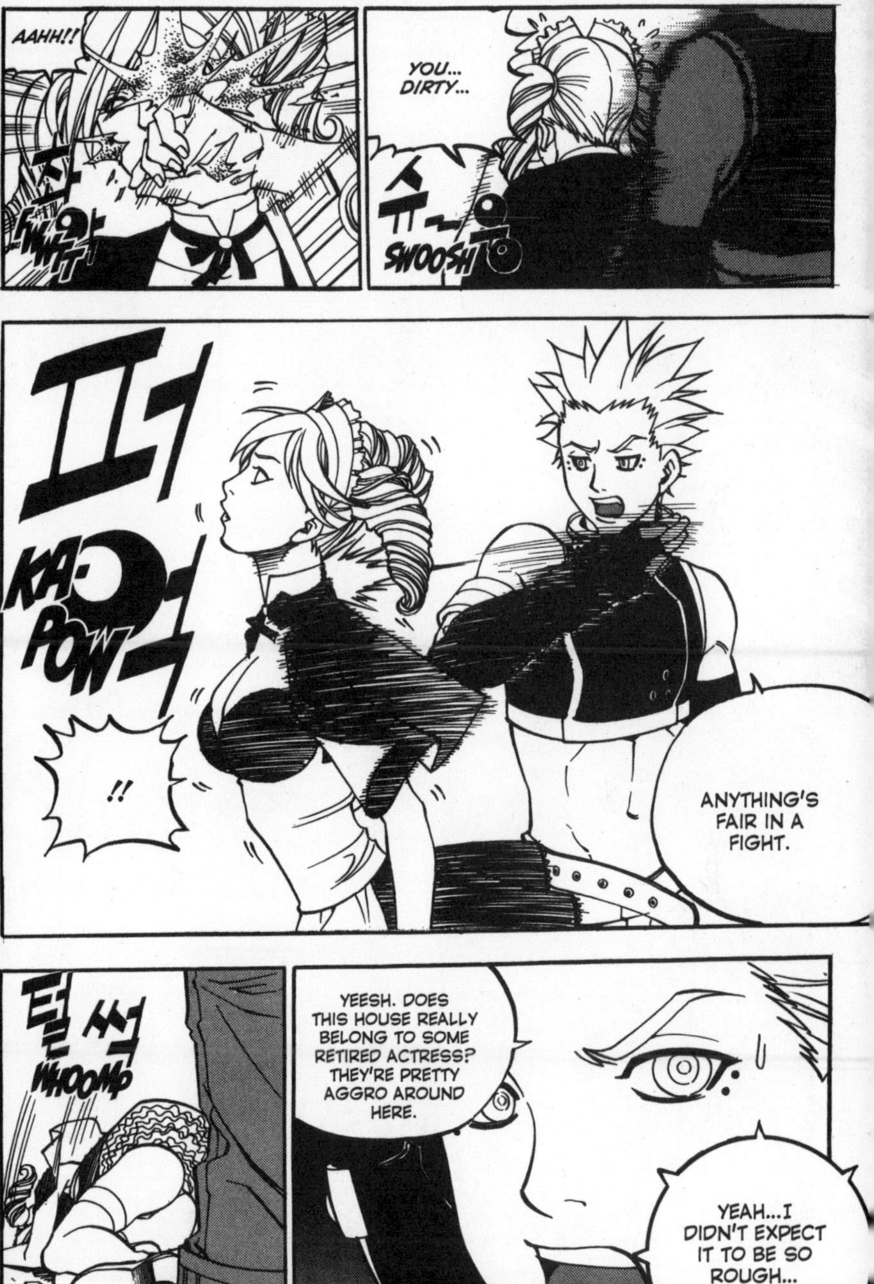

AAHH!!
FWWIT
YOU... DIRTY...
SWOOSH
KA-POW
!!
ANYTHING'S FAIR IN A FIGHT.
WHOOMP
YEESH. DOES THIS HOUSE REALLY BELONG TO SOME RETIRED ACTRESS? THEY'RE PRETTY AGGRO AROUND HERE.
YEAH...I DIDN'T EXPECT IT TO BE SO ROUGH...

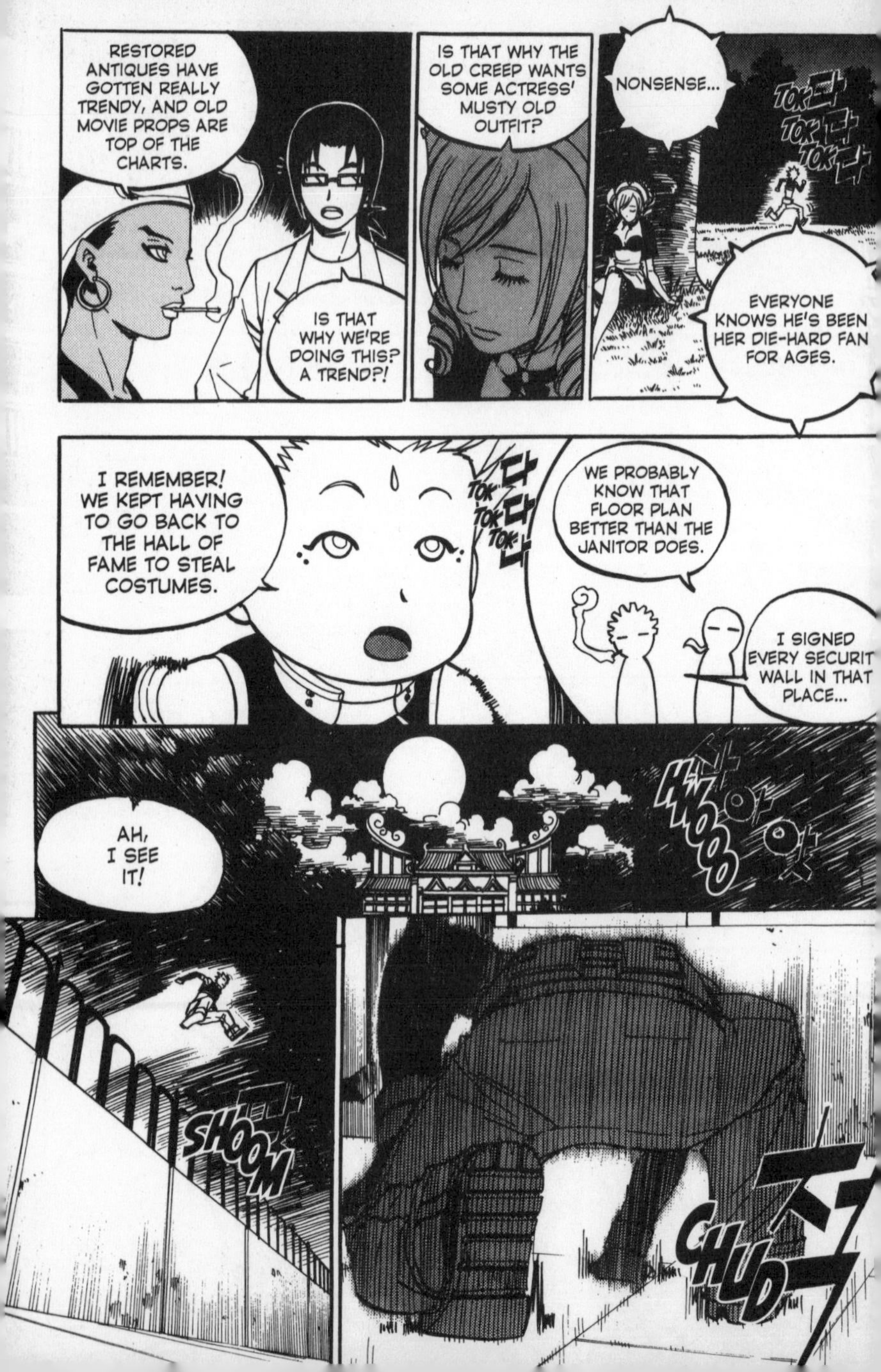
RESTORED ANTIQUES HAVE GOTTEN REALLY TRENDY, AND OLD MOVIE PROPS ARE TOP OF THE CHARTS.
IS THAT WHY WE'RE DOING THIS? A TREND?!
IS THAT WHY THE OLD CREEP WANTS SOME ACTRESS' MUSTY OLD OUTFIT?
NONSENSE...
TOK TOK TOK
EVERYONE KNOWS HE'S BEEN HER DIE-HARD FAN FOR AGES.
I REMEMBER! WE KEPT HAVING TO GO BACK TO THE HALL OF FAME TO STEAL COSTUMES.
TOK TOK TOK
WE PROBABLY KNOW THAT FLOOR PLAN BETTER THAN THE JANITOR DOES.
I SIGNED EVERY SECURIT WALL IN THAT PLACE...
AH, I SEE IT!
HWOOO
SHOOM
CHUD

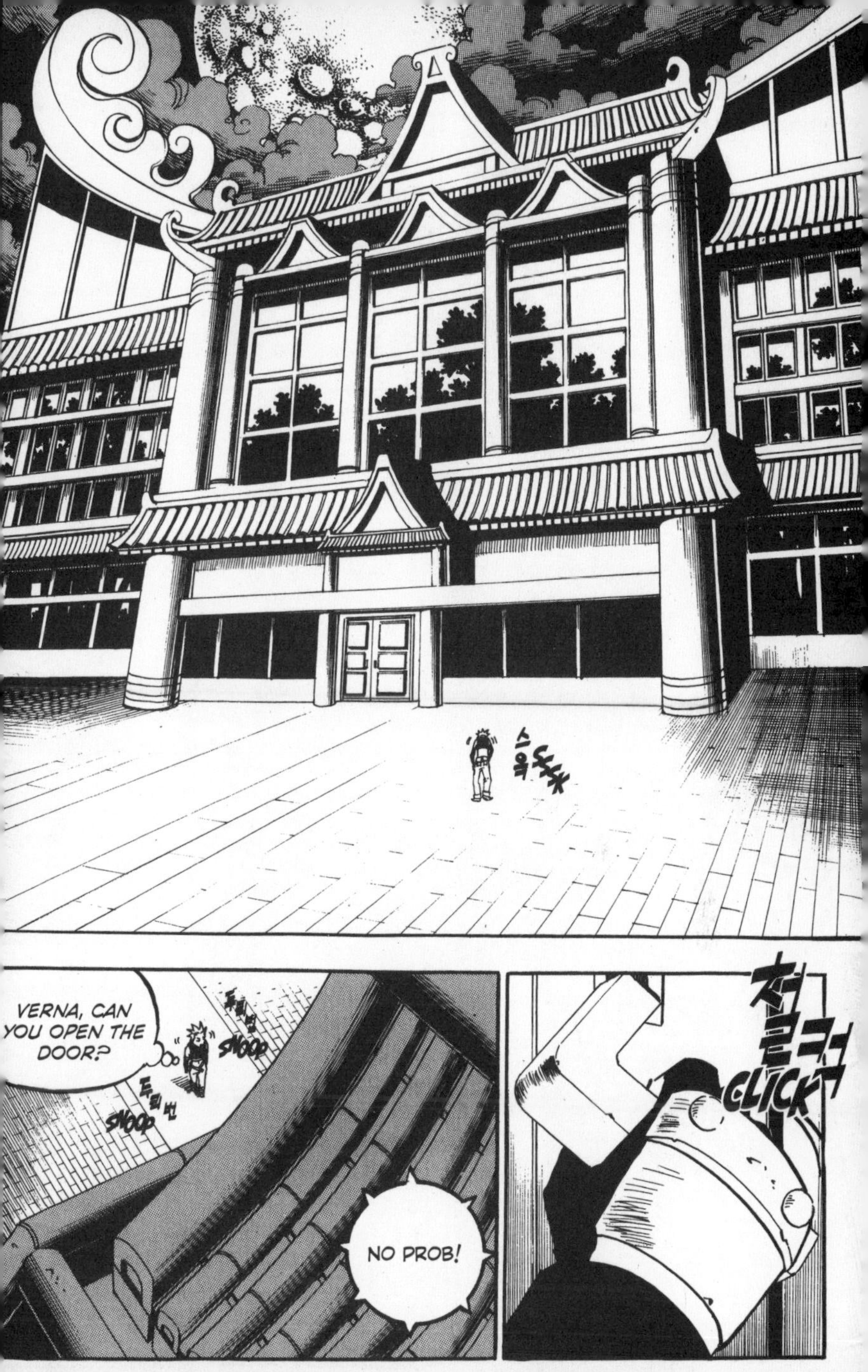
스윽
VERNA, CAN YOU OPEN THE DOOR?
SNOOP
두리번
SNOOP
NO PROB!
CLICK

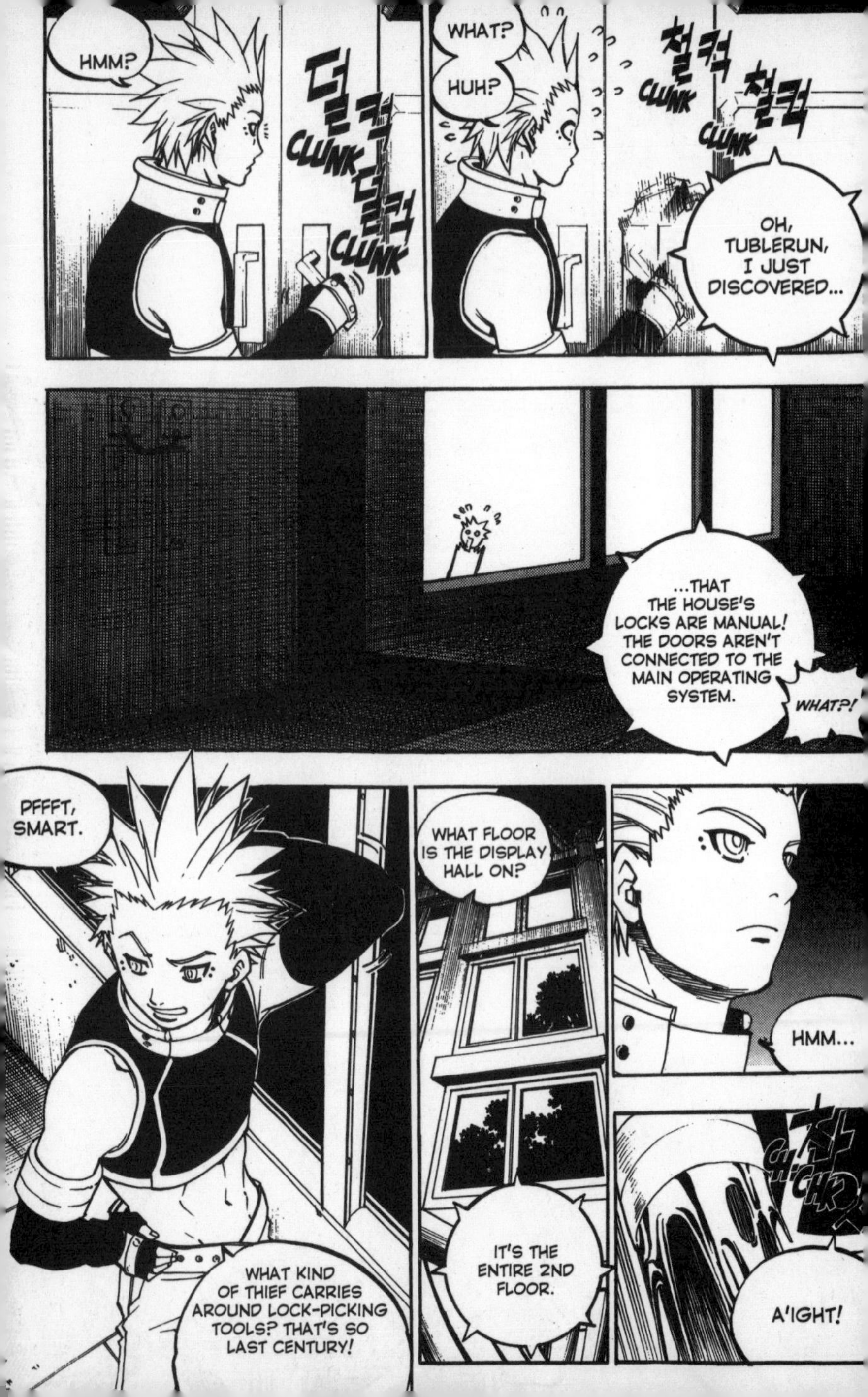
HMM?
덜컥
CLUNK
덜컥
CLUNK
WHAT?
HUH?
철컥
CLUNK
철컥
CLUNK
OH, TUBLERUN, I JUST DISCOVERED...
...THAT THE HOUSE'S LOCKS ARE MANUAL! THE DOORS AREN'T CONNECTED TO THE MAIN OPERATING SYSTEM.
WHAT?!
PFFFT, SMART.
WHAT KIND OF THIEF CARRIES AROUND LOCK-PICKING TOOLS? THAT'S SO LAST CENTURY!
WHAT FLOOR IS THE DISPLAY HALL ON?
IT'S THE ENTIRE 2ND FLOOR.
HMM...
착
CH-CHK
A'IGHT!

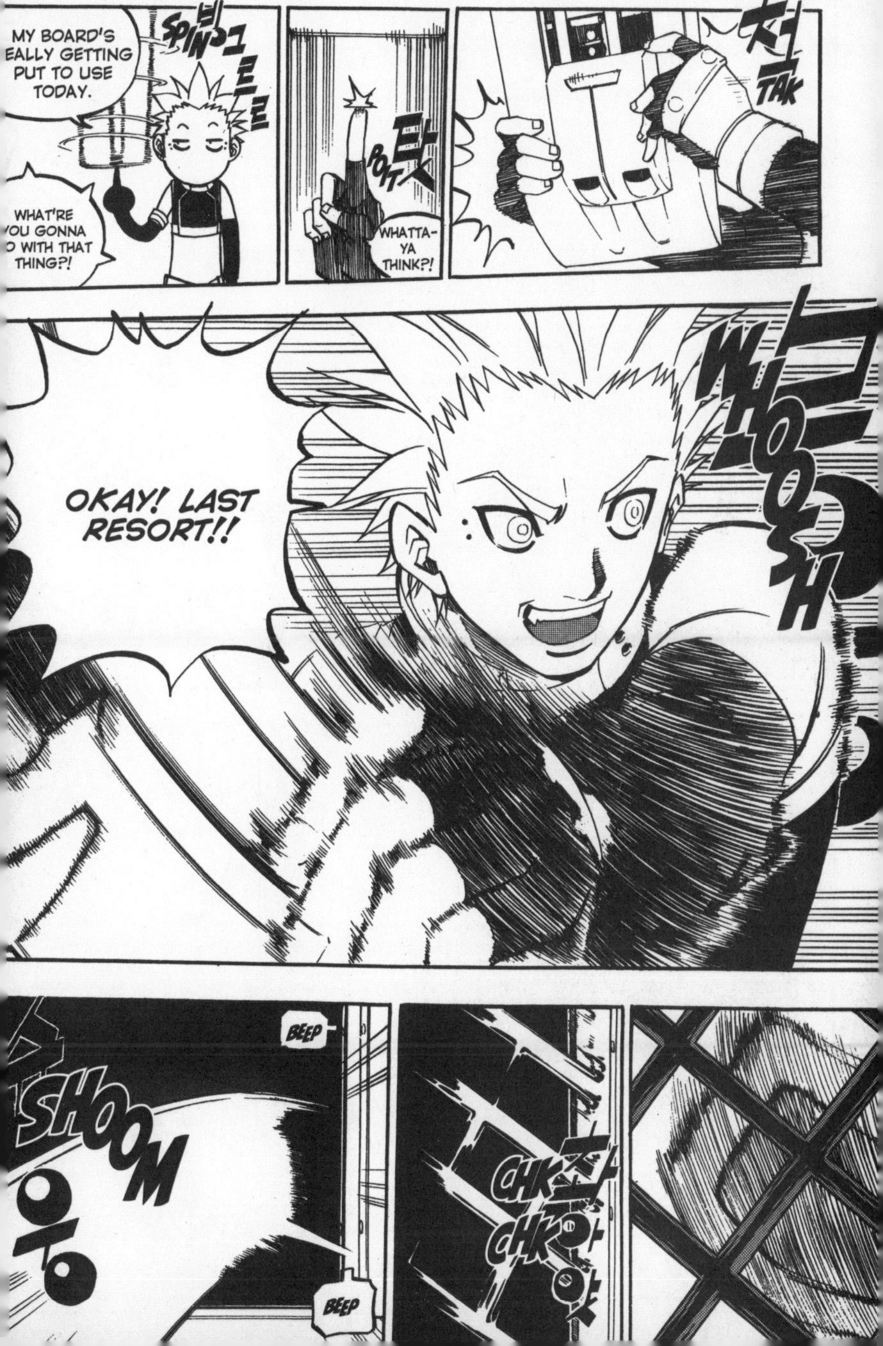
MY BOARD'S EALLY GETTING PUT TO USE TODAY.
SPIN
WHAT'RE OU GONNA O WITH THAT THING?!
POIT
WHATTA-YA THINK?!
TAK
OKAY! LAST RESORT!!
WHOOSH
SHOOM
BEEP
BEEP
CHK
CHK

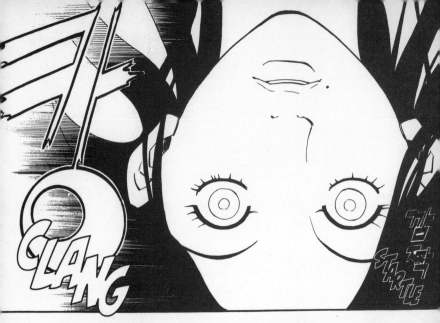

CLANG

STARTLE

BEEP
BEEP
BEEP

!!

ZNNN

CHK

CHK

CHK

AAAAHHH--

BZT

BZT

BZT
BZT
BZT

LAST RESORT,
MY BUTT! YOU
DON'T HAVE ANY
IDEA WHAT YOU'RE
TALKING ABOUT,
IDIOT!

THE
WINDOW
SENSOR'S
BEEN
TRIGGERED!

INTRU-
DER?!

TOK
TOK
TOK

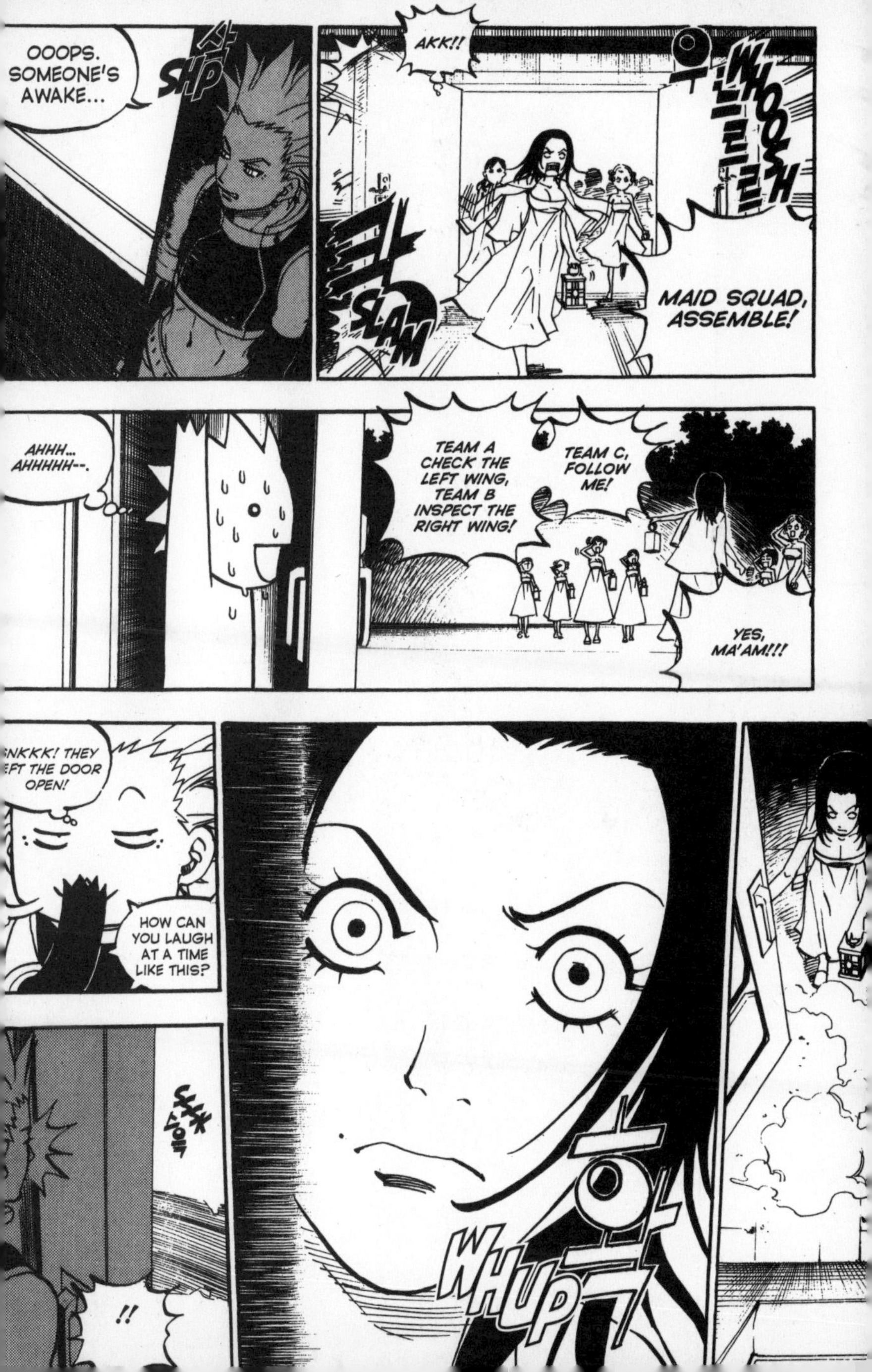
OOOPS. SOMEONE'S AWAKE...
SHP
AKK!!
WHOOOSH
SLAM
MAID SQUAD, ASSEMBLE!
AHHH... AHHHHH--.
TEAM A CHECK THE LEFT WING, TEAM B INSPECT THE RIGHT WING!
TEAM C, FOLLOW ME!
YES, MA'AM!!!
SNKKK! THEY LEFT THE DOOR OPEN!
HOW CAN YOU LAUGH AT A TIME LIKE THIS?
!!
WHUP

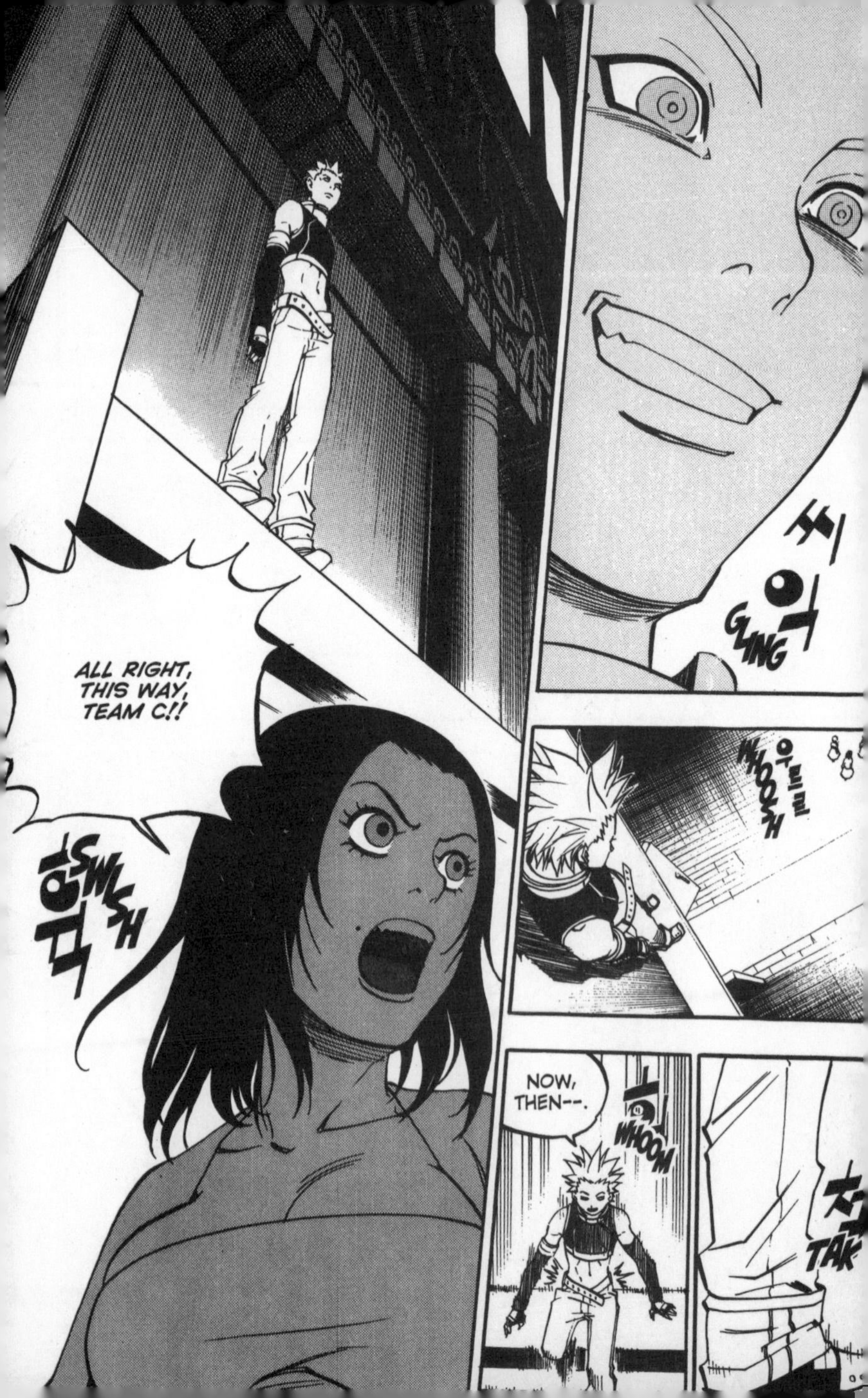
ALL RIGHT, THIS WAY, TEAM C!!
SWISH
GLING
WHOOSH
NOW, THEN--.
WHOOM
TAK

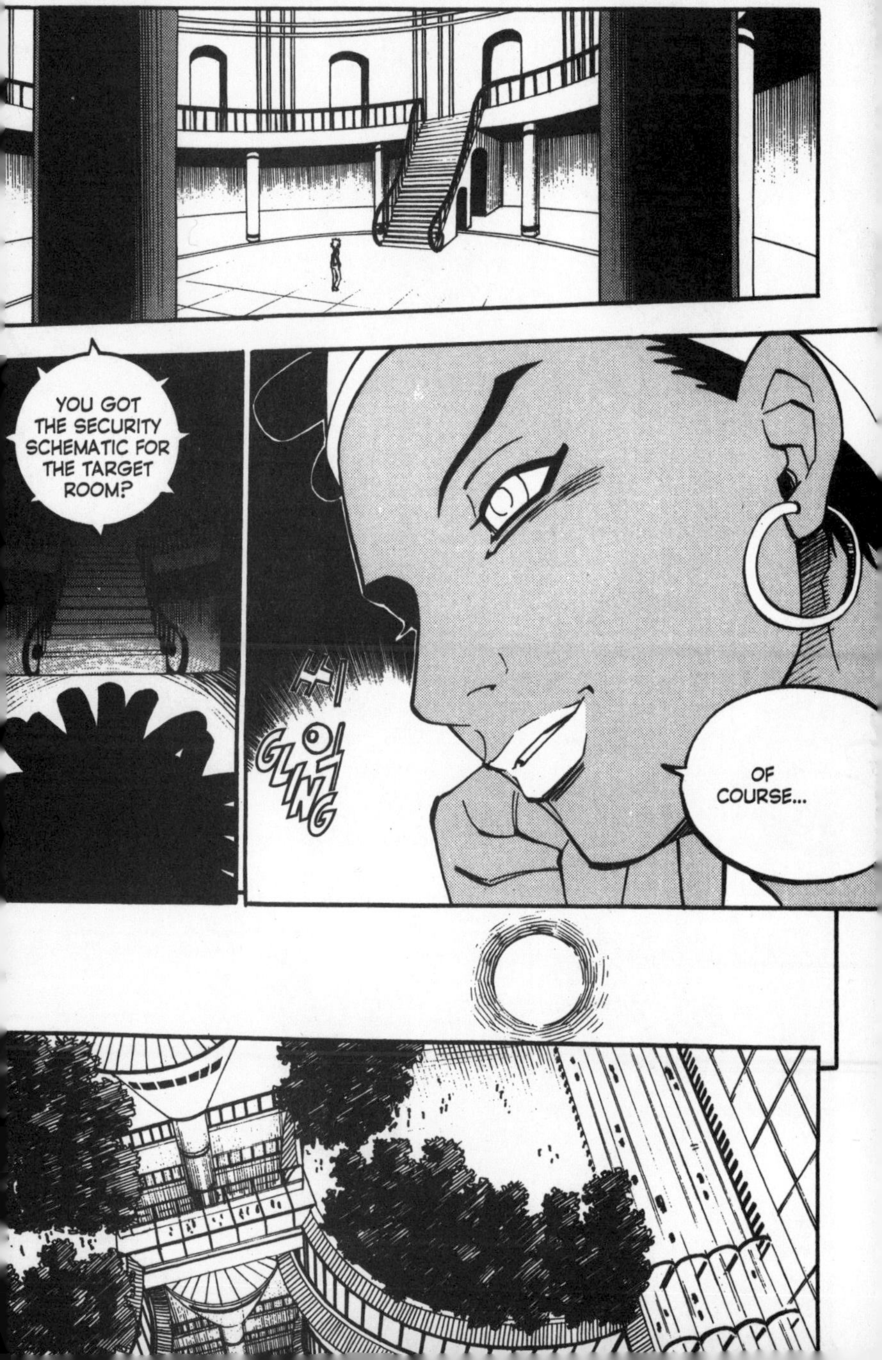
YOU GOT THE SECURITY SCHEMATIC FOR THE TARGET ROOM?
GLING GLING
OF COURSE...

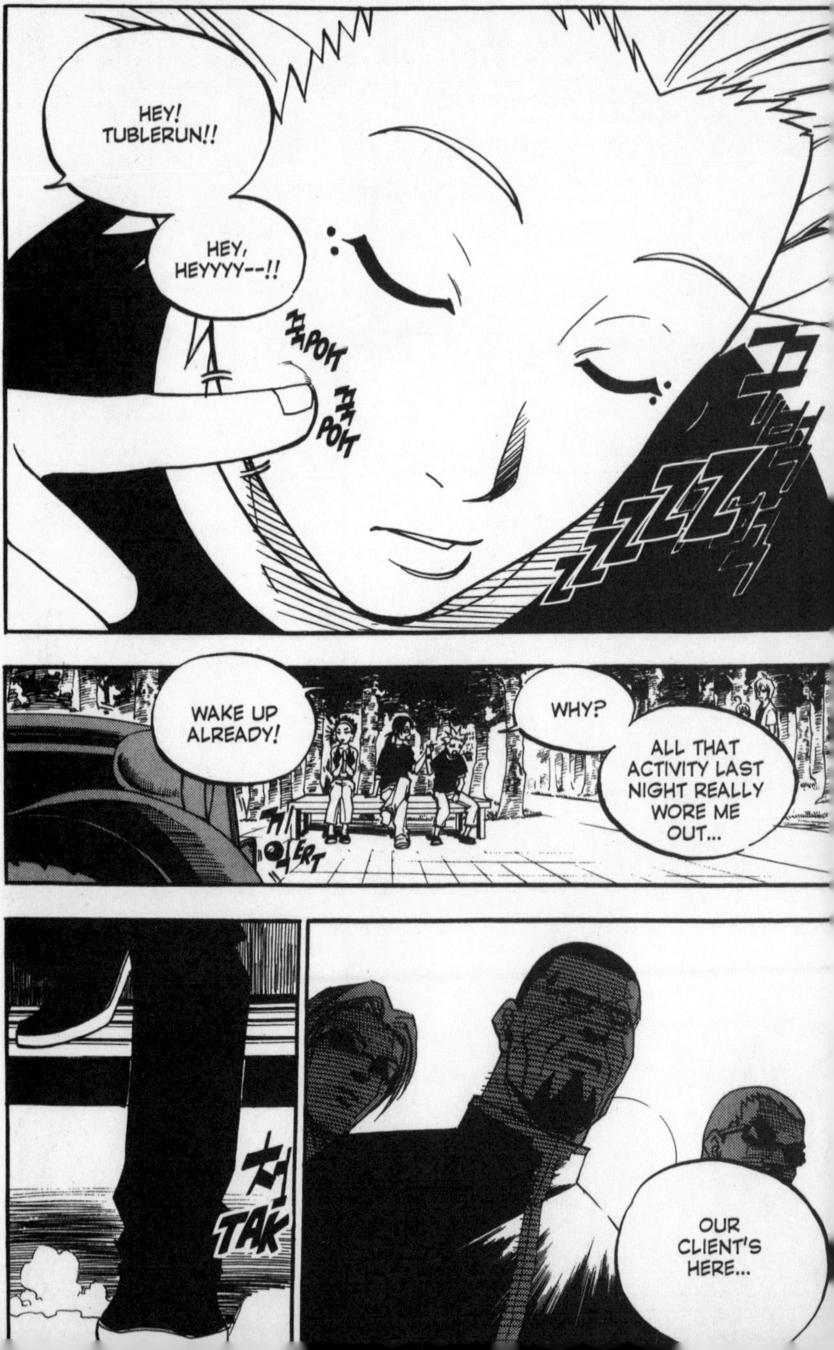
HEY! TUBLERUN!!
HEY, HEYYYY--!!
POK
POK
WAKE UP ALREADY!
ERT
WHY?
ALL THAT ACTIVITY LAST NIGHT REALLY WORE ME OUT...
TAK
OUR CLIENT'S HERE...

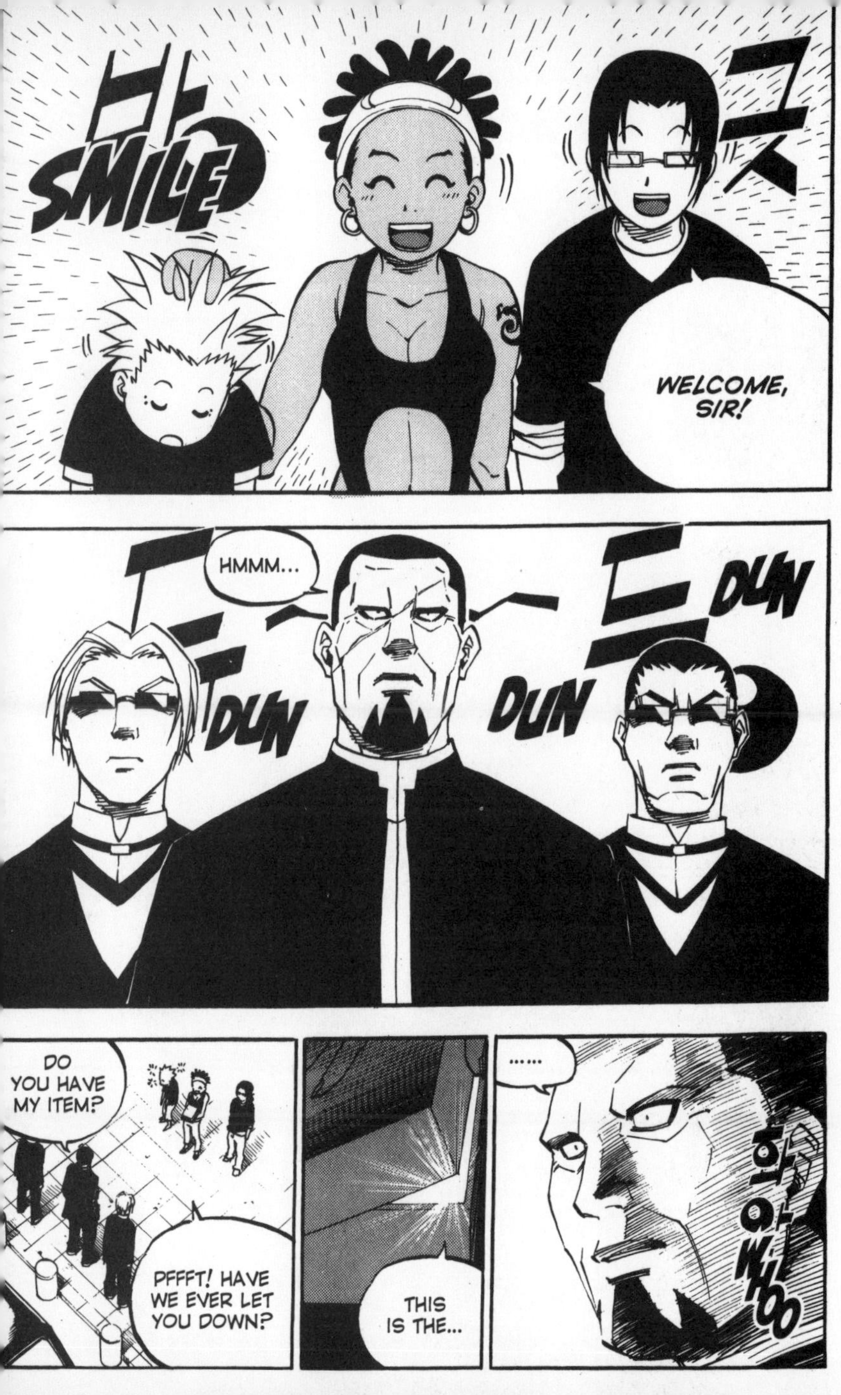
SMILE
WELCOME, SIR!
HMMM...
DUN
DUN
DUN
DO YOU HAVE MY ITEM?
PFFFT! HAVE WE EVER LET YOU DOWN?
THIS IS THE...
......
WHOO

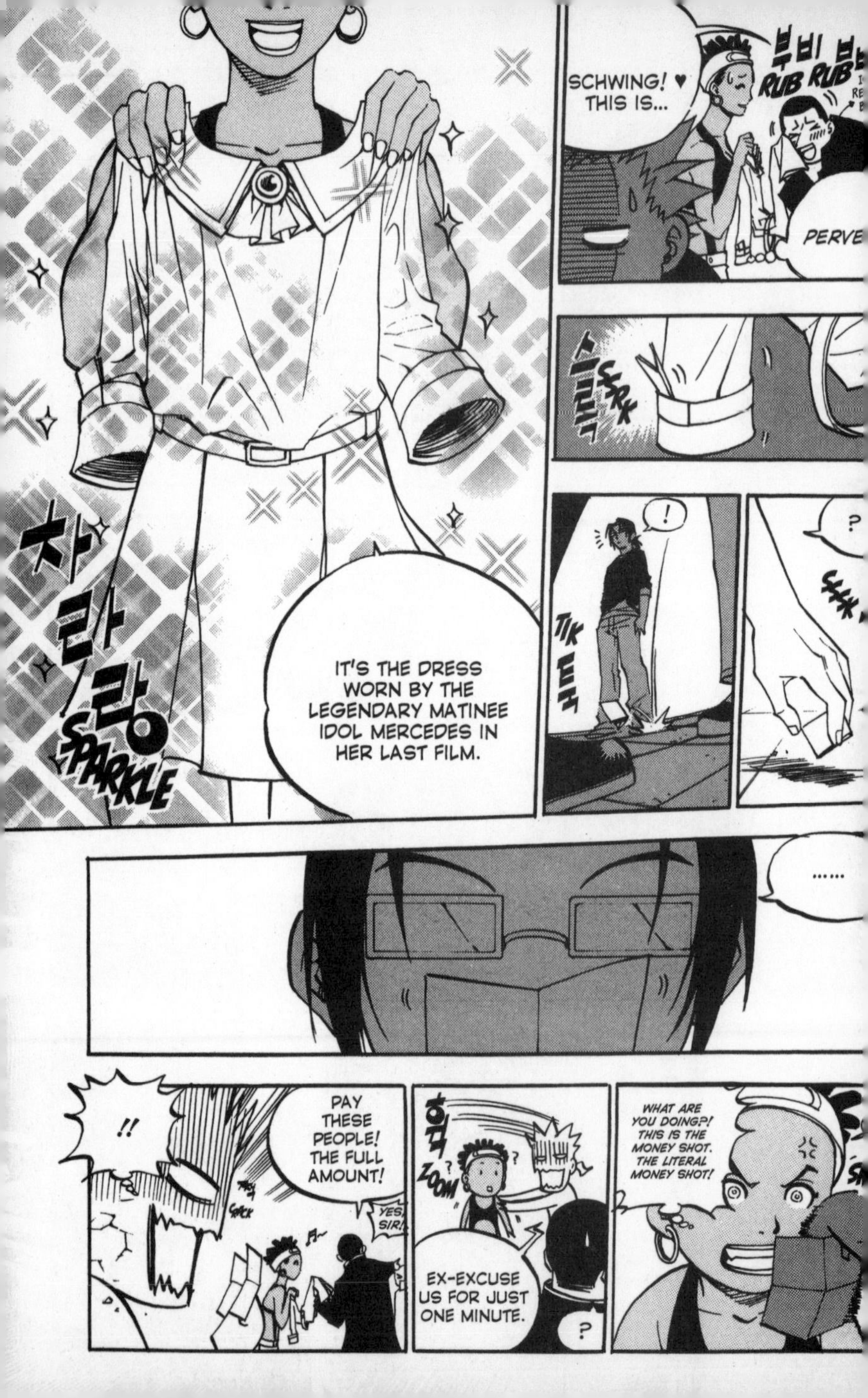
SPARKLE
IT'S THE DRESS WORN BY THE LEGENDARY MATINEE IDOL MERCEDES IN HER LAST FILM.
SCHWING! ♥ THIS IS...
RUB RUB
PERVE
SCRK
!
TIK
?
SCRK
......
!!
PAY THESE PEOPLE! THE FULL AMOUNT!
YES, SIR!
ZOOM
?
?
EX-EXCUSE US FOR JUST ONE MINUTE.
?
WHAT ARE YOU DOING?! THIS IS THE MONEY SHOT. THE LITERAL MONEY SHOT!

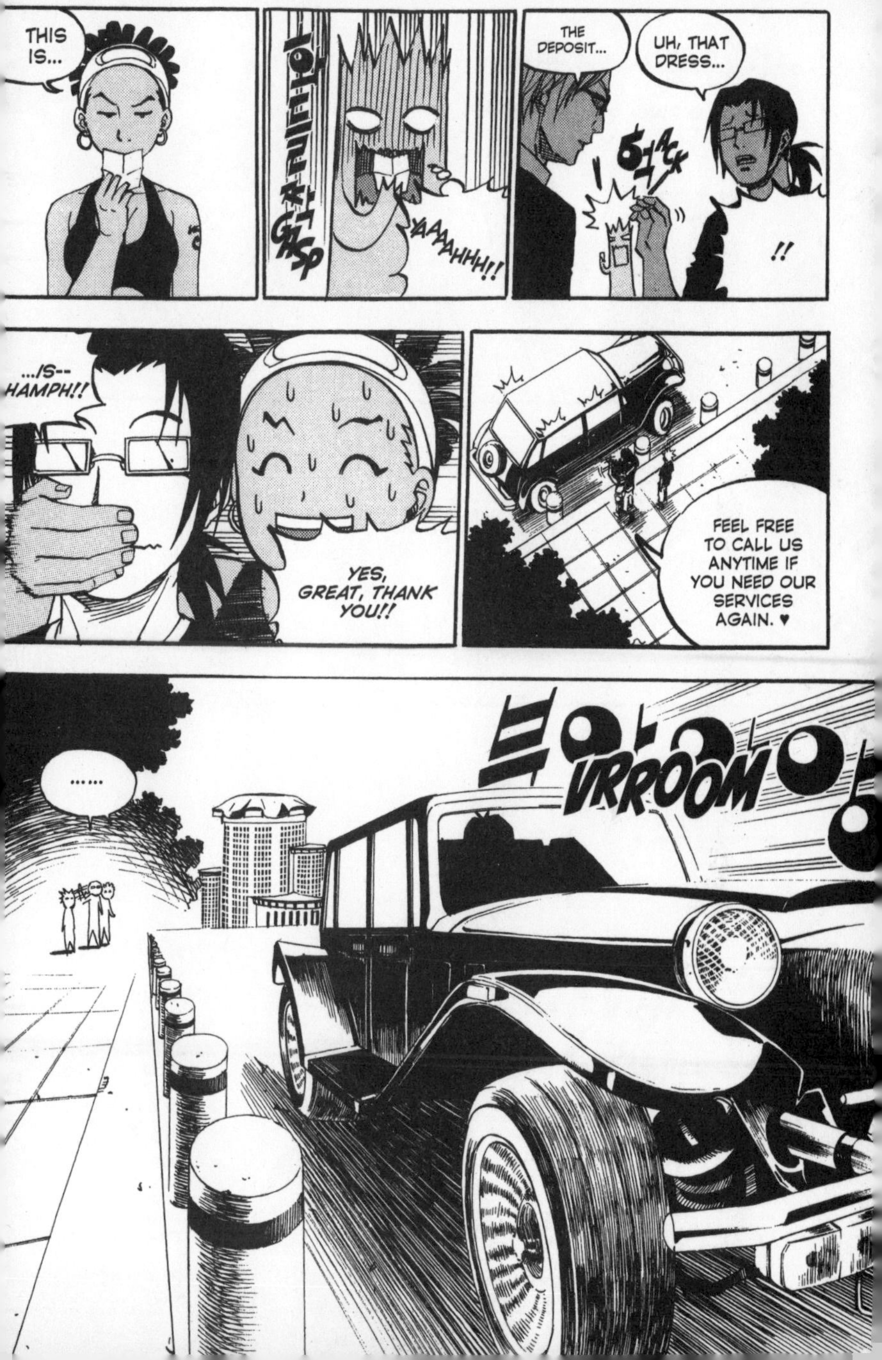

THIS IS...
GASP
YAAAAAHHH!!
THE DEPOSIT...
UH, THAT DRESS...
!!
...IS-- HAMPH!!
YES, GREAT, THANK YOU!!
FEEL FREE TO CALL US ANYTIME IF YOU NEED OUR SERVICES AGAIN. ♥
......
VRROOM

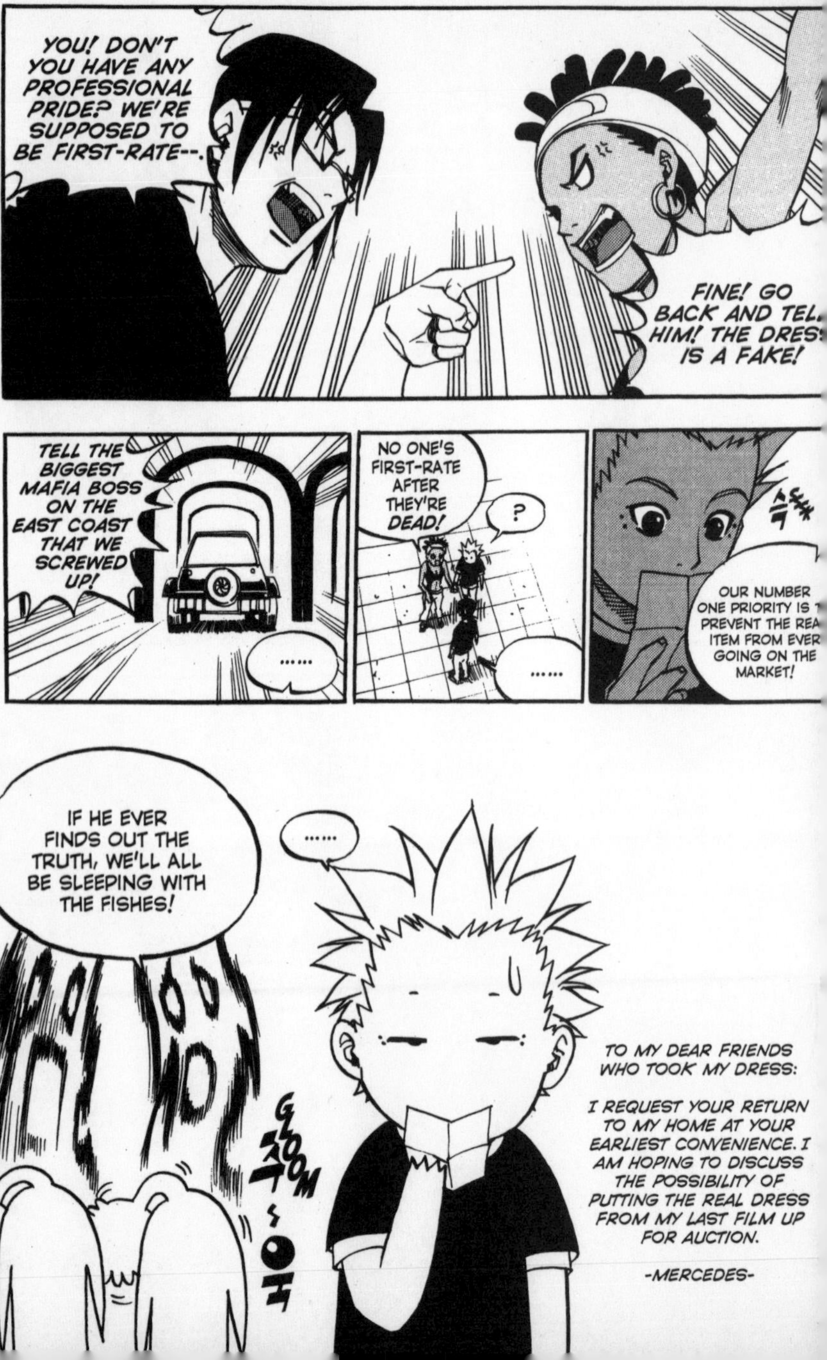
YOU! DON'T YOU HAVE ANY PROFESSIONAL PRIDE? WE'RE SUPPOSED TO BE FIRST-RATE--.
FINE! GO BACK AND TEL HIM! THE DRES IS A FAKE!
TELL THE BIGGEST MAFIA BOSS ON THE EAST COAST THAT WE SCREWED UP!
......
NO ONE'S FIRST-RATE AFTER THEY'RE DEAD!
?
......
OUR NUMBER ONE PRIORITY IS T PREVENT THE REA ITEM FROM EVER GOING ON THE MARKET!
IF HE EVER FINDS OUT THE TRUTH, WE'LL ALL BE SLEEPING WITH THE FISHES!
......
GLOOM
TO MY DEAR FRIENDS WHO TOOK MY DRESS:
I REQUEST YOUR RETURN TO MY HOME AT YOUR EARLIEST CONVENIENCE. I AM HOPING TO DISCUSS THE POSSIBILITY OF PUTTING THE REAL DRESS FROM MY LAST FILM UP FOR AUCTION.
-MERCEDES-

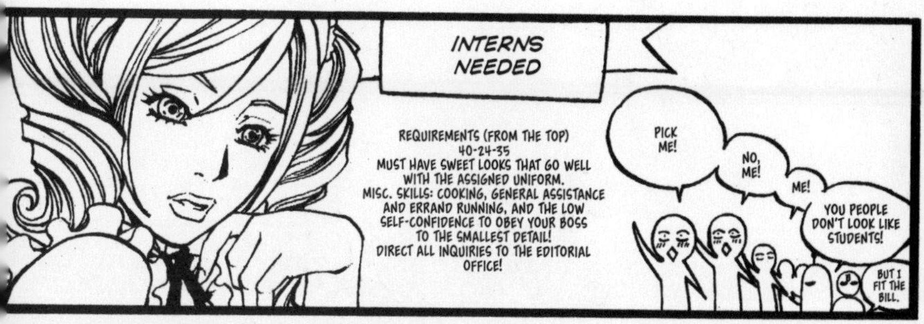
INTERNS NEEDED
REQUIREMENTS (FROM THE TOP)
40-24-35
MUST HAVE SWEET LOOKS THAT GO WELL WITH THE ASSIGNED UNIFORM.
MISC. SKILLS: COOKING, GENERAL ASSISTANCE AND ERRAND RUNNING, AND THE LOW SELF-CONFIDENCE TO OBEY YOUR BOSS TO THE SMALLEST DETAIL!
DIRECT ALL INQUIRIES TO THE EDITORIAL OFFICE!
PICK ME!
NO, ME!
ME!
YOU PEOPLE DON'T LOOK LIKE STUDENTS!
BUT I FIT THE BILL.

BACK TALK...
NO, NO...AFTER WORD?!

THAT WAS CHAPTER 3. YUP...CHAPTER 3.

THIS TIME, LET ME TALK ABOUT LIQUID METAL (WHICH I'LL JUST CALL "LM").

LM IS A METAL THAT BEHAVES LIKE WATER. I GOT THE IDEA QUITE BY HAPPENSTANCE. I WAS WATCHING A TV PROGRAM ON HOW BABY'S DIAPERS WORK. IT WAS A FLASH OF INSPIRATION! AN INFANT DIAPER CONTAINS A "HIGH ABSORPTION TISSUE" THAT INSTANTLY MAKES LIQUIDS SOLID. WATCHING IT MADE ME REMEMBER AN OLD IDEA I HAD ABOUT WEAPONS MADE FROM WATER. UNDER NORMAL CONDITIONS, IT WOULD JUST BE STANDARD WATER, BUT ON CONTACT WITH OPEN AIR, THE WATER WOULD TURN INTO A WEAPON, CONFORMING TO A PRE-PROGRAMMED SHAPE. BUT THE NEW INSPIRATION WAS THAT IT WASN'T WATER AT ALL, BUT SOME KIND OF METAL IN THE FORM OF FLUID. LM WOULD REMAIN IN LIQUID FORM AS LONG AS IT'S IN ITS SPECIFIED CONTAINER, ONLY TURNING INTO METAL WHEN IT'S TAKEN OUT. KNIVES, BULLETS, TOOLS...CONVERTIBLE SECURITY BARRIERS AND DOORS...AND WHILE IT'S LIQUID, LM IS EASY TO STORE, TAKING UP HARDLY ANY SPACE. LM IS TOUGH AND PRACTICAL, AMONGST MANY OTHER BENEFITS. LATER IN THE BOOK, YOU'LL MEET ECLIPTOR. HE HAS TWO SHORT SWORDS TUCKED INTO THE BACK OF HIS WAISTBAND. THE BLADES ARE FORMED OUT OF LM AND BECOME FULL-LENGTH WEAPONS WHEN HE NEEDS THEM. (THE BLADES CAN HAVE VARIABLE LENGTHS.)

ANOTHER THING THAT MAKES LM CONVENIENT IS THAT IT'S CONTROLLED BY THE BRAINWAVES OF ITS OWNER. IN FANTASY GENRE STORIES, IT WOULD BE A KIND OF ESP, BUT I PREFER TO THINK OF IT AS MORE SCIENTIFIC. THE BAND THAT TUBLERUN'S BOARD COMES OUT OF, FOR INSTANCE, HAS A DEVICE ATTUNED TO HIS BRAINWAVES. AT FIRST, I THOUGHT MAYBE THE DEVICE SHOULD BE IMPLANTED IN HIS BRAIN, BUT THEN EVERYONE COULD HAVE ESP, AND THEY'D BE THROWING ALL SORTS OF RANDOM THINGS AT EACH OTHER AND MAKING A REAL MESS. SO, I GAVE UP ON THAT IDEA, INSTEAD PUTTING THE RECEPTOR IN THE LM CONTAINER ITSELF. ABOVE ALL, THE THING THAT GIVES LM ITS EDGE IS THAT IT CAN CHANGE INTO ALL SORTS OF DIFFERENT OBJECTS. YOU JUST HAVE TO INSTALL SEPARATE PROGRAMS FOR THEM ALL. ONE LM CONTAINER CAN PRODUCE FIVE OR MORE WEAPONS. WE HAVE YET TO TEST ITS LIMITS, BUT I HOPE WE CAN SEE HOW FAR LM CAN GO ONE OF THESE DAYS!

INTERESTINGLY, AFTER I HAD HATCHED MY LM IDEA AND SHOWED IT TO SOME PUBLISHERS, I HAPPENED TO SEE ON THE SUBWAY TV THAT RESEARCH IS ALREADY UNDERWAY TO FIND A WAY TO CONTROL EXTERNAL OBJECTS WITH THE POWER OF THOUGHT. ALL THAT'S LEFT IS FOR SOMEONE TO DEVELOP THE LM ITSELF.

CAR 3. VALENTINE'S BRAIN, PART 2

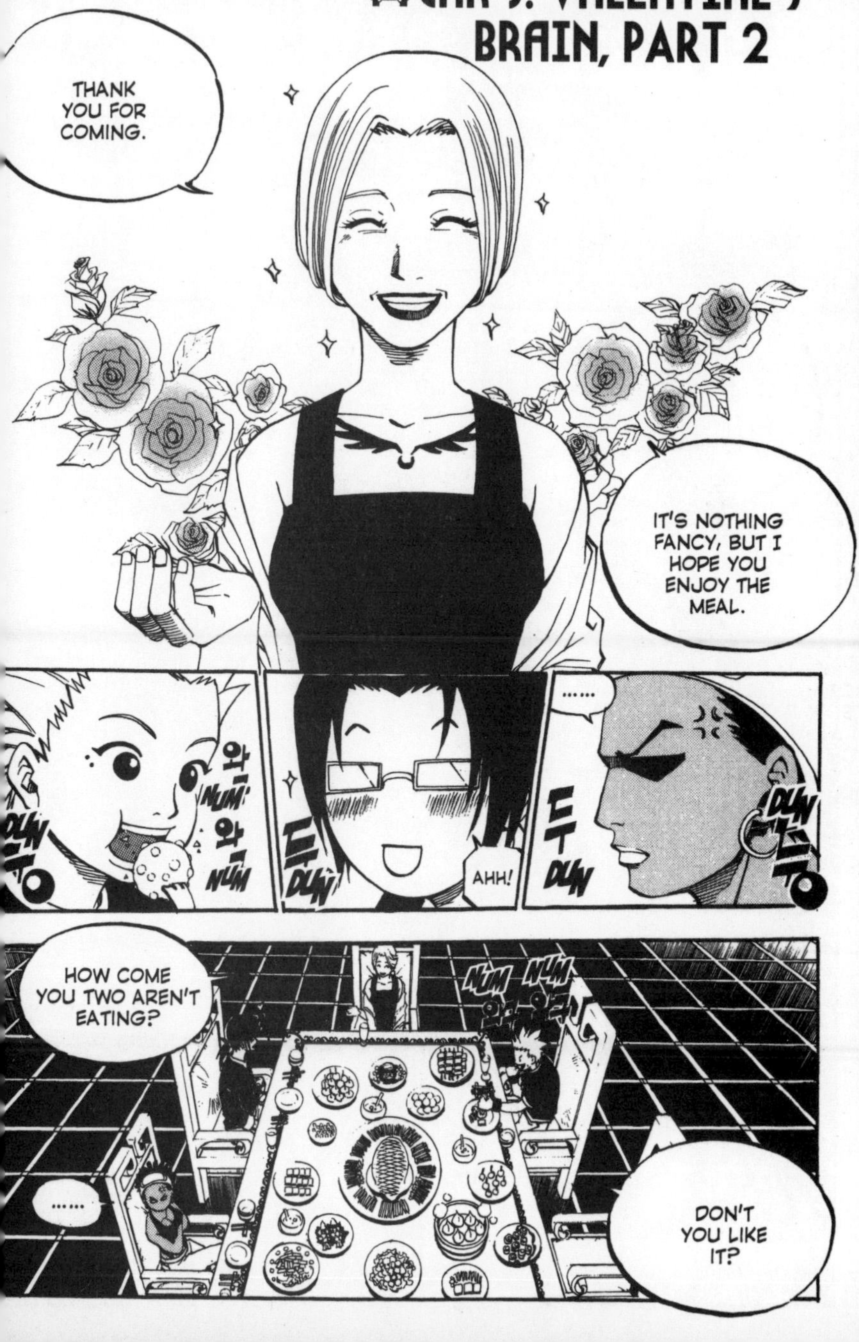

THANK YOU FOR COMING.
IT'S NOTHING FANCY, BUT I HOPE YOU ENJOY THE MEAL.
NUM NUM
DUN
DUN
AHH!
......
DUN
DUN
NUM NUM
HOW COME YOU TWO AREN'T EATING?
......
DON'T YOU LIKE IT?

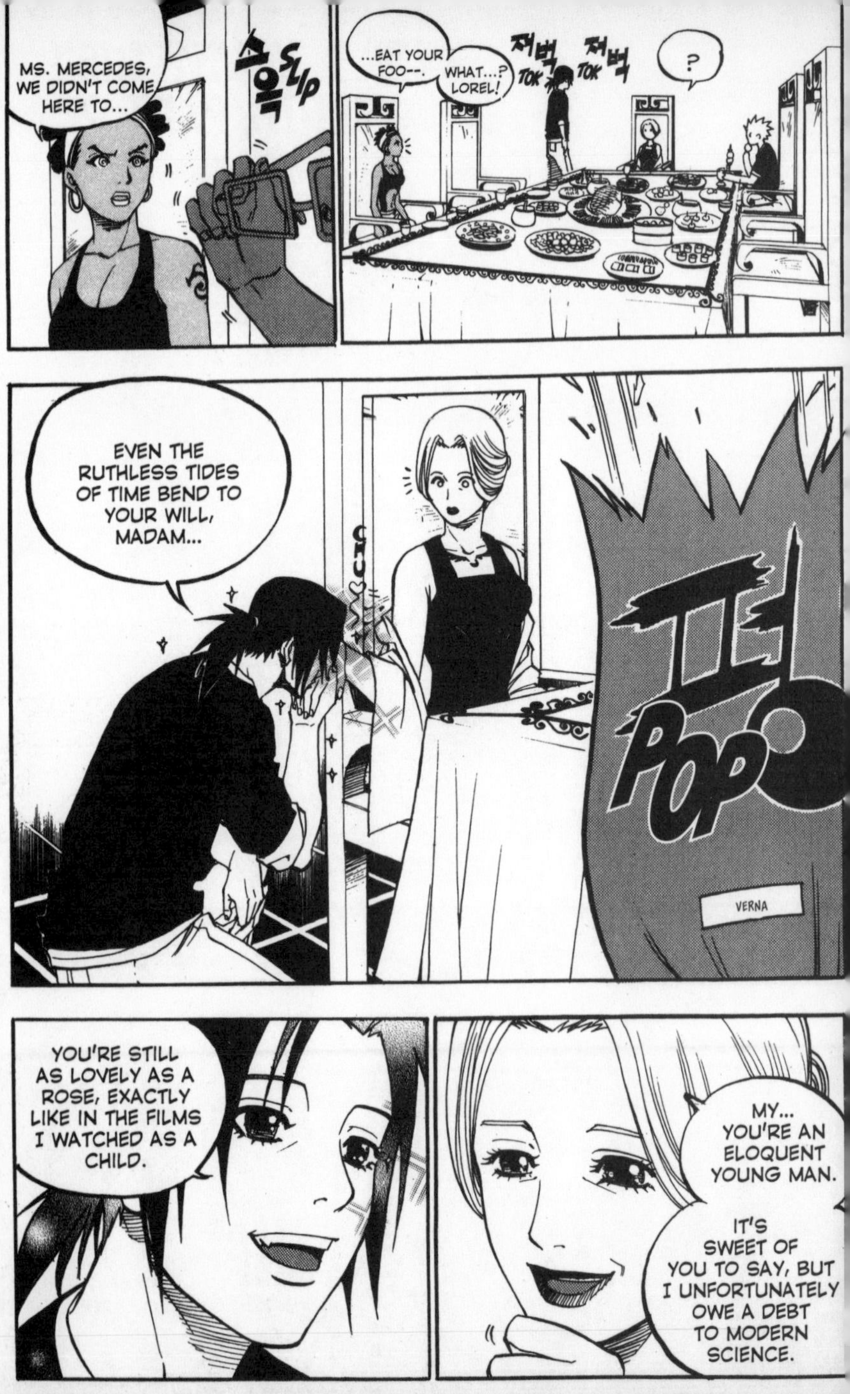
MS. MERCEDES, WE DIDN'T COME HERE TO...
스윽 SLIP
...EAT YOUR FOO--.
WHAT...? LOREL!
저벅 TOK
저벅 TOK
?
EVEN THE RUTHLESS TIDES OF TIME BEND TO YOUR WILL, MADAM...
펑 POP
VERNA
YOU'RE STILL AS LOVELY AS A ROSE, EXACTLY LIKE IN THE FILMS I WATCHED AS A CHILD.
MY... YOU'RE AN ELOQUENT YOUNG MAN.
IT'S SWEET OF YOU TO SAY, BUT I UNFORTUNATELY OWE A DEBT TO MODERN SCIENCE.

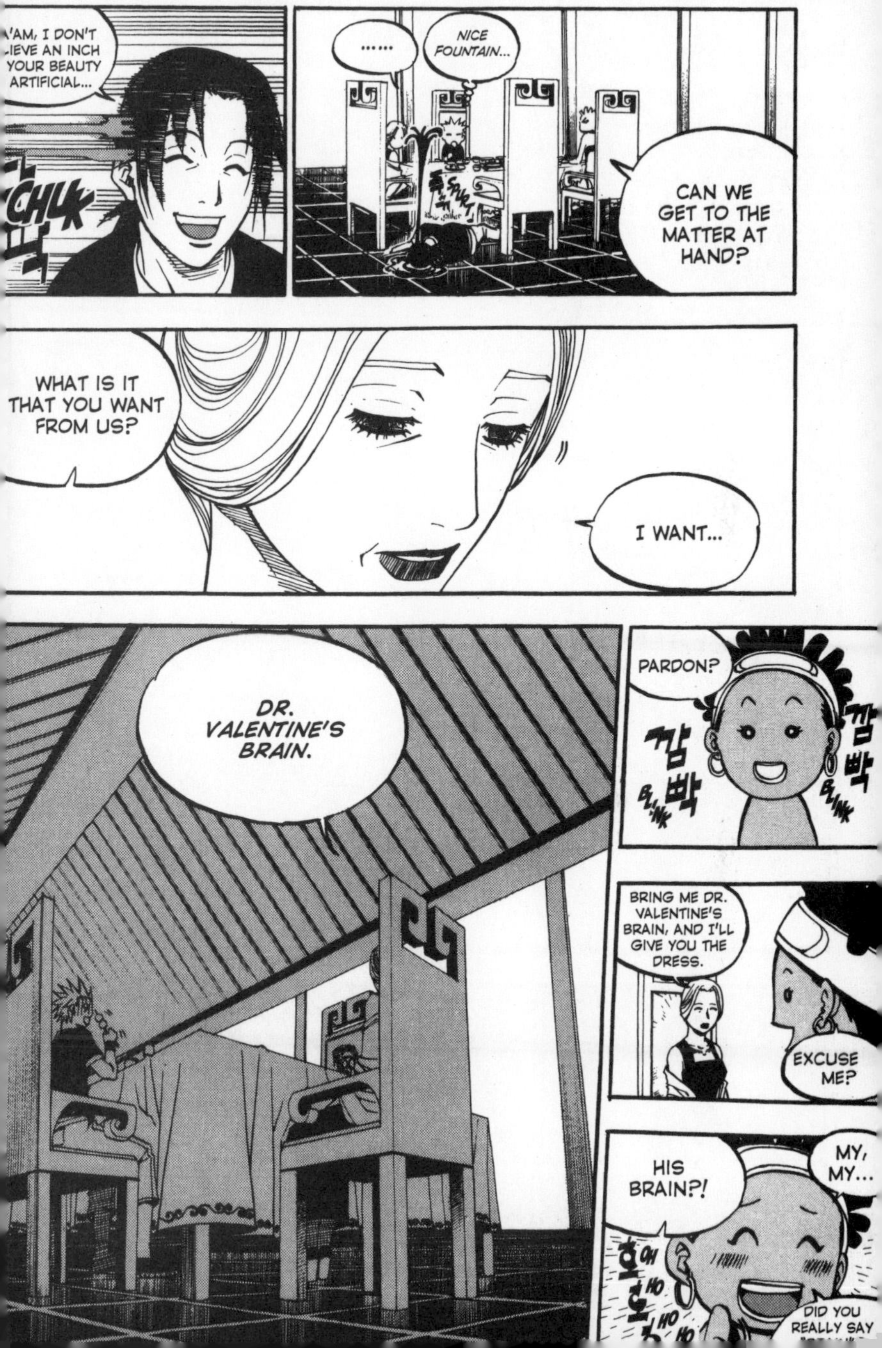
'AM, I DON'T
IEVE AN INCH
YOUR BEAUTY
ARTIFICIAL...
CHUK
......
NICE FOUNTAIN...
SPURT
CAN WE GET TO THE MATTER AT HAND?
WHAT IS IT THAT YOU WANT FROM US?
I WANT...
DR. VALENTINE'S BRAIN.
PARDON?
깜빡 BLINK
깜빡 BLINK
BRING ME DR. VALENTINE'S BRAIN, AND I'LL GIVE YOU THE DRESS.
EXCUSE ME?
HIS BRAIN?!
MY, MY...
OH HO HO HO
DID YOU REALLY SAY

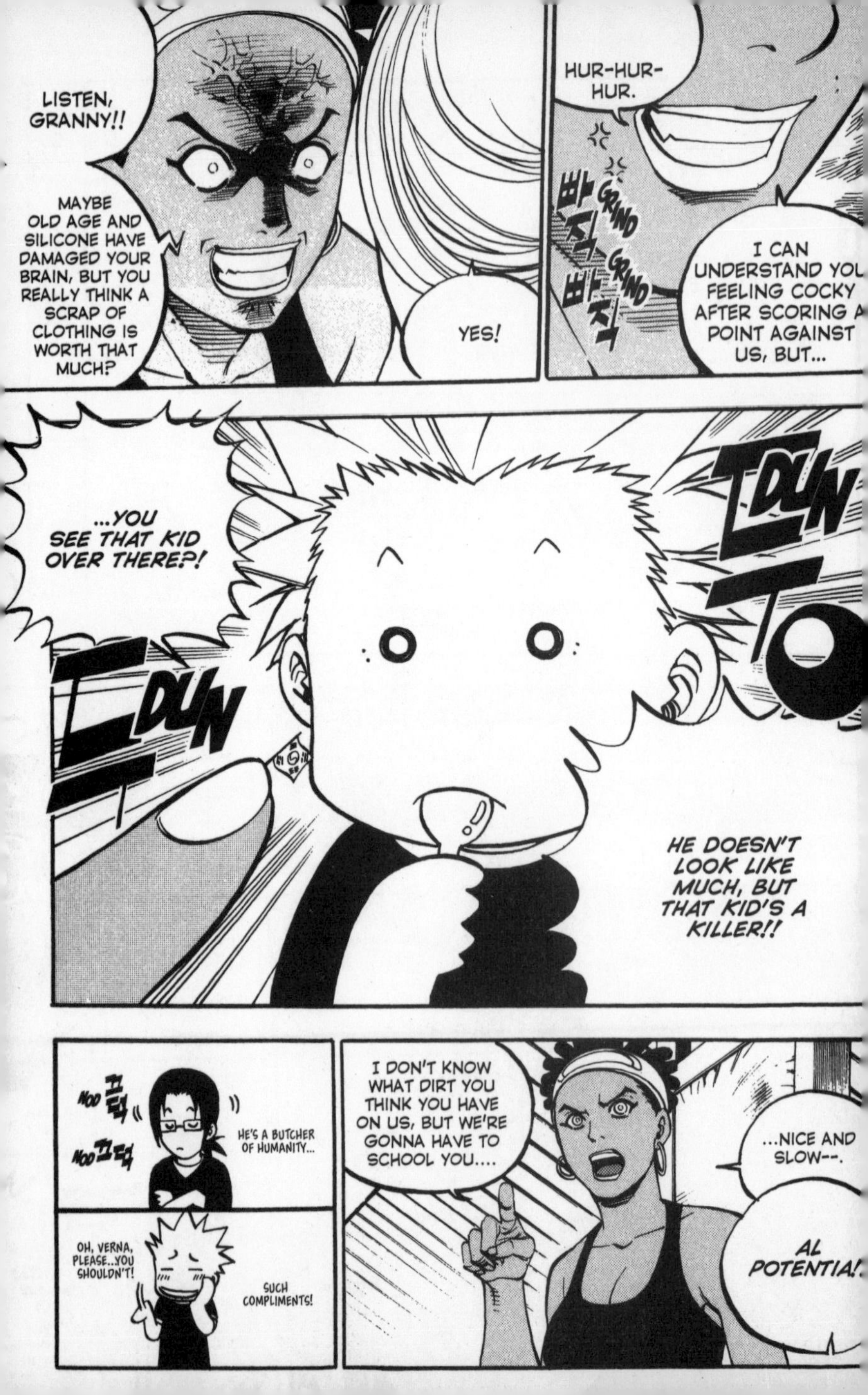
LISTEN, GRANNY!!
MAYBE OLD AGE AND SILICONE HAVE DAMAGED YOUR BRAIN, BUT YOU REALLY THINK A SCRAP OF CLOTHING IS WORTH THAT MUCH?
YES!
HUR-HUR-HUR.
GRIND GRIND
I CAN UNDERSTAND YOU FEELING COCKY AFTER SCORING A POINT AGAINST US, BUT...
...YOU SEE THAT KID OVER THERE?!
DUN
DUN
HE DOESN'T LOOK LIKE MUCH, BUT THAT KID'S A KILLER!!
NOD
NOD
HE'S A BUTCHER OF HUMANITY...
OH, VERNA, PLEASE...YOU SHOULDN'T!
SUCH COMPLIMENTS!
I DON'T KNOW WHAT DIRT YOU THINK YOU HAVE ON US, BUT WE'RE GONNA HAVE TO SCHOOL YOU....
...NICE AND SLOW--.
AL POTENTIA!

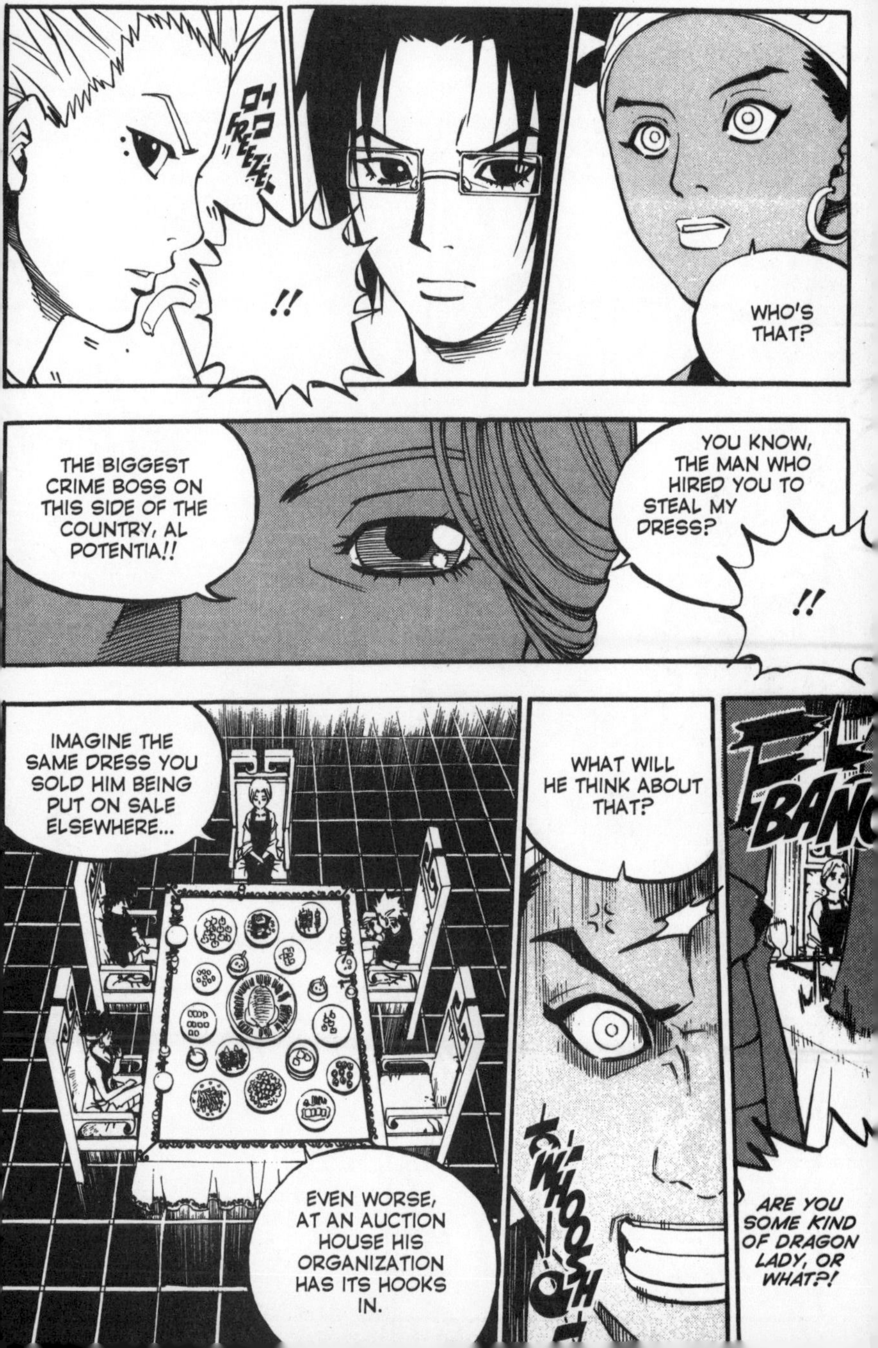
OI FREEZE!
!!
WHO'S THAT?
THE BIGGEST CRIME BOSS ON THIS SIDE OF THE COUNTRY, AL POTENTIA!!
YOU KNOW, THE MAN WHO HIRED YOU TO STEAL MY DRESS?
!!
IMAGINE THE SAME DRESS YOU SOLD HIM BEING PUT ON SALE ELSEWHERE...
EVEN WORSE, AT AN AUCTION HOUSE HIS ORGANIZATION HAS ITS HOOKS IN.
WHAT WILL HE THINK ABOUT THAT?
WHOOSH
ARE YOU SOME KIND OF DRAGON LADY, OR WHAT?!

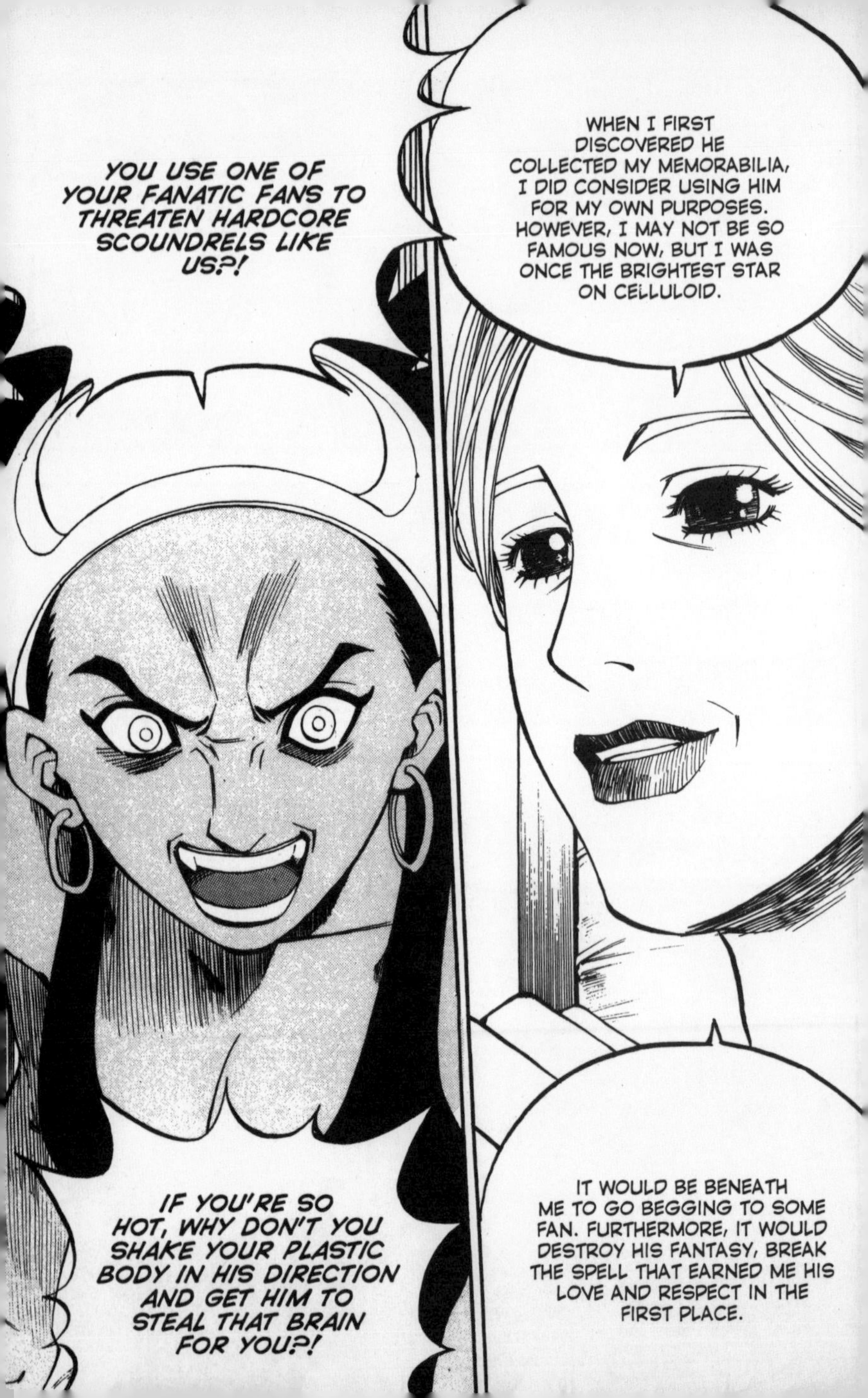
YOU USE ONE OF YOUR FANATIC FANS TO THREATEN HARDCORE SCOUNDRELS LIKE US?!
IF YOU'RE SO HOT, WHY DON'T YOU SHAKE YOUR PLASTIC BODY IN HIS DIRECTION AND GET HIM TO STEAL THAT BRAIN FOR YOU?!
WHEN I FIRST DISCOVERED HE COLLECTED MY MEMORABILIA, I DID CONSIDER USING HIM FOR MY OWN PURPOSES. HOWEVER, I MAY NOT BE SO FAMOUS NOW, BUT I WAS ONCE THE BRIGHTEST STAR ON CELLULOID.
IT WOULD BE BENEATH ME TO GO BEGGING TO SOME FAN. FURTHERMORE, IT WOULD DESTROY HIS FANTASY, BREAK THE SPELL THAT EARNED ME HIS LOVE AND RESPECT IN THE FIRST PLACE.

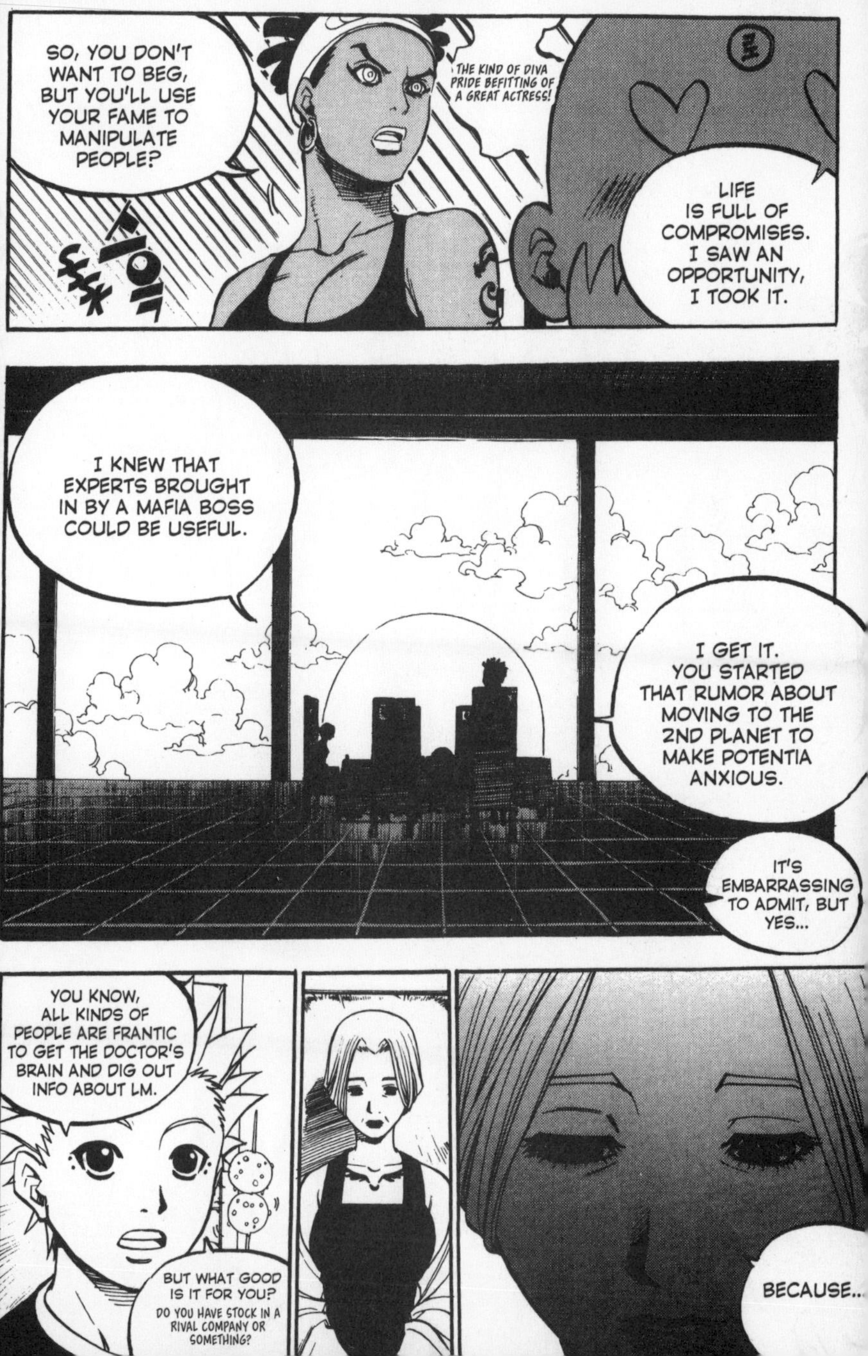
SO, YOU DON'T WANT TO BEG, BUT YOU'LL USE YOUR FAME TO MANIPULATE PEOPLE?
THE KIND OF DIVA PRIDE BEFITTING OF A GREAT ACTRESS!
LIFE IS FULL OF COMPROMISES. I SAW AN OPPORTUNITY, I TOOK IT.
I KNEW THAT EXPERTS BROUGHT IN BY A MAFIA BOSS COULD BE USEFUL.
I GET IT. YOU STARTED THAT RUMOR ABOUT MOVING TO THE 2ND PLANET TO MAKE POTENTIA ANXIOUS.
IT'S EMBARRASSING TO ADMIT, BUT YES...
YOU KNOW, ALL KINDS OF PEOPLE ARE FRANTIC TO GET THE DOCTOR'S BRAIN AND DIG OUT INFO ABOUT LM.
BUT WHAT GOOD IS IT FOR YOU?
DO YOU HAVE STOCK IN A RIVAL COMPANY OR SOMETHING?
BECAUSE...

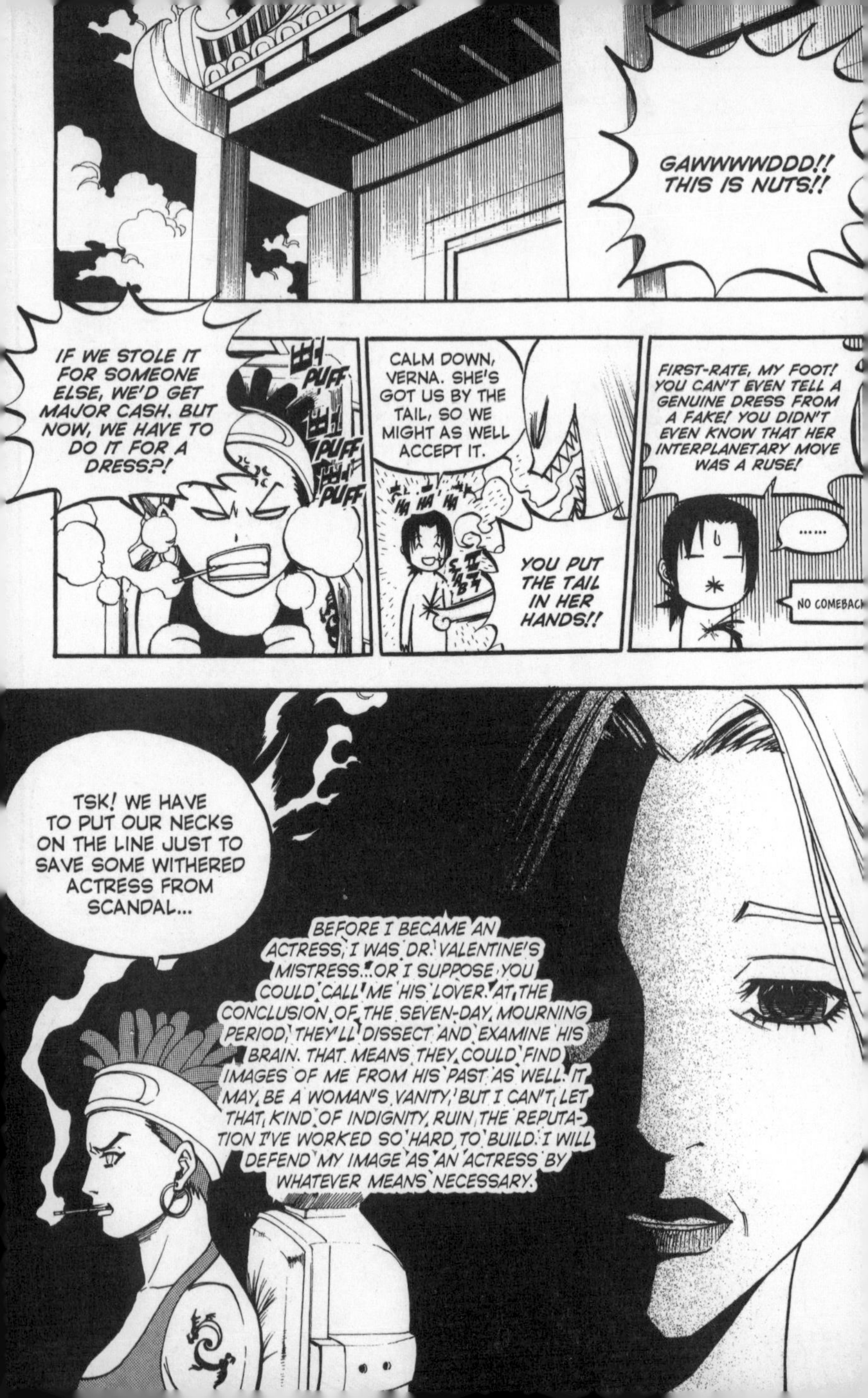
GAWWWWDDD!! THIS IS NUTS!!
IF WE STOLE IT FOR SOMEONE ELSE, WE'D GET MAJOR CASH. BUT NOW, WE HAVE TO DO IT FOR A DRESS?!
PUFF
PUFF
PUFF
CALM DOWN, VERNA. SHE'S GOT US BY THE TAIL, SO WE MIGHT AS WELL ACCEPT IT.
HA HA HA
YOU PUT THE TAIL IN HER HANDS!!
FIRST-RATE, MY FOOT! YOU CAN'T EVEN TELL A GENUINE DRESS FROM A FAKE! YOU DIDN'T EVEN KNOW THAT HER INTERPLANETARY MOVE WAS A RUSE!
......
NO COMEBACK
TSK! WE HAVE TO PUT OUR NECKS ON THE LINE JUST TO SAVE SOME WITHERED ACTRESS FROM SCANDAL...
BEFORE I BECAME AN ACTRESS, I WAS DR. VALENTINE'S MISTRESS...OR I SUPPOSE YOU COULD CALL ME HIS LOVER. AT THE CONCLUSION OF THE SEVEN-DAY MOURNING PERIOD, THEY'LL DISSECT AND EXAMINE HIS BRAIN. THAT MEANS THEY COULD FIND IMAGES OF ME FROM HIS PAST AS WELL. IT MAY BE A WOMAN'S VANITY, BUT I CAN'T LET THAT KIND OF INDIGNITY RUIN THE REPUTATION I'VE WORKED SO HARD TO BUILD. I WILL DEFEND MY IMAGE AS AN ACTRESS BY WHATEVER MEANS NECESSARY.

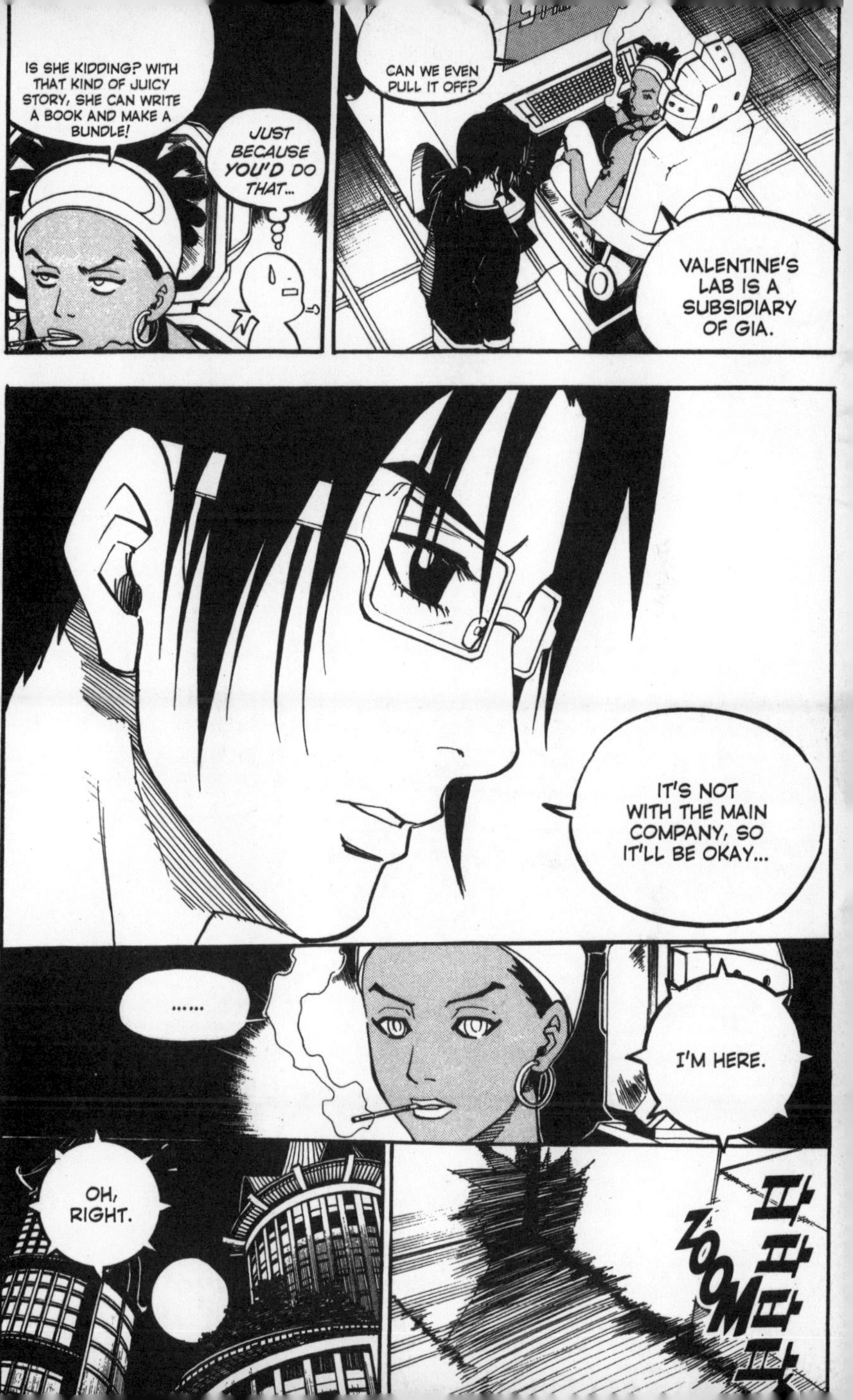
IS SHE KIDDING? WITH THAT KIND OF JUICY STORY, SHE CAN WRITE A BOOK AND MAKE A BUNDLE!
JUST BECAUSE YOU'D DO THAT...
CAN WE EVEN PULL IT OFF?
VALENTINE'S LAB IS A SUBSIDIARY OF GIA.
IT'S NOT WITH THE MAIN COMPANY, SO IT'LL BE OKAY...
......
I'M HERE.
OH, RIGHT.
ZOOM
파파파팍

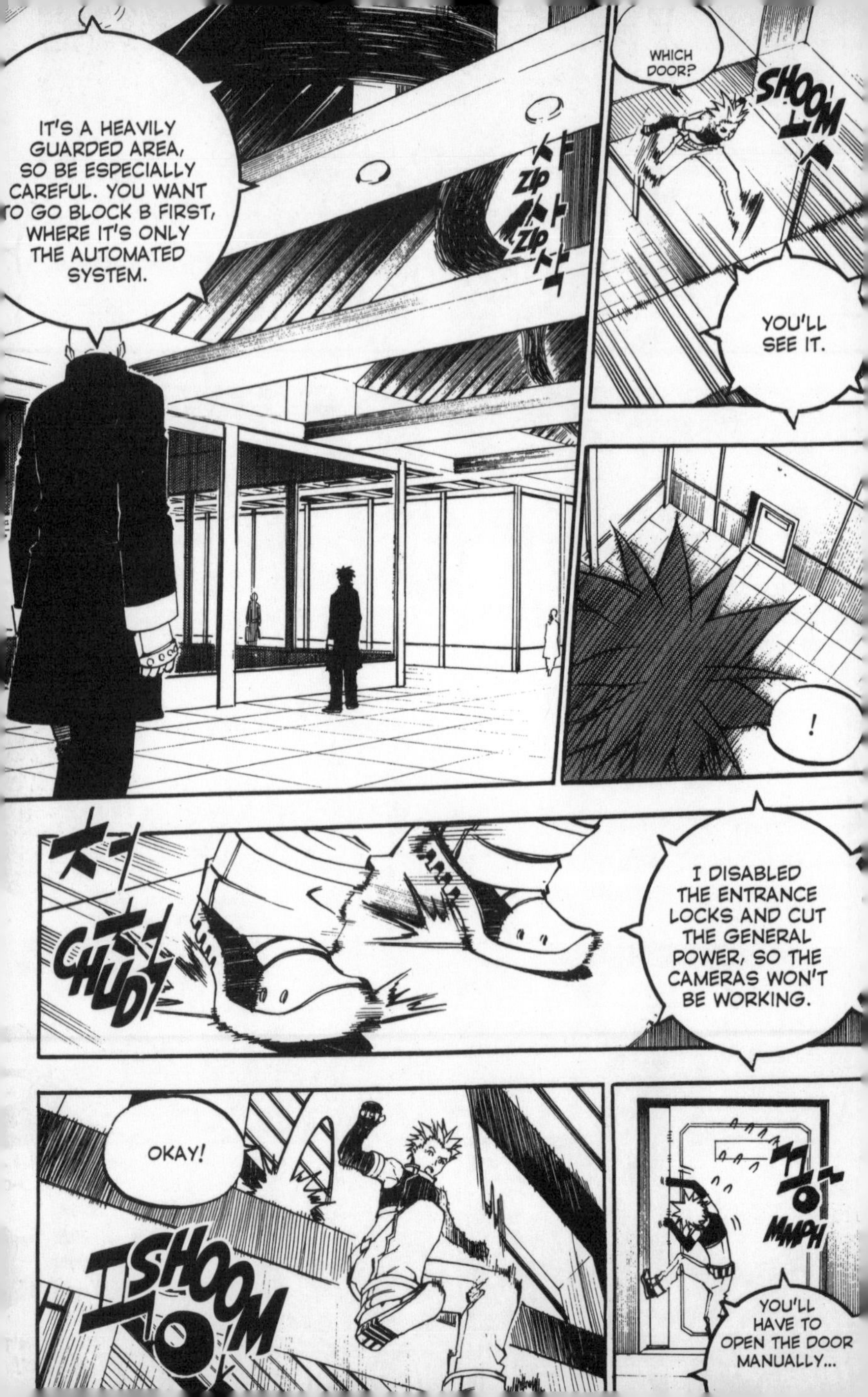
IT'S A HEAVILY GUARDED AREA, SO BE ESPECIALLY CAREFUL. YOU WANT TO GO BLOCK B FIRST, WHERE IT'S ONLY THE AUTOMATED SYSTEM.
ZIP ZIP
WHICH DOOR?
SHOOM
YOU'LL SEE IT.
!
CHUD
I DISABLED THE ENTRANCE LOCKS AND CUT THE GENERAL POWER, SO THE CAMERAS WON'T BE WORKING.
OKAY!
SHOOM
MMPH
YOU'LL HAVE TO OPEN THE DOOR MANUALLY...

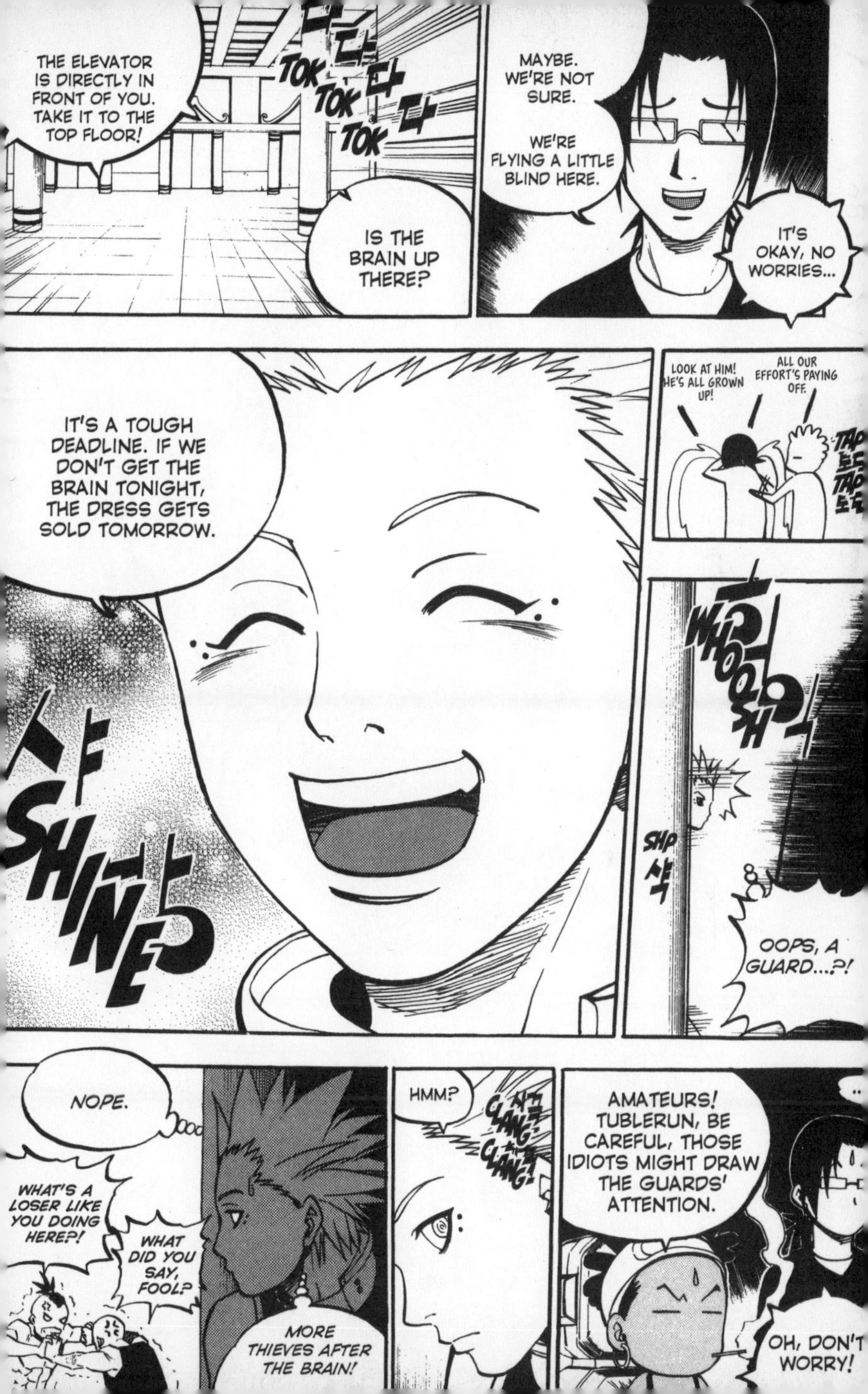

THE ELEVATOR IS DIRECTLY IN FRONT OF YOU. TAKE IT TO THE TOP FLOOR!
TOK TOK TOK
IS THE BRAIN UP THERE?
MAYBE. WE'RE NOT SURE.
WE'RE FLYING A LITTLE BLIND HERE.
IT'S OKAY, NO WORRIES...
IT'S A TOUGH DEADLINE. IF WE DON'T GET THE BRAIN TONIGHT, THE DRESS GETS SOLD TOMORROW.
SHINE
LOOK AT HIM! HE'S ALL GROWN UP!
ALL OUR EFFORT'S PAYING OFF.
TAP TAP
WHOOSH
SHP 삭
OOPS, A GUARD...?!
NOPE.
WHAT'S A LOSER LIKE YOU DOING HERE?!
WHAT DID YOU SAY, FOOL?
MORE THIEVES AFTER THE BRAIN!
HMM?
CLANG CLANG!
AMATEURS! TUBLERUN, BE CAREFUL, THOSE IDIOTS MIGHT DRAW THE GUARDS' ATTENTION.
...
OH, DON'T WORRY!

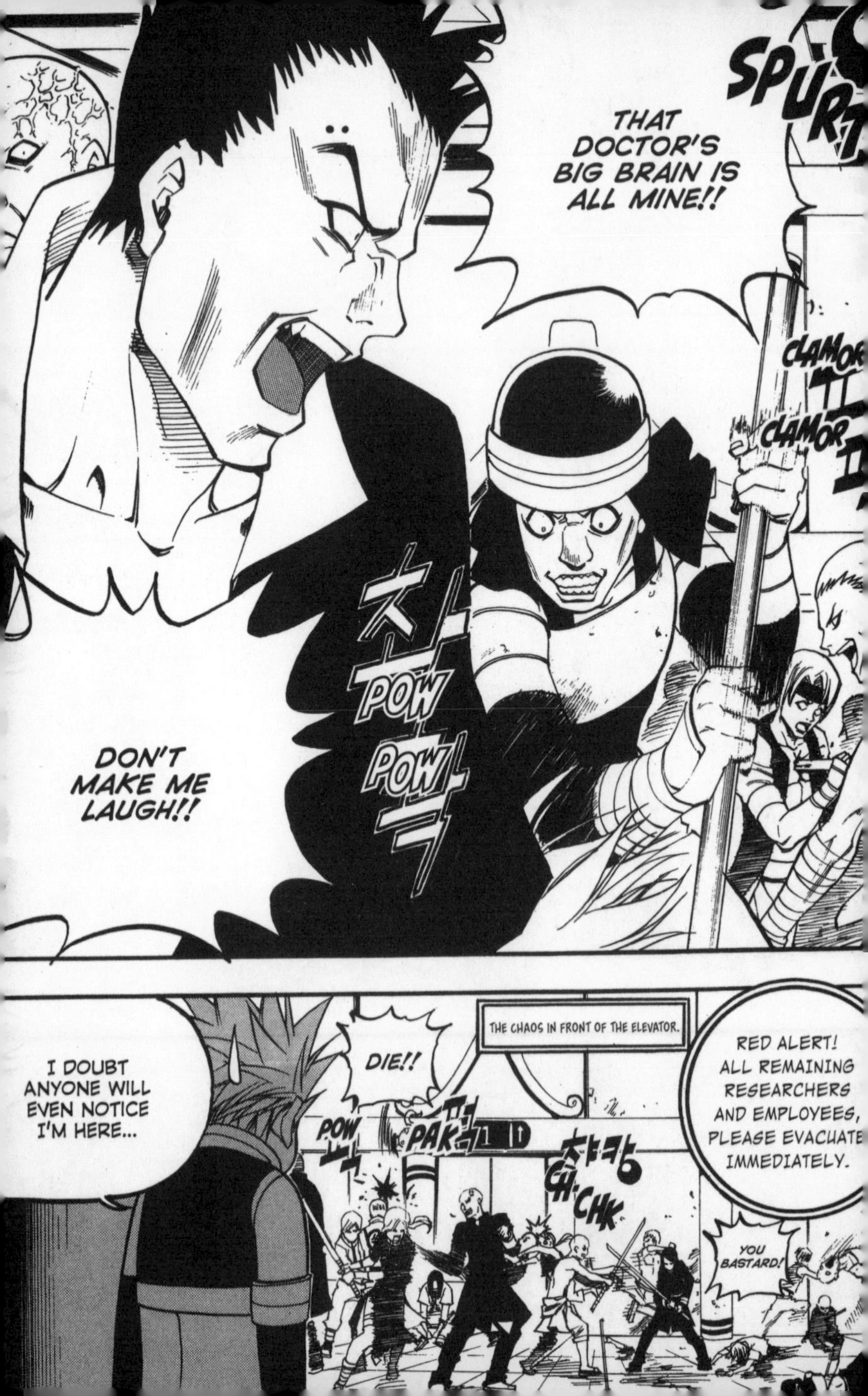

THAT DOCTOR'S BIG BRAIN IS ALL MINE!!
SPURT
CLAMOR
CLAMOR
DON'T MAKE ME LAUGH!!
POW
POW
I DOUBT ANYONE WILL EVEN NOTICE I'M HERE...
DIE!!
THE CHAOS IN FRONT OF THE ELEVATOR.
RED ALERT! ALL REMAINING RESEARCHERS AND EMPLOYEES, PLEASE EVACUATE IMMEDIATELY.
POW
PAK
CH-CHK
YOU BASTARD!

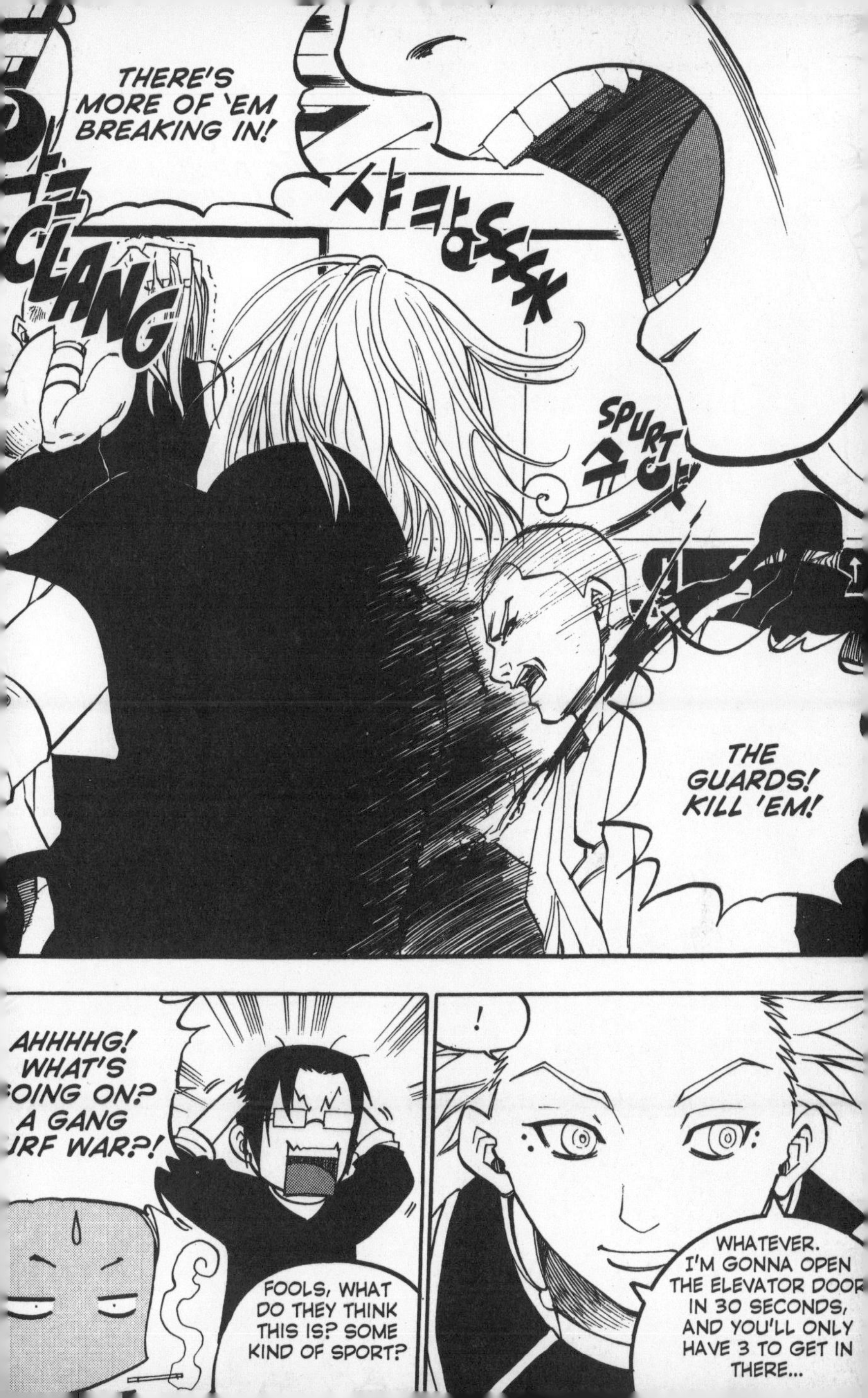
THERE'S MORE OF 'EM BREAKING IN!
CLANG
샤캉
SSSK
SPURT
THE GUARDS! KILL 'EM!
AHHHHG! WHAT'S OING ON? A GANG URF WAR?!
FOOLS, WHAT DO THEY THINK THIS IS? SOME KIND OF SPORT?
!
WHATEVER. I'M GONNA OPEN THE ELEVATOR DOOR IN 30 SECONDS, AND YOU'LL ONLY HAVE 3 TO GET IN THERE...

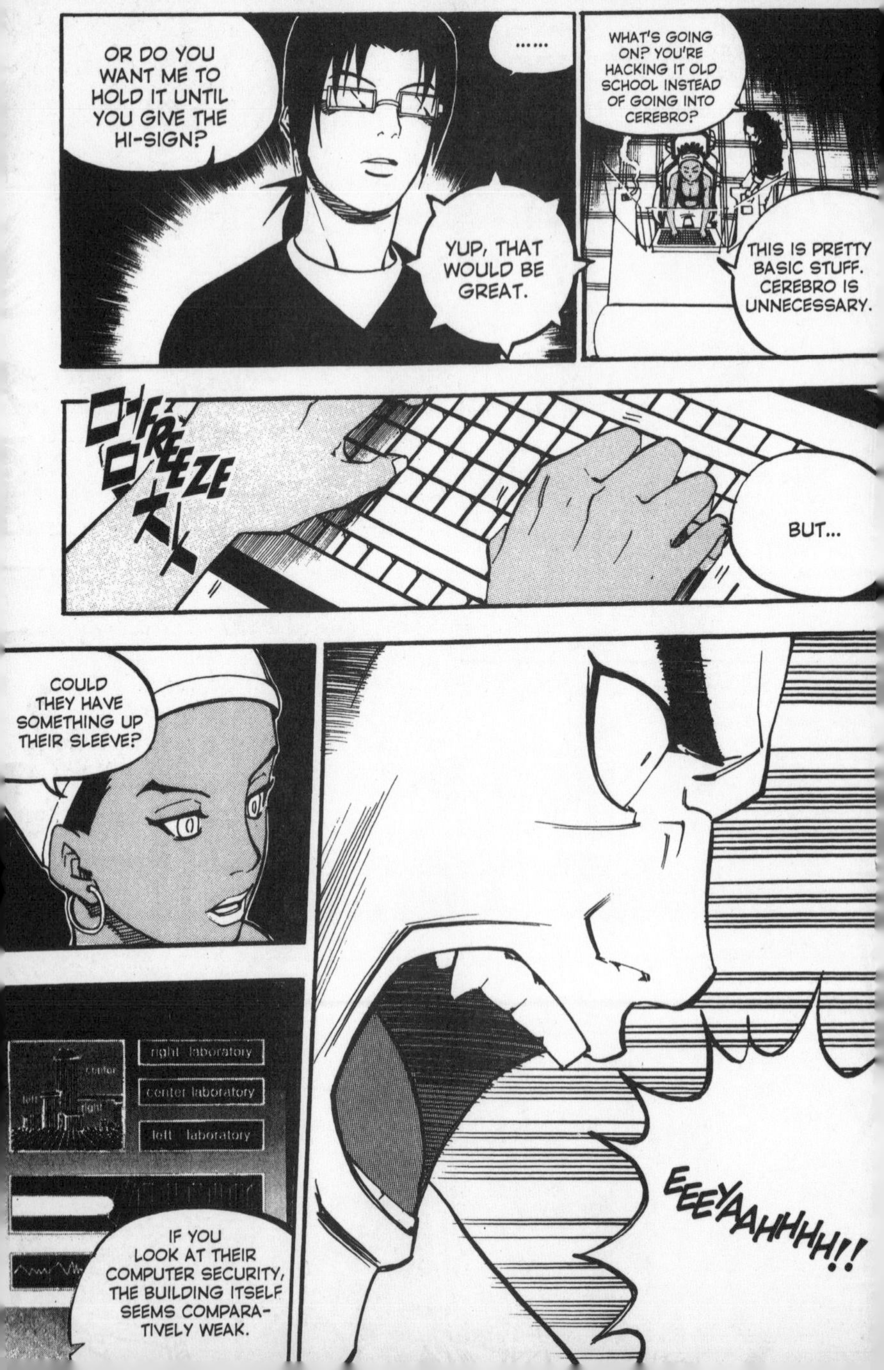
OR DO YOU WANT ME TO HOLD IT UNTIL YOU GIVE THE HI-SIGN?
......
YUP, THAT WOULD BE GREAT.
WHAT'S GOING ON? YOU'RE HACKING IT OLD SCHOOL INSTEAD OF GOING INTO CEREBRO?
THIS IS PRETTY BASIC STUFF. CEREBRO IS UNNECESSARY.
FREEZE
BUT...
COULD THEY HAVE SOMETHING UP THEIR SLEEVE?
right laboratory
center laboratory
left laboratory
center
left
right
IF YOU LOOK AT THEIR COMPUTER SECURITY, THE BUILDING ITSELF SEEMS COMPARATIVELY WEAK.
EEEYAAHHHH!!

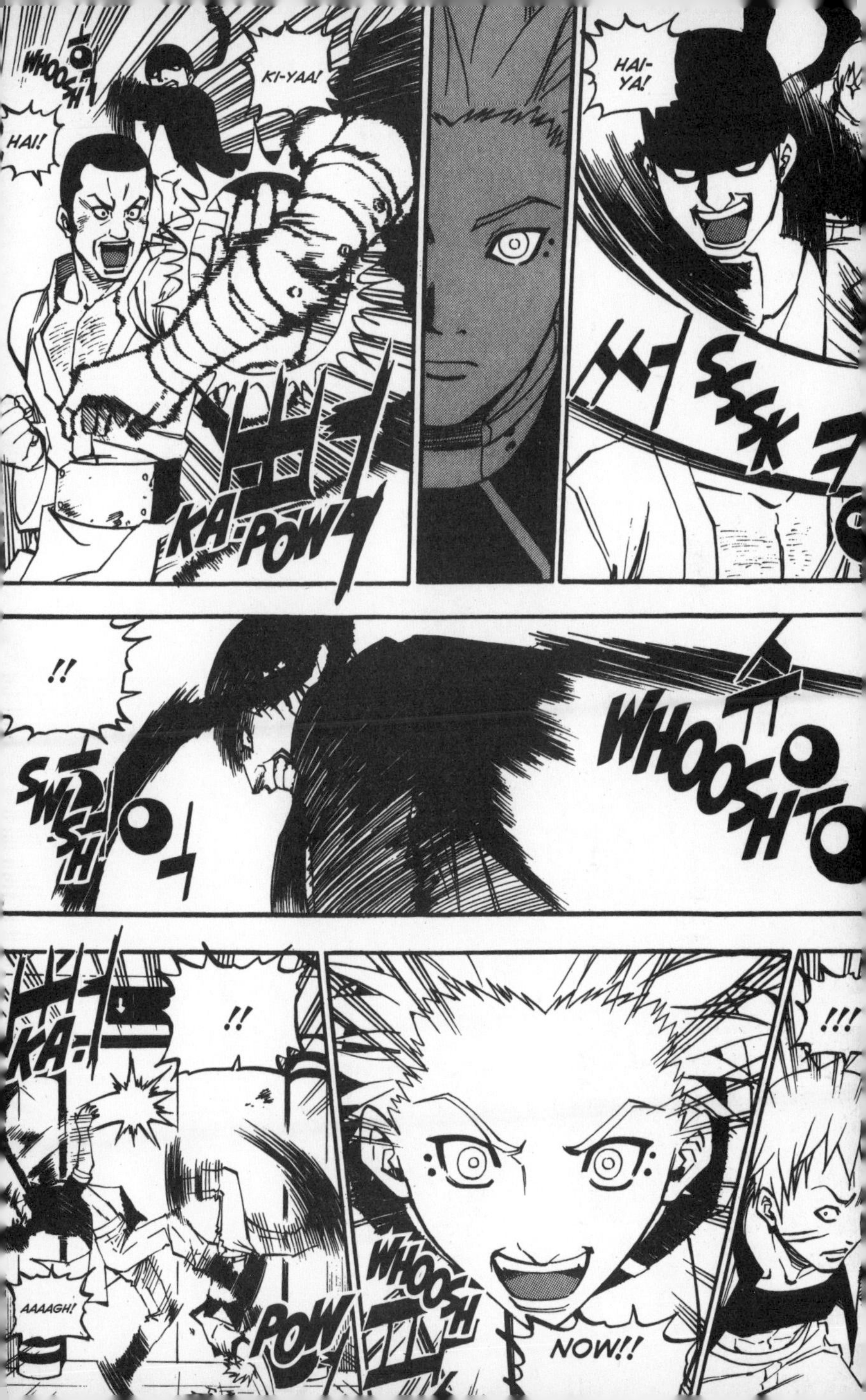
WHOOSH
HAI!
KI-YAA!
KA-POW
HAI-YA!
SSSK
!!
SWISH
WHOOSH
KA-
!!
AAAAGH!
POW
WHOOSH
NOW!!
!!!

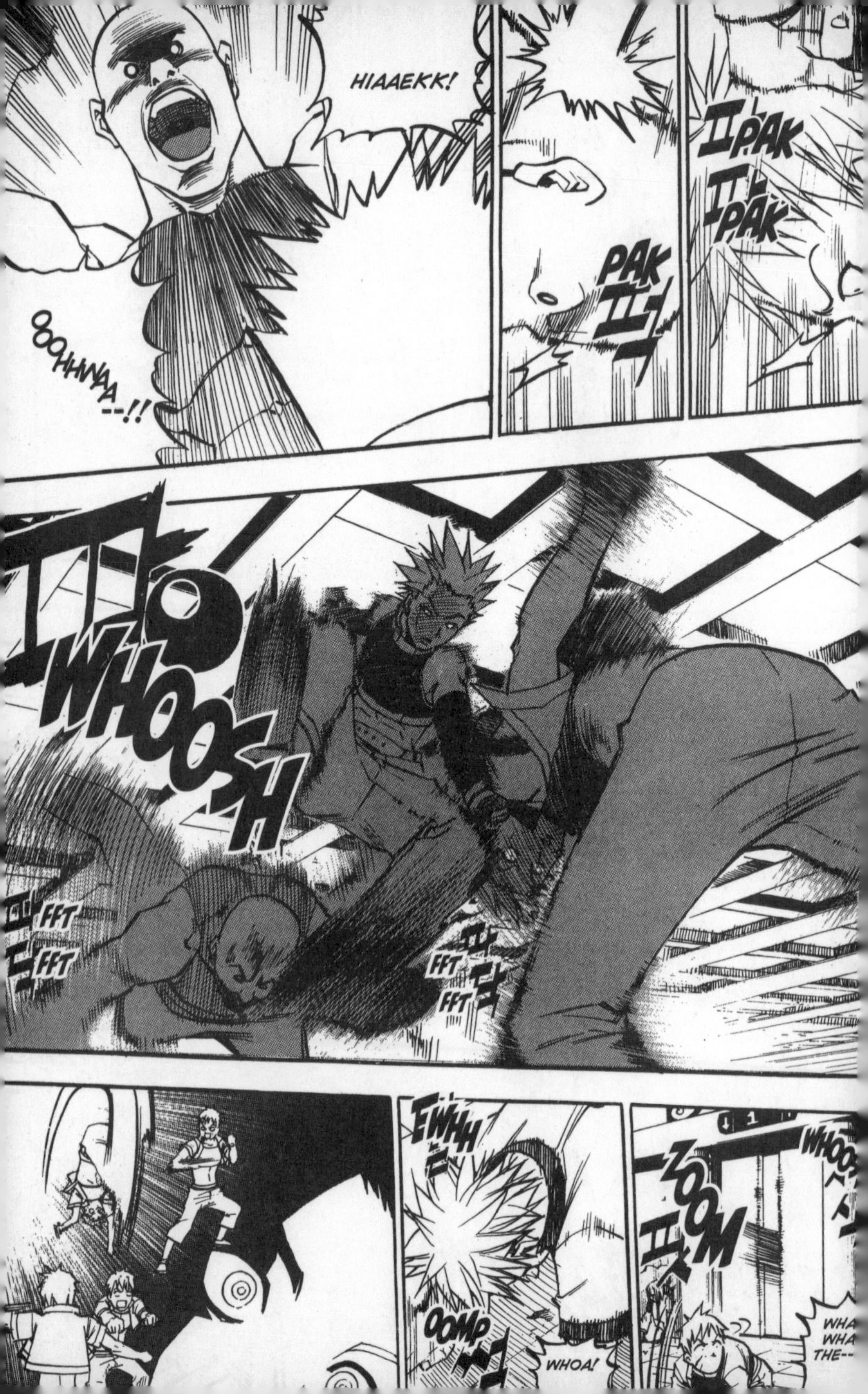
HIAAAEKK!
OOOHHWAA--!!
PAK
PAK
PAK
WHOOSH
FFT
FFT
FFT
FFT
EWHH
OOMP
WHOA!
ZOOM
WHOOSH
WHA
WHA
THE--

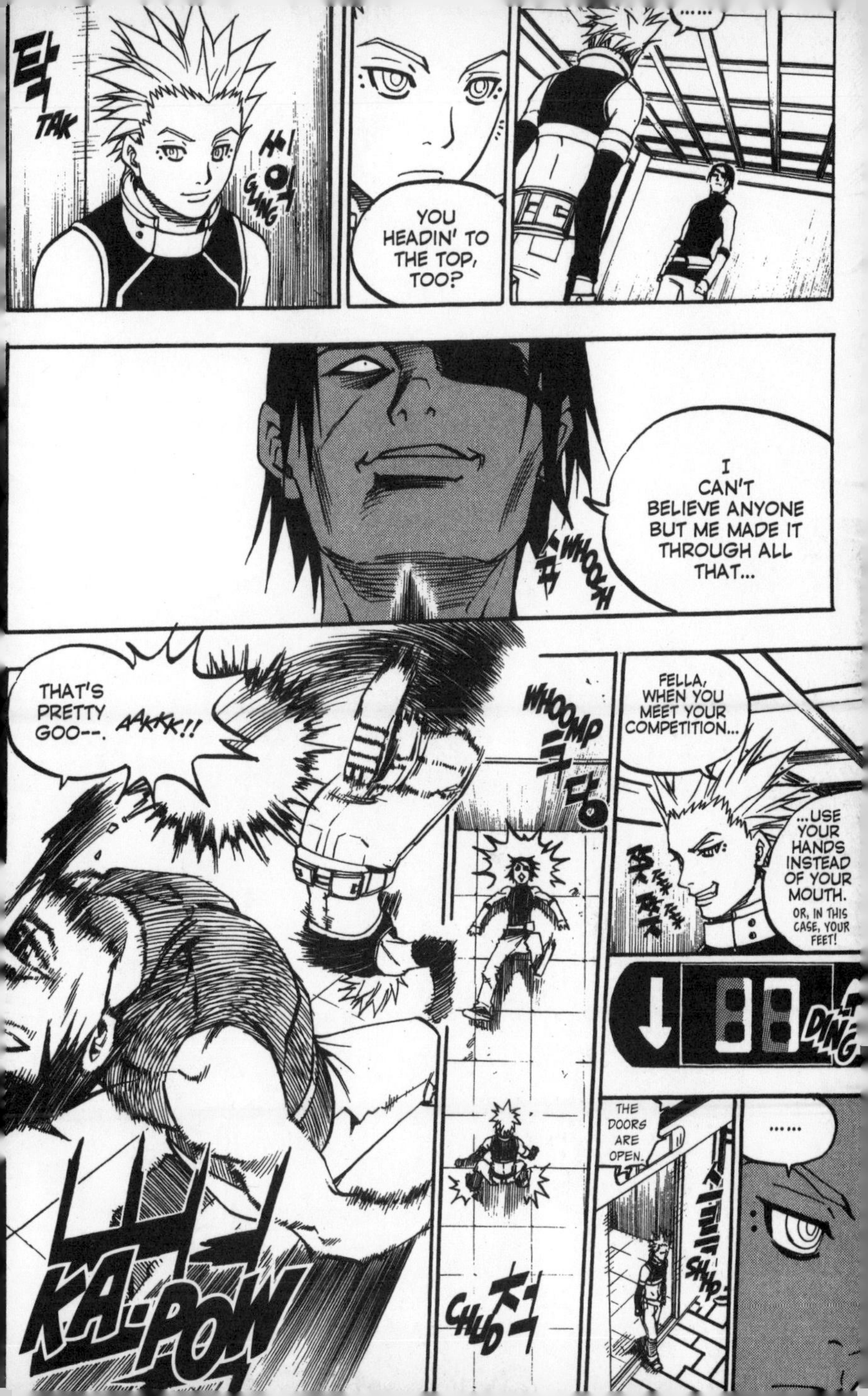

탁
TAK
휘오잉
HI-OO-GUING
YOU HEADIN' TO THE TOP, TOO?
......
I CAN'T BELIEVE ANYONE BUT ME MADE IT THROUGH ALL THAT...
WHOOSH
THAT'S PRETTY GOO--.
AAKKK!!
KA-POW
WHOOMP
쿠당
CHUD
FELLA, WHEN YOU MEET YOUR COMPETITION...
...USE YOUR HANDS INSTEAD OF YOUR MOUTH.
OR, IN THIS CASE, YOUR FEET!
DING
THE DOORS ARE OPEN.
SHHP
......

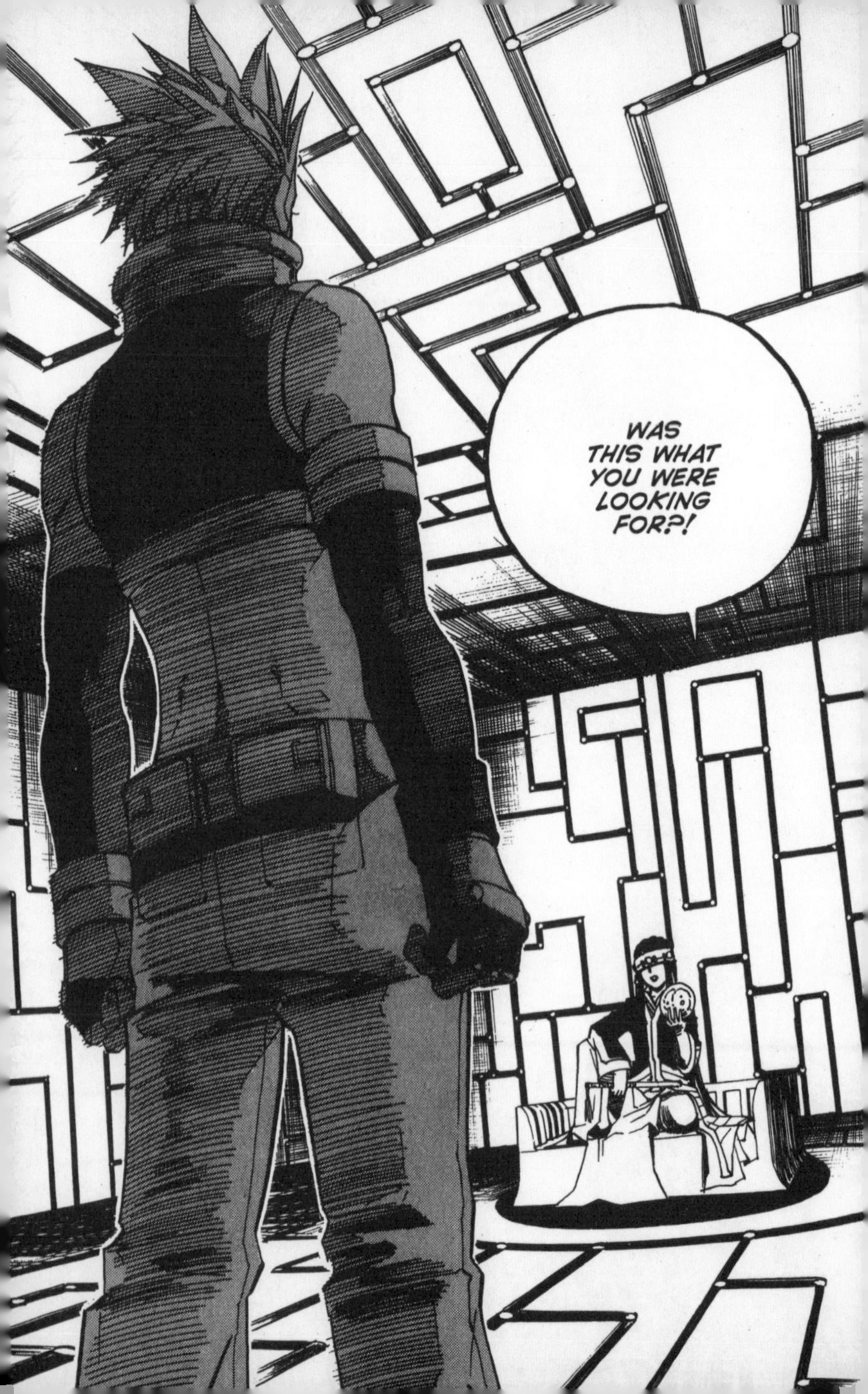
WAS THIS WHAT YOU WERE LOOKING FOR?!

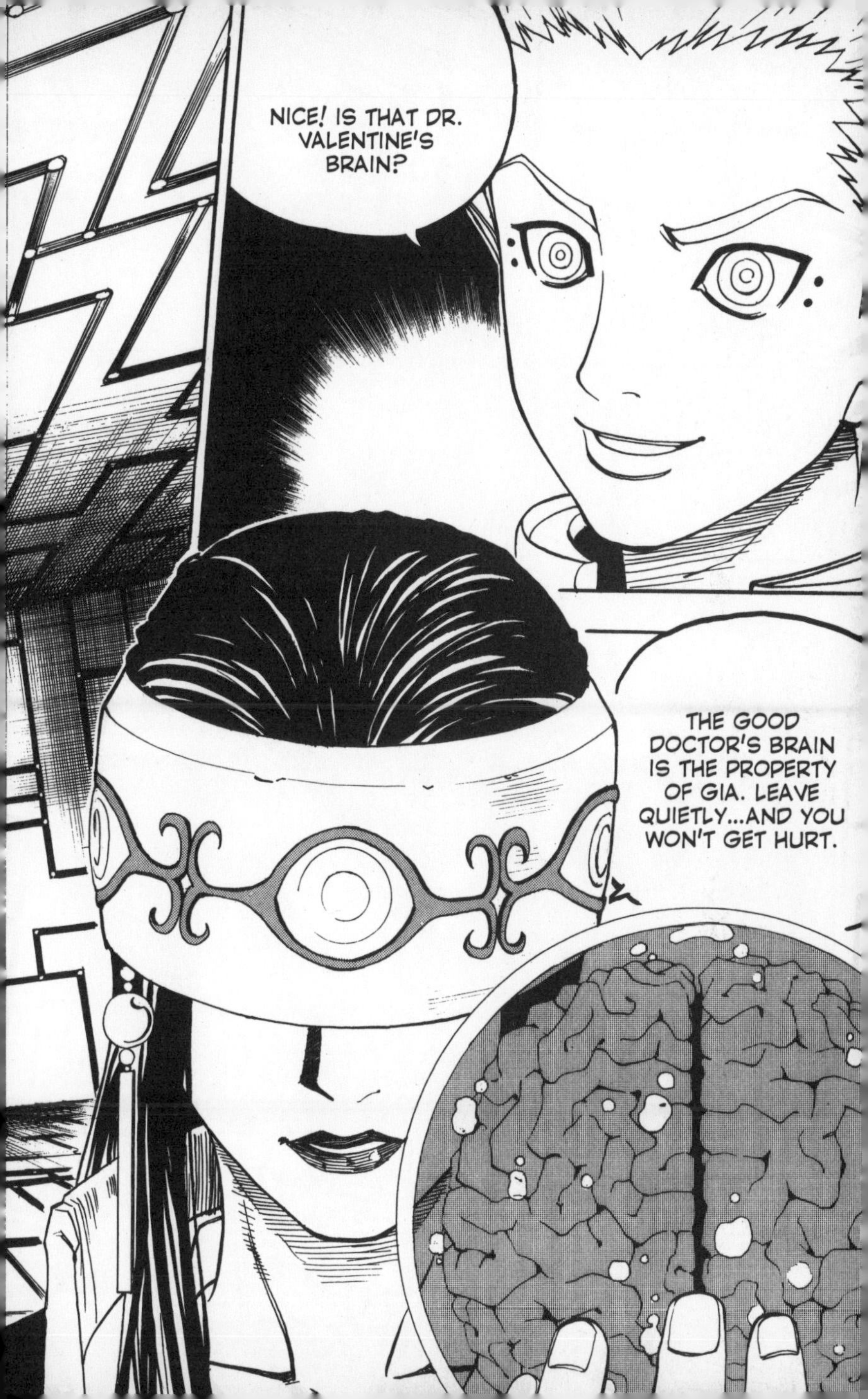
NICE! IS THAT DR. VALENTINE'S BRAIN?
THE GOOD DOCTOR'S BRAIN IS THE PROPERTY OF GIA. LEAVE QUIETLY...AND YOU WON'T GET HURT.

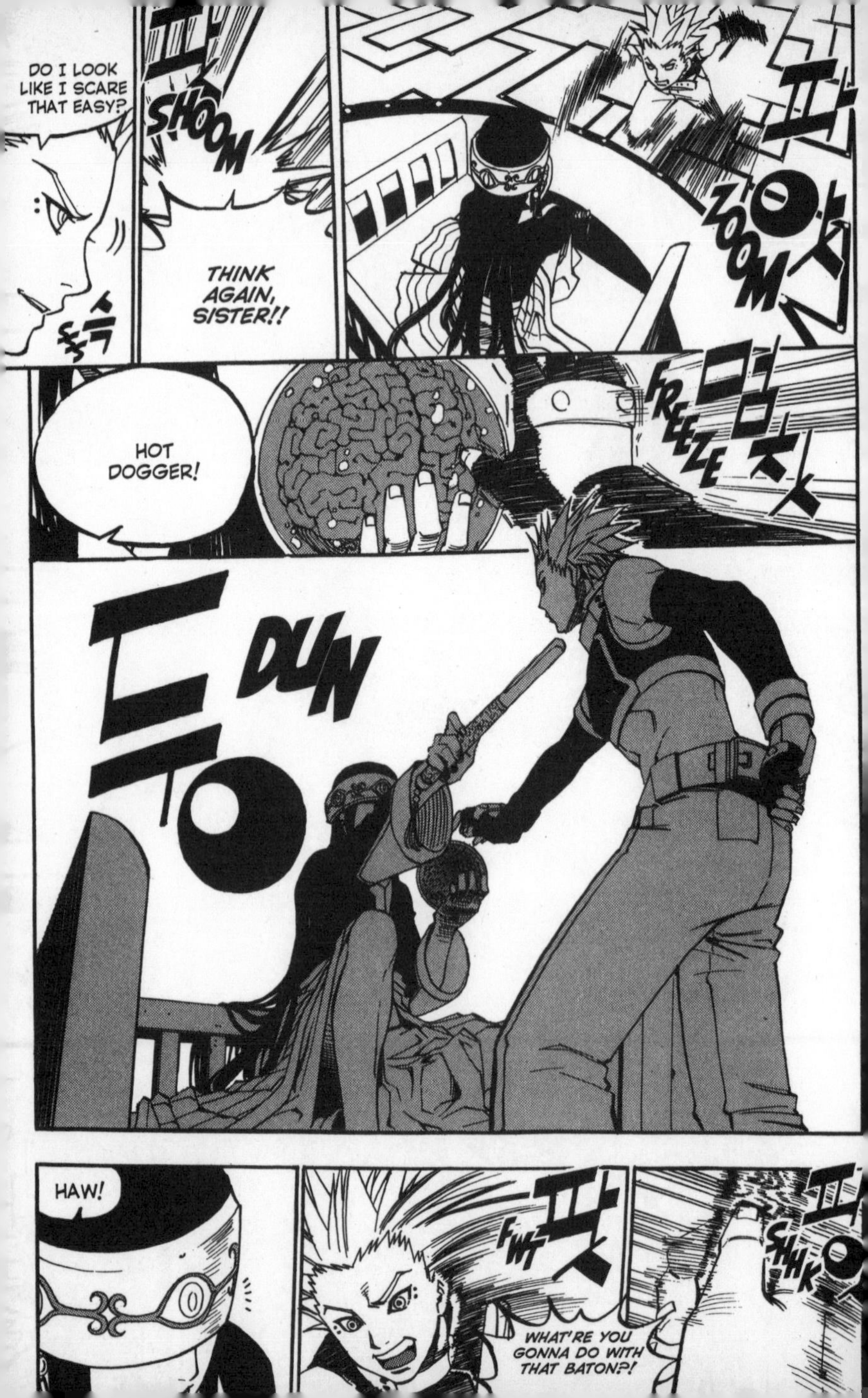
DO I LOOK LIKE I SCARE THAT EASY?
SHOOM
THINK AGAIN, SISTER!!
ZOOM
HOT DOGGER!
FREEZE
DUN
HAW!
FWT
WHAT'RE YOU GONNA DO WITH THAT BATON?!
SHHK

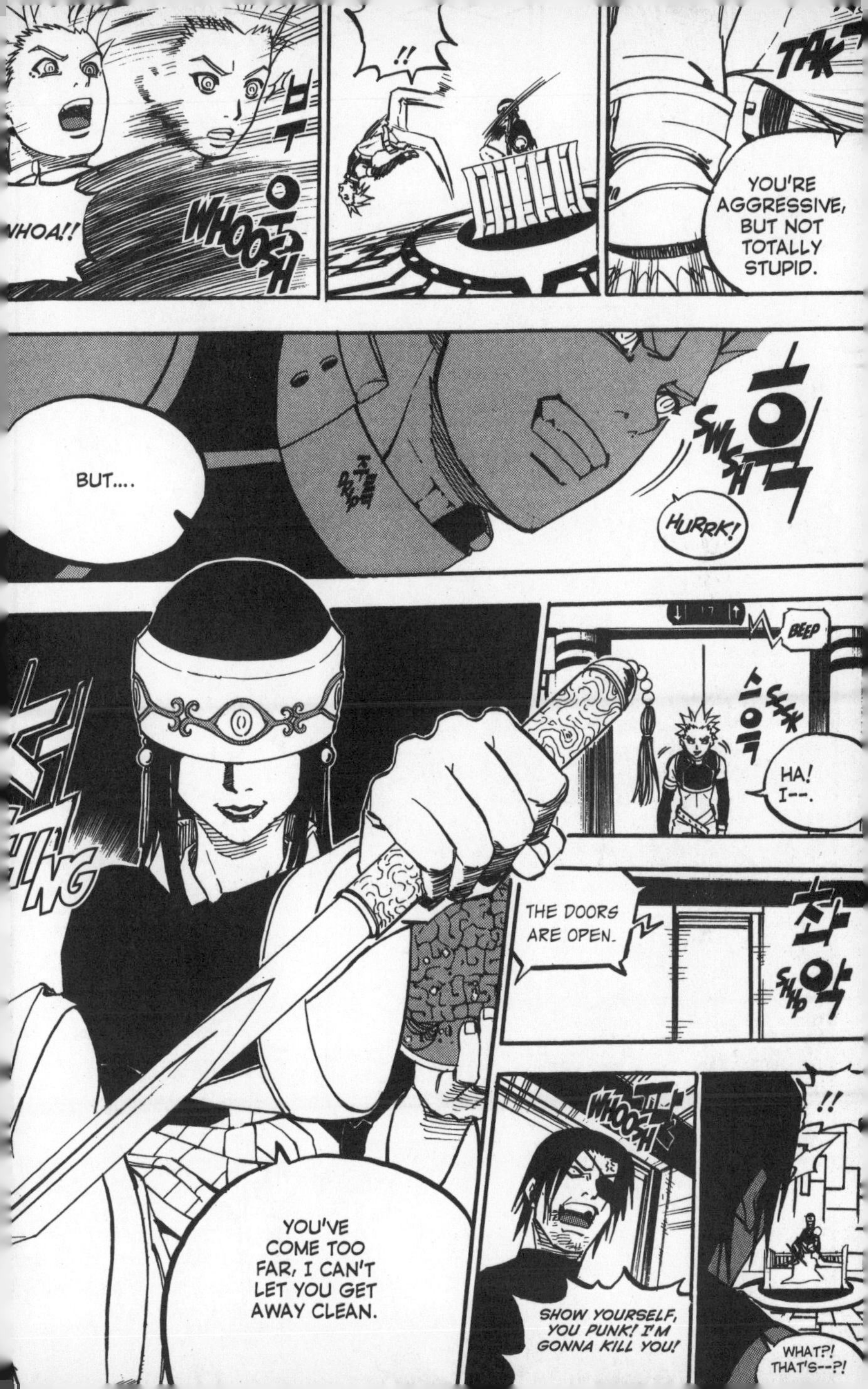
WHOA!!
WHOOSH
!!
TAK
YOU'RE AGGRESSIVE, BUT NOT TOTALLY STUPID.
BUT....
SWISH
HURRK!
BEEP
SEEK
HA! I--.
THE DOORS ARE OPEN.
SHIP
YOU'VE COME TOO FAR, I CAN'T LET YOU GET AWAY CLEAN.
WHOOSH
SHOW YOURSELF, YOU PUNK! I'M GONNA KILL YOU!
!!
WHAT?! THAT'S--?!

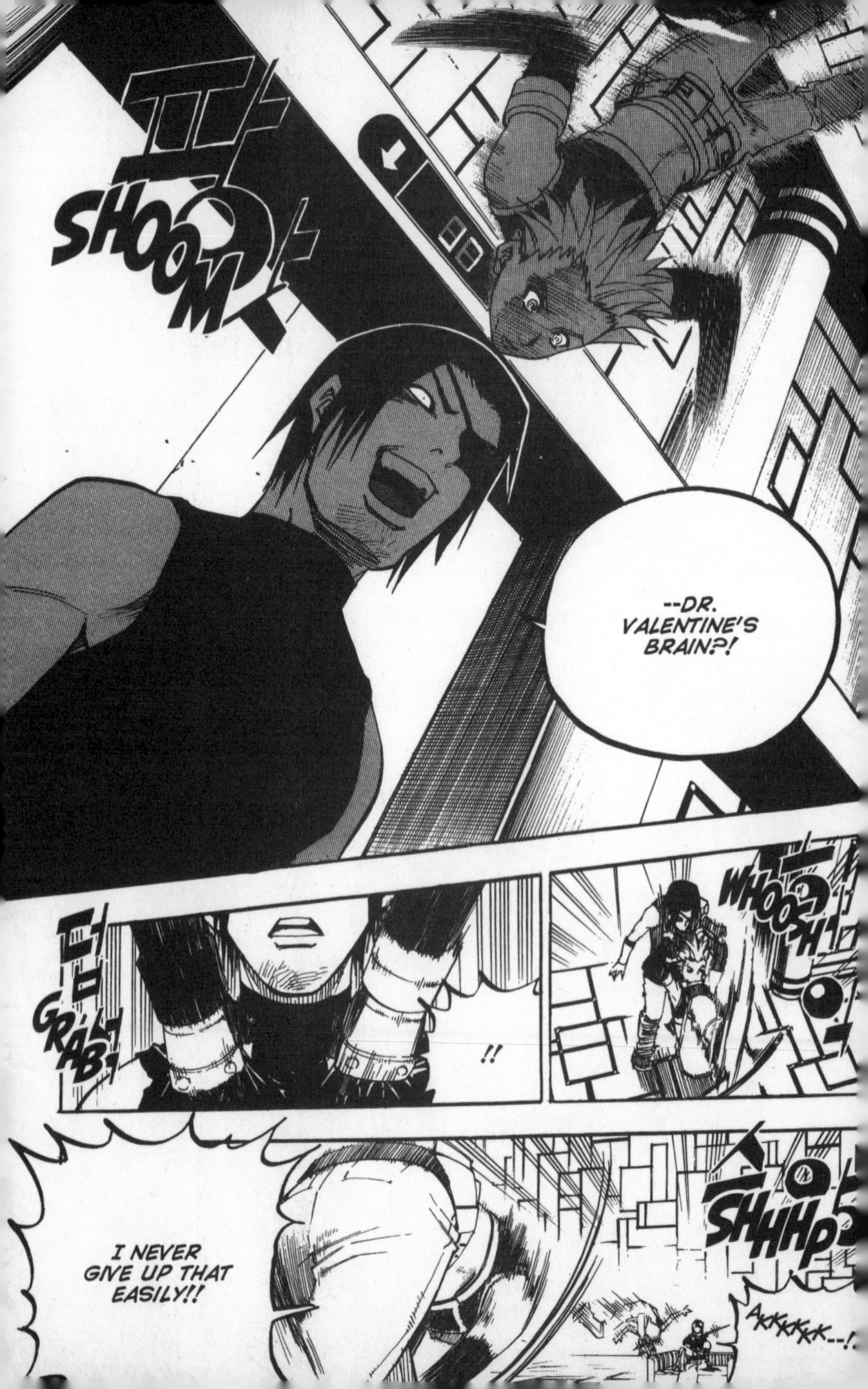
SHOOM
--DR. VALENTINE'S BRAIN?!
GRAB
!!
WHOOSH
I NEVER GIVE UP THAT EASILY!!
SHHHP
AKKKKKK--!

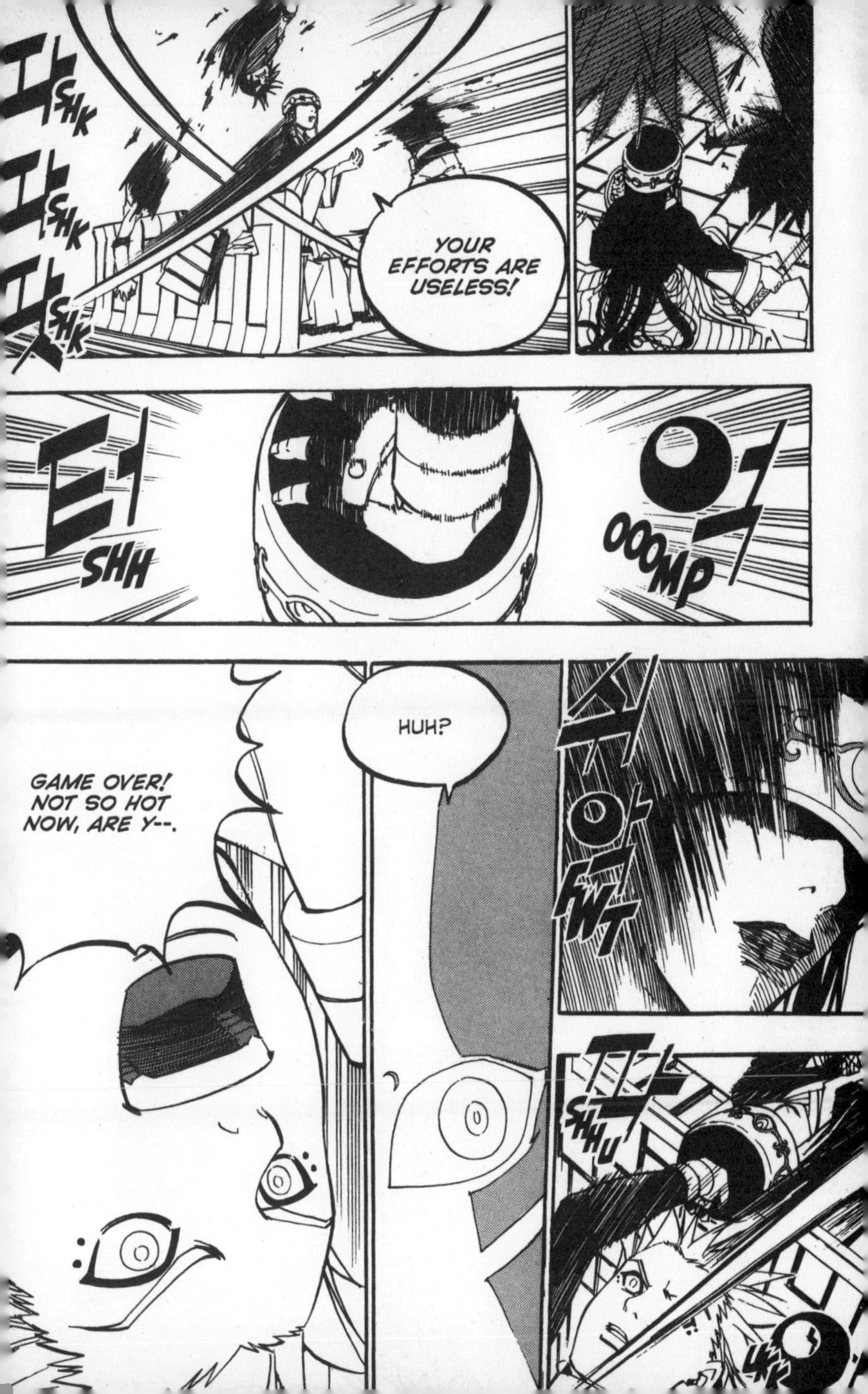
SHK
SHK
SHK
YOUR EFFORTS ARE USELESS!
SHH
OOOMP
GAME OVER! NOT SO HOT NOW, ARE Y--.
HUH?
FWT
SHHU

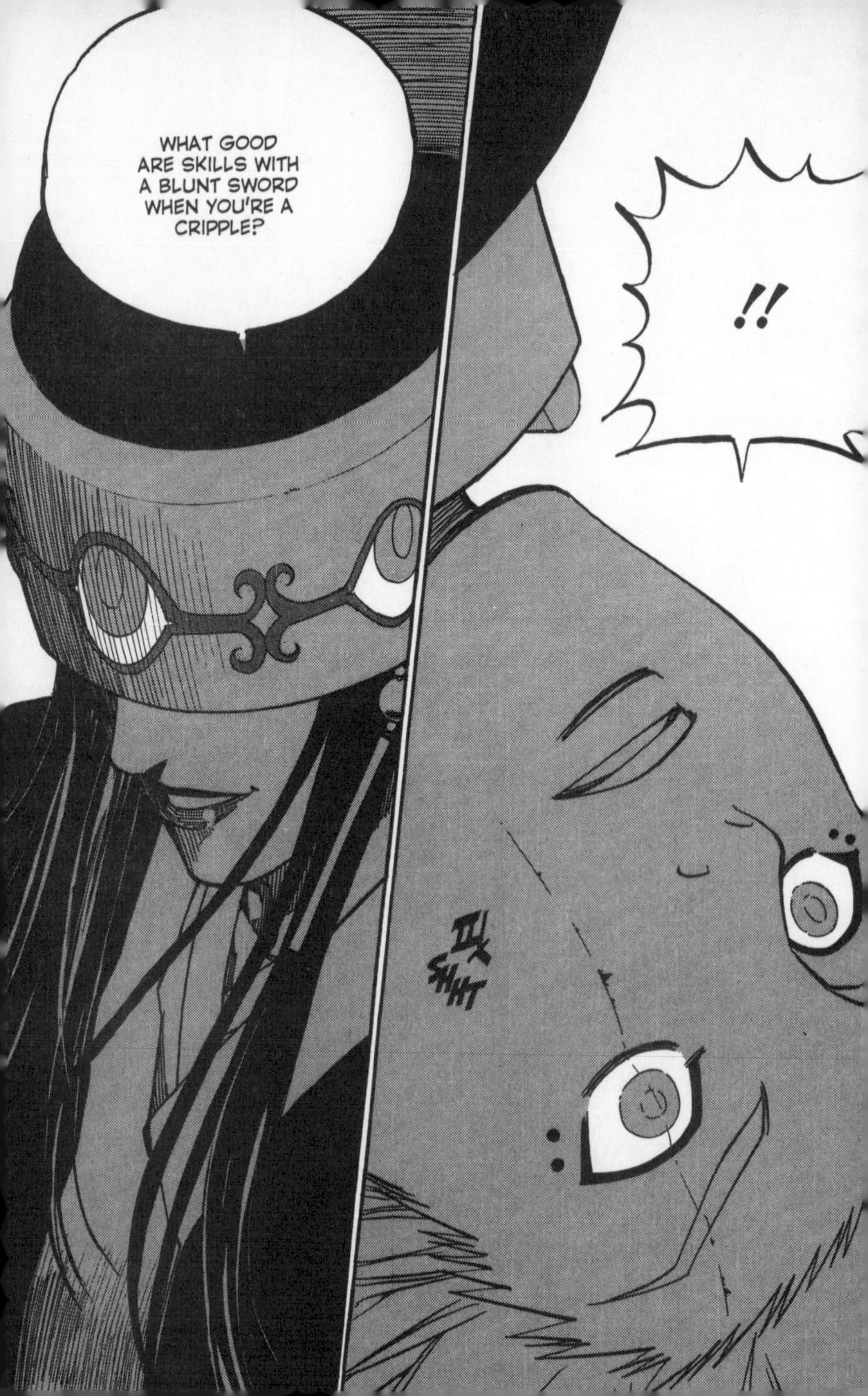
WHAT GOOD ARE SKILLS WITH A BLUNT SWORD WHEN YOU'RE A CRIPPLE?
!!
SHHT

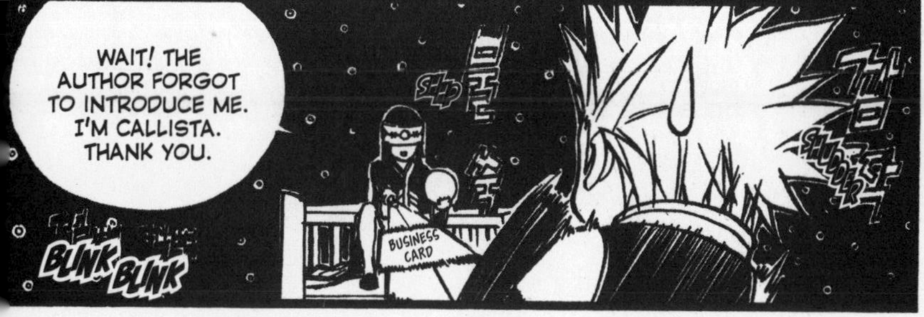
WAIT! THE AUTHOR FORGOT TO INTRODUCE ME. I'M CALLISTA. THANK YOU.
BLINK BLINK
BUSINESS CARD
SHUDDER

BACK TALK...
NO, NO...AFTER WORD?!

NOT MUCH TO SAY ABOUT CHAPTER 4. I WAS GOING TO
TALK ABOUT CALLISTA, BUT I FEEL LIKE I'D BE CHATTING HER UP ONE CHAPTER TOO
SOON, SO I'LL LEAVE THAT FOR THE NEXT ENTRY. JUST FOR FUN, LET ME TALK ABOUT
THE TYPE OF CIGARETTES THAT VERNA SMOKES.

IN THIS AGE, CIGARETTES HAVE THE FOLLOWING STRUCTURE. THEY ARE KNOWN AS
"WATER CIGARETTES".

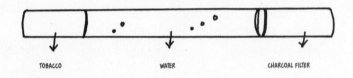

TOBACCO   WATER   CHARCOAL FILTER

I REALLY JUST TURNED A WATER PIPE INTO A CIGARETTE FOR FUN.

AS I WAS BROWSING THE INTERNET TO RESEARCH THE CONCEPT, I READ THAT WATER
PIPES HAVE A FRUITY SMELL...HOW BIZARRE. ALSO, IT HAS THE ADVANTAGE OF
LASTING A LOT LONGER THAN YOUR AVERAGE CIGARETTE. I THOUGHT, "WOULDN'T IT
BE NICE TO HAVE ONE CIGARETTE LAST FOR THE WHOLE WORK PERIOD?" AND THE
WATER CIGARETTE WAS THE RESULT. IT WOULD BE CONVENIENT TO CARRY AROUND,
AND YOU COULD TAKE YOUR TIME SMOKING ONE, BUT I WORRY IT MIGHT LEAD TO
PEOPLE SMOKING MORE...EXCEPT, IT'S ALL MADE UP ANYWAY, SO WHY WORRY?! OH,
I FORGOT TO MENTION TUBLERUN'S POWERS.

TUBLERUN'S SPECIAL ABILITIES ARE AN ADAPTATION OF THE PSYCHO-MATRIX: HE CAN
PUT HIS HAND ON HIS OPPONENT'S HEAD, READ HIS BATTLE PATTERN, AND THEN USE
IT HIMSELF. THE THING TO REMEMBER HERE IS THAT HIS CAPACITY TO REPRODUCE HIS
OPPONENT'S STRATEGY IS TEMPORARY. AFTER A CERTAIN AMOUNT OF TIME, TUBLE-
RUN FORGETS EVERYTHING HE ABSORBS (OR, PERHAPS IT GETS TUCKED AWAY AND
LOST IN SOME REMOTE CORNER OF HIS MIND...).

UNLIKE THE AVERAGE PSYCHO MATRIX, IT'S NOT POSSIBLE TO READ THE REST
OF THEIR THOUGHTS. IT'S ONLY DESIGNED FOR BATTLE...AND THE REASON WHY HE
CAN READ THE DOCTOR'S BRAIN IN CHAPTER 6 IS BECAUSE IT'S A 'PURE' BRAIN. AS
FOR HOW TUBLERUN ACQUIRED THIS POWER, I WOULDN'T SAY IT'S ANYTHING
DRAMATIC, BUT THE PAST WILL GRADUALLY COME OUT INTO THE OPEN...SO SIT TIGHT
AND WAIT.

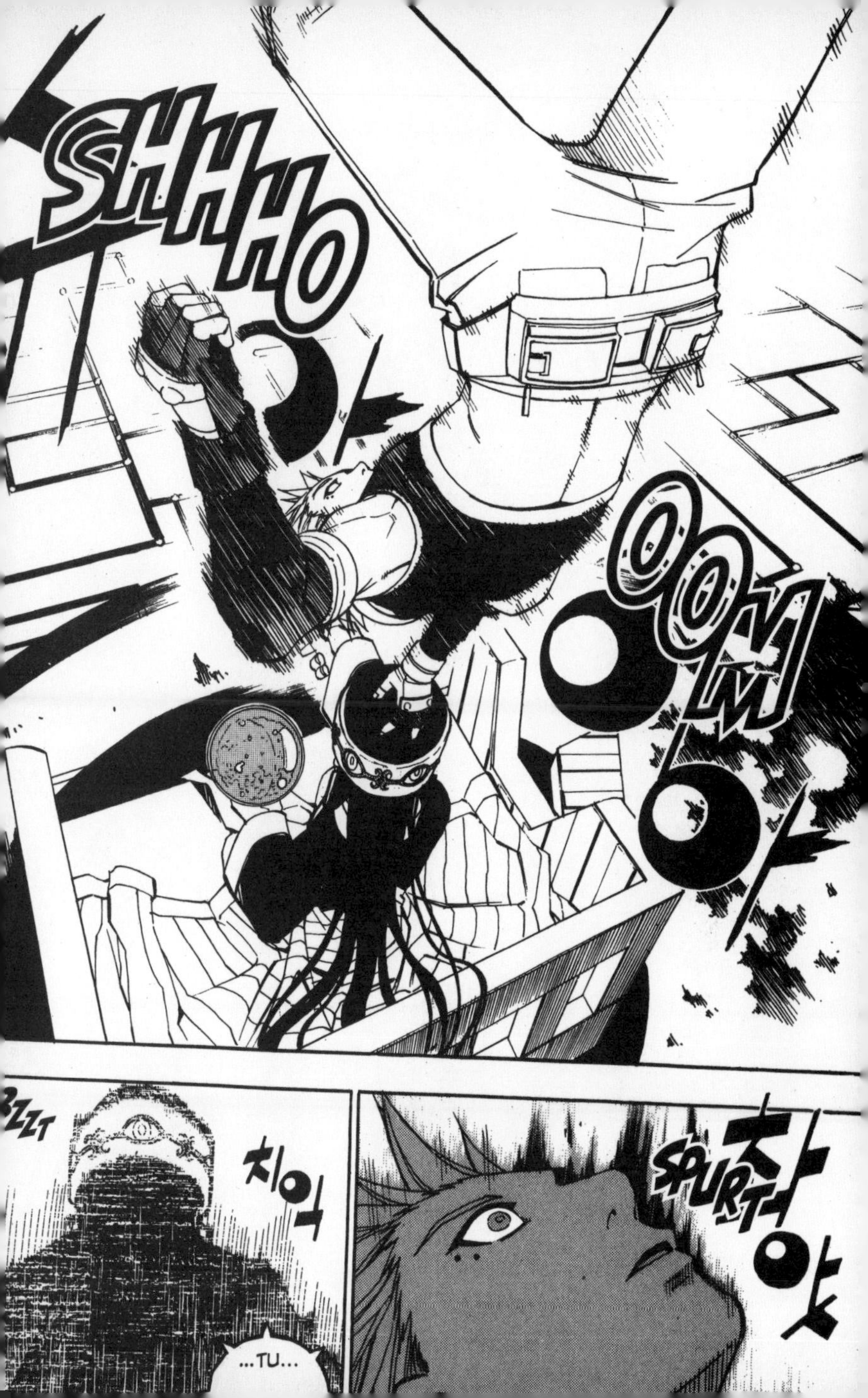
SHHHO
OOOM
ZZZT
...TU...
SPURT

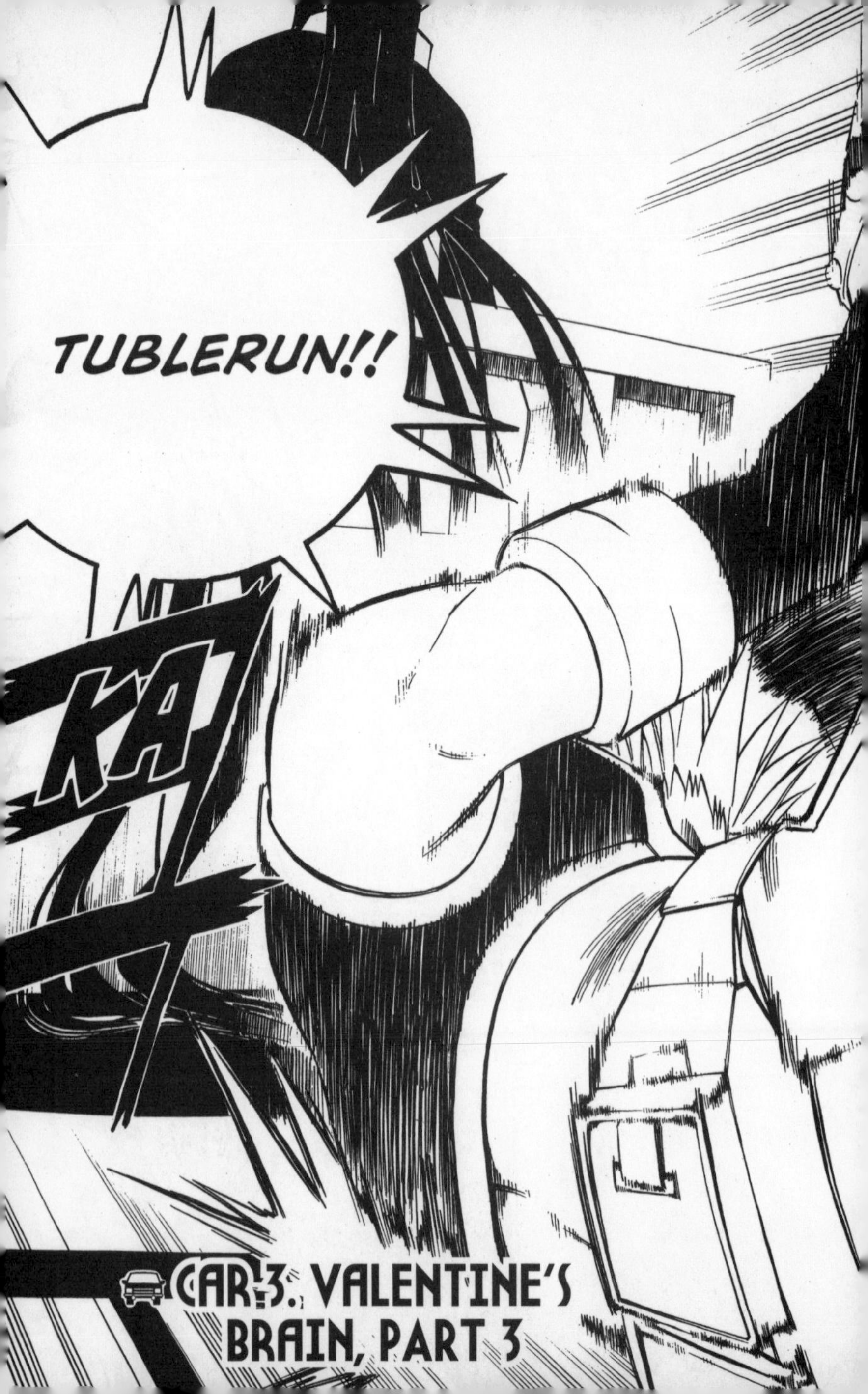
TUBLERUN!!
KA
CAR 3. VALENTINE'S BRAIN, PART 3

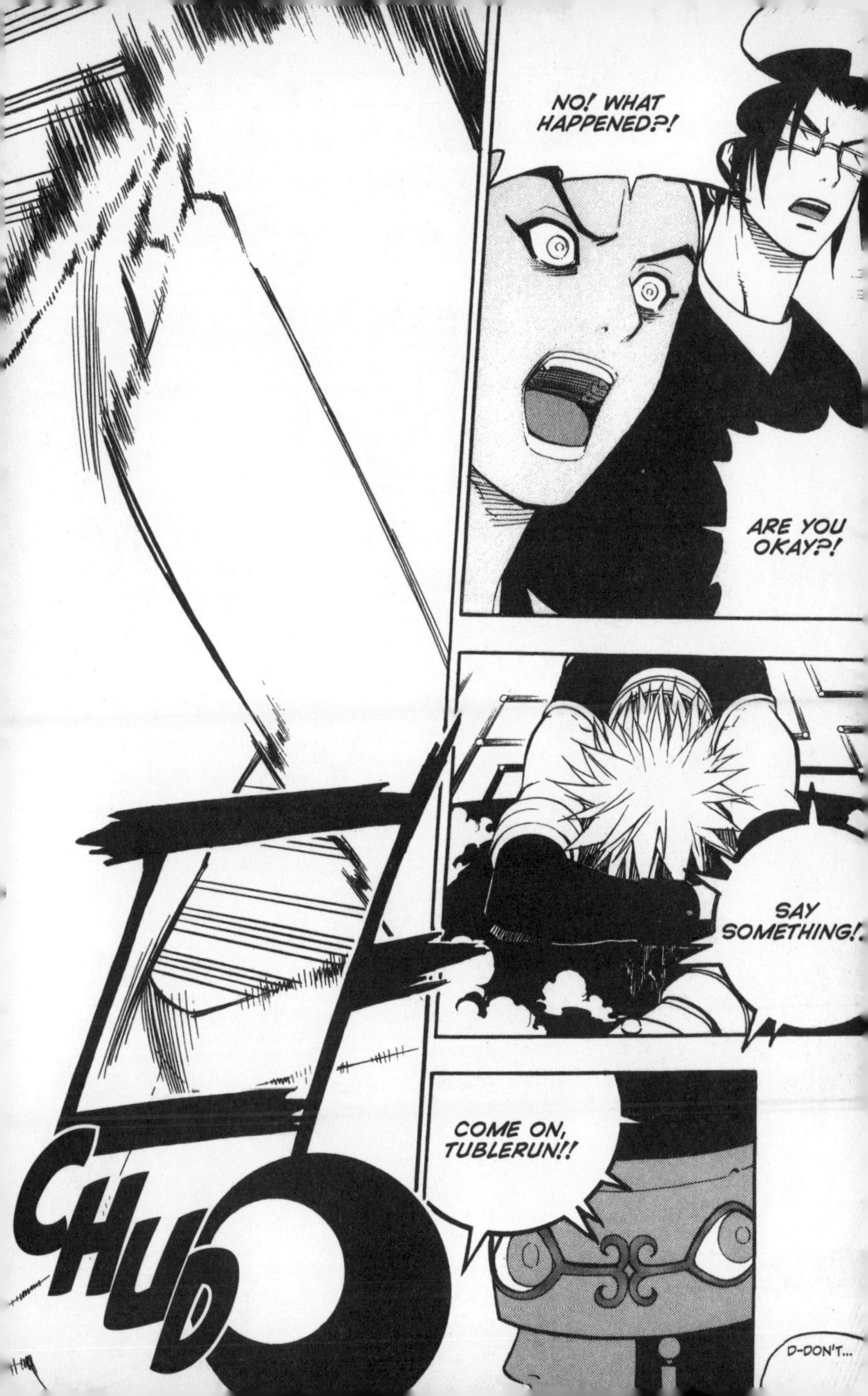
CHUD
NO! WHAT HAPPENED?!
ARE YOU OKAY?!
SAY SOMETHING!!
COME ON, TUBLERUN!!
D-DON'T...

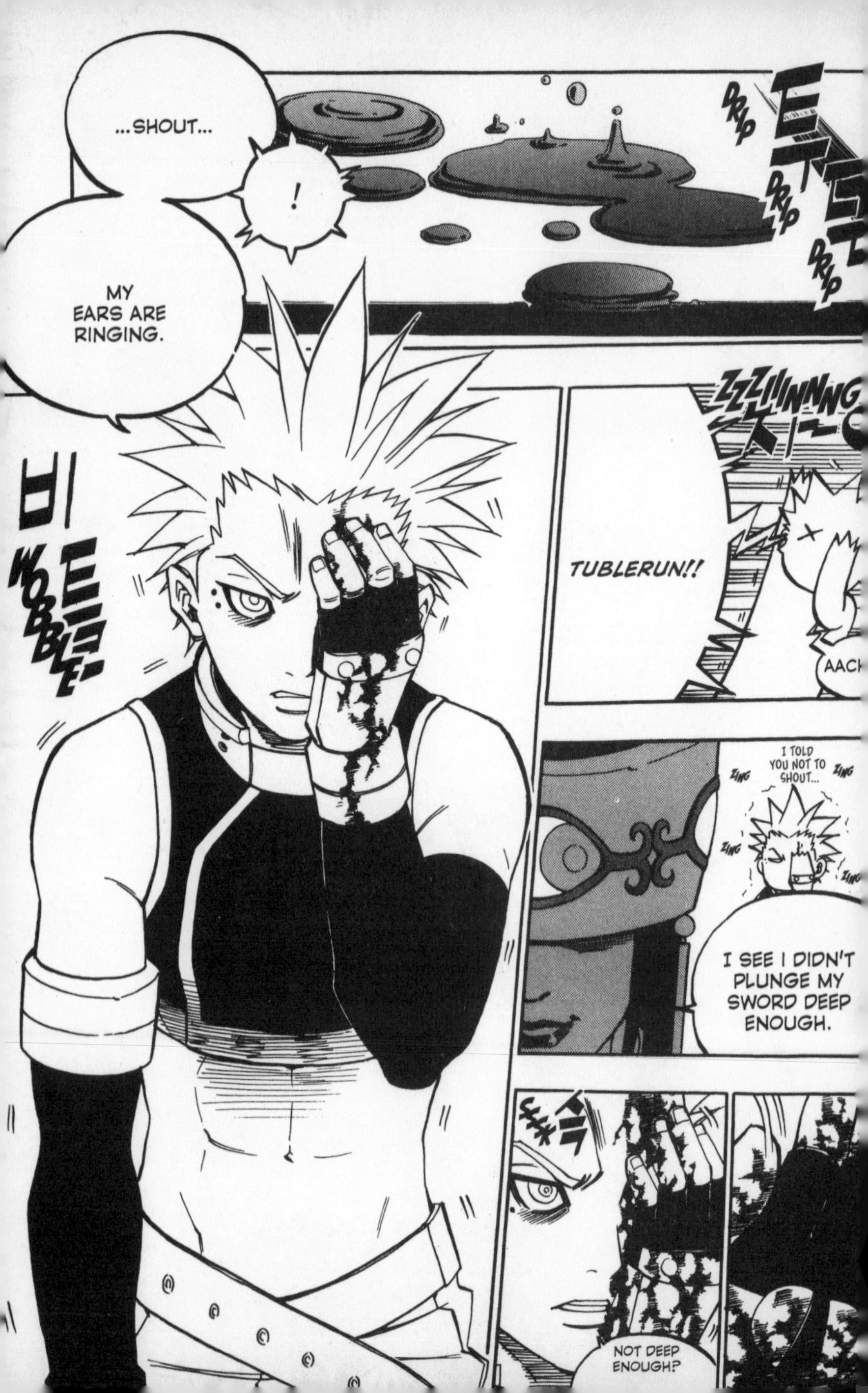
...SHOUT...
!
MY EARS ARE RINGING.
DRIP
DRIP
DRIP
WOBBLE-
ZZZIIINNNG
TUBLERUN!!
AACK
ZING
I TOLD YOU NOT TO SHOUT...
ZING
ZING
ZING
I SEE I DIDN'T PLUNGE MY SWORD DEEP ENOUGH.
SKK
NOT DEEP ENOUGH?

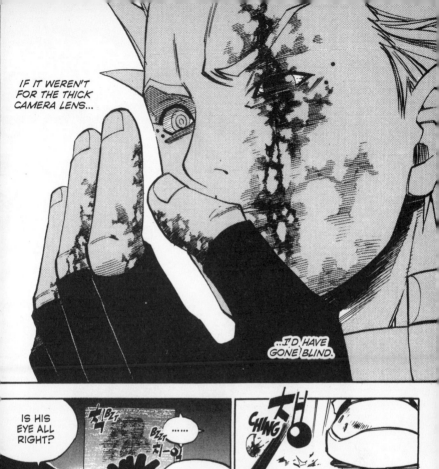

IF IT WEREN'T FOR THE THICK CAMERA LENS...

...I'D HAVE GONE BLIND.

IS HIS EYE ALL RIGHT?

......

HIS VISION IS LIMITED TO THE ONE LENS.

CHING

...BUT...

NEXT TIME...

...YOU WON'T BE SO LUCKY!

SHHH!

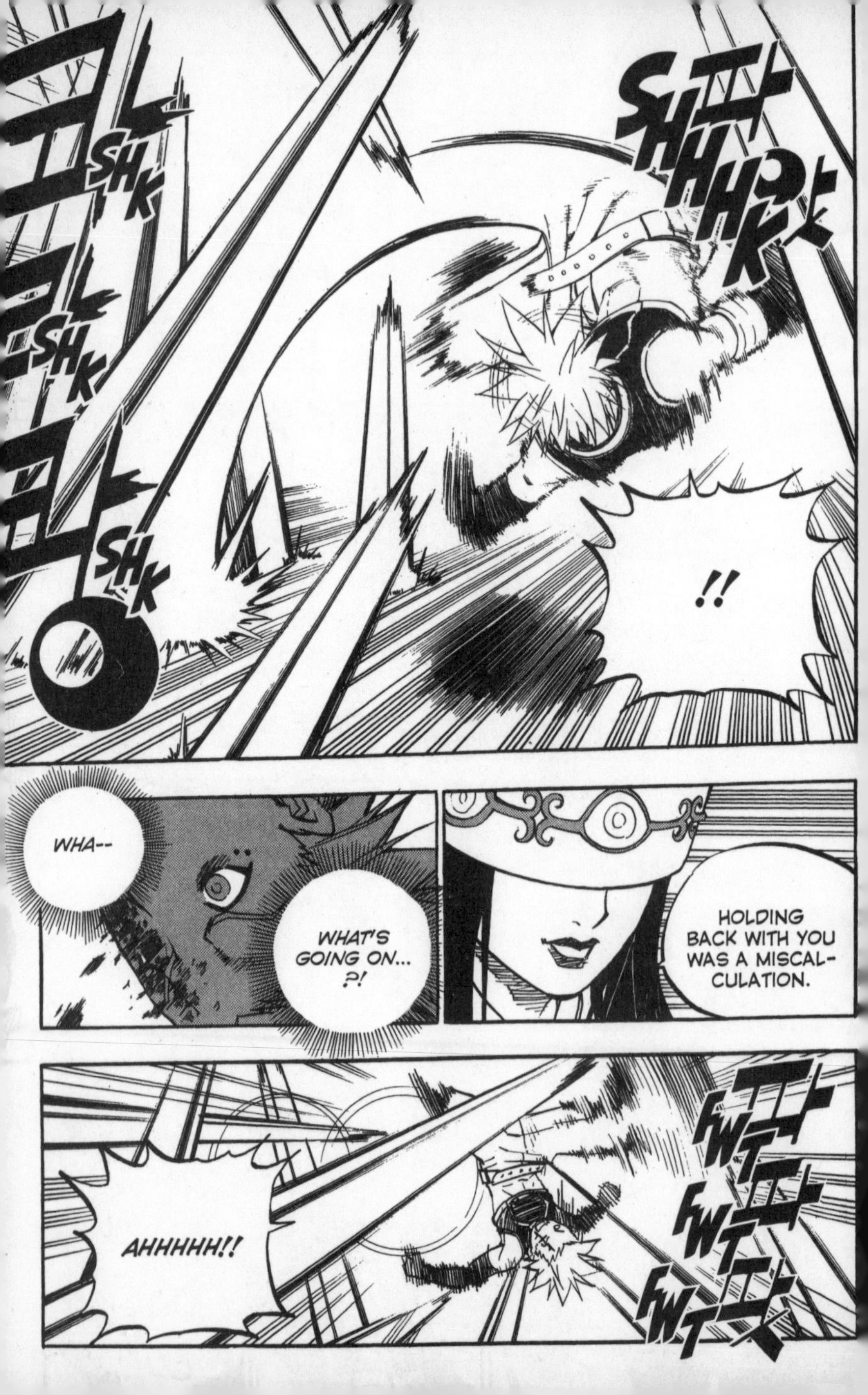

SHK
SHK
SHK
SHHHHK
!!
WHA--
WHAT'S GOING ON... ?!
HOLDING BACK WITH YOU WAS A MISCALCULATION.
AHHHHH!!
FWT
FWT
FWT

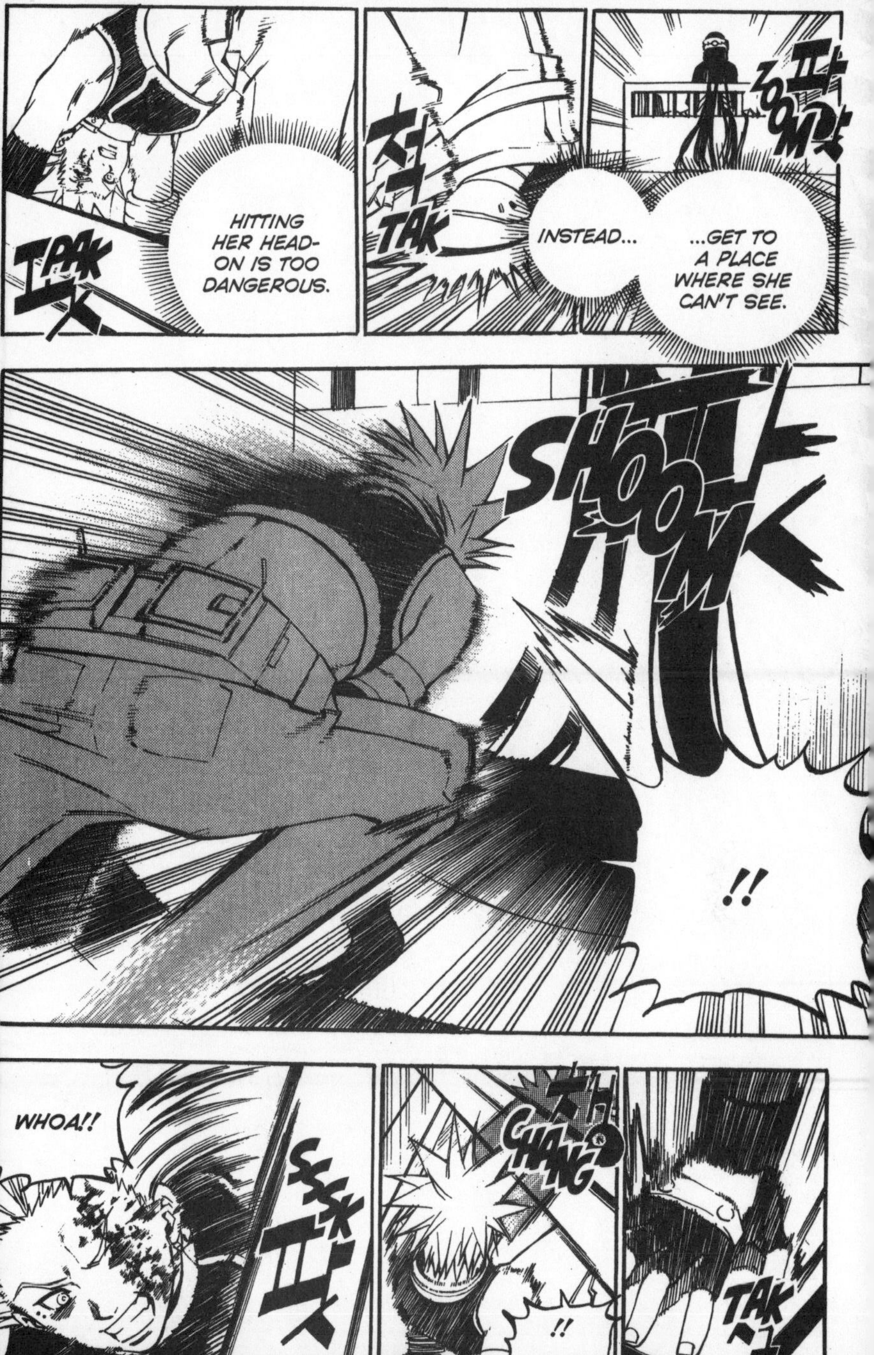
PAK
HITTING HER HEAD-ON IS TOO DANGEROUS.
TAK
INSTEAD...
...GET TO A PLACE WHERE SHE CAN'T SEE.
ZOOOM
SHOOOM
!!
WHOA!!
SSSK
CHANG
!!
TAK

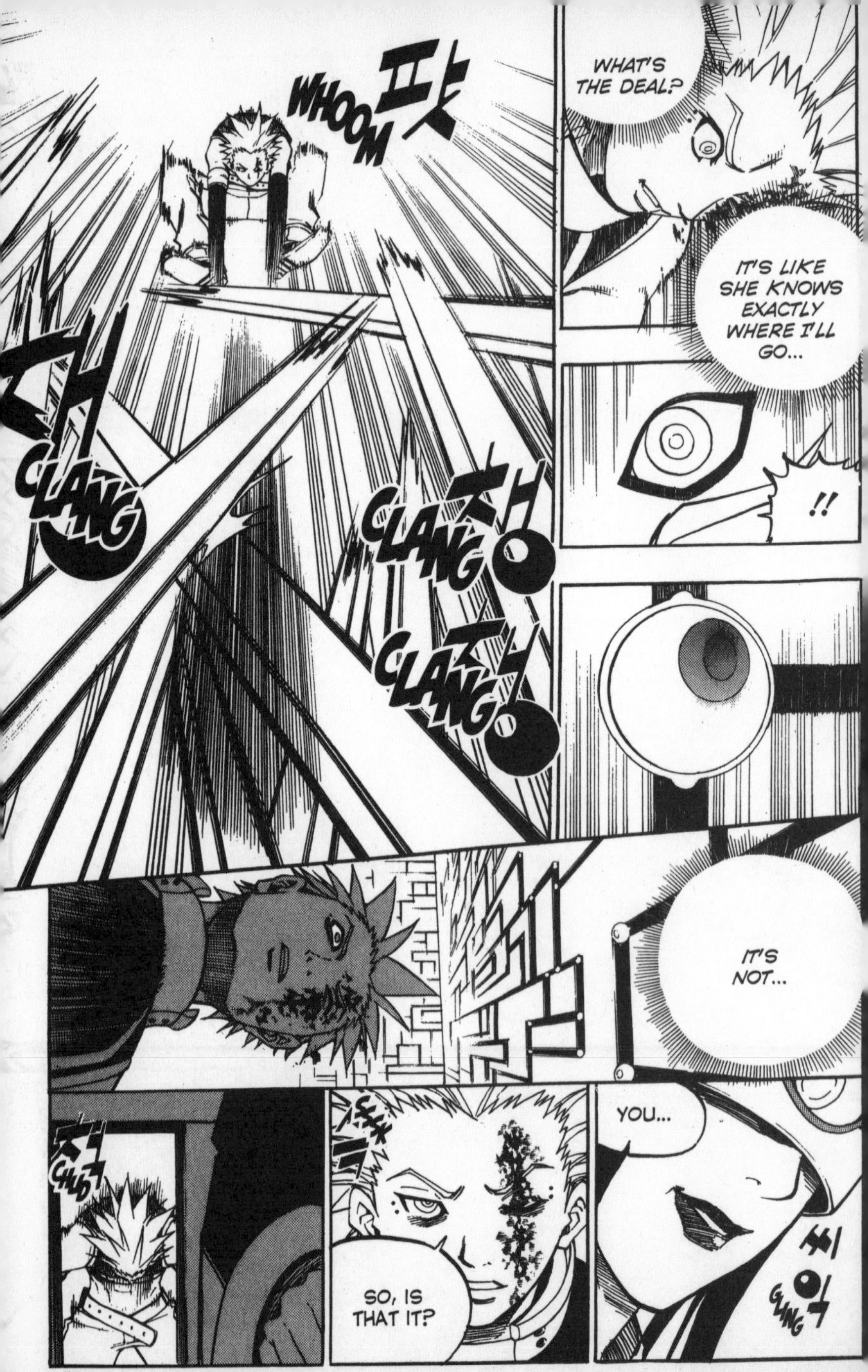
WHOOM
CLANG
CLANG
CLANG
WHAT'S THE DEAL?
IT'S LIKE SHE KNOWS EXACTLY WHERE I'LL GO...
!!
IT'S NOT...
CHUD
SO, IS THAT IT?
YOU...
GLING

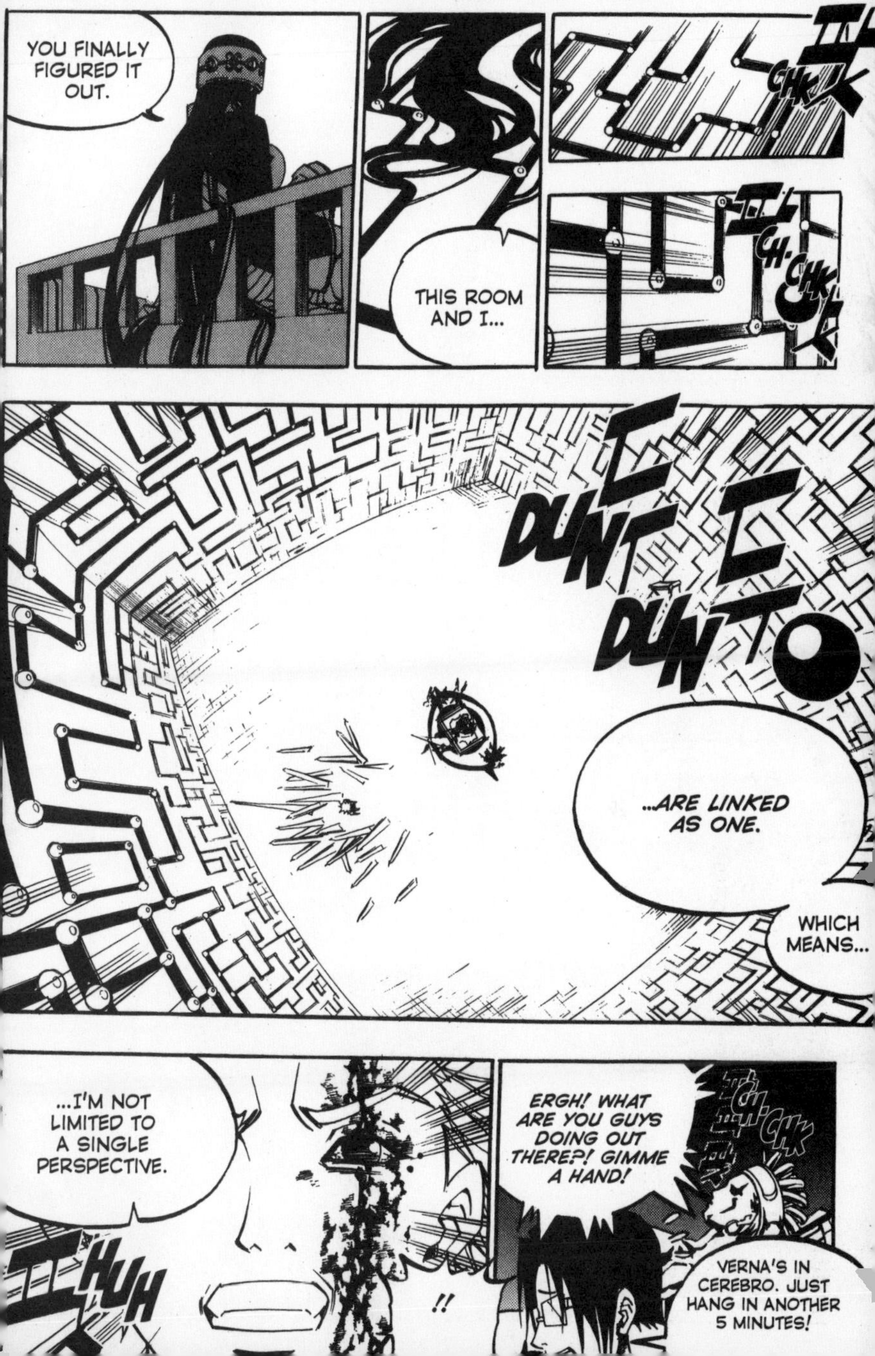
YOU FINALLY FIGURED IT OUT.
THIS ROOM AND I...
...ARE LINKED AS ONE.
WHICH MEANS...
...I'M NOT LIMITED TO A SINGLE PERSPECTIVE.
HUH
!!
ERGH! WHAT ARE YOU GUYS DOING OUT THERE?! GIMME A HAND!
VERNA'S IN CEREBRO. JUST HANG IN ANOTHER 5 MINUTES!

5 MINUTES! WITH THIS CRAZY LADY?! RIIIIGHT!!
FLASH
ZNNNNN
ZNNNNN
FLASH

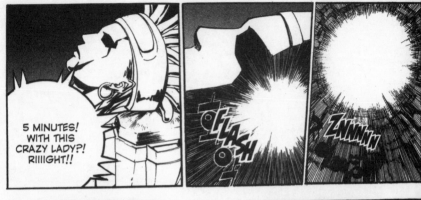

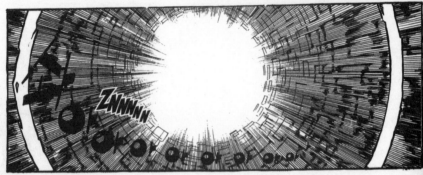

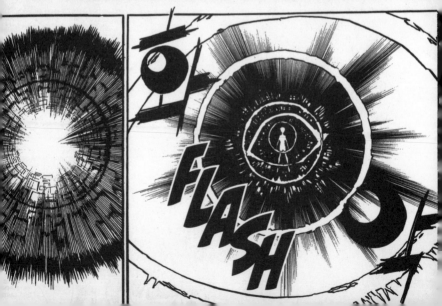

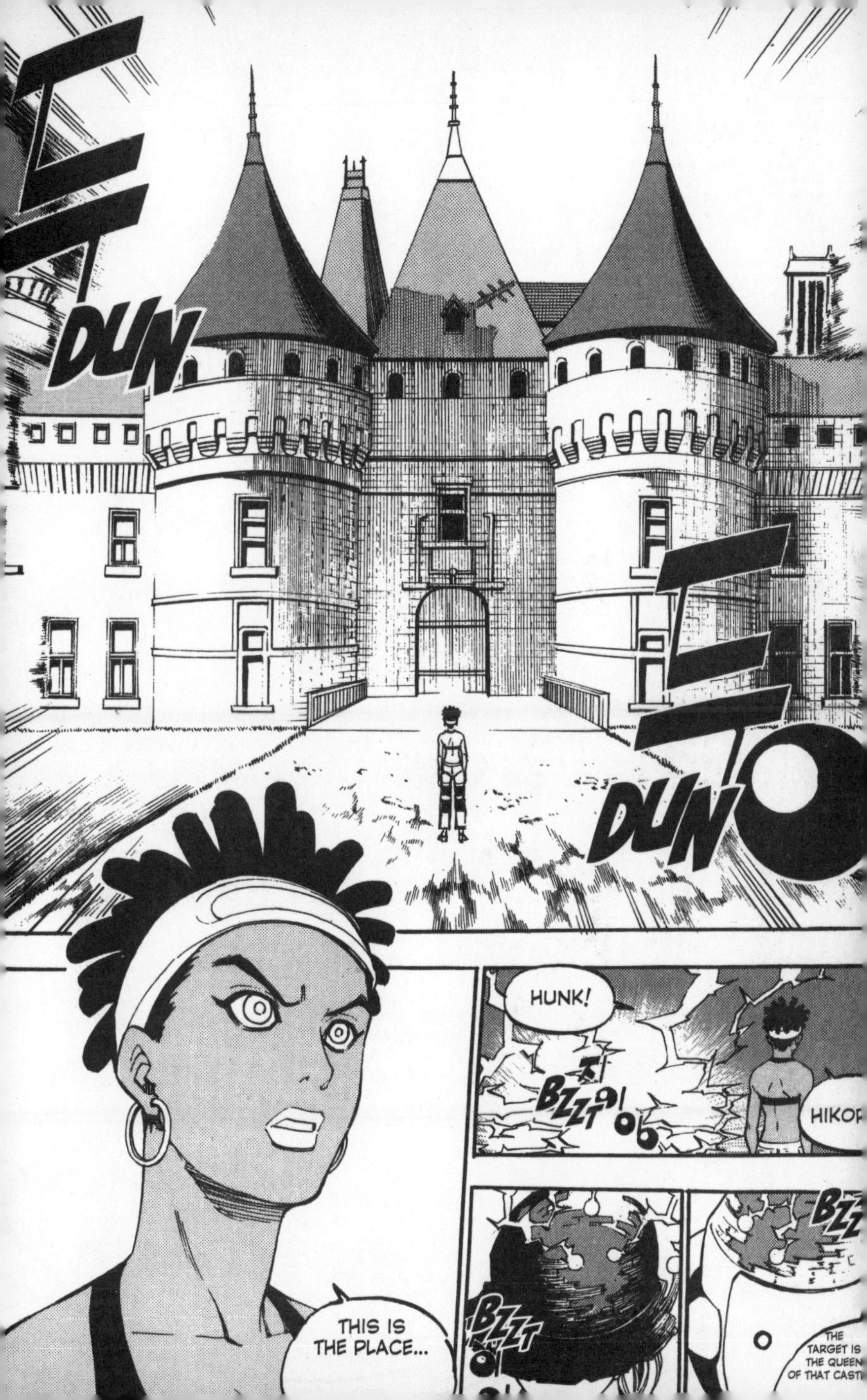
DUN
DUN
HUNK!
BZZT
HIKO
THIS IS THE PLACE...
BZZT
THE TARGET IS THE QUEEN OF THAT CAST

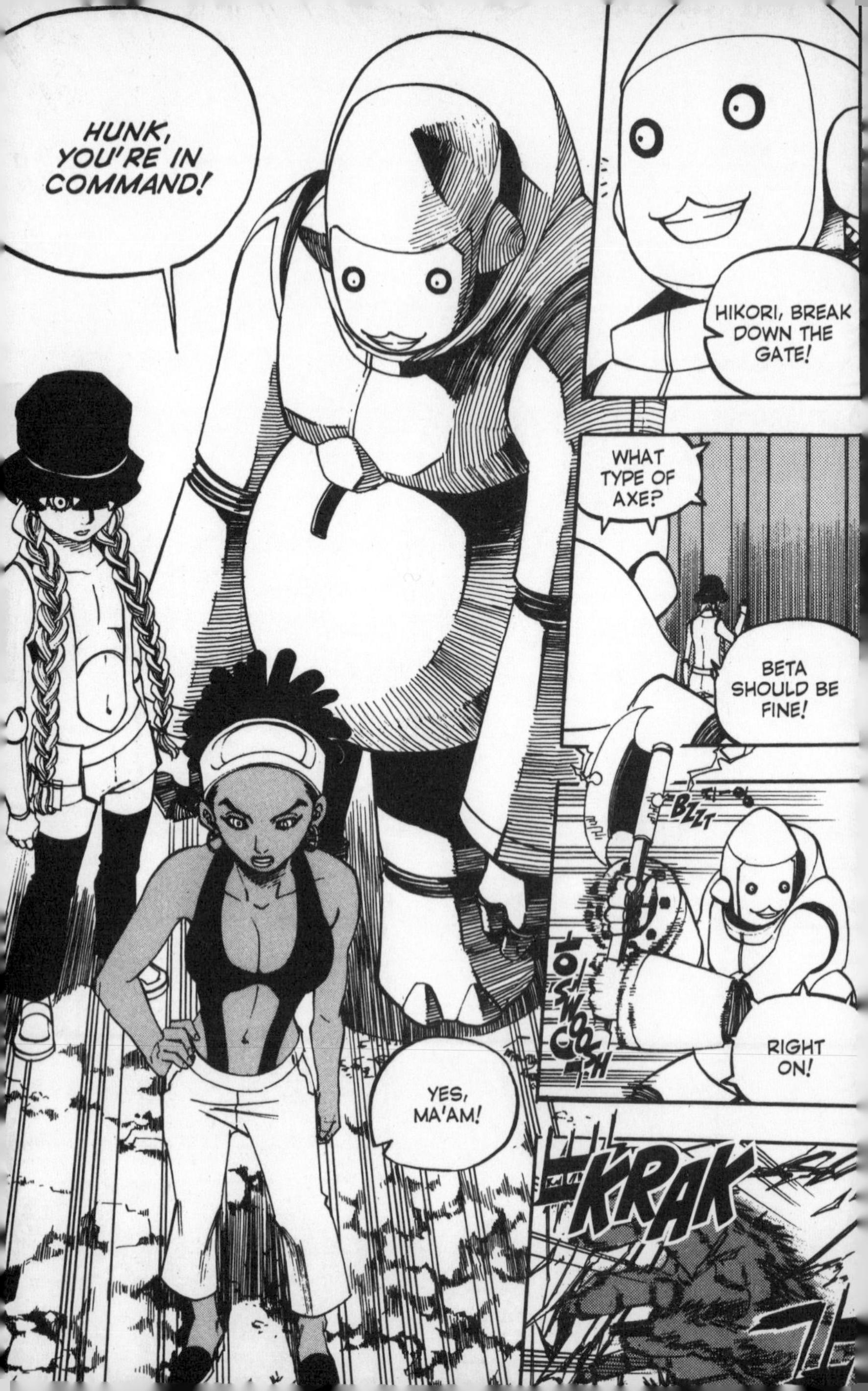
HUNK, YOU'RE IN COMMAND!
YES, MA'AM!
HIKORI, BREAK DOWN THE GATE!
WHAT TYPE OF AXE?
BETA SHOULD BE FINE!
BZZT
SWOOSH
RIGHT ON!
KRAK

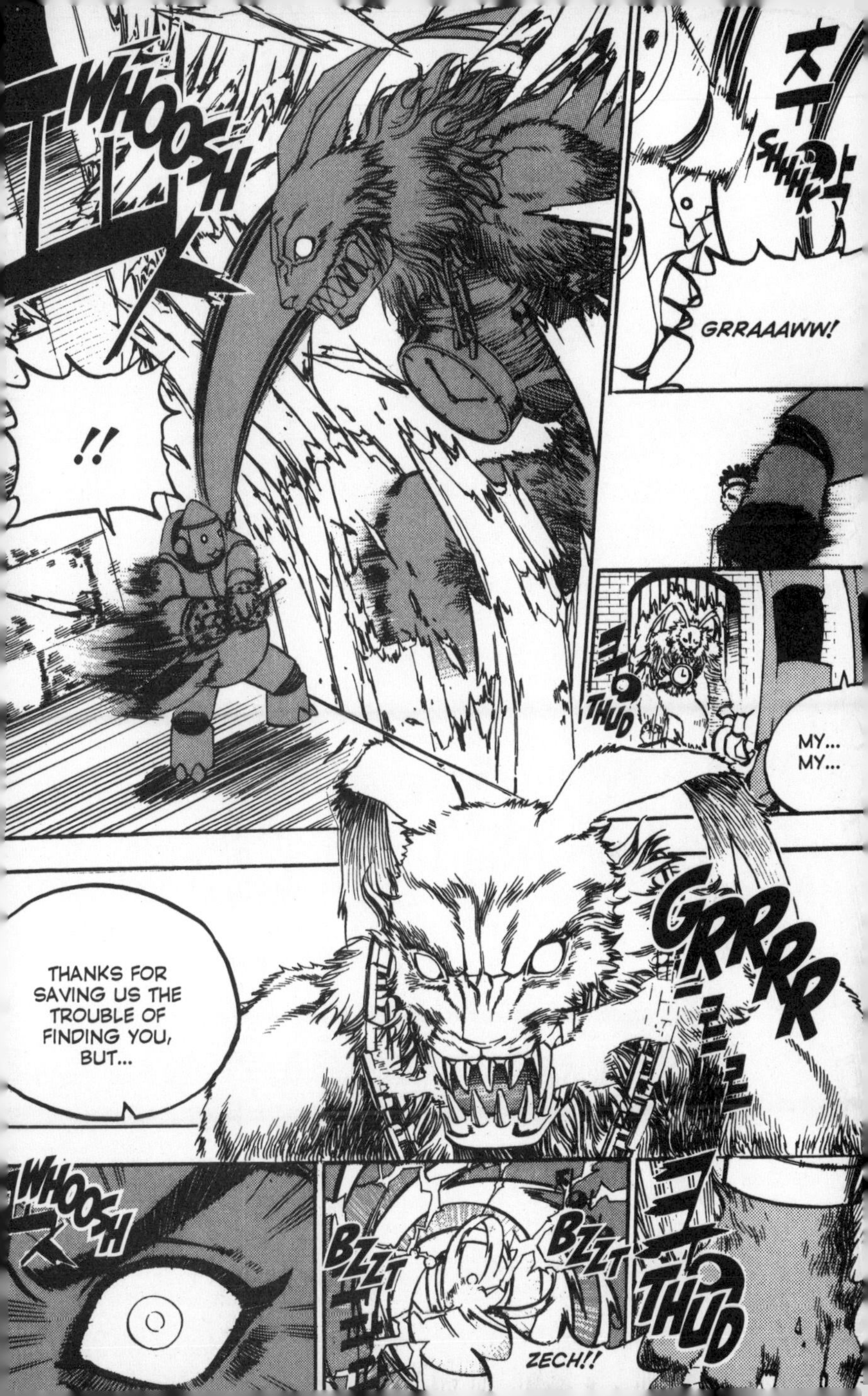
WHOOSH
!!
SHHIK
GRRAAAWW!
THUD
MY... MY...
THANKS FOR SAVING US THE TROUBLE OF FINDING YOU, BUT...
GRRRR
WHOOSH
BZZT
BZZT
ZECH!!
THUD

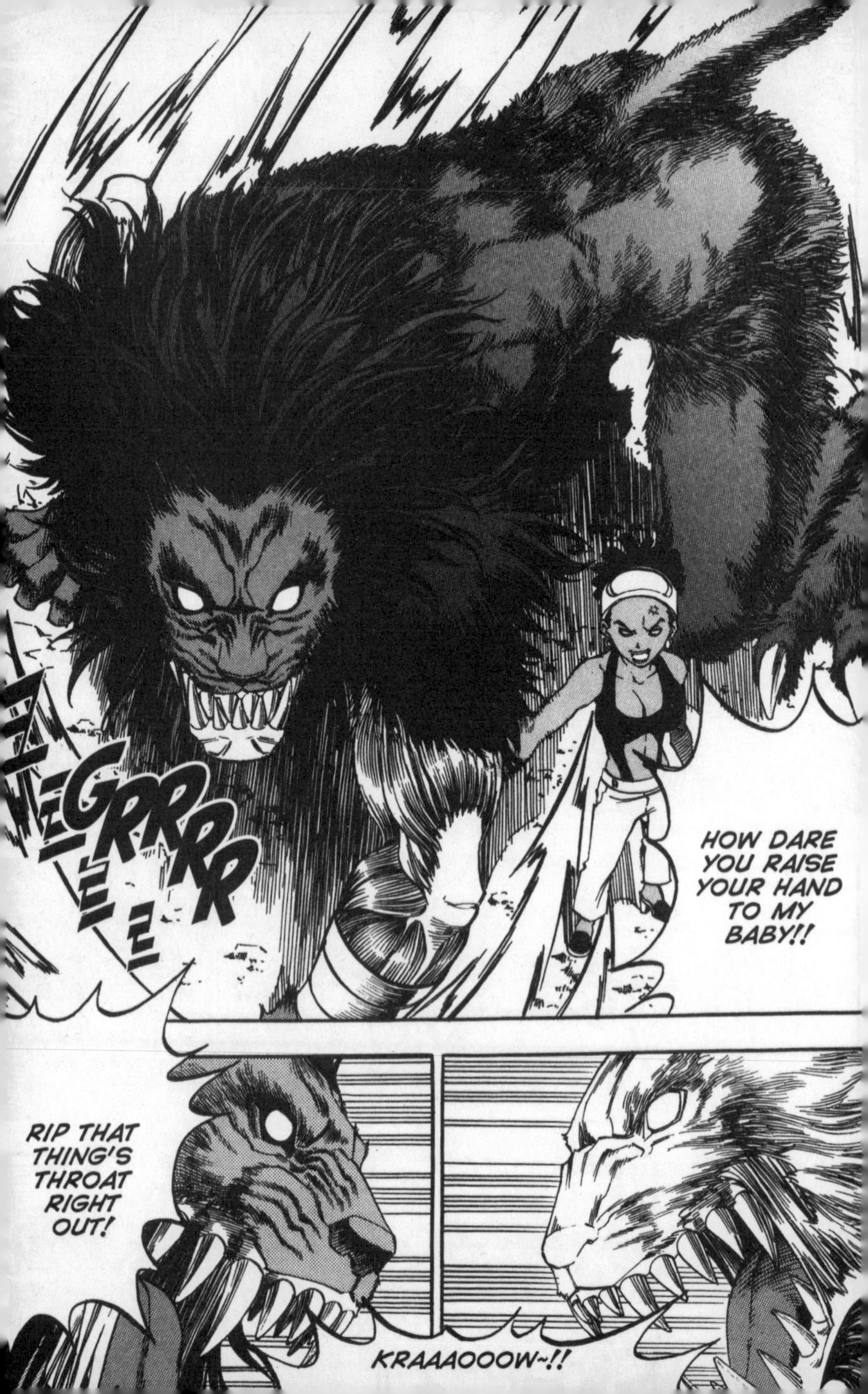
GRRRR
HOW DARE YOU RAISE YOUR HAND TO MY BABY!!
RIP THAT THING'S THROAT RIGHT OUT!
KRAAAOOOW~!!

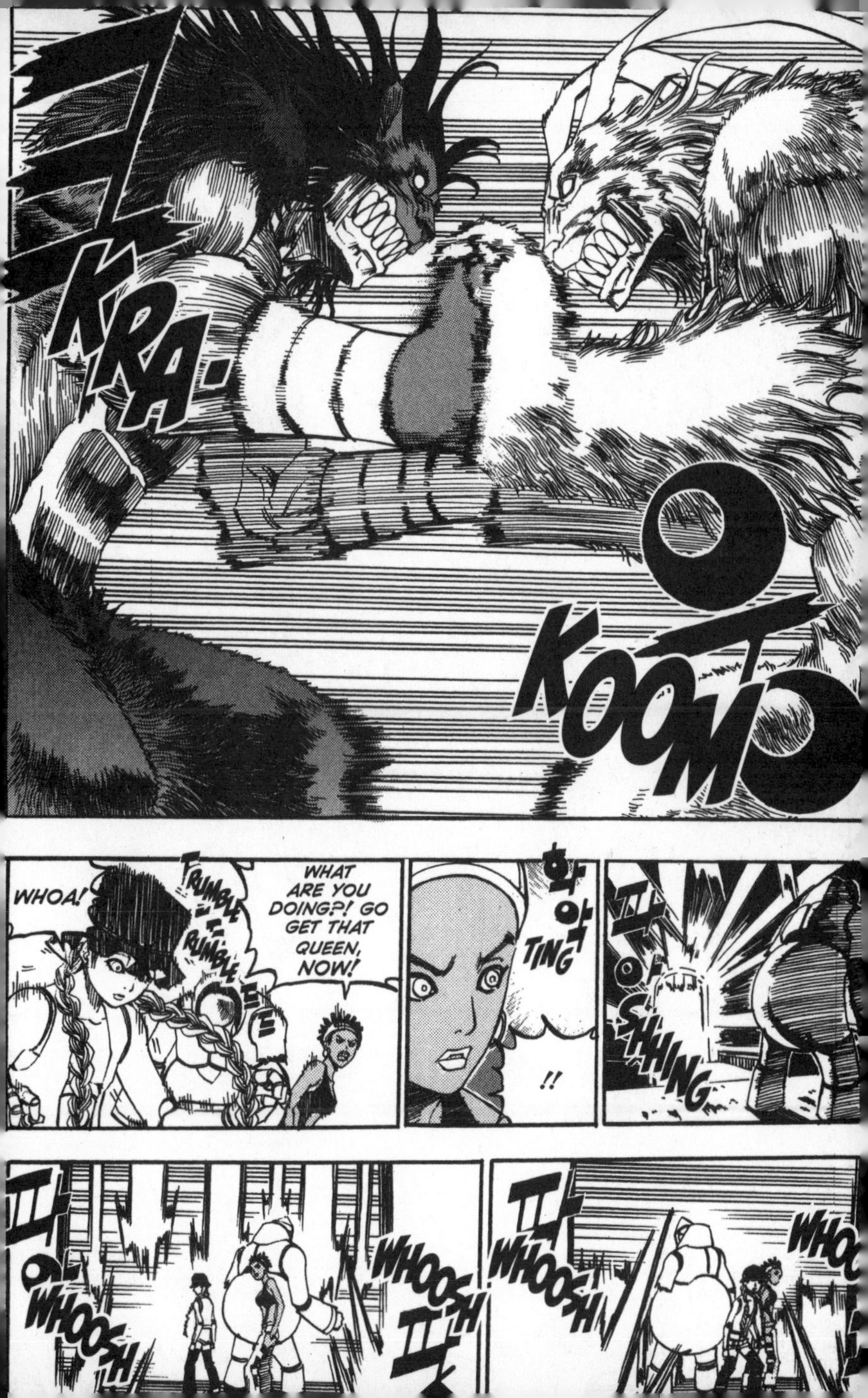
KRA-
KOOM
WHOA!
RUMBLE RUMBLE
WHAT ARE YOU DOING?! GO GET THAT QUEEN, NOW!
TING
!!
SHHING
WHOOSH
WHOOSH
WHOOSH
WHOOSH

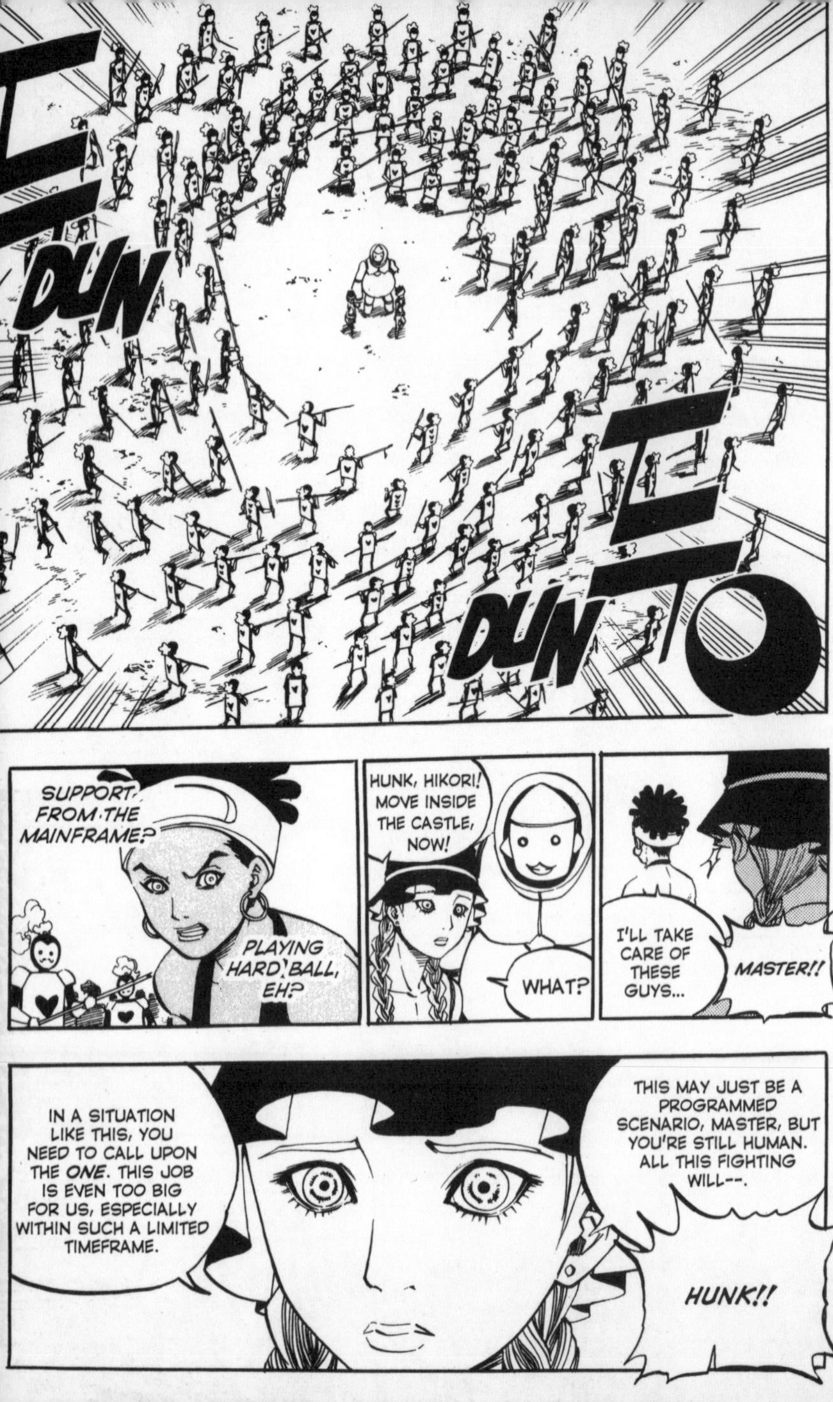

DUN
DUN
SUPPORT FROM THE MAINFRAME?
PLAYING HARD BALL, EH?
HUNK, HIKORI! MOVE INSIDE THE CASTLE, NOW!
WHAT?
I'LL TAKE CARE OF THESE GUYS...
MASTER!!
IN A SITUATION LIKE THIS, YOU NEED TO CALL UPON THE *ONE*. THIS JOB IS EVEN TOO BIG FOR US, ESPECIALLY WITHIN SUCH A LIMITED TIMEFRAME.
THIS MAY JUST BE A PROGRAMMED SCENARIO, MASTER, BUT YOU'RE STILL HUMAN. ALL THIS FIGHTING WILL--.
HUNK!!

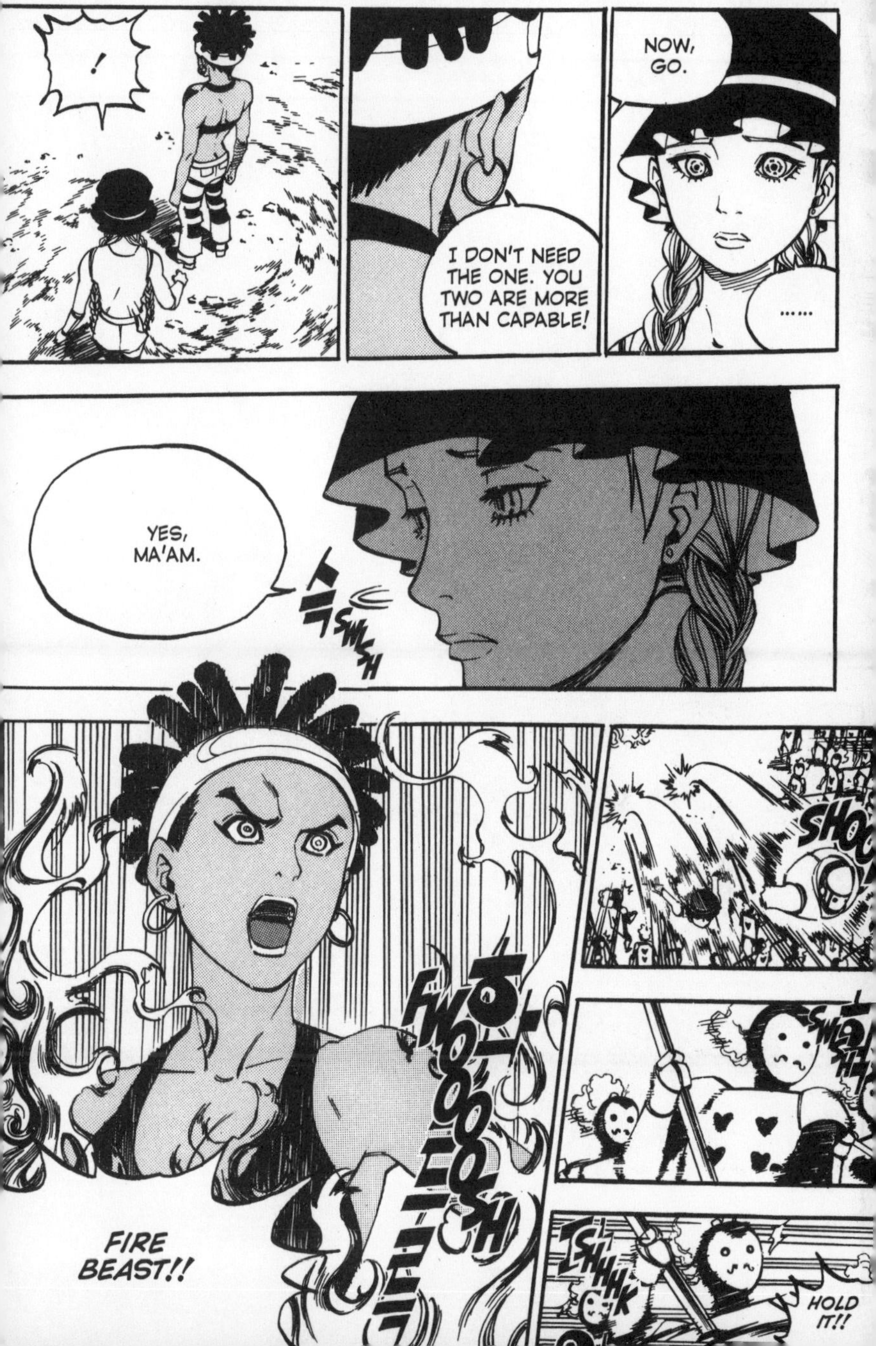
!
I DON'T NEED THE ONE. YOU TWO ARE MORE THAN CAPABLE!
NOW, GO.
......
YES, MA'AM.
SWISH
FWOOOOOSH
FIRE BEAST!!
SHOO
SWISH
TSHHHK
HOLD IT!!

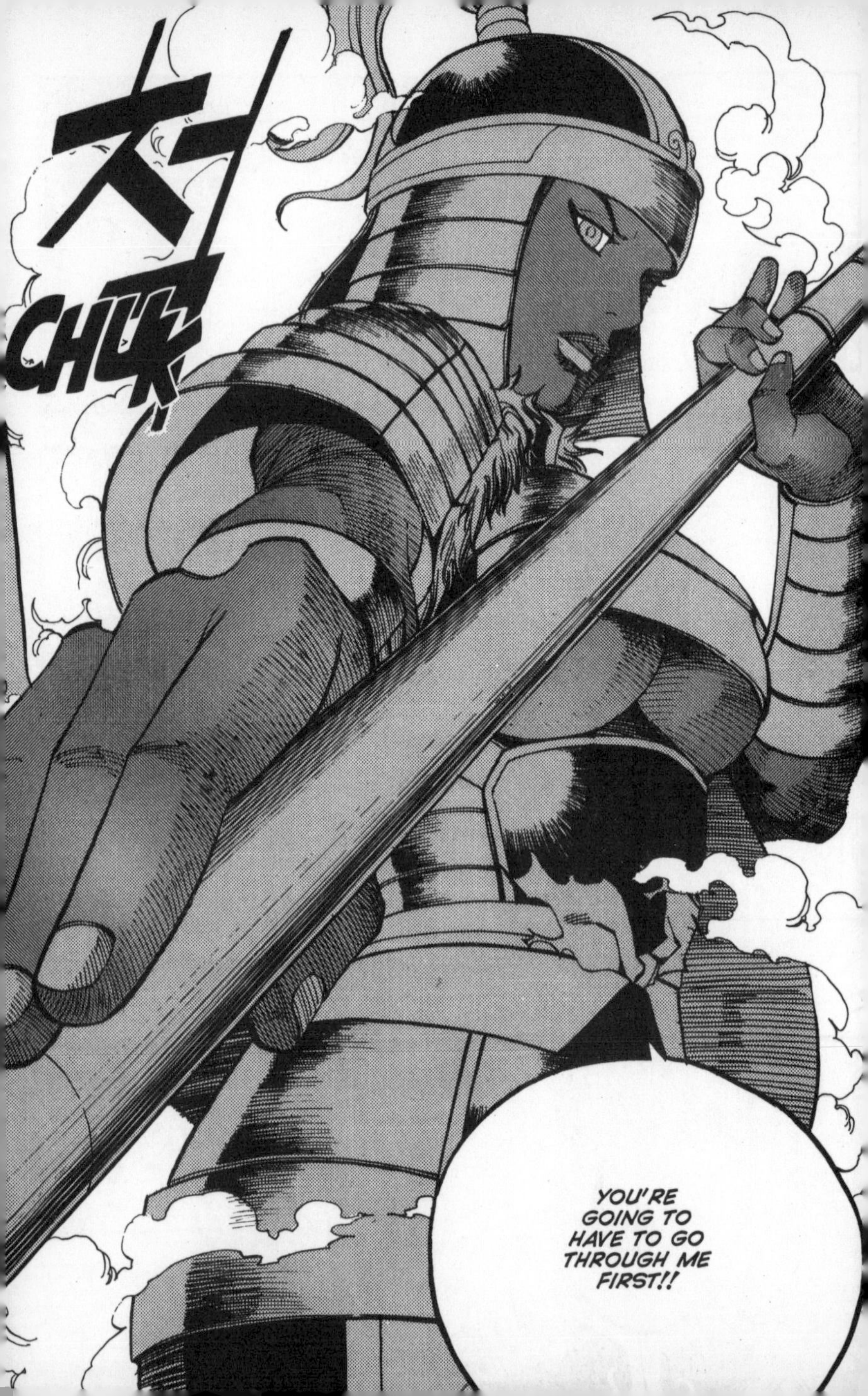
CHUK
YOU'RE GOING TO HAVE TO GO THROUGH ME FIRST!!

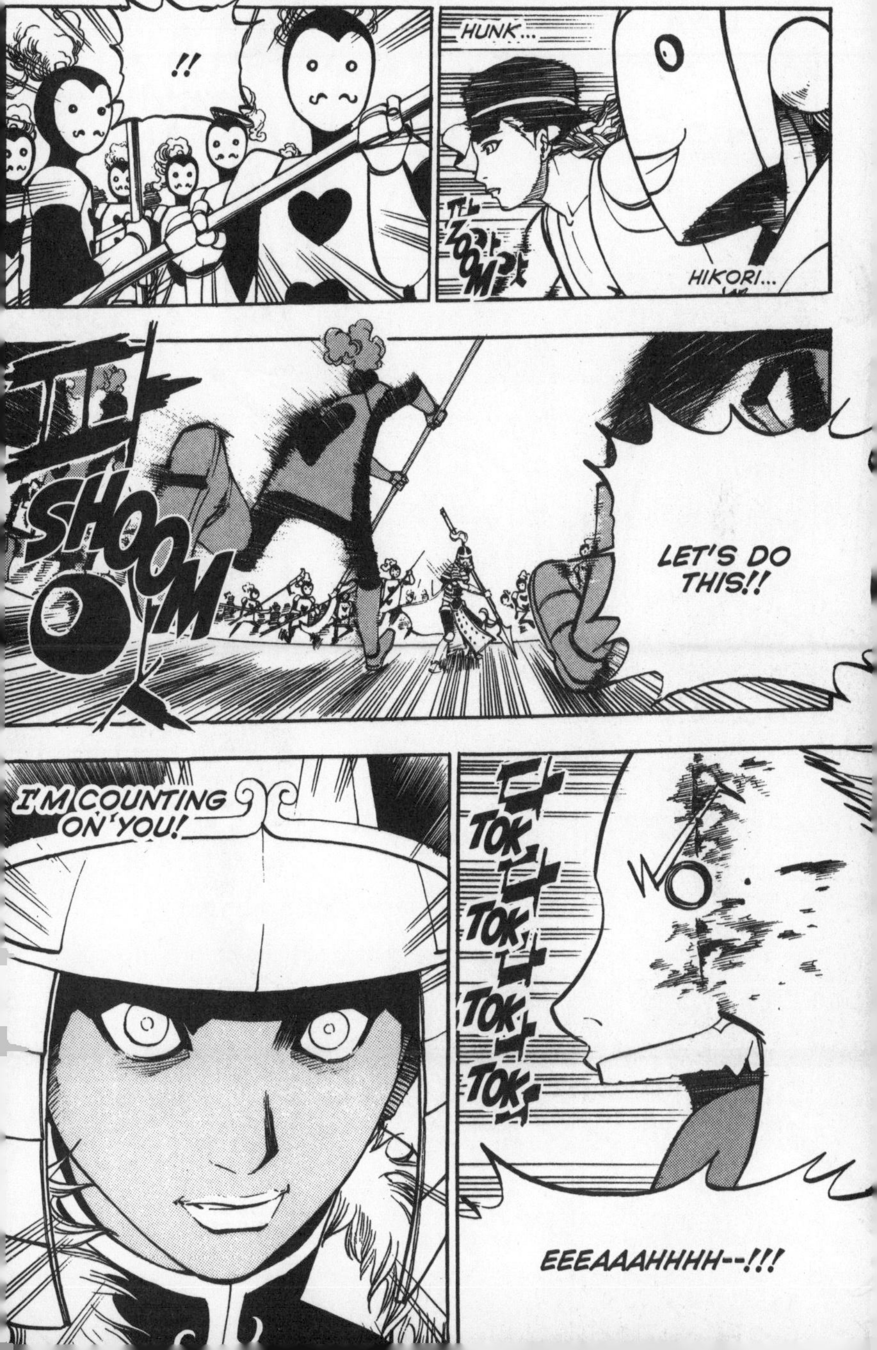
!!
HUNK...
ZOOM
HIKORI...
SHOOM
LET'S DO THIS!!
I'M COUNTING ON YOU!
TOK TOK TOK TOK TOK
EEEAAAHHHH--!!!

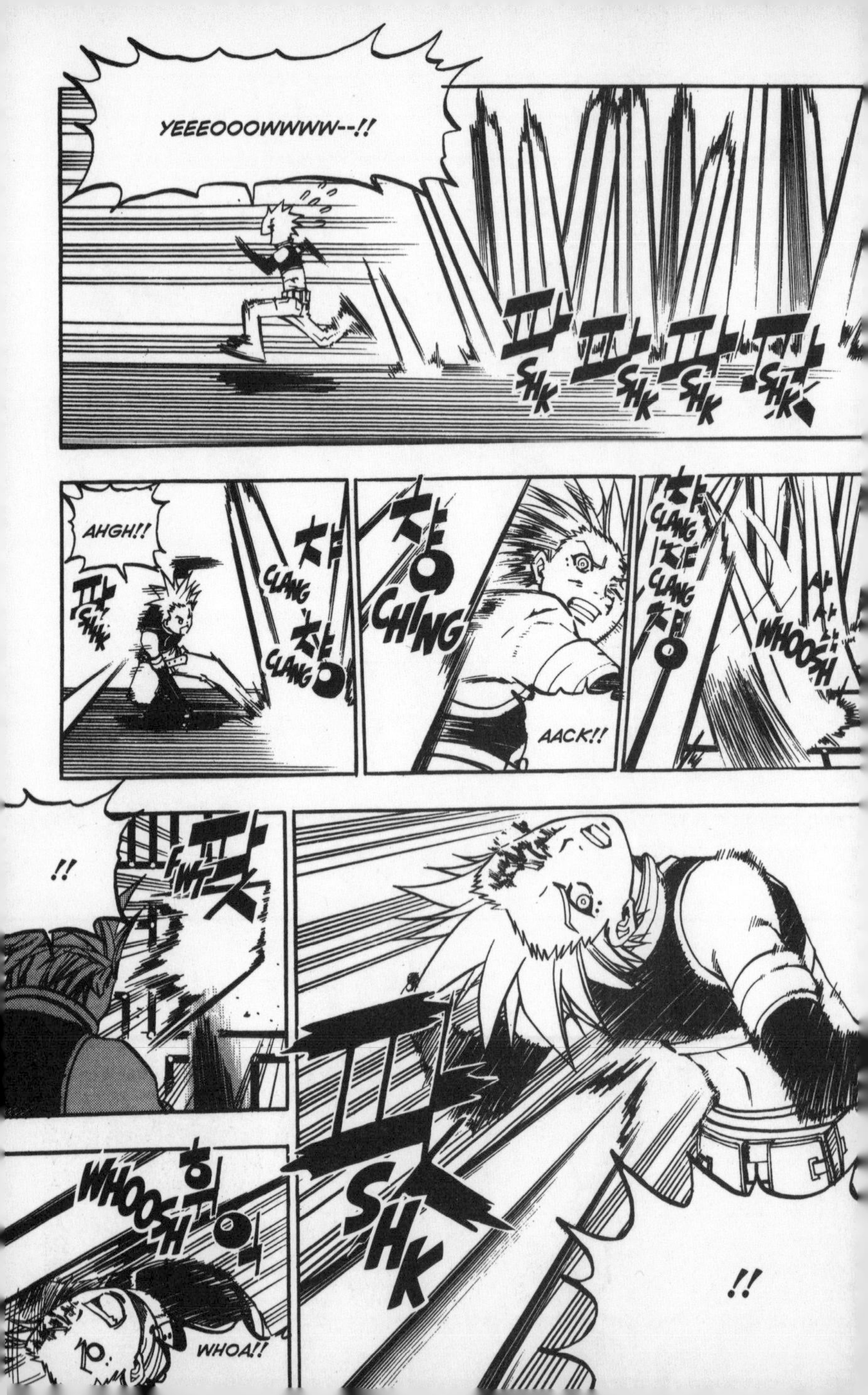
YEEEOOOWWWW--!!
SHK
SHK
SHK
SHK
AHGH!!
SHK
CLANG
CLANG
CHING
AACK!!
CLANG
CLANG
WHOOSH
!!
FWT
WHOOSH
WHOA!!
SHK
!!

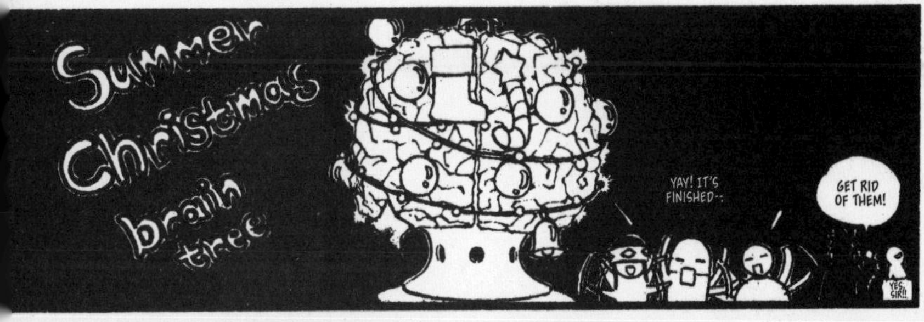
Summer Christmas brain tree
YAY! IT'S FINISHED--.
GET RID OF THEM!
YES, SIR!!

BACK TALK...
NO, NO...AFTER WORD?!

OKAY...NOW I CAN FINALLY TALK ABOUT CALLISTA.

CALLISTA IS BLIND.

IT IS FASTER TO PROCESS INFORMATION BY RECEIVING IT DIRECTLY INTO THE BRAIN
RATHER THAN RECEIVING IT THROUGH THE VISUAL NERVES FIRST AND THEN LETTING
THEM TRANSPORT IT TO THE BRAIN SECOND. SO, CALLISTA IS DESIGNED TO RECEIVE
INPUT DIRECTLY THROUGH HER EYE-LIKE SENSORS THAT SURROUND HER IN HER
ROOM. THE EYE ON THE BAND AROUND HER HEAD ALSO FUNCTIONS THE SAME WAY.
WHAT APPEARS TO BE CALLISTA'S HAIR TRAILING ACROSS THE FLOOR IS ACTUALLY
HAIR-THIN CIRCUIT LINES THAT ARE CONNECTED TO THE EYES IN THE ROOM, AND THE
WALLS ARE MADE OF LM SO THAT THEY CAN BE PROGRAMMED TO MORPH INTO
PROTECTIVE WEAPONS. THESE MULTIPLE EYES SEND HER DATA FROM ALL OVER THE
ROOM, GOING DIRECTLY TO HER BRAIN AND ACTUALLY INCREASING HER VISUAL
RANGE, MAKING HER AN INCREDIBLY FAST FIGHTER.
WHEN I FIRST DESIGNED HER, CALLISTA WAS MORE OF A WARRIOR-TYPE WOMAN, AND
SHE FUNCTIONED WITHOUT WIRES. IN THE CURRENT VERSION, SHE IS WIRED, BUT HER
ABILITIES HAVE ESSENTIALLY STAYED THE SAME...
I THOUGHT SHE WAS TOO COOL TO BE JUST A ONE-OFF CHARACTER, SO I DECIDED TO
BRING HER BACK AT LEAST ONE MORE TIME.

AND NEXT TIME SHE'LL HAVE WIRELESS UPGRADES! HEE-HEE!

- VERNA, A CYBER CEREBRO HUMAN -

AT FIRST, VERNA WAS JUST A FASTER-THAN-AVERAGE COMPUTER GEEK.

THEN I SAW THE TERM "CYBER CEREBRO SPACE" SOMEWHERE AND GOT THE IDEA FOR
A WOMAN WHO COULD PROGRAM HER BODY TO ENTER IT. (I DON'T KNOW WHY A
WOMAN WITH THIS CAPACITY SEEMED MORE ATTRACTIVE THAN A MAN WITH THE SAME
ABILITY.)
THIS CYBER CEREBRO SPACE IS NOT A VIRTUAL SPACE, LIKE IN A VIDEO GAME OR THE
MATRIX, IT'S A NETWORK. YOU ENTER THE NETWORK AND RIDE IT TO BREAK INTO
WHEREVER YOU WANT TO GO...
THE REASON WHY THE SPACE THAT WE SEE IS POPULATED WITH SO MANY DIFFERENT
PEOPLE AND ANIMALS IS BECAUSE WE ARE SEEING IT FROM VERNA'S PERSPECTIVE.
DIGITALIZING HER BRAINWAVES, VERNA'S SENSES TURN INTO FUNCTIONAL PROGRAMS
INSIDE THE CYBER CEREBRO SPACE; HOWEVER, ANY INJURIES YOU INCUR IN CYBER
CEREBRO SPACE TRANSLATE INTO REAL DAMAGE TO YOUR PHYSICAL BODY.
THOUGH, IT'S NOT UNCOMMON FOR THE ACTUAL INJURIES TO APPEAR IN DIFFERENT
PLACES ON YOUR BODY IN REAL LIFE.
BUT WHY, YOU ASK, IS VERNA WEARING BANDAGES????
SHE'S FAKING IT...PROBABLY...

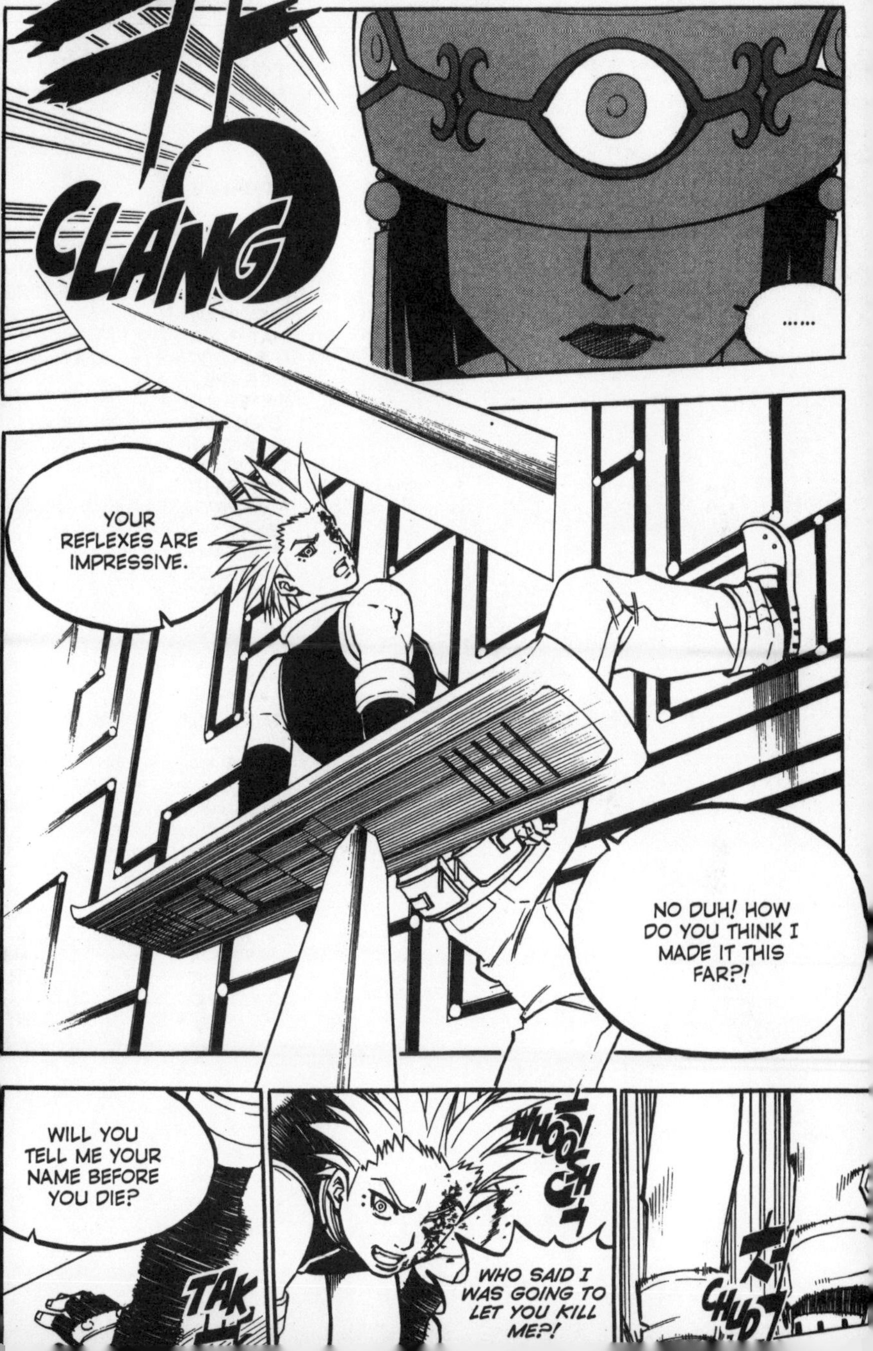
CLANG
......
YOUR REFLEXES ARE IMPRESSIVE.
NO DUH! HOW DO YOU THINK I MADE IT THIS FAR?!
WILL YOU TELL ME YOUR NAME BEFORE YOU DIE?
TAK
WHOOSH
WHO SAID I WAS GOING TO LET YOU KILL ME?!
CHUD

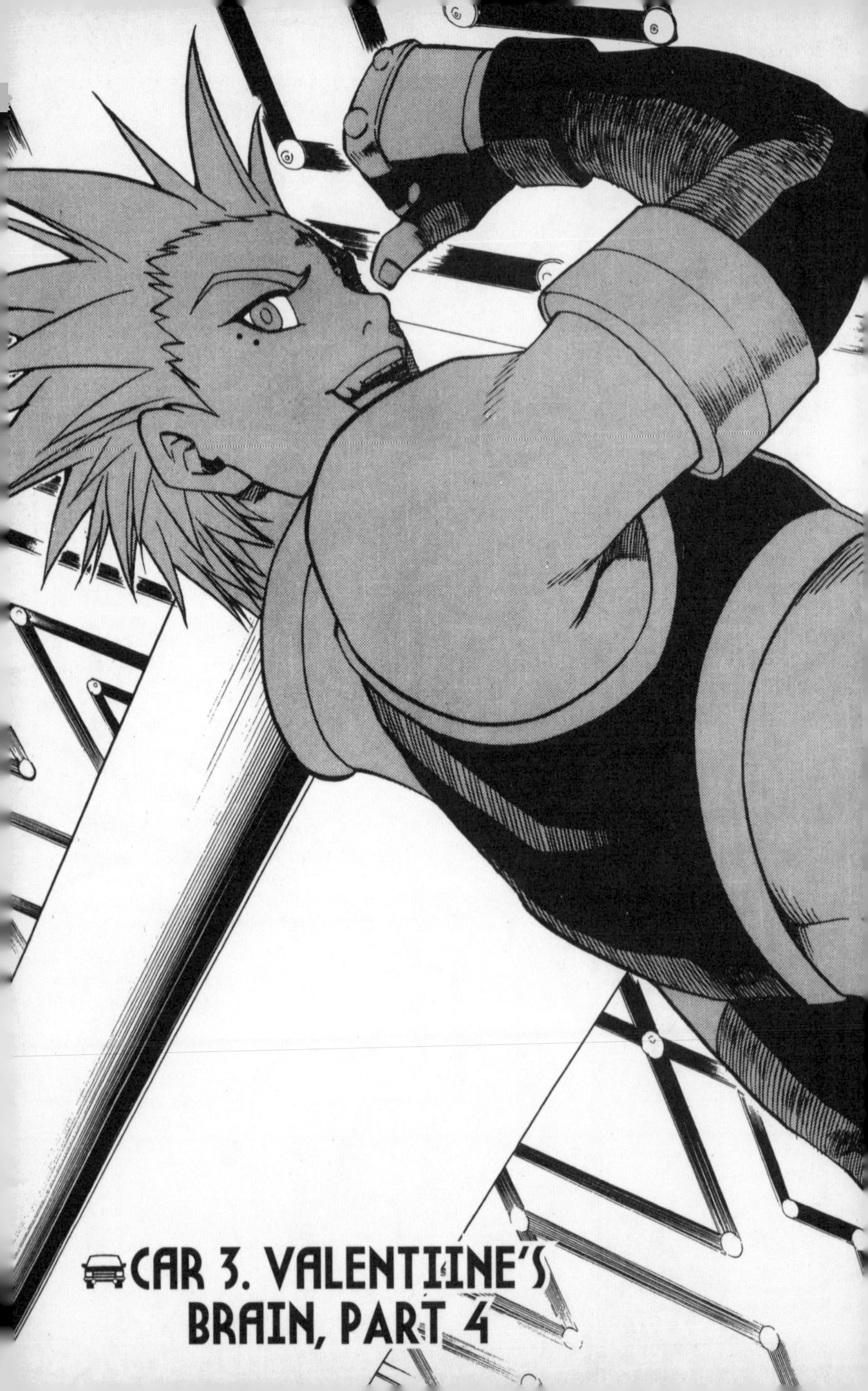

CAR 3. VALENTIINE'S BRAIN, PART 4

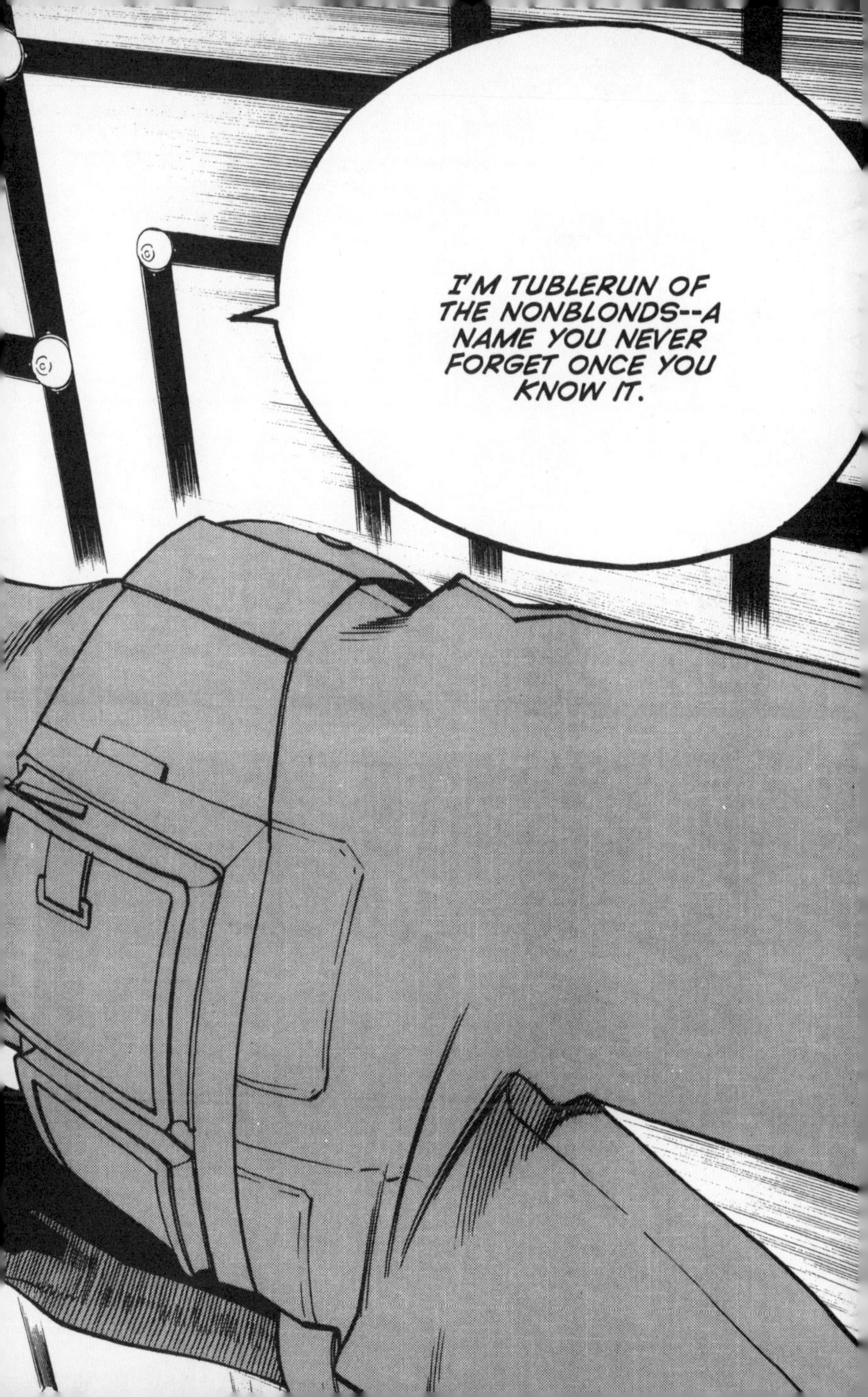
I'M TUBLERUN OF THE NONBLONDS--A NAME YOU NEVER FORGET ONCE YOU KNOW IT.

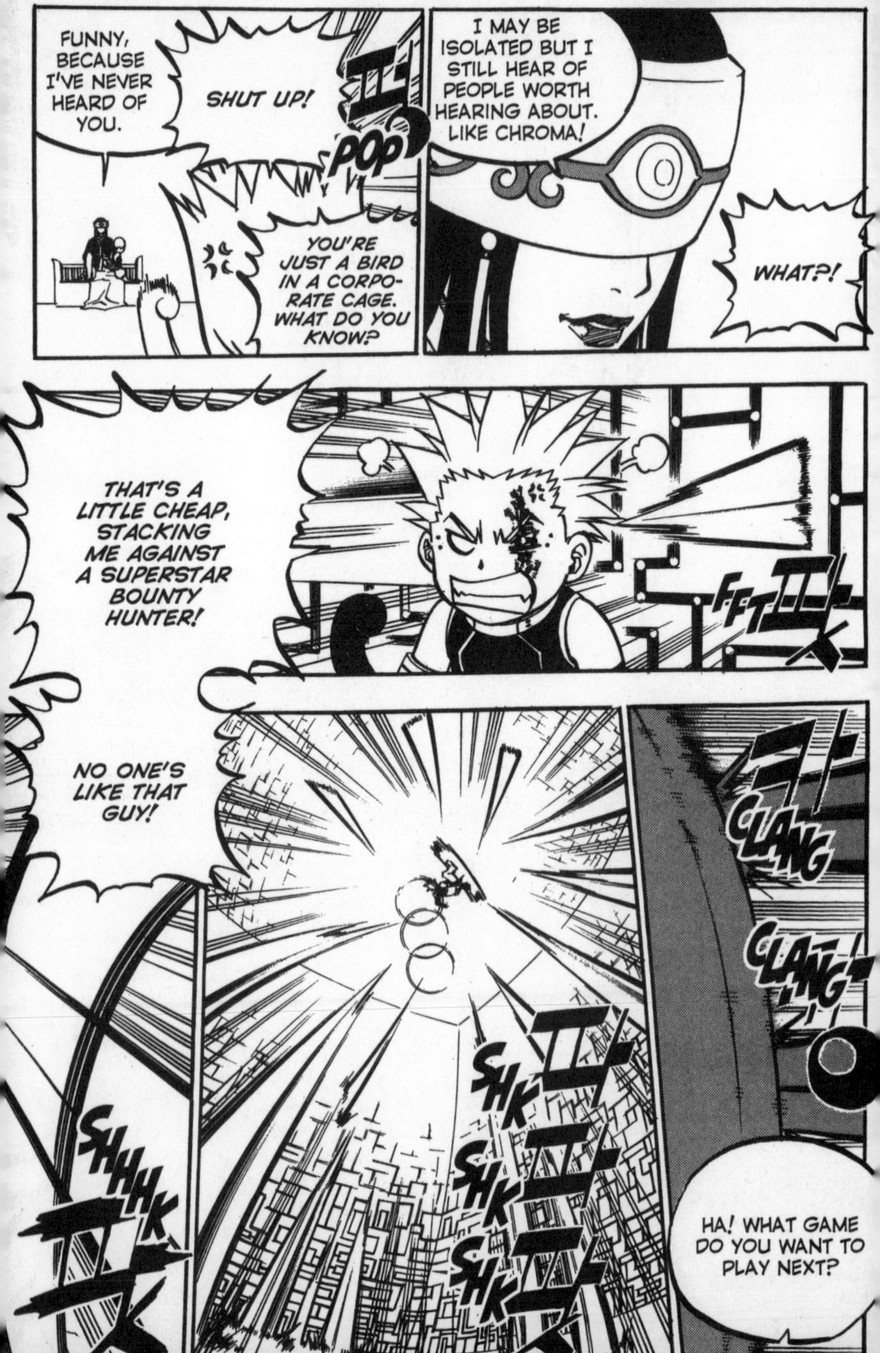
FUNNY, BECAUSE I'VE NEVER HEARD OF YOU.
SHUT UP!
POP
YOU'RE JUST A BIRD IN A CORPO-RATE CAGE. WHAT DO YOU KNOW?
I MAY BE ISOLATED BUT I STILL HEAR OF PEOPLE WORTH HEARING ABOUT. LIKE CHROMA!
WHAT?!
THAT'S A LITTLE CHEAP, STACKING ME AGAINST A SUPERSTAR BOUNTY HUNTER!
FFT
NO ONE'S LIKE THAT GUY!
CLANG
CLANG
SHHHHK
SHK
SHK
SHK
HA! WHAT GAME DO YOU WANT TO PLAY NEXT?

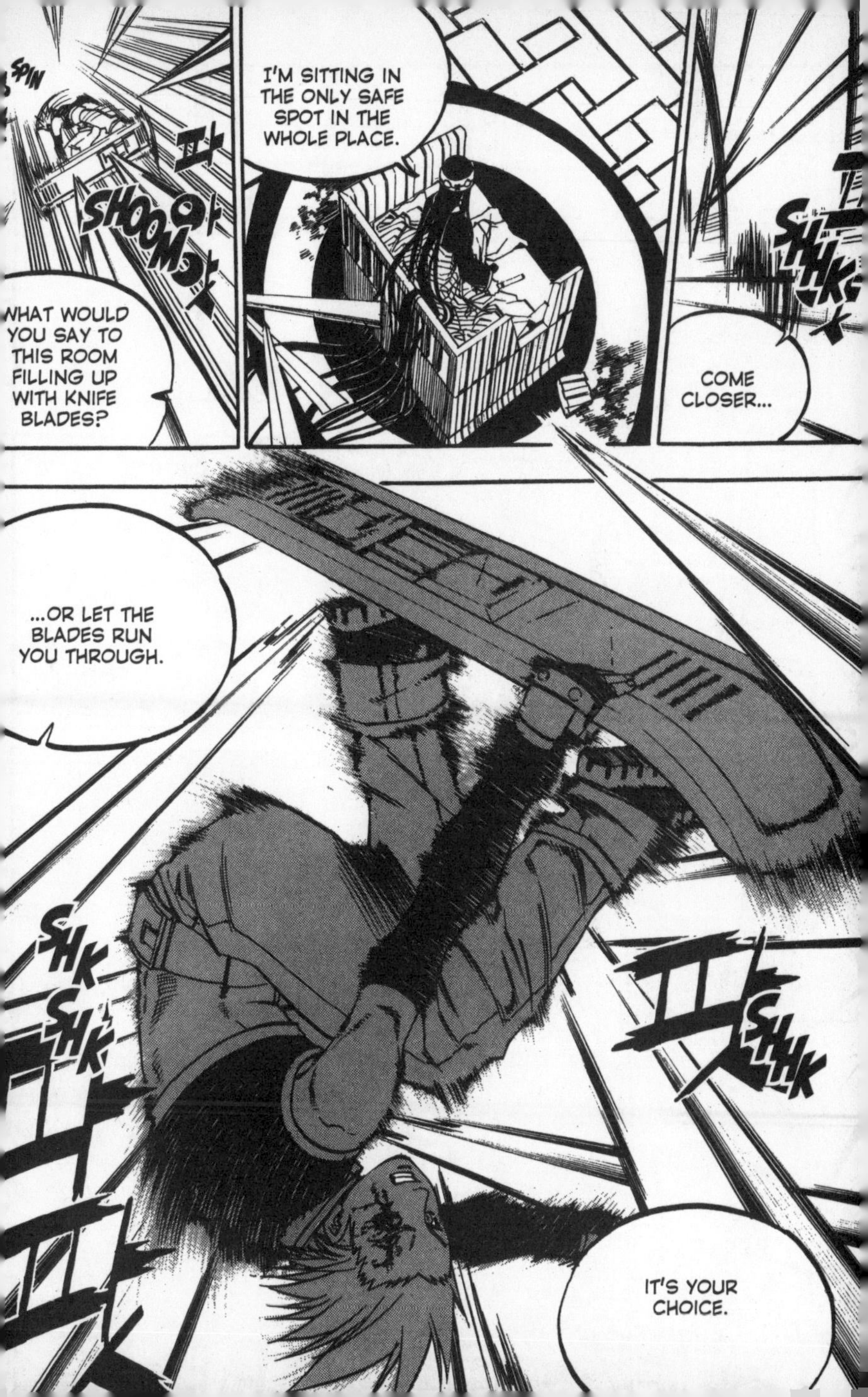
SPIN
SHOOOM
WHAT WOULD YOU SAY TO THIS ROOM FILLING UP WITH KNIFE BLADES?
I'M SITTING IN THE ONLY SAFE SPOT IN THE WHOLE PLACE.
SHHKK
COME CLOSER...
...OR LET THE BLADES RUN YOU THROUGH.
SHK
SHK
SHHK
IT'S YOUR CHOICE.

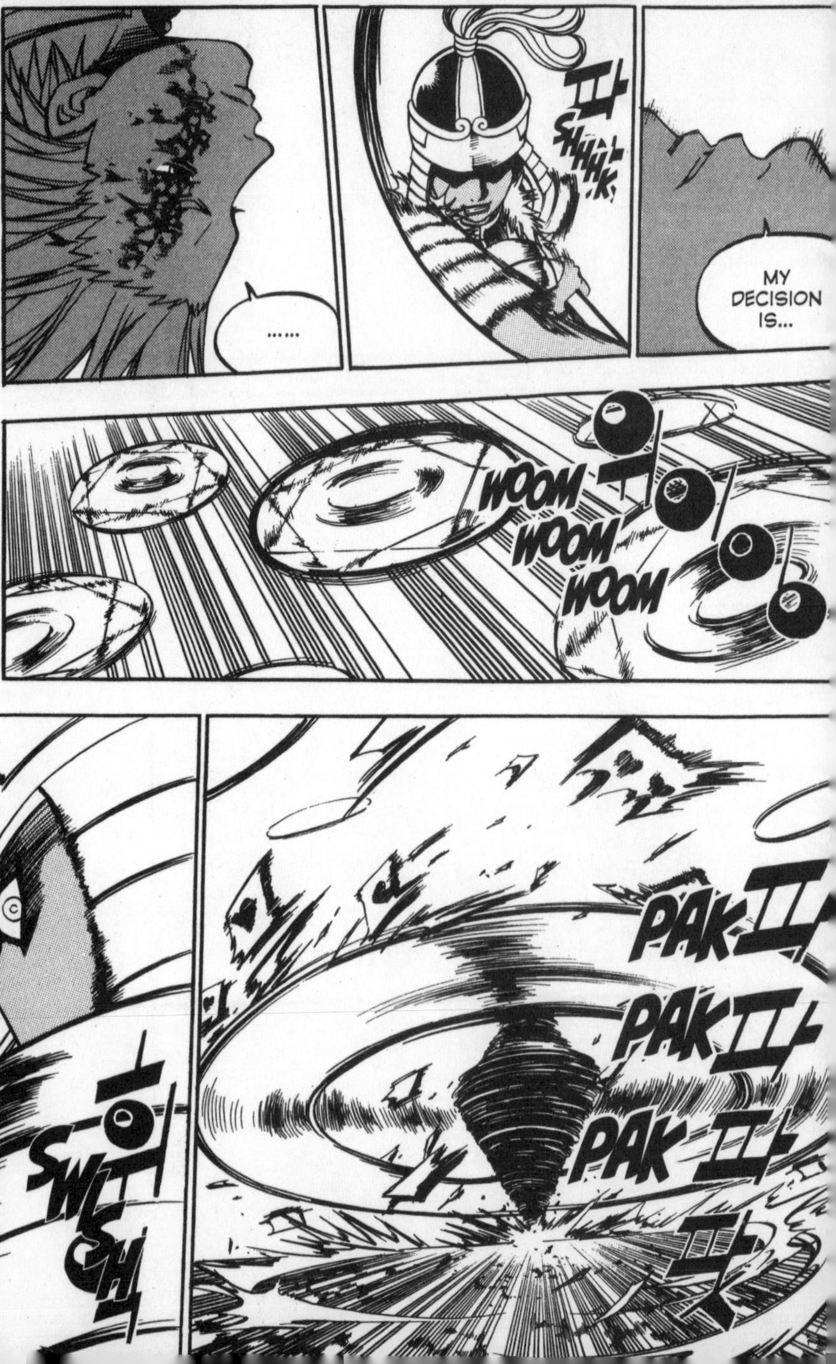
MY DECISION IS...
SHHHK
......
WOOM
WOOM
WOOM
PAK
PAK
PAK
SWISH

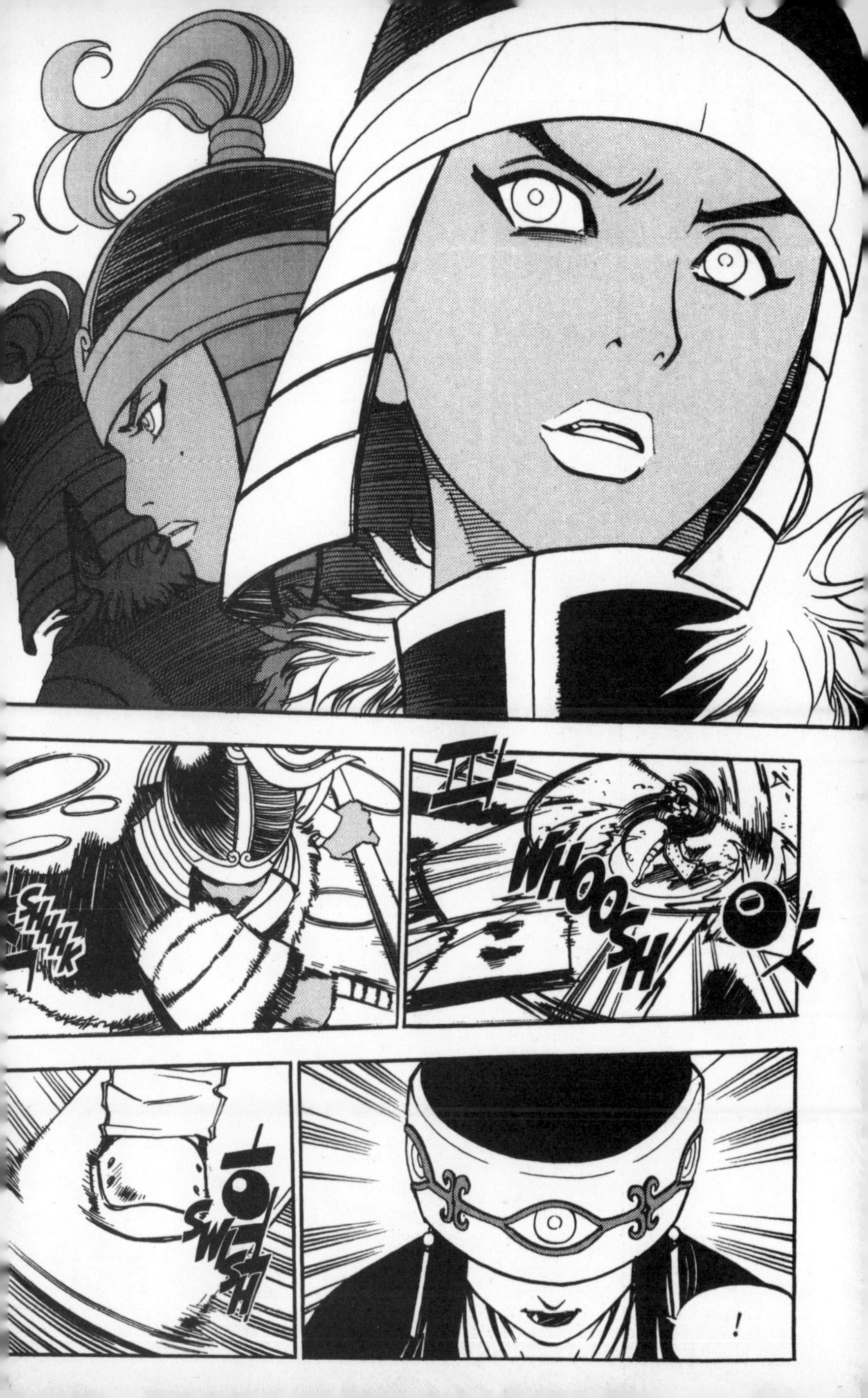
SHHHK
WHOOSH
SWISH
!

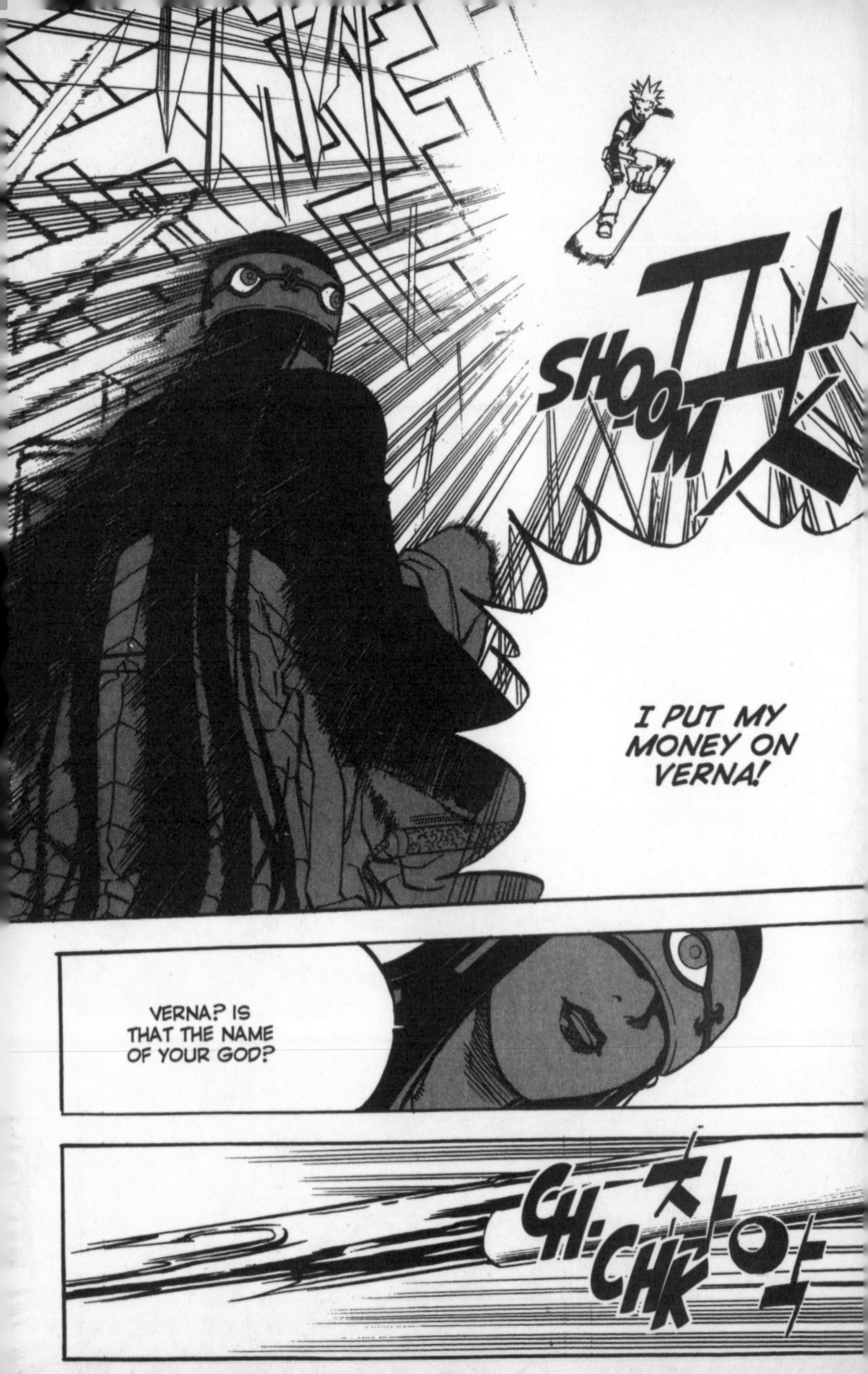
SHOOM
I PUT MY MONEY ON VERNA!
VERNA? IS THAT THE NAME OF YOUR GOD?
CH-CHK

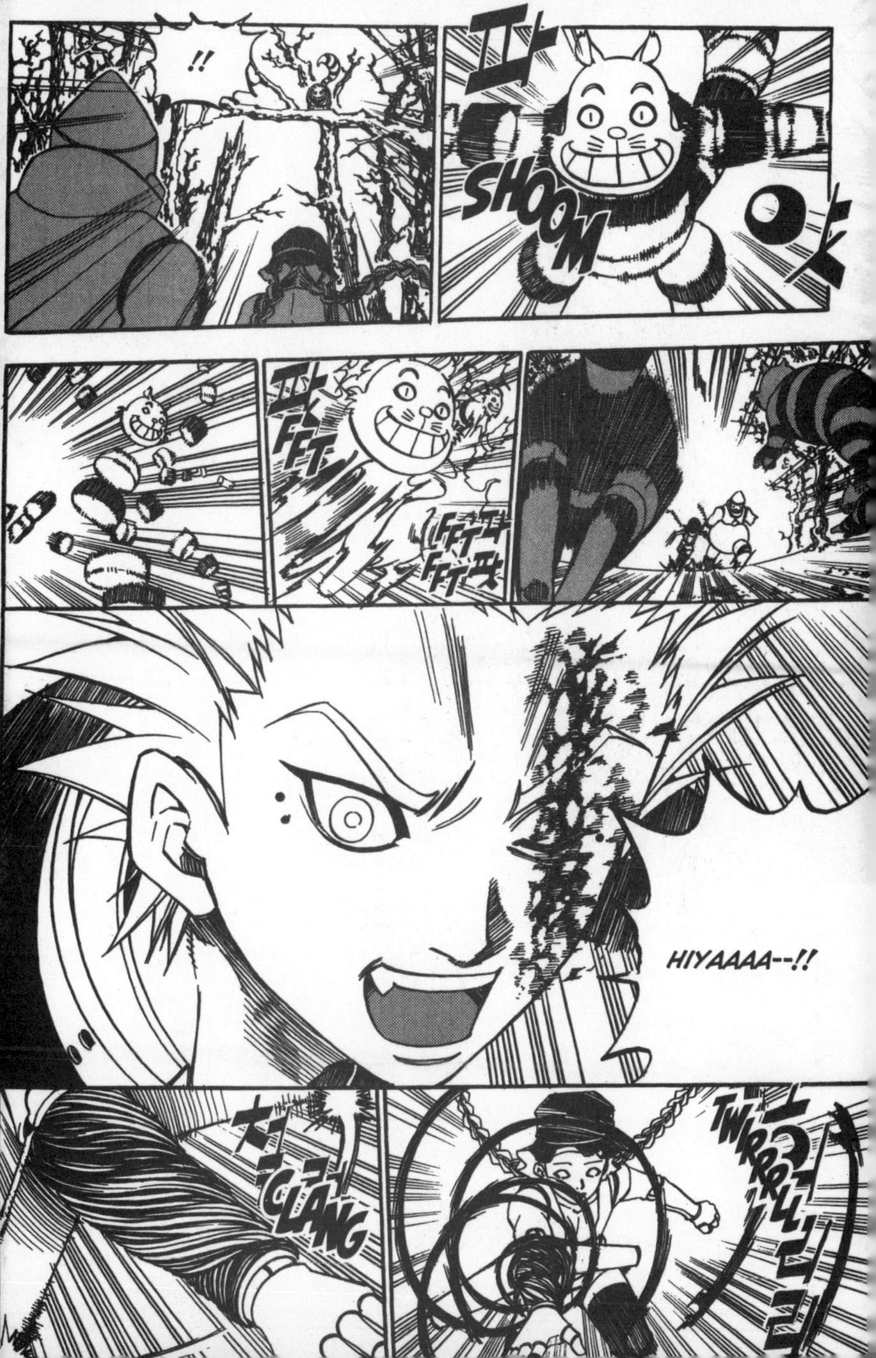
!!
SHOOM
HIYAAAA--!!
CLANG
TWIRRRLLL

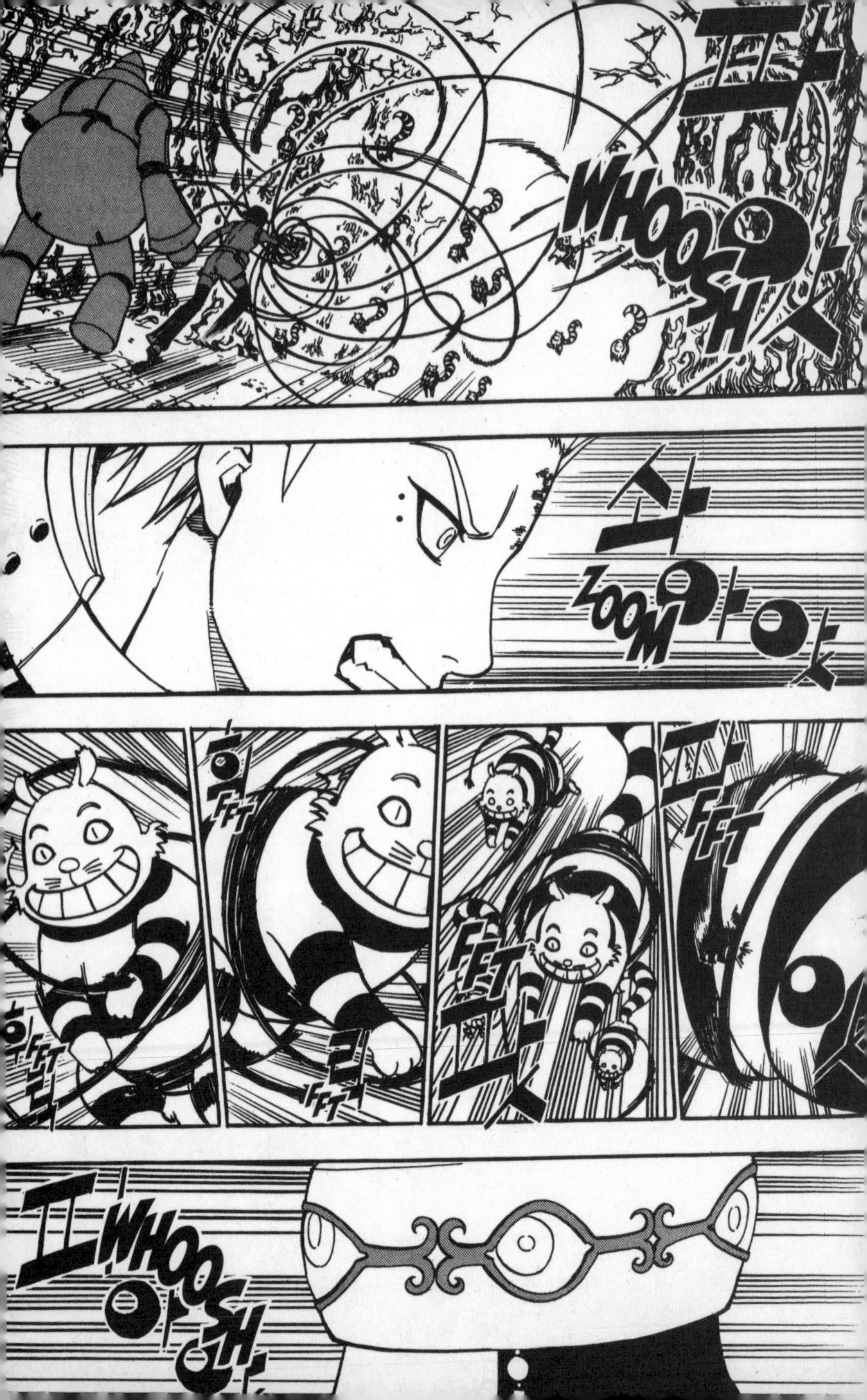
WHOOSH
ZOOM
FFT
FFT
FFT
FFT
FFT
WHOOSH

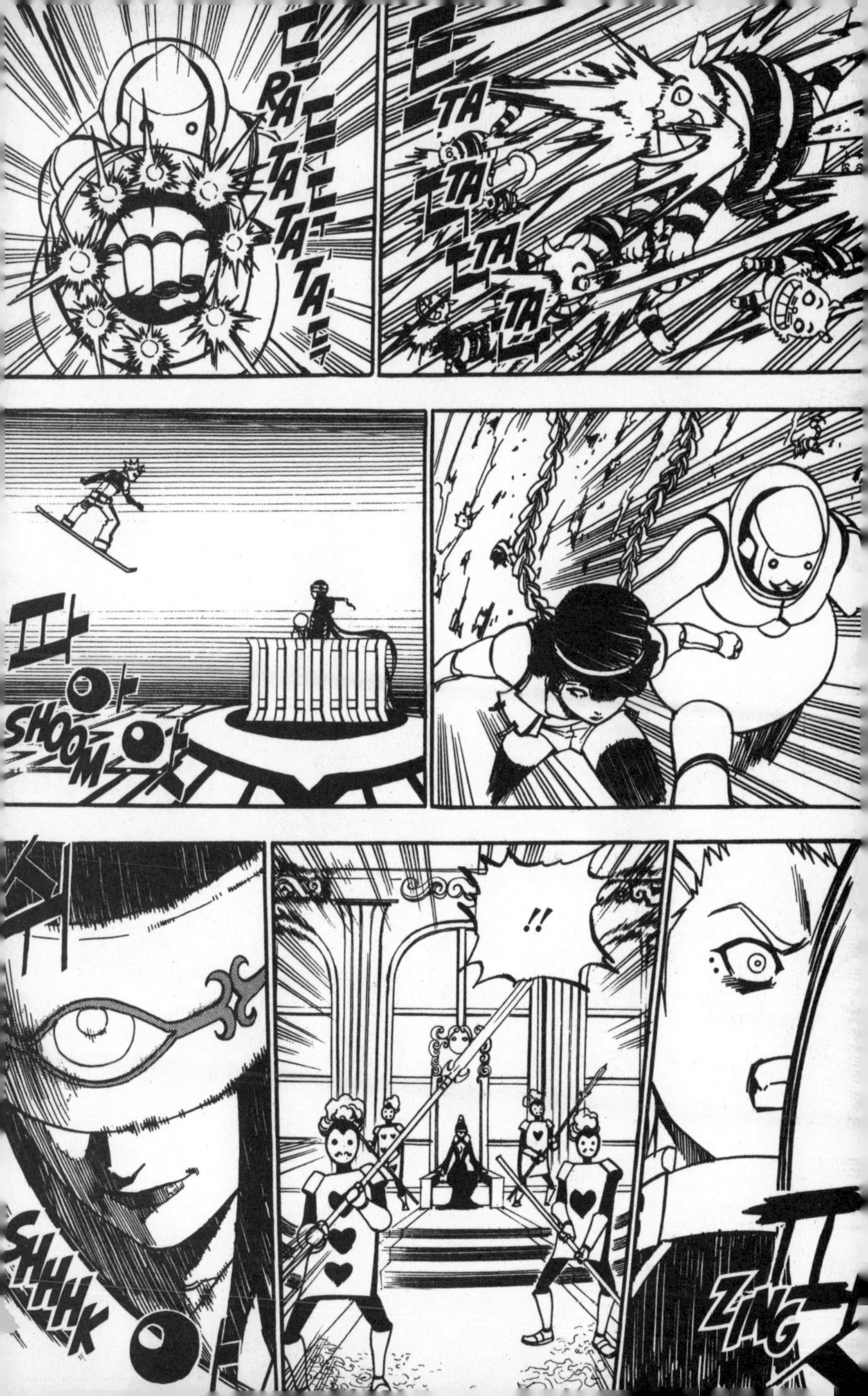
RATATATATA
TA TA TA TA TA
SHOOM
SHHHK
!!
ZING

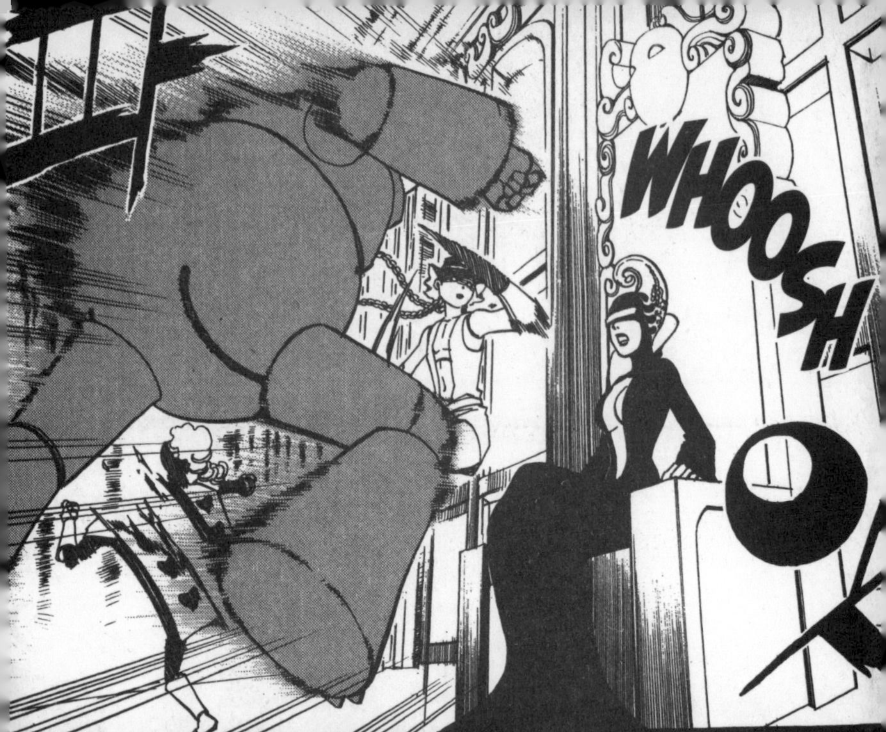
WHOOSH

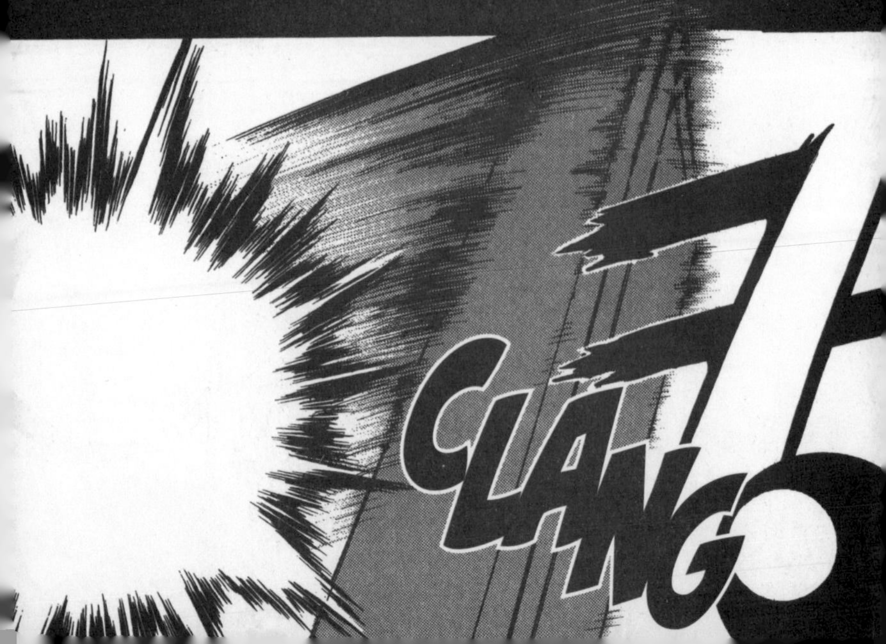
CLANG

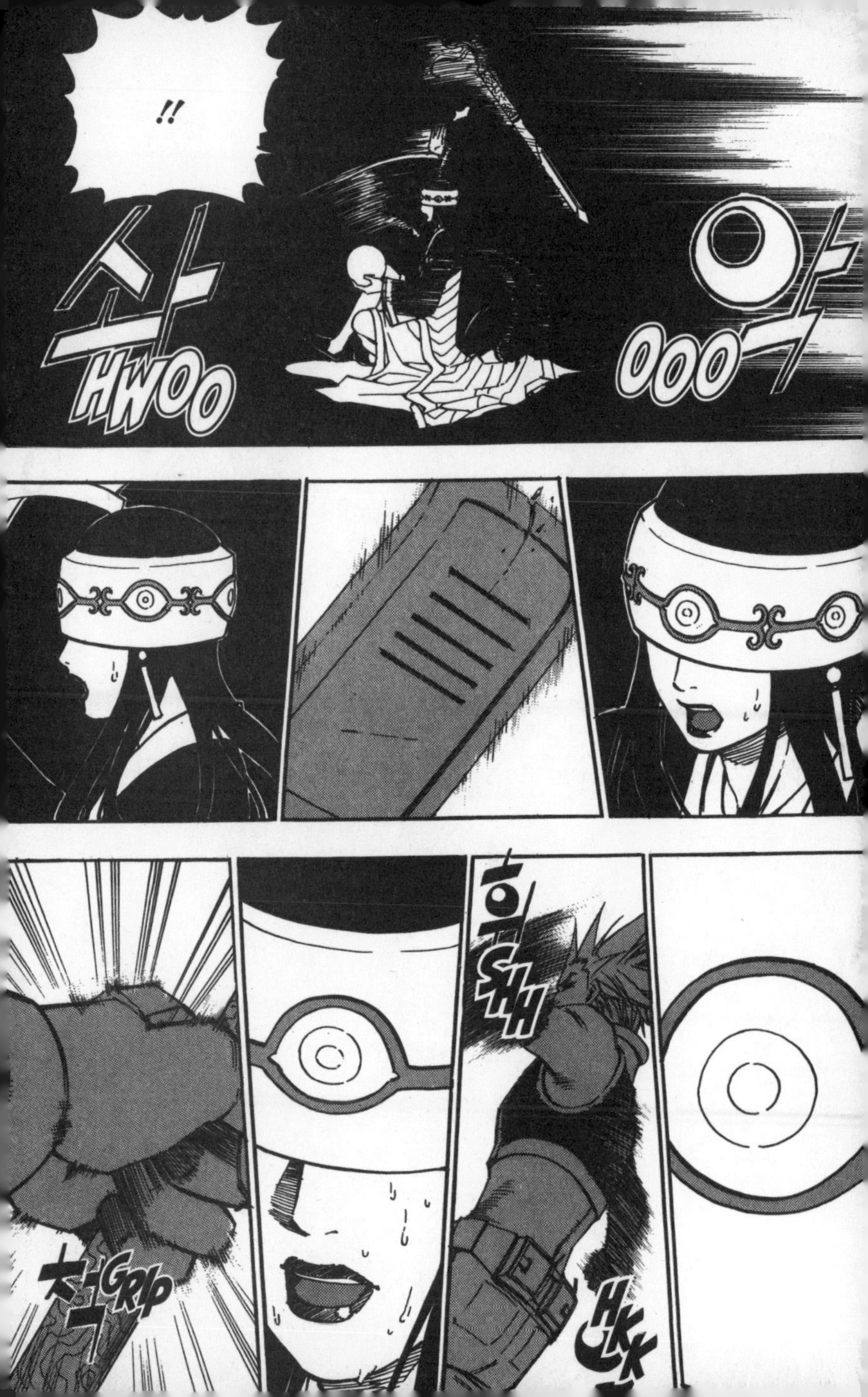

!!
HWOO
OOO
GRIP
SHH
HKK

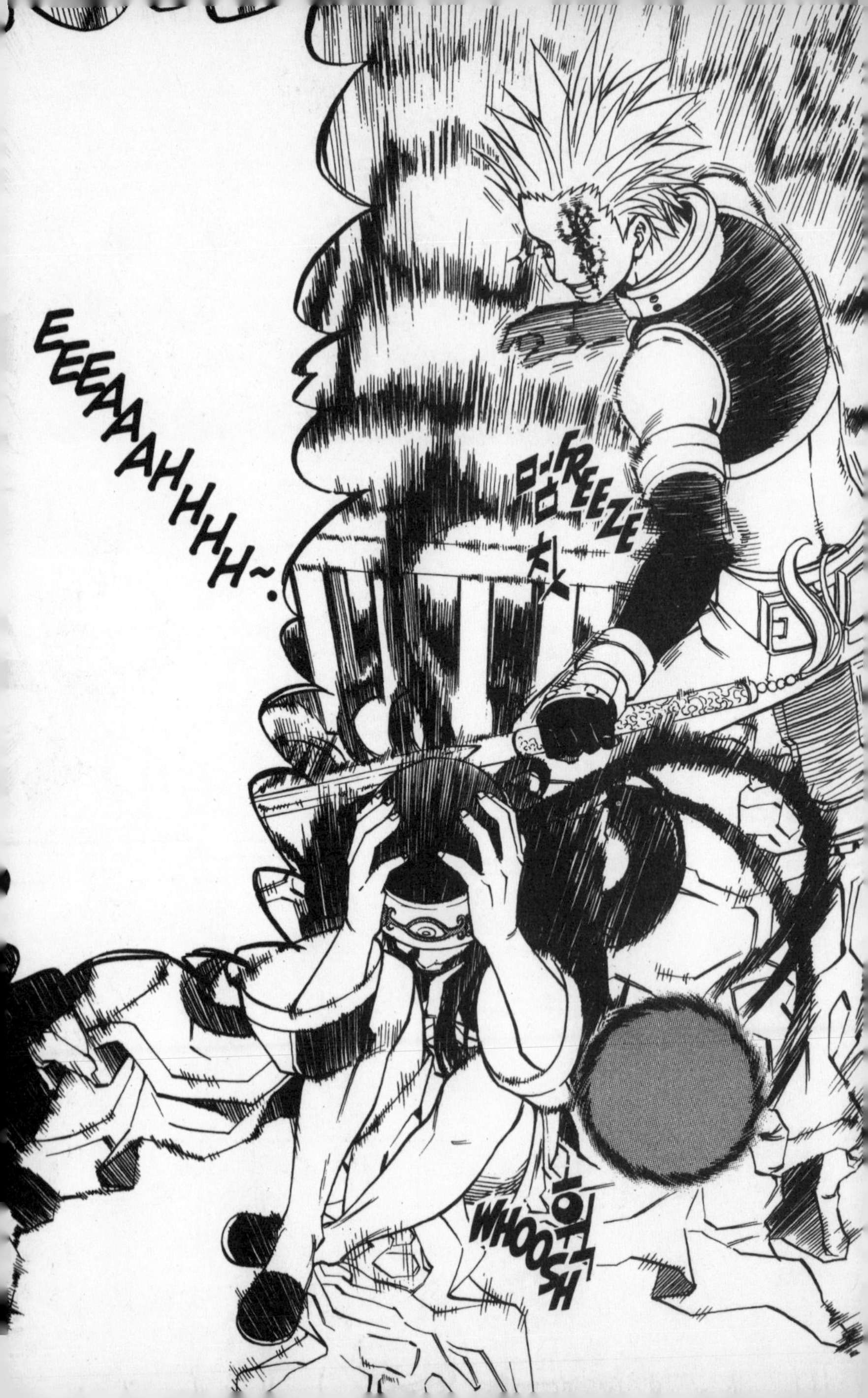
EEEAAAAHHHH~!
멈칫
FREEZE
후아
WHOOSH

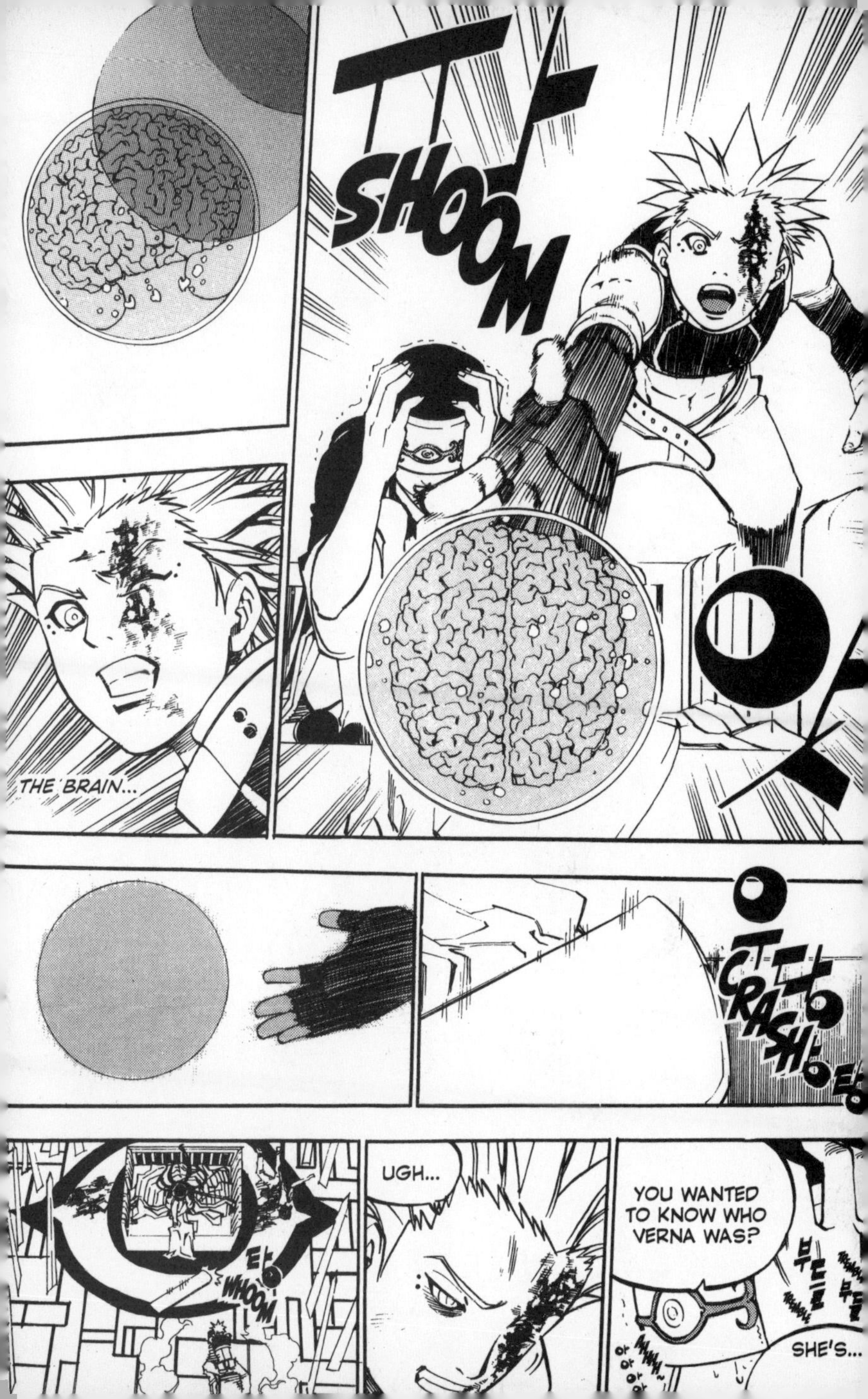
THE BRAIN...
SHOOM
CRASH
WHOOM
UGH...
YOU WANTED TO KNOW WHO VERNA WAS?
SHE'S...

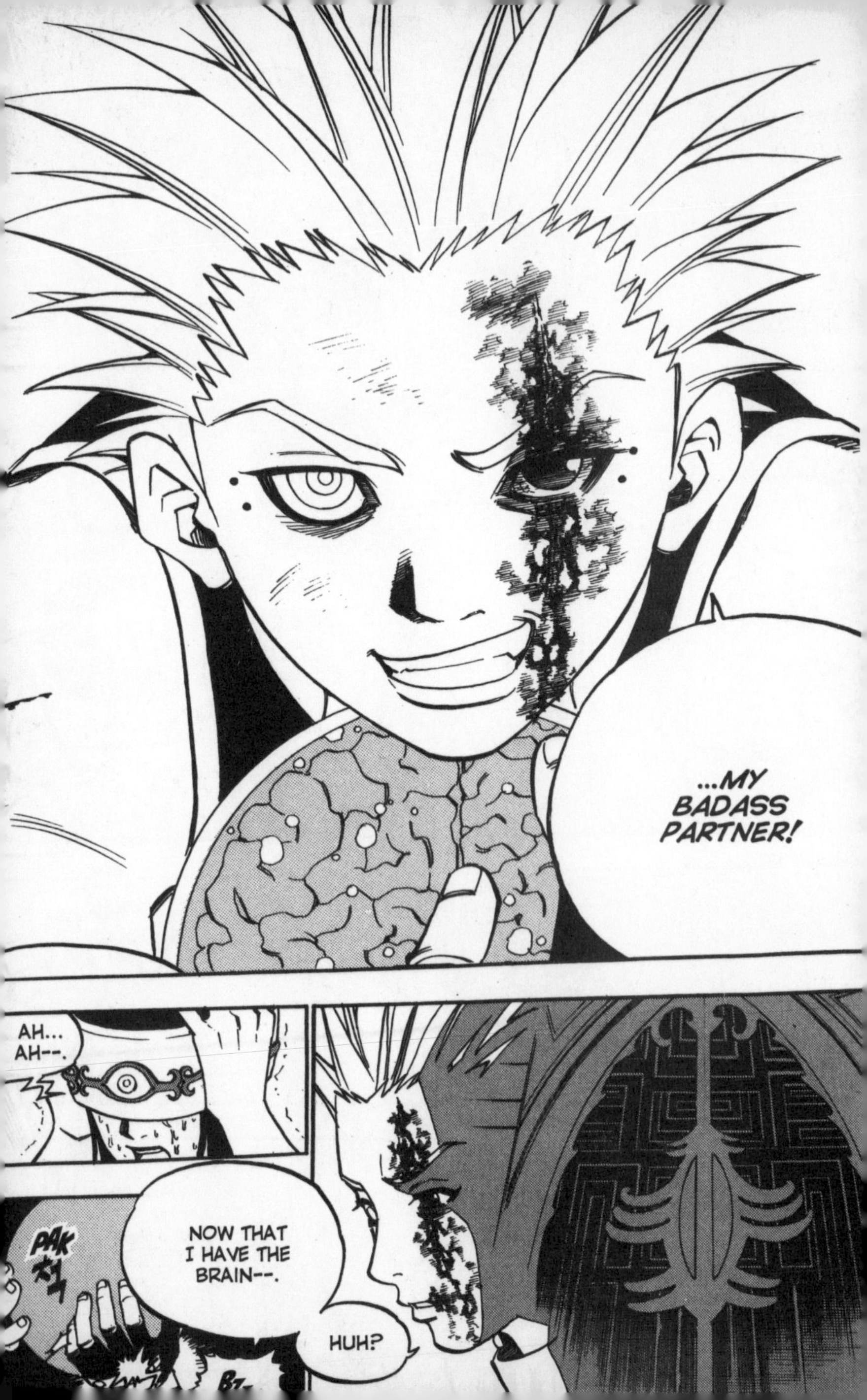
...MY BADASS PARTNER!
AH... AH--.
PAK
NOW THAT I HAVE THE BRAIN--.
HUH?

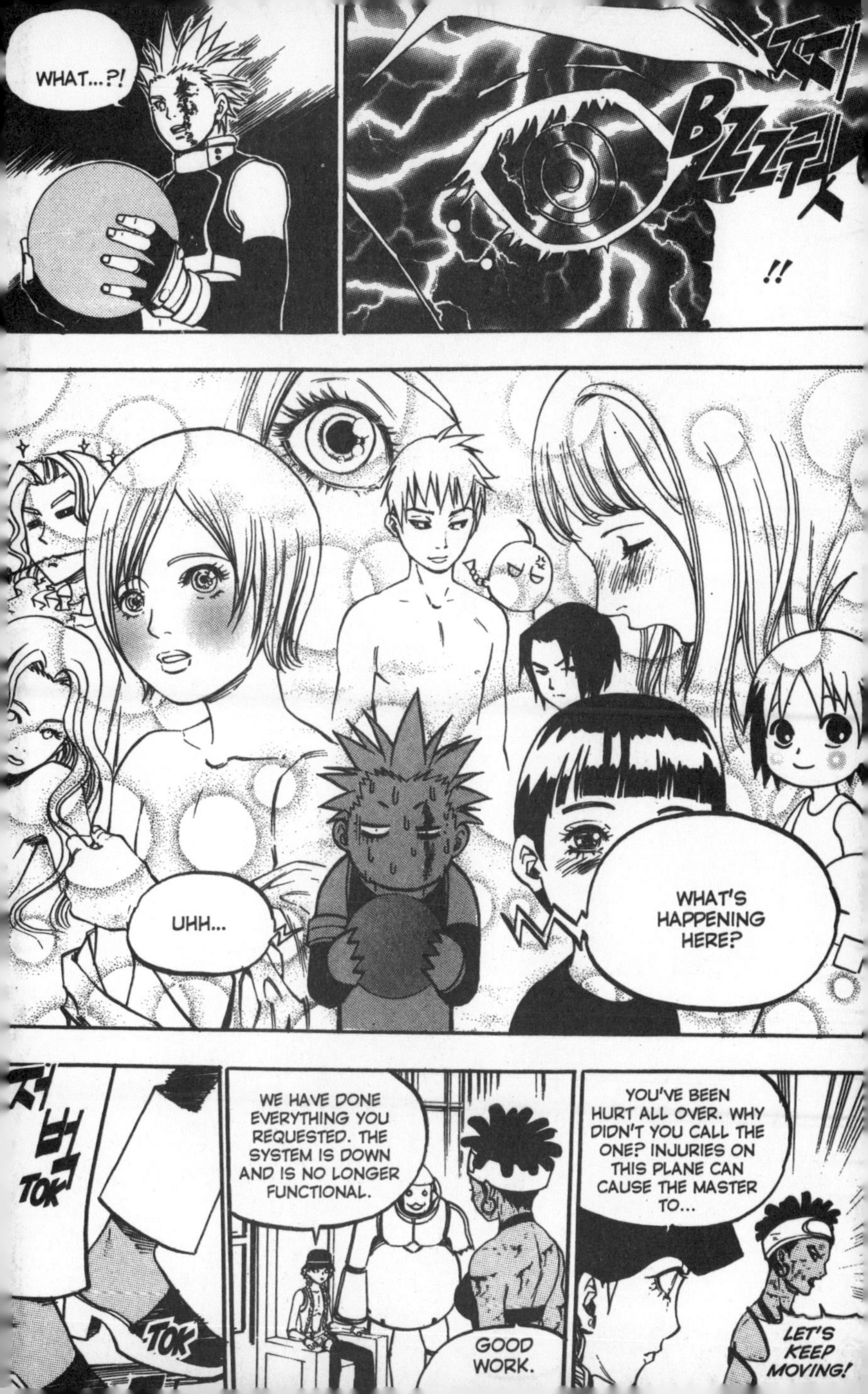
WHAT...?!
BZZT
!!
UHH...
WHAT'S HAPPENING HERE?
TOK
WE HAVE DONE EVERYTHING YOU REQUESTED. THE SYSTEM IS DOWN AND IS NO LONGER FUNCTIONAL.
GOOD WORK.
TOK
YOU'VE BEEN HURT ALL OVER. WHY DIDN'T YOU CALL THE ONE? INJURIES ON THIS PLANE CAN CAUSE THE MASTER TO...
LET'S KEEP MOVING!

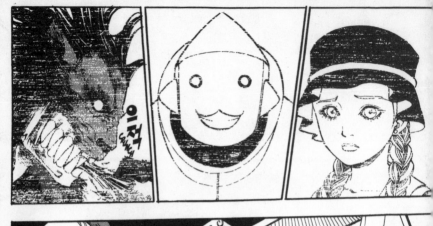

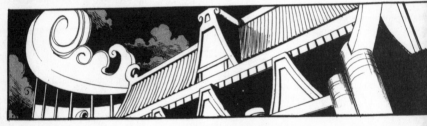

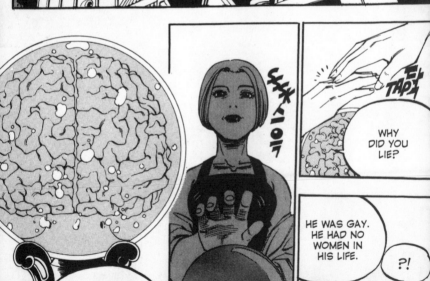

CRUNCH
IS IT REALLY DR. VALENTINE'S BRAIN?
SSSK
TAP
WHY DID YOU LIE?
HE WAS GAY. HE HAD NO WOMEN IN HIS LIFE.
?!
HOW DID YOU KNOW HE WAS GAY?

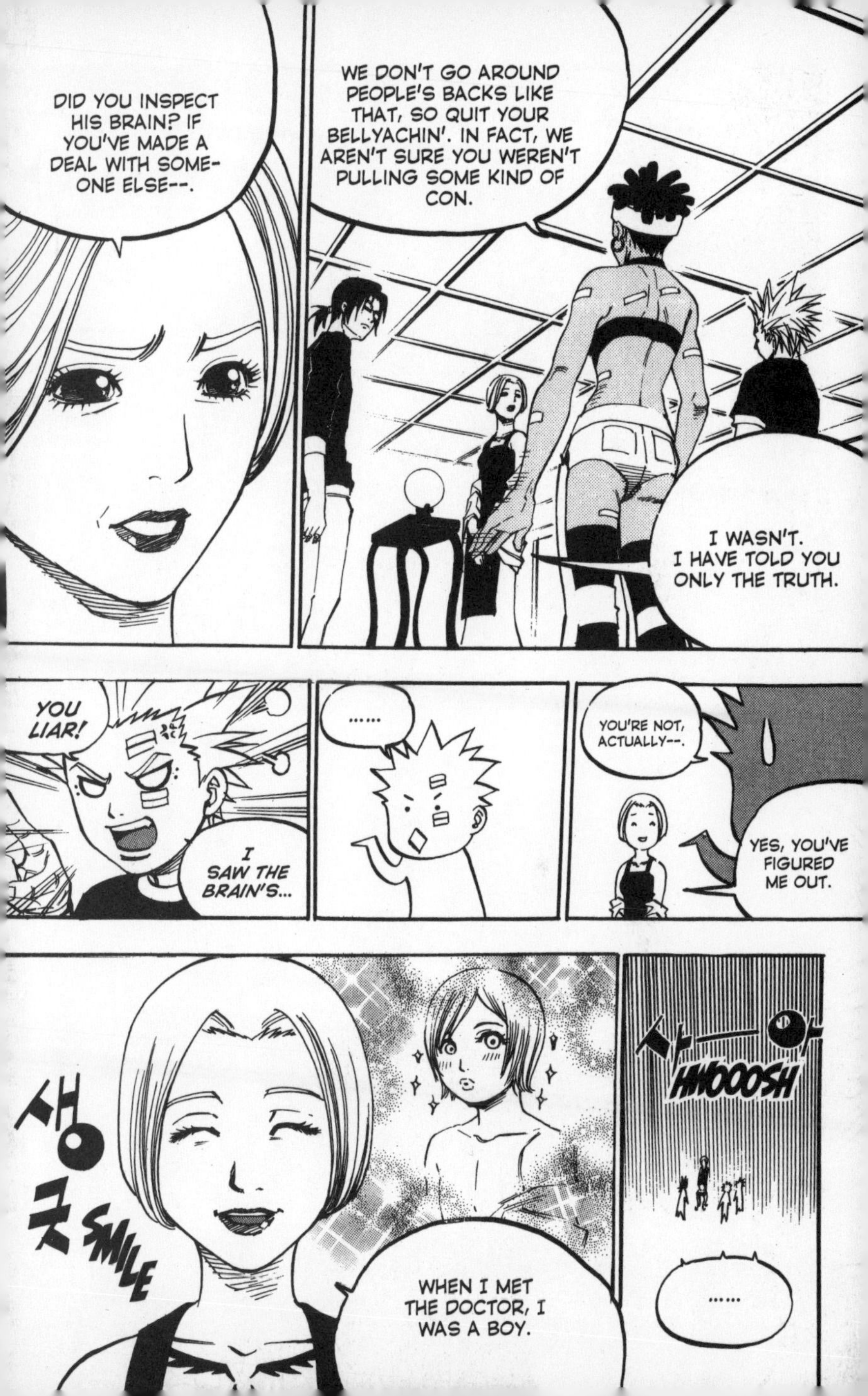
DID YOU INSPECT HIS BRAIN? IF YOU'VE MADE A DEAL WITH SOME-ONE ELSE--.
WE DON'T GO AROUND PEOPLE'S BACKS LIKE THAT, SO QUIT YOUR BELLYACHIN'. IN FACT, WE AREN'T SURE YOU WEREN'T PULLING SOME KIND OF CON.
I WASN'T. I HAVE TOLD YOU ONLY THE TRUTH.
YOU LIAR!
I SAW THE BRAIN'S...
......
YOU'RE NOT, ACTUALLY--.
YES, YOU'VE FIGURED ME OUT.
생긋
SMILE
WHEN I MET THE DOCTOR, I WAS A BOY.
샤—아
HWOOOSH
......

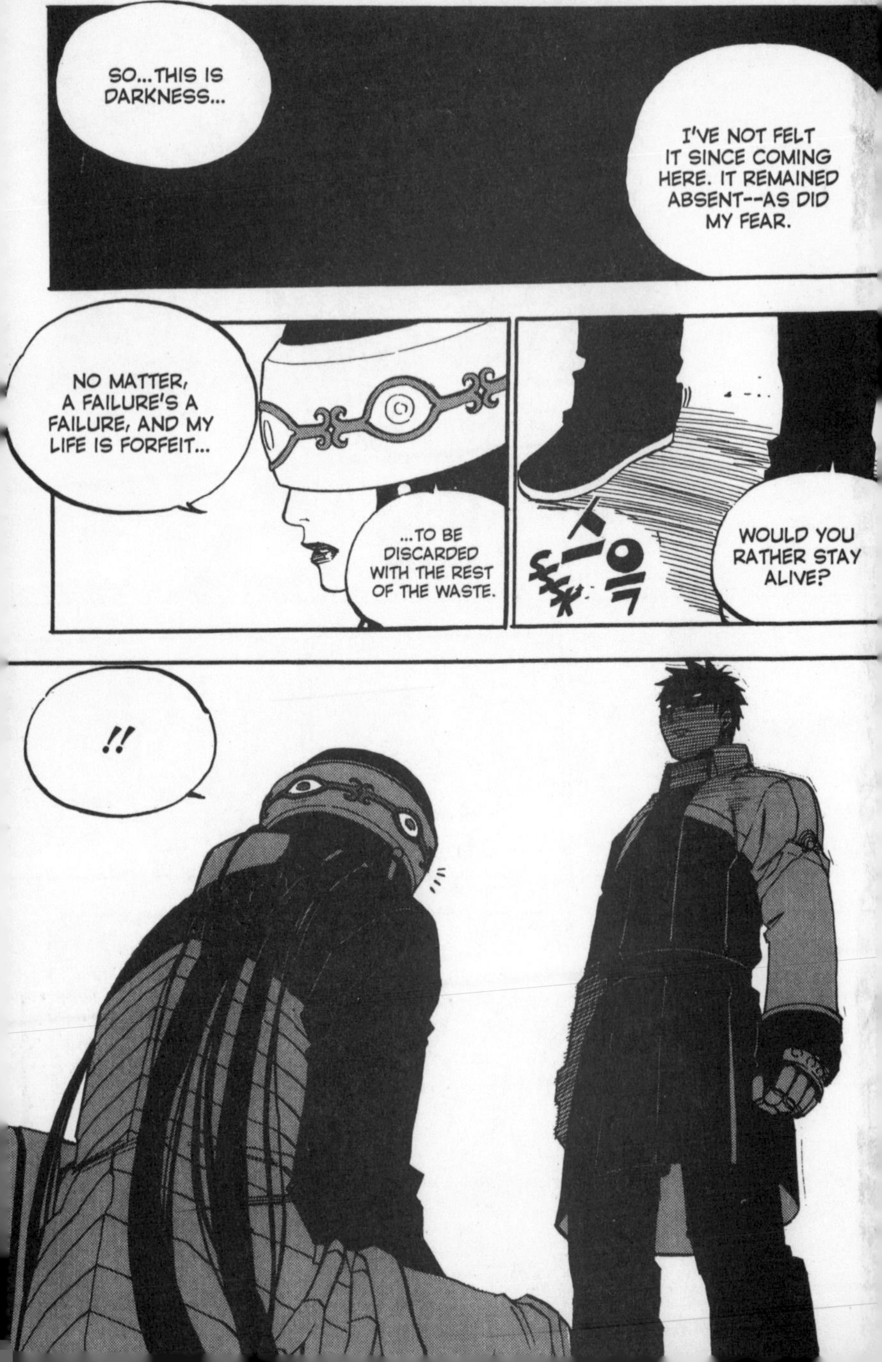
SO...THIS IS DARKNESS...
I'VE NOT FELT IT SINCE COMING HERE. IT REMAINED ABSENT--AS DID MY FEAR.
NO MATTER, A FAILURE'S A FAILURE, AND MY LIFE IS FORFEIT...
...TO BE DISCARDED WITH THE REST OF THE WASTE.
WOULD YOU RATHER STAY ALIVE?
!!

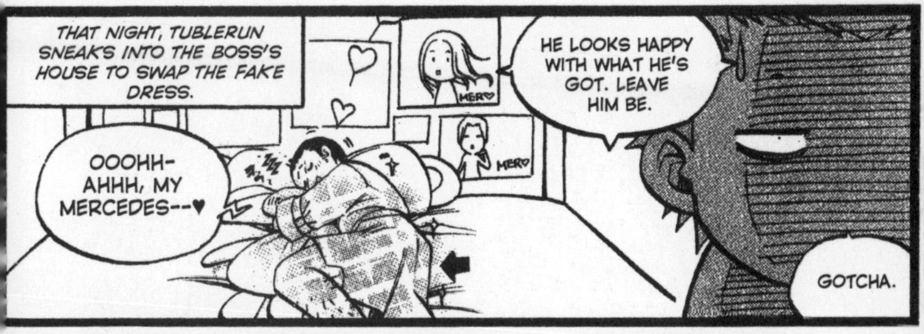
THAT NIGHT, TUBLERUN SNEAKS INTO THE BOSS'S HOUSE TO SWAP THE FAKE DRESS.
MER♡
MER♡
OOOHH-AHHH, MY MERCEDES--♥
HE LOOKS HAPPY WITH WHAT HE'S GOT. LEAVE HIM BE.
GOTCHA.

BACK TALK...
NO, NO...AFTER WORD?!

I'LL END CHAPTER 6 WITH SMALL TALK. THE CHARACTER DESIGNS BEHIND THE CYBER CEREBRO SPACE BATTLE WERE 'THE WIZARD OF OZ' FOR VERNA AND 'ALICE IN WONDERLAND' FOR HER OPPONENTS.

AT FIRST, I FOUGHT WITH DONG-EUN OVER THIS IDEA. I ARGUED THAT 'ALICE IN WONDERLAND' WAS SUPERIOR, WHILE DONG-EUN ROOTED FOR OZ. IN THE END, THE COMPROMISE WAS TO USE ONE FOR THE ENEMY AND ONE FOR VERNA.

AS YOU CAN SEE, THEY RESEMBLE THE SCARECROW, TIN WOODSMAN, AND COWARDLY LION. HUNK IS BASED ON STRUCTURAL JOINT PUPPETS, BUT I STRUGGLED REALLY HARD WITH THE TIN WOODSMAN. I DEBATED WHETHER I SHOULD INTRODUCE UNIQUE MECHANICAL STRUCTURES OR USE CLASSICAL MECHANICS. FOR THE FINAL DESIGN, I CHOSE TO GO WITH ROUND FORMS. ;) FOR THE LION, I THOUGHT OF AN ABSTRACT DESIGN WITHOUT A FACE OR LIMBS, BUT WITH ITS MUSCLES VISIBLE. ORIGINALLY, THIS WAS SOMETHING I HAD IN MIND FOR THE MONSTER RABBIT. I THOUGHT "RABBIT =MONSTER" WAS A BETTER EQUATION THAN "LION=MONSTER"...BUT WHY MESS WITH SOMETHING WHEN IT'S ALREADY SO GOOD? LIKE CATS WHOSE BODIES DISASSEMBLE...AND LASTLY, THE QUEEN OF CARDS. CARD-SHAPED SOLDIERS EVEN SHOWED UP IN THE MIDDLE THERE.

I GAVE VERNA THE ABILITY TO CHANGE DESIGNS WHILE INSIDE THE CYBER CEREBRO SPACE JUST LIKE ONE MIGHT IN A VIDEO GAME, APPEARING IN A COMPOSITE OF GENERAL LEE SUN-SHIN'S ARMOR AND OTHER MILITARY ARMORS. AT FIRST, IT WAS SIMPLE AND REPRESENTATIVE OF ARMOR WORN BY A MILITARY GENERAL, BUT I LATER ADDED FEATHERS ON THE HELMET AND MANTLE. SADLY, THE EDITORS DIDN'T AGREE, SO I HAD TO GET RID OF THEM. ;(
I DON'T KNOW IF WE'LL GET TO SEE THE CYBER CEREBRO SPACE AGAIN.

WE STILL HAVE PLENTY OF TRICKS UP OUR SLEEVES! ☺

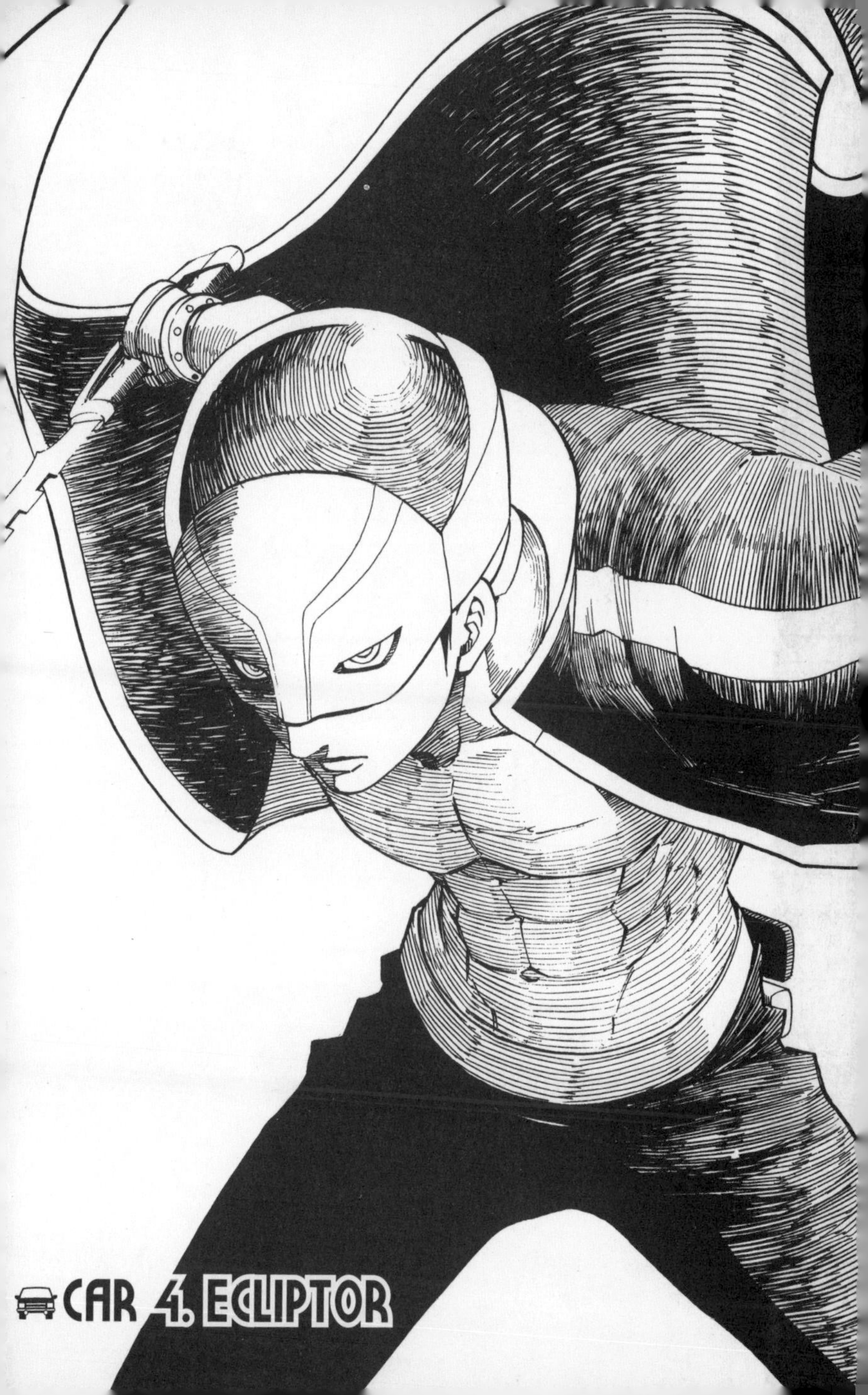

CAR 4. ECLIPTOR

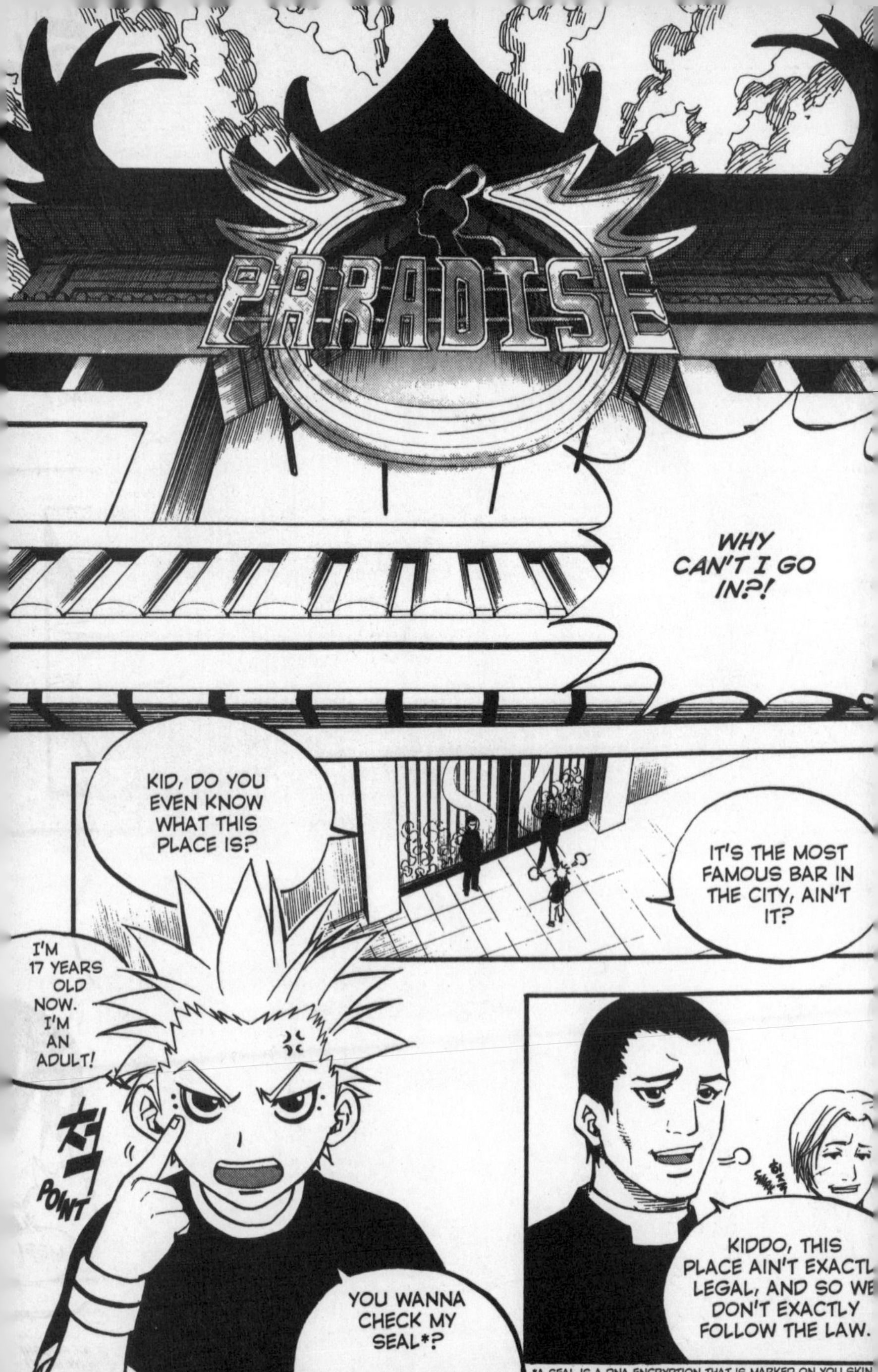
PARADISE
WHY CAN'T I GO IN?!
KID, DO YOU EVEN KNOW WHAT THIS PLACE IS?
IT'S THE MOST FAMOUS BAR IN THE CITY, AIN'T IT?
I'M 17 YEARS OLD NOW. I'M AN ADULT!
POINT
YOU WANNA CHECK MY SEAL*?
KIDDO, THIS PLACE AIN'T EXACTL LEGAL, AND SO WE DON'T EXACTLY FOLLOW THE LAW.

*A SEAL IS A DNA ENCRYPTION THAT IS MARKED ON YOU SKIN LIKE A TATTOO. IT IS OFTEN USED IN LIEU OF AN ID.

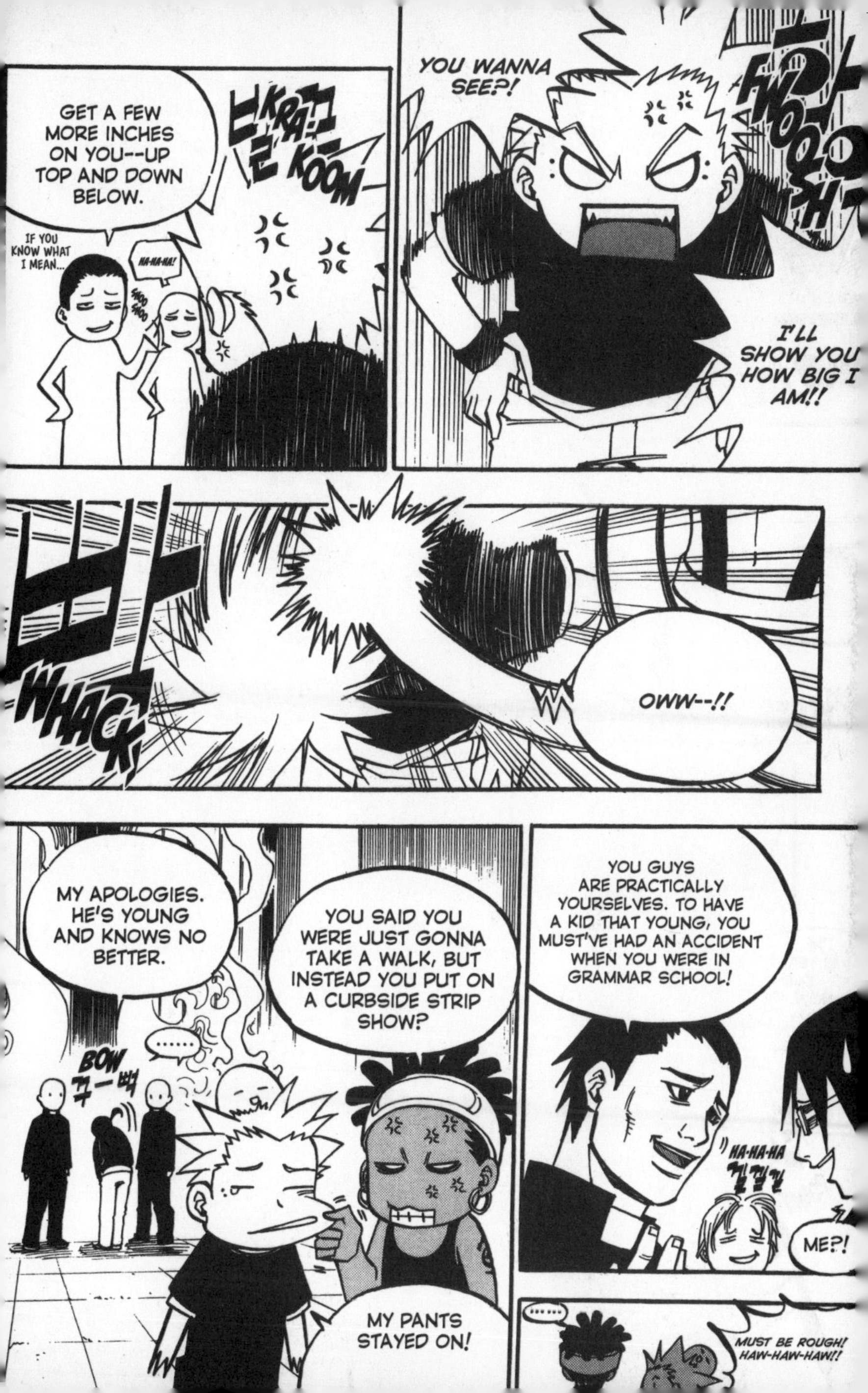
GET A FEW MORE INCHES ON YOU--UP TOP AND DOWN BELOW.
IF YOU KNOW WHAT I MEAN...
HA-HA-HA!
KRA-KOOM
YOU WANNA SEE?!
FWOOOSH
I'LL SHOW YOU HOW BIG I AM!!
WHACK
OWW--!!
MY APOLOGIES. HE'S YOUNG AND KNOWS NO BETTER.
......
BOW
꾸-벅
YOU SAID YOU WERE JUST GONNA TAKE A WALK, BUT INSTEAD YOU PUT ON A CURBSIDE STRIP SHOW?
MY PANTS STAYED ON!
YOU GUYS ARE PRACTICALLY YOURSELVES. TO HAVE A KID THAT YOUNG, YOU MUST'VE HAD AN ACCIDENT WHEN YOU WERE IN GRAMMAR SCHOOL!
HA-HA-HA
ME?!
......
MUST BE ROUGH! HAW-HAW-HAW!!

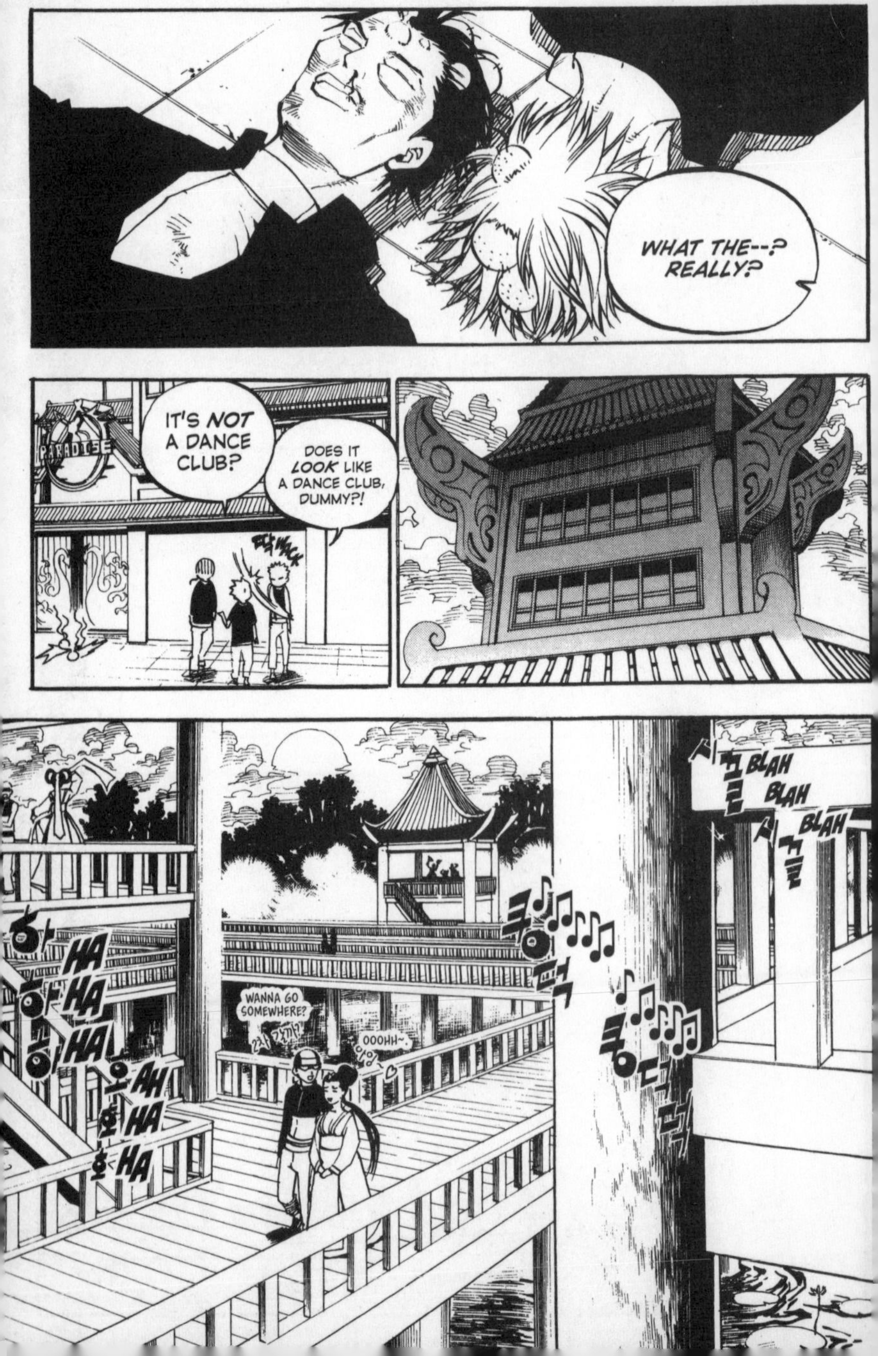
WHAT THE--? REALLY?
PARADISE
IT'S NOT A DANCE CLUB?
DOES IT LOOK LIKE A DANCE CLUB, DUMMY?!
WACK
HA HA HA
AH HA HA
WANNA GO SOMEWHERE?
OOOHH~
BLAH BLAH BLAH

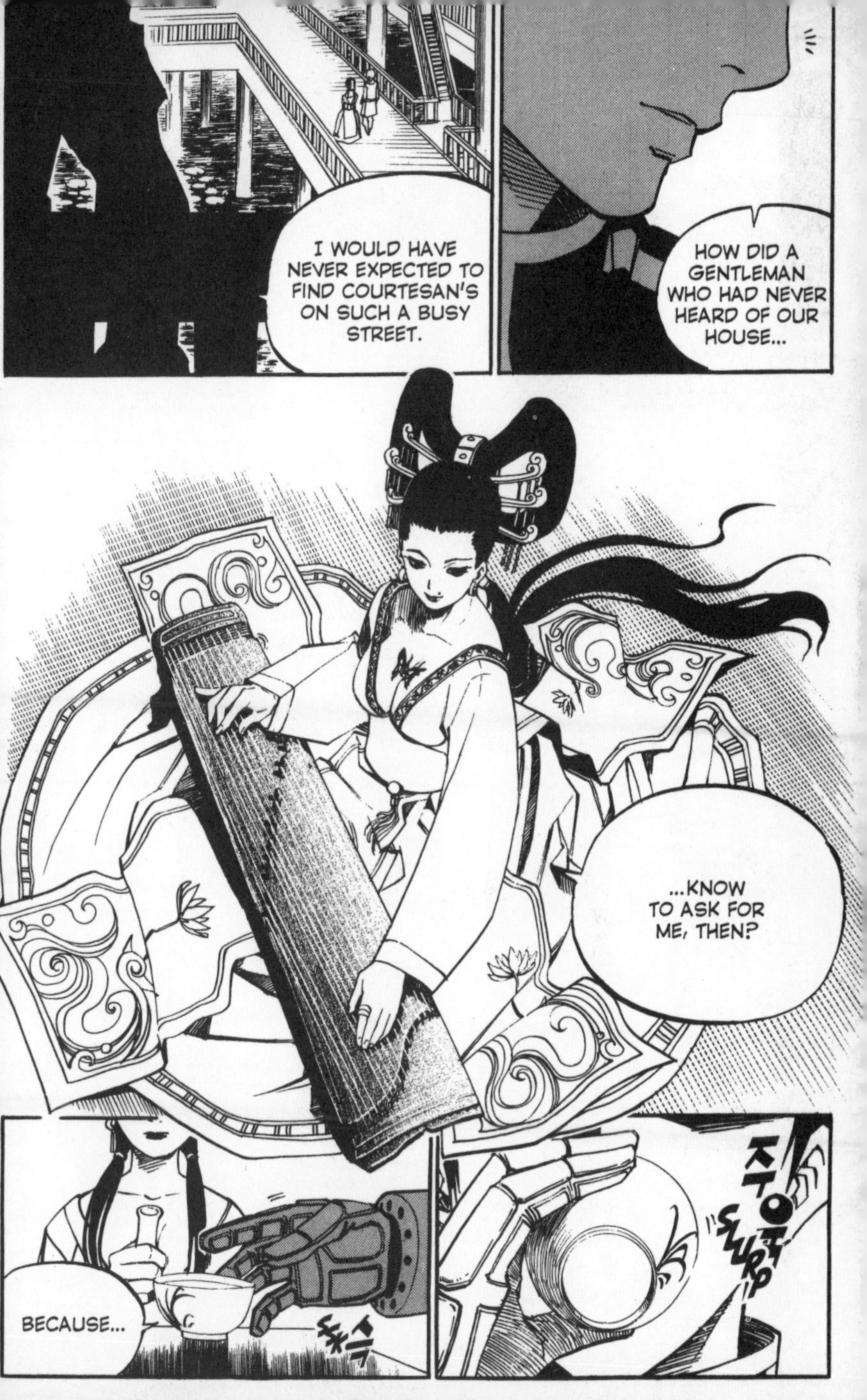
I WOULD HAVE NEVER EXPECTED TO FIND COURTESAN'S ON SUCH A BUSY STREET.
HOW DID A GENTLEMAN WHO HAD NEVER HEARD OF OUR HOUSE...
...KNOW TO ASK FOR ME, THEN?
BECAUSE...
SLURP!

...I FOLLOWED YOU.

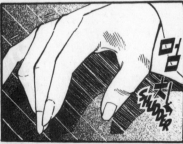

DOES THAT MEAN YOU WERE LOOKING FOR ME TO--.

FOUND HER!!

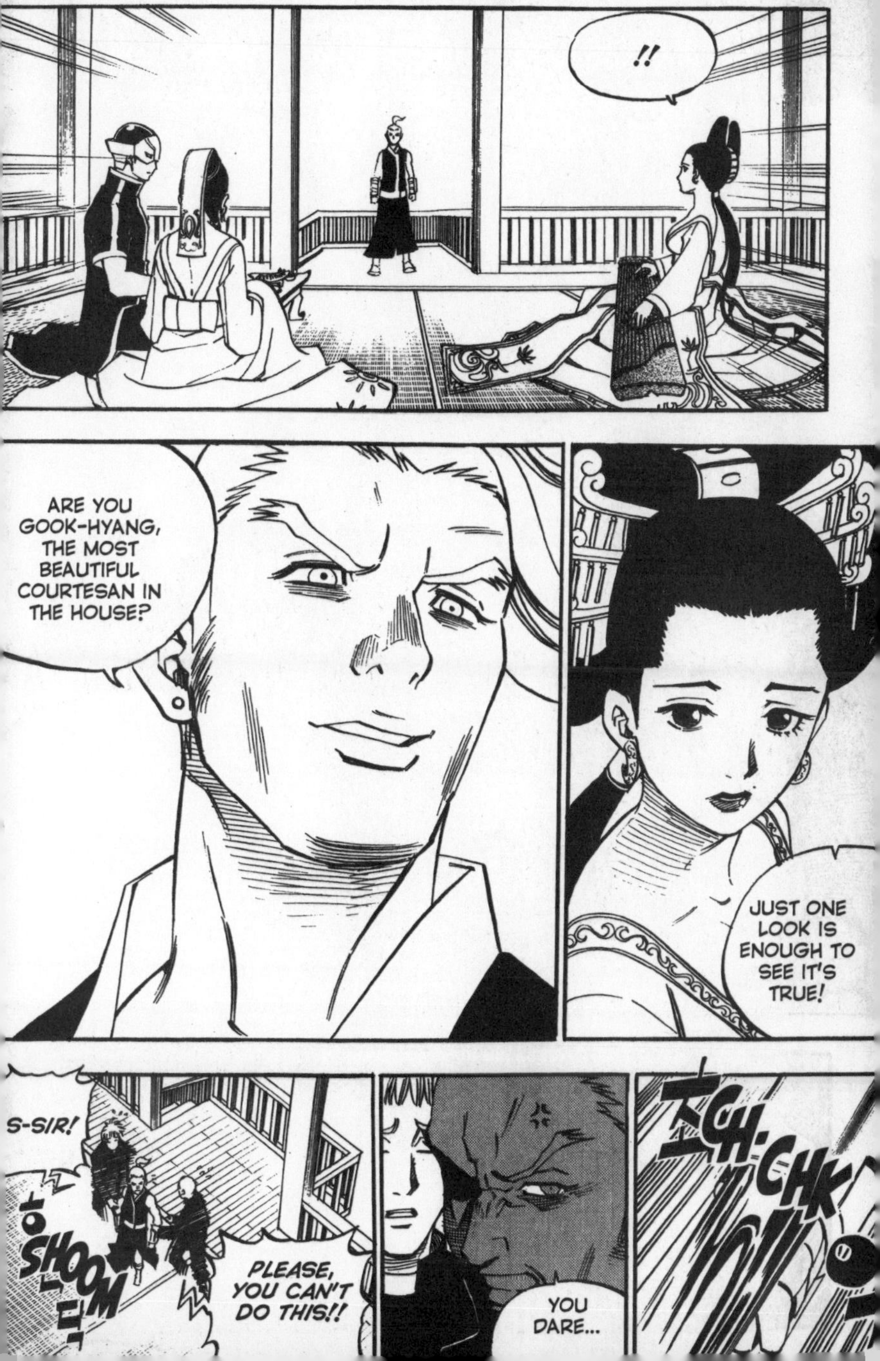

!!
ARE YOU GOOK-HYANG, THE MOST BEAUTIFUL COURTESAN IN THE HOUSE?
JUST ONE LOOK IS ENOUGH TO SEE IT'S TRUE!
S-SIR!
SHOOM
PLEASE, YOU CAN'T DO THIS!!
YOU DARE...
CH-CHK

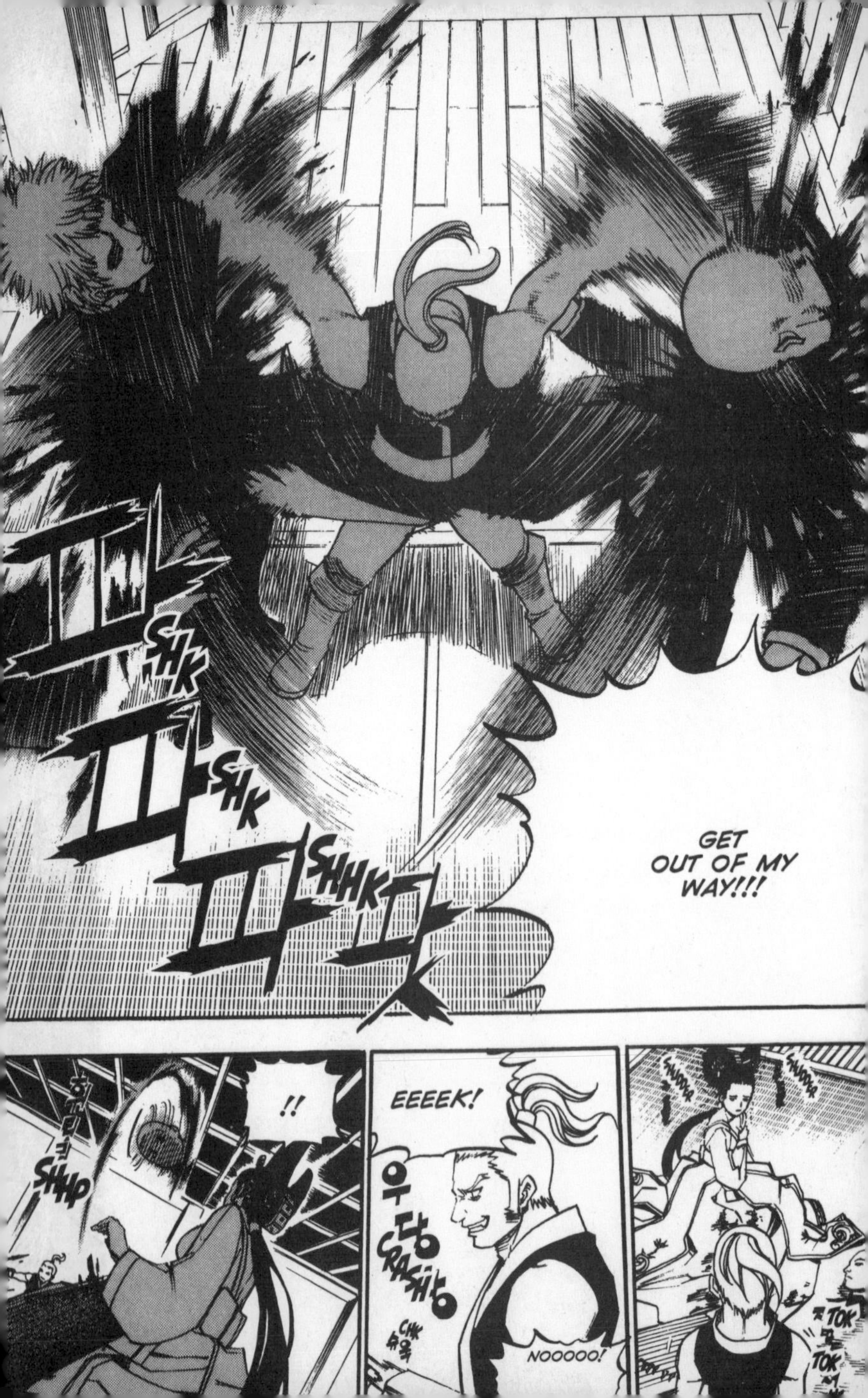
SHK
SHK
SHHK
GET OUT OF MY WAY!!!
SHHP
!!
EEEEK!
CRASH
CHK
NOOOOO!
SHUDDER
SHUDDER
TOK
TOK

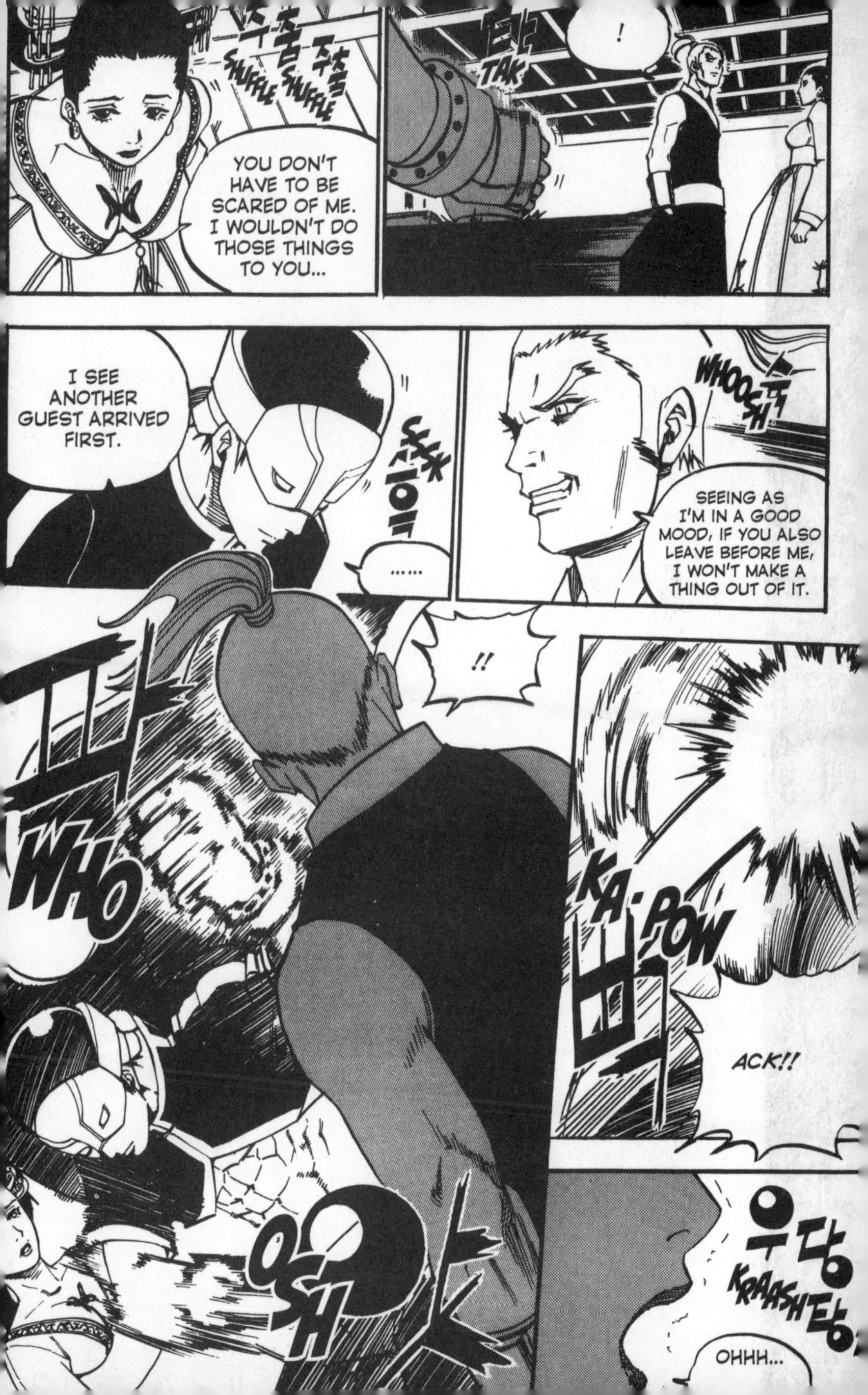
SHUFFLE SHUFFLE
YOU DON'T HAVE TO BE SCARED OF ME. I WOULDN'T DO THOSE THINGS TO YOU...
TAK
!
I SEE ANOTHER GUEST ARRIVED FIRST.
SEEK
......
WHOOSH
SEEING AS I'M IN A GOOD MOOD, IF YOU ALSO LEAVE BEFORE ME, I WON'T MAKE A THING OUT OF IT.
!!
WHOOSH
KA-POW
ACK!!
KRAASH
OHHH...

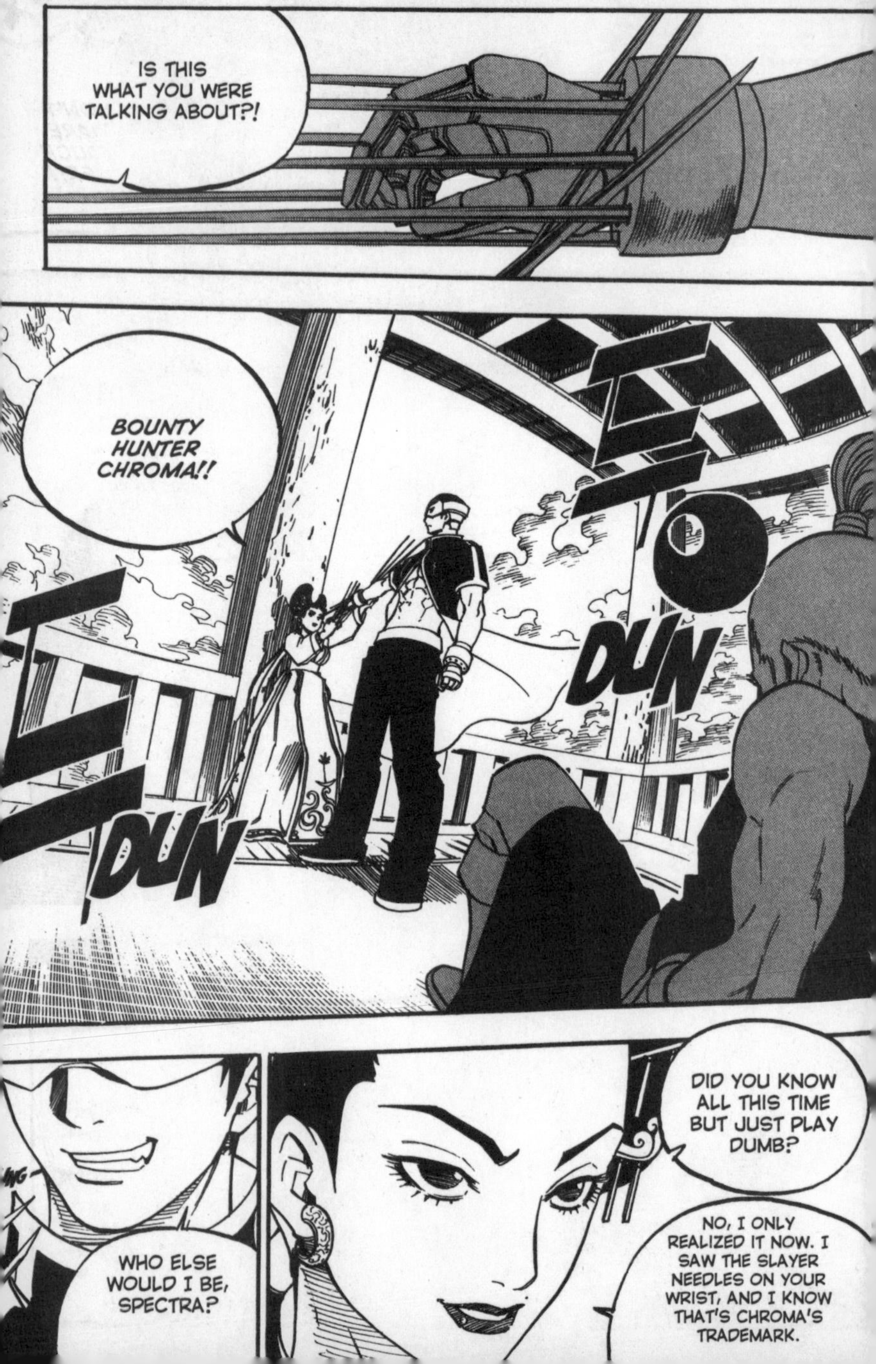
IS THIS WHAT YOU WERE TALKING ABOUT?!
BOUNTY HUNTER CHROMA!!
DUN
DUN
WHO ELSE WOULD I BE, SPECTRA?
DID YOU KNOW ALL THIS TIME BUT JUST PLAY DUMB?
NO, I ONLY REALIZED IT NOW. I SAW THE SLAYER NEEDLES ON YOUR WRIST, AND I KNOW THAT'S CHROMA'S TRADEMARK.

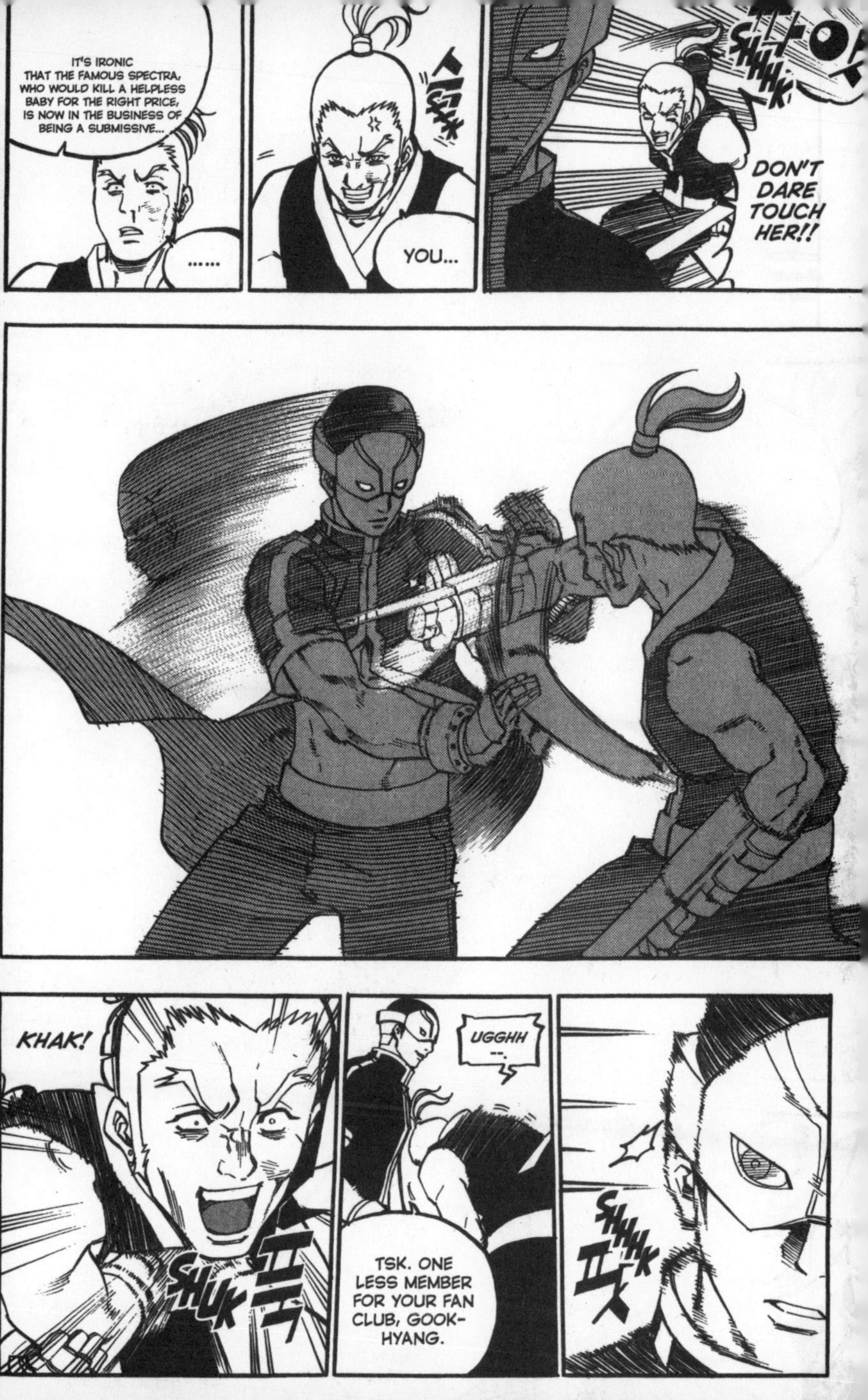
IT'S IRONIC THAT THE FAMOUS SPECTRA, WHO WOULD KILL A HELPLESS BABY FOR THE RIGHT PRICE, IS NOW IN THE BUSINESS OF BEING A SUBMISSIVE...
......
YOU...
SHHHK
DON'T DARE TOUCH HER!!
KHAK!
SHUK
UGGHH --.
TSK. ONE LESS MEMBER FOR YOUR FAN CLUB, GOOK-HYANG.
SHHHK

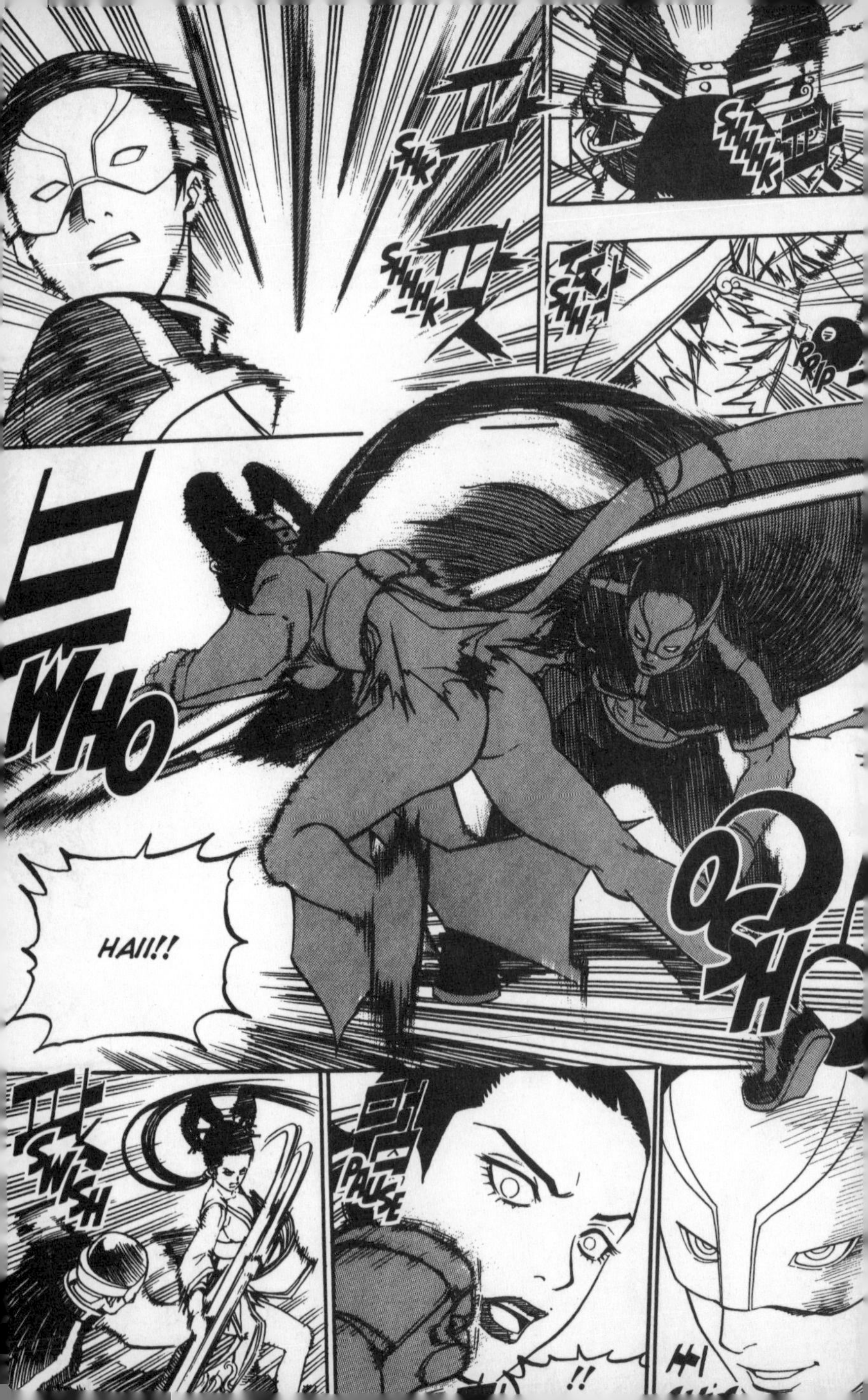
SHK
SHHHK
SHHHK
SHH
RRIP
WHO
HAII!!
OSH
SWISH
PAUSE
!!

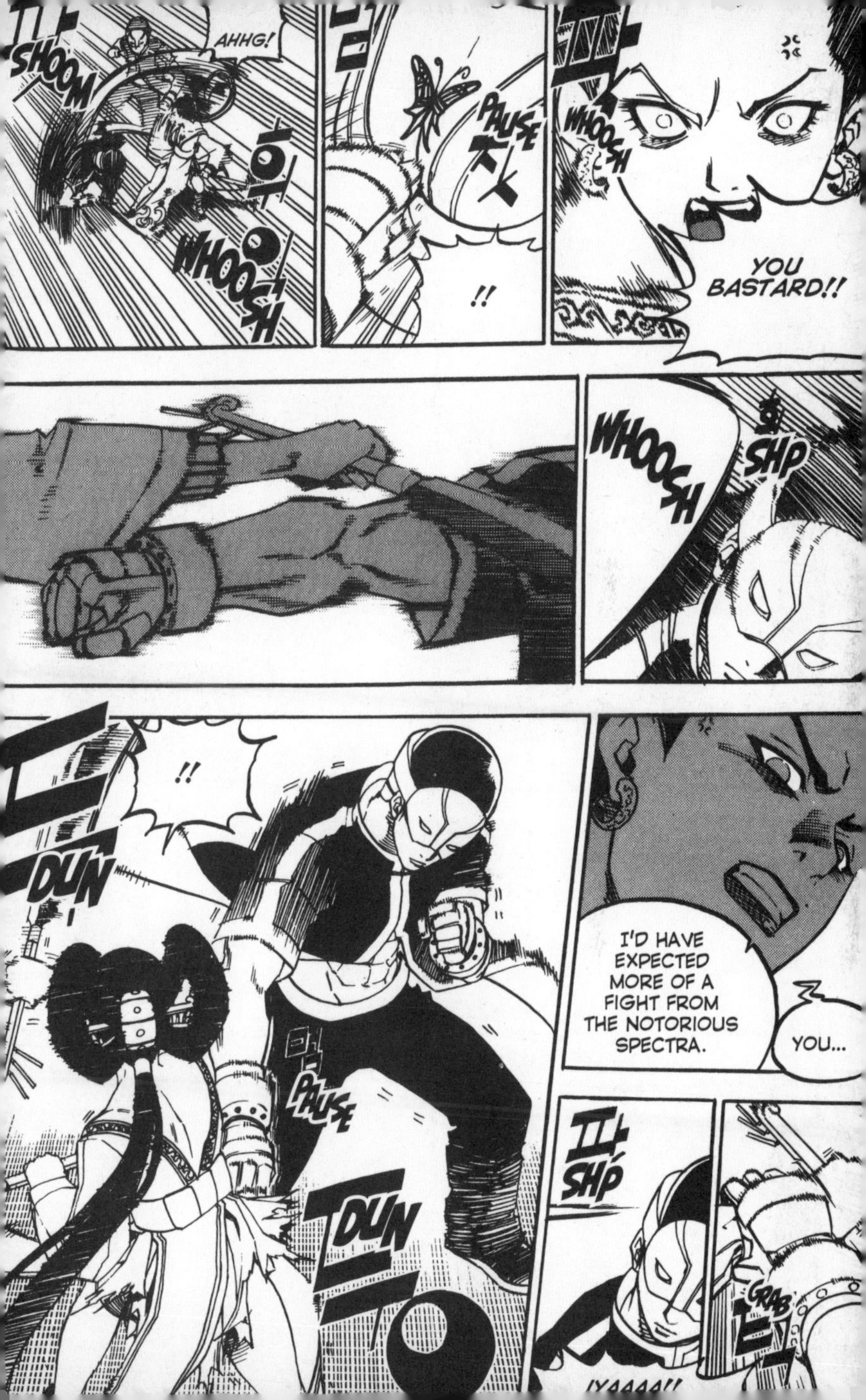
SHOOM
AHHG!
WHOOSH
PAUSE
!!
WHOOSH
YOU BASTARD!!
WHOOSH
SHP
!!
DUN
PAUSE
DUN
I'D HAVE EXPECTED MORE OF A FIGHT FROM THE NOTORIOUS SPECTRA.
YOU...
SHP
GRAB

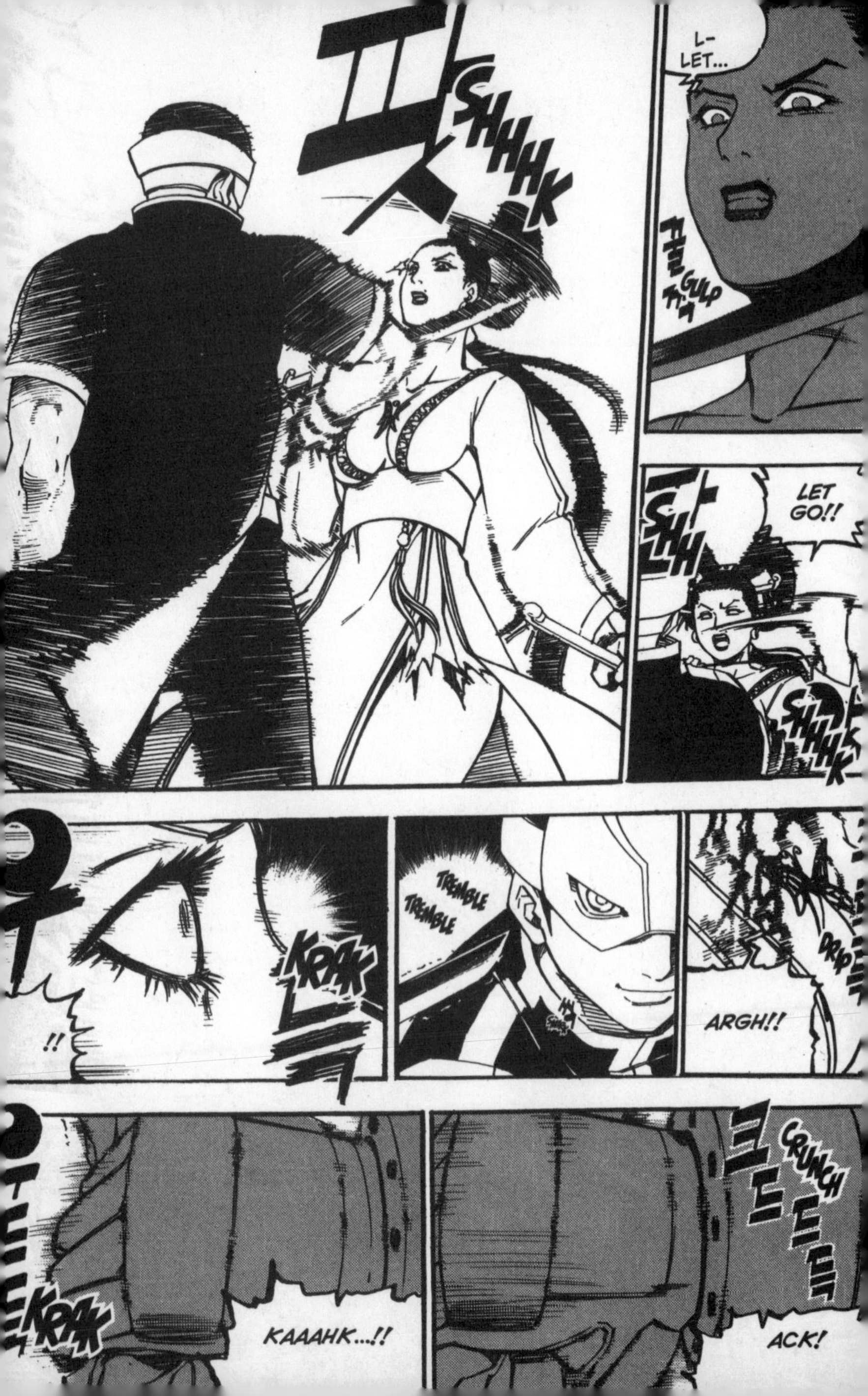
SHHHHK
L-
LET...
GULP
SHHH
LET GO!!
SHHHHK
!!
KRAK
TREMBLE
TREMBLE
DRIP
ARGH!!
KRAK
KAAAHK...!!
CRUNCH
ACK!

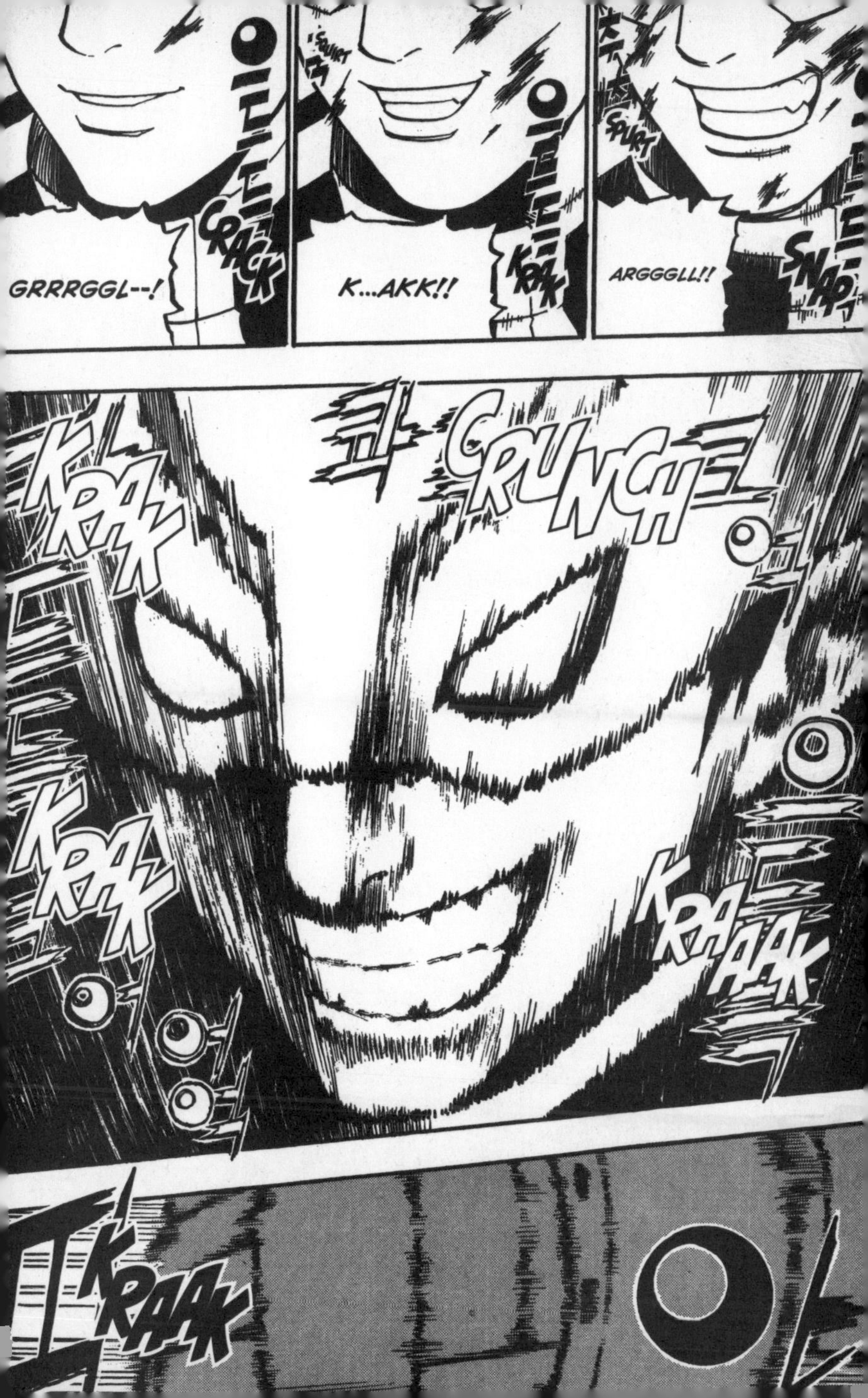
GRRRGGL--!
CRACK
SQUIRT
K...AKK!!
KRAK
SPURT
ARGGGLL!!
SNAP
KRAK
CRUNCH
KRAK
KRAAK
KRAAK

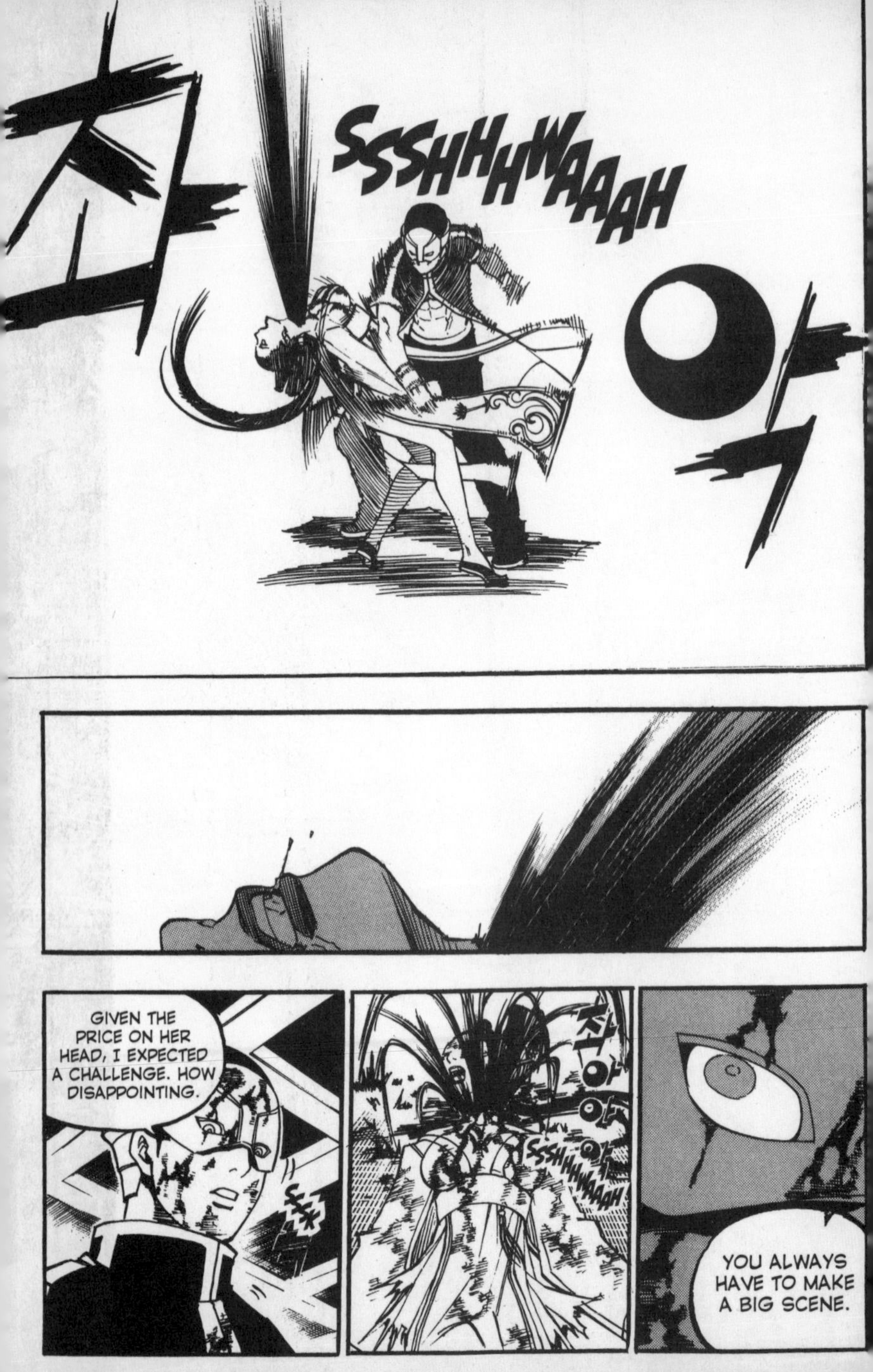
SSSHHHWAAAAH
GIVEN THE PRICE ON HER HEAD, I EXPECTED A CHALLENGE. HOW DISAPPOINTING.
SSSHHWAAAH
YOU ALWAYS HAVE TO MAKE A BIG SCENE.

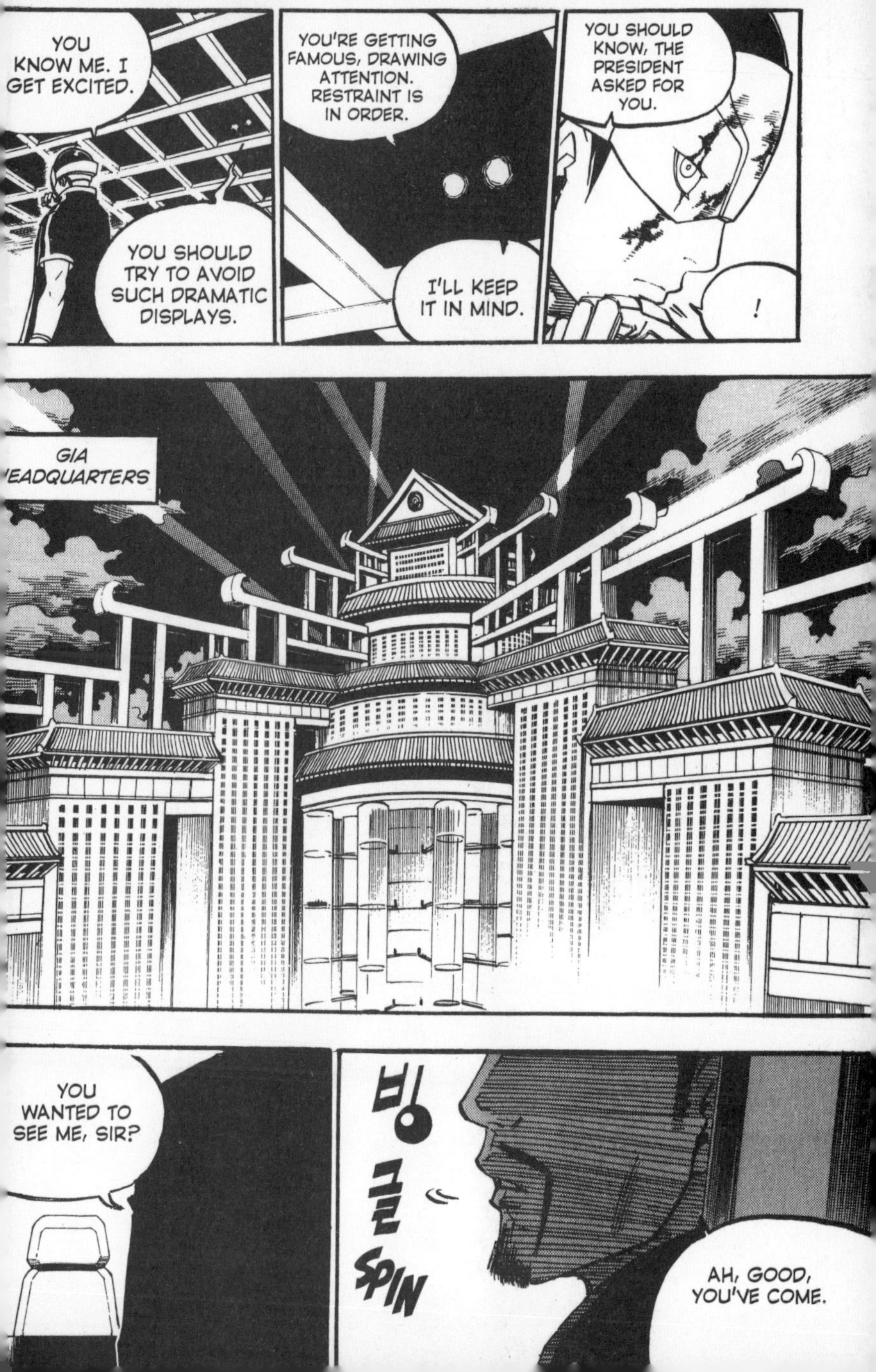
YOU KNOW ME. I GET EXCITED.
YOU SHOULD TRY TO AVOID SUCH DRAMATIC DISPLAYS.
YOU'RE GETTING FAMOUS, DRAWING ATTENTION. RESTRAINT IS IN ORDER.
I'LL KEEP IT IN MIND.
YOU SHOULD KNOW, THE PRESIDENT ASKED FOR YOU.
!
GIA HEADQUARTERS
YOU WANTED TO SEE ME, SIR?
빙글
SPIN
AH, GOOD, YOU'VE COME.

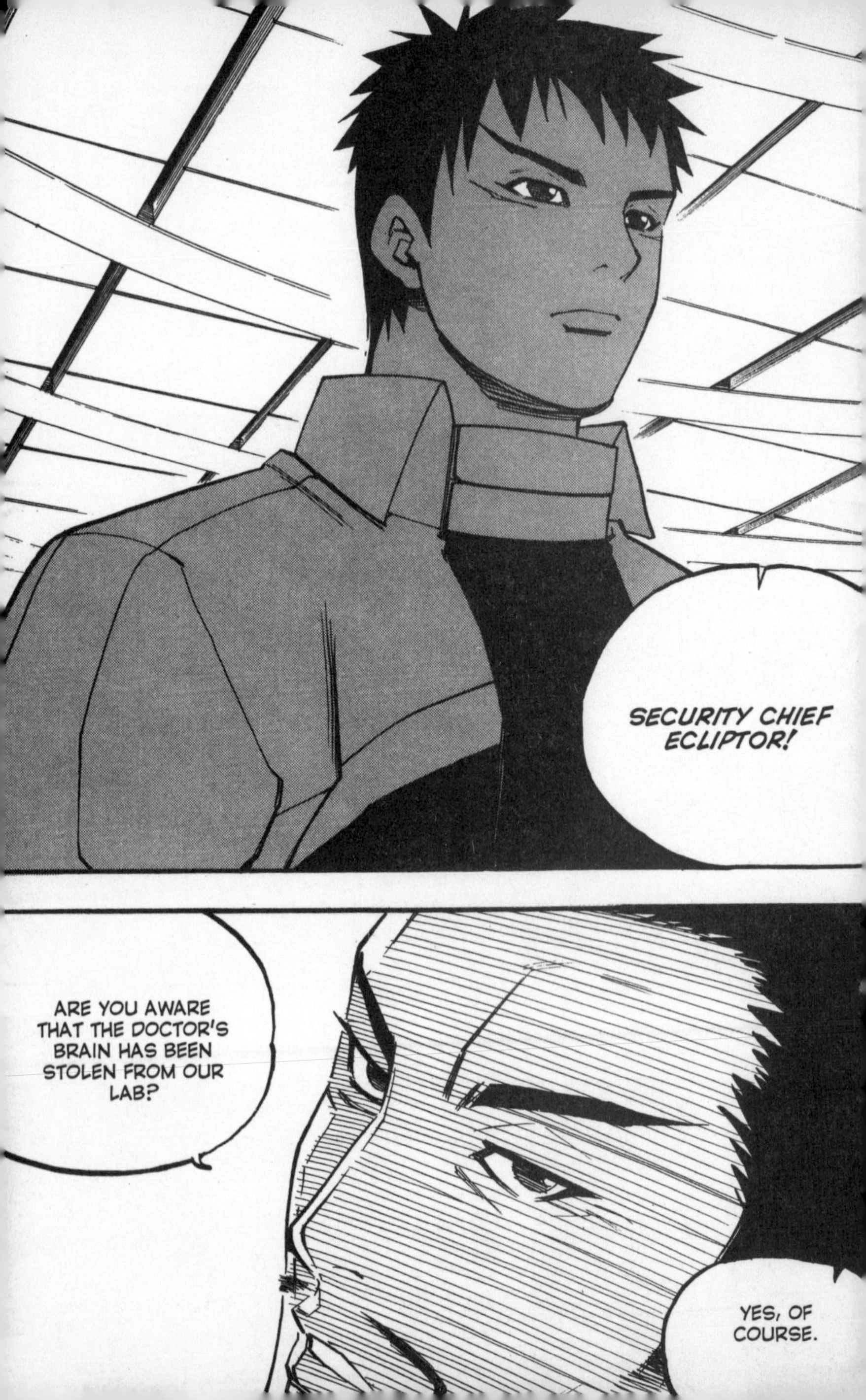
SECURITY CHIEF ECLIPTOR!
ARE YOU AWARE THAT THE DOCTOR'S BRAIN HAS BEEN STOLEN FROM OUR LAB?
YES, OF COURSE.

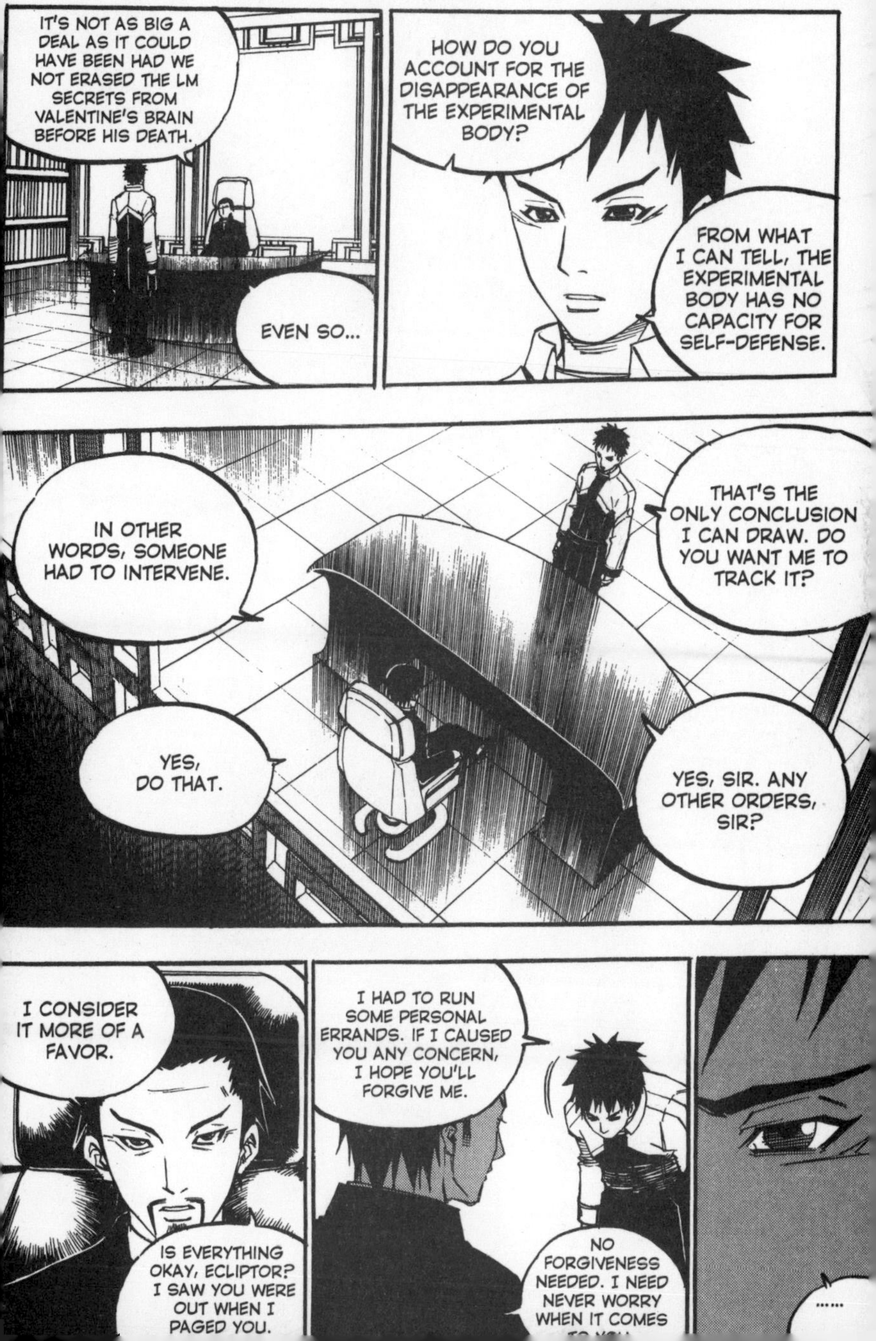
IT'S NOT AS BIG A DEAL AS IT COULD HAVE BEEN HAD WE NOT ERASED THE LM SECRETS FROM VALENTINE'S BRAIN BEFORE HIS DEATH.
EVEN SO...
HOW DO YOU ACCOUNT FOR THE DISAPPEARANCE OF THE EXPERIMENTAL BODY?
FROM WHAT I CAN TELL, THE EXPERIMENTAL BODY HAS NO CAPACITY FOR SELF-DEFENSE.
IN OTHER WORDS, SOMEONE HAD TO INTERVENE.
THAT'S THE ONLY CONCLUSION I CAN DRAW. DO YOU WANT ME TO TRACK IT?
YES, DO THAT.
YES, SIR. ANY OTHER ORDERS, SIR?
I CONSIDER IT MORE OF A FAVOR.
IS EVERYTHING OKAY, ECLIPTOR? I SAW YOU WERE OUT WHEN I PAGED YOU.
I HAD TO RUN SOME PERSONAL ERRANDS. IF I CAUSED YOU ANY CONCERN, I HOPE YOU'LL FORGIVE ME.
NO FORGIVENESS NEEDED. I NEED NEVER WORRY WHEN IT COMES
......

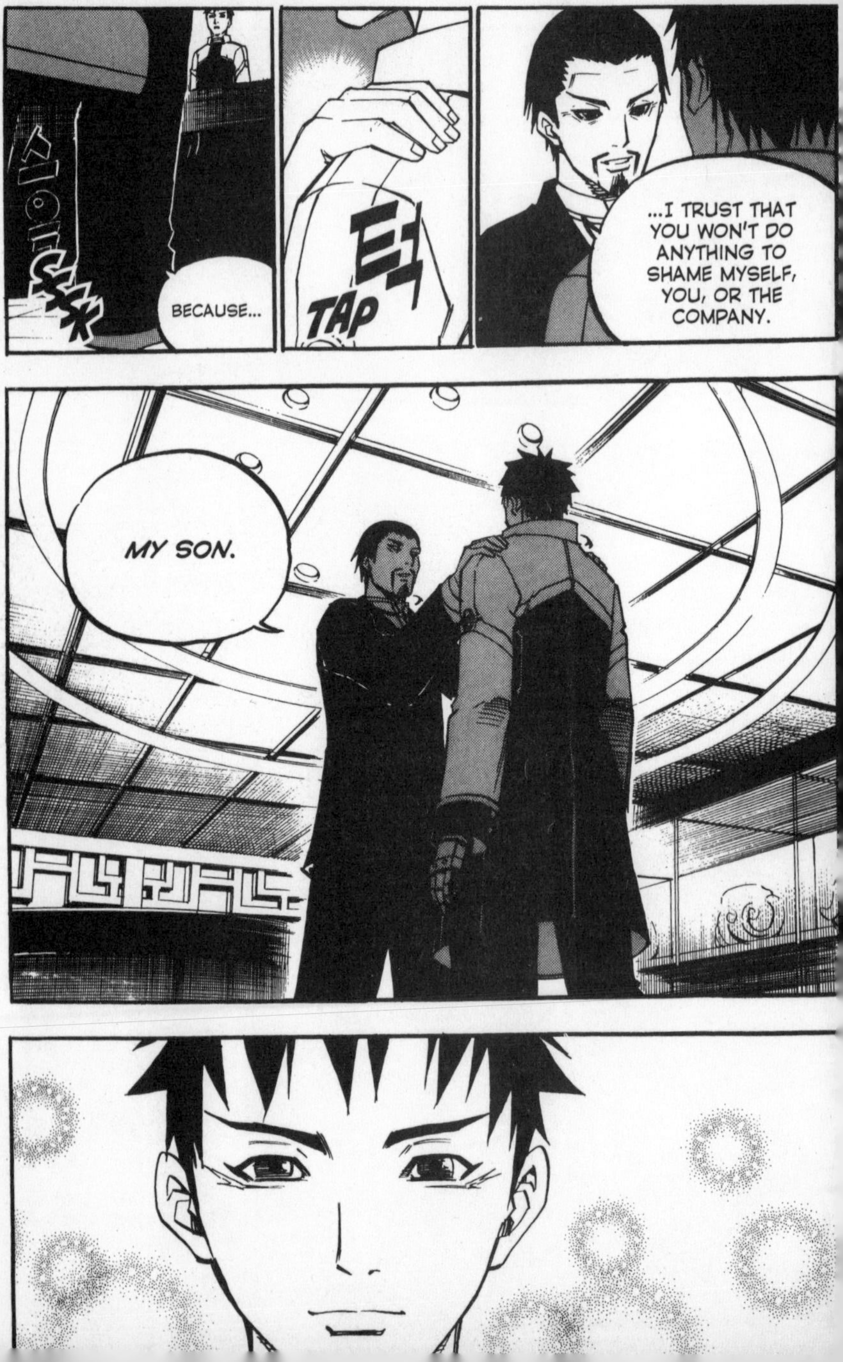
BECAUSE...
TAP
...I TRUST THAT YOU WON'T DO ANYTHING TO SHAME MYSELF, YOU, OR THE COMPANY.
MY SON.

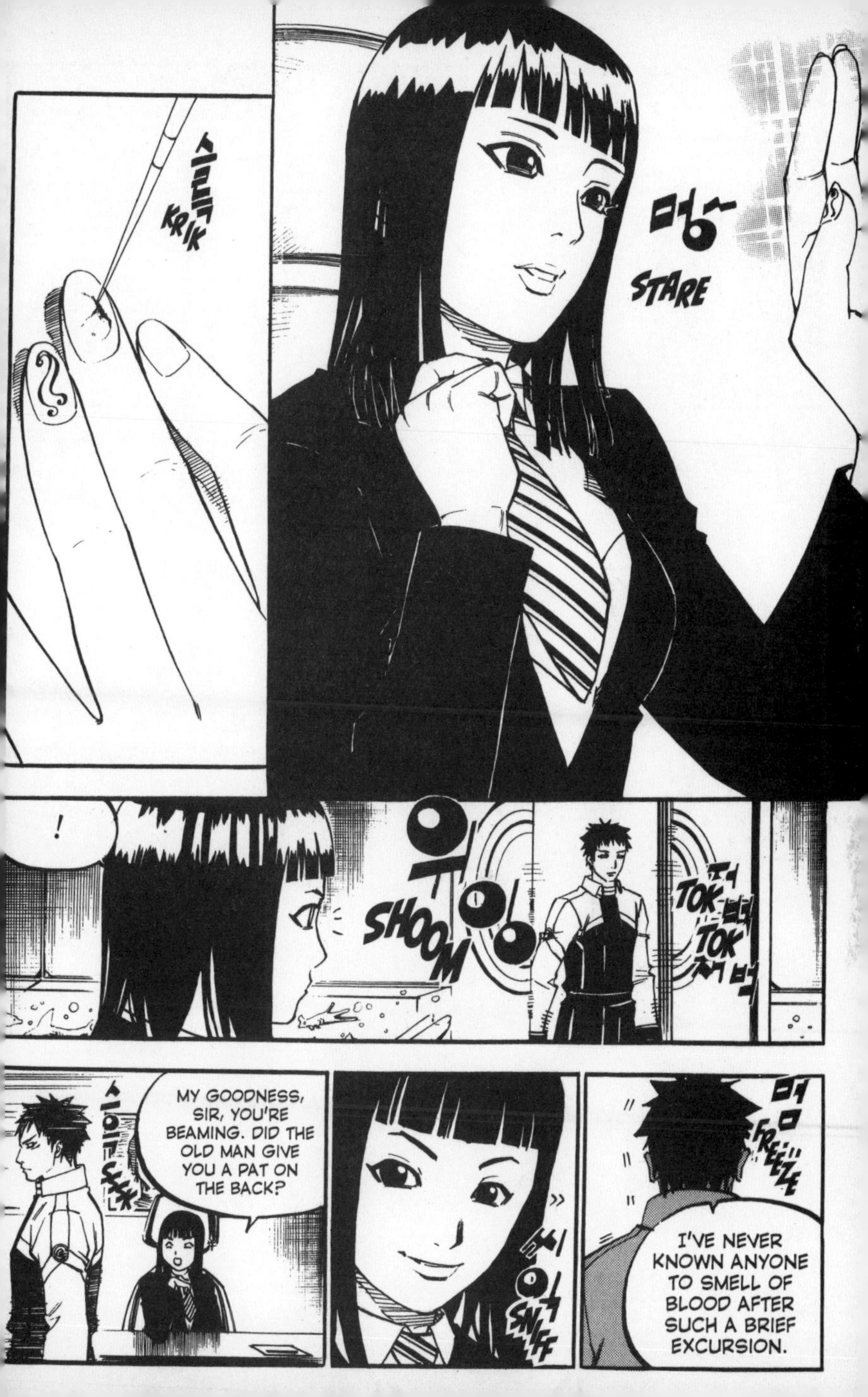

KRIK
STARE
!
SHOOM
TOK TOK
SKK
MY GOODNESS, SIR, YOU'RE BEAMING. DID THE OLD MAN GIVE YOU A PAT ON THE BACK?
SNIFF
FREEZE
I'VE NEVER KNOWN ANYONE TO SMELL OF BLOOD AFTER SUCH A BRIEF EXCURSION.

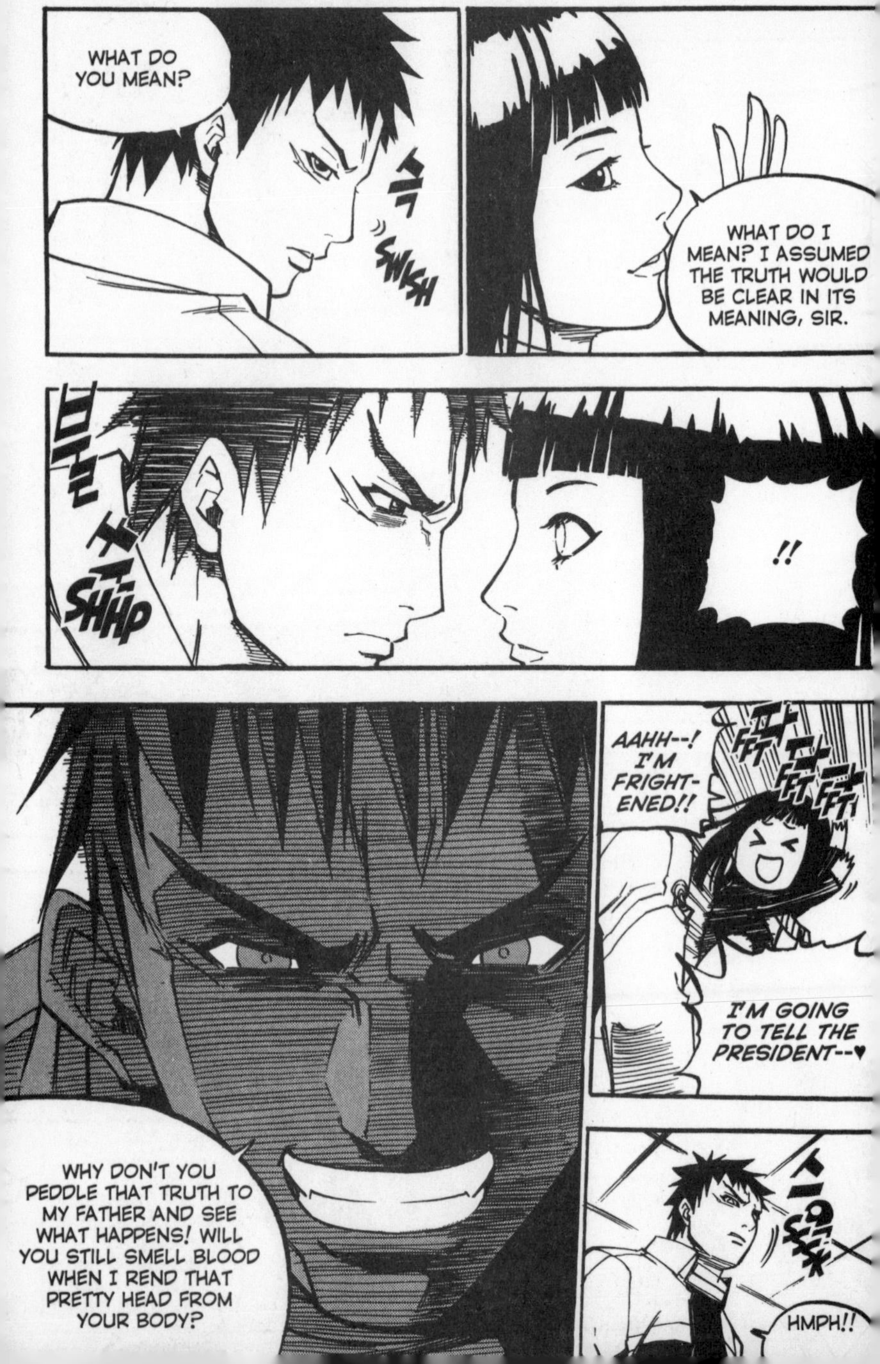
WHAT DO YOU MEAN?
SWISH
WHAT DO I MEAN? I ASSUMED THE TRUTH WOULD BE CLEAR IN ITS MEANING, SIR.
SHHP
!!
WHY DON'T YOU PEDDLE THAT TRUTH TO MY FATHER AND SEE WHAT HAPPENS! WILL YOU STILL SMELL BLOOD WHEN I REND THAT PRETTY HEAD FROM YOUR BODY?
AAHH--! I'M FRIGHT-ENED!!
FFT
FFT
FFT
I'M GOING TO TELL THE PRESIDENT--♥
HMPH!!

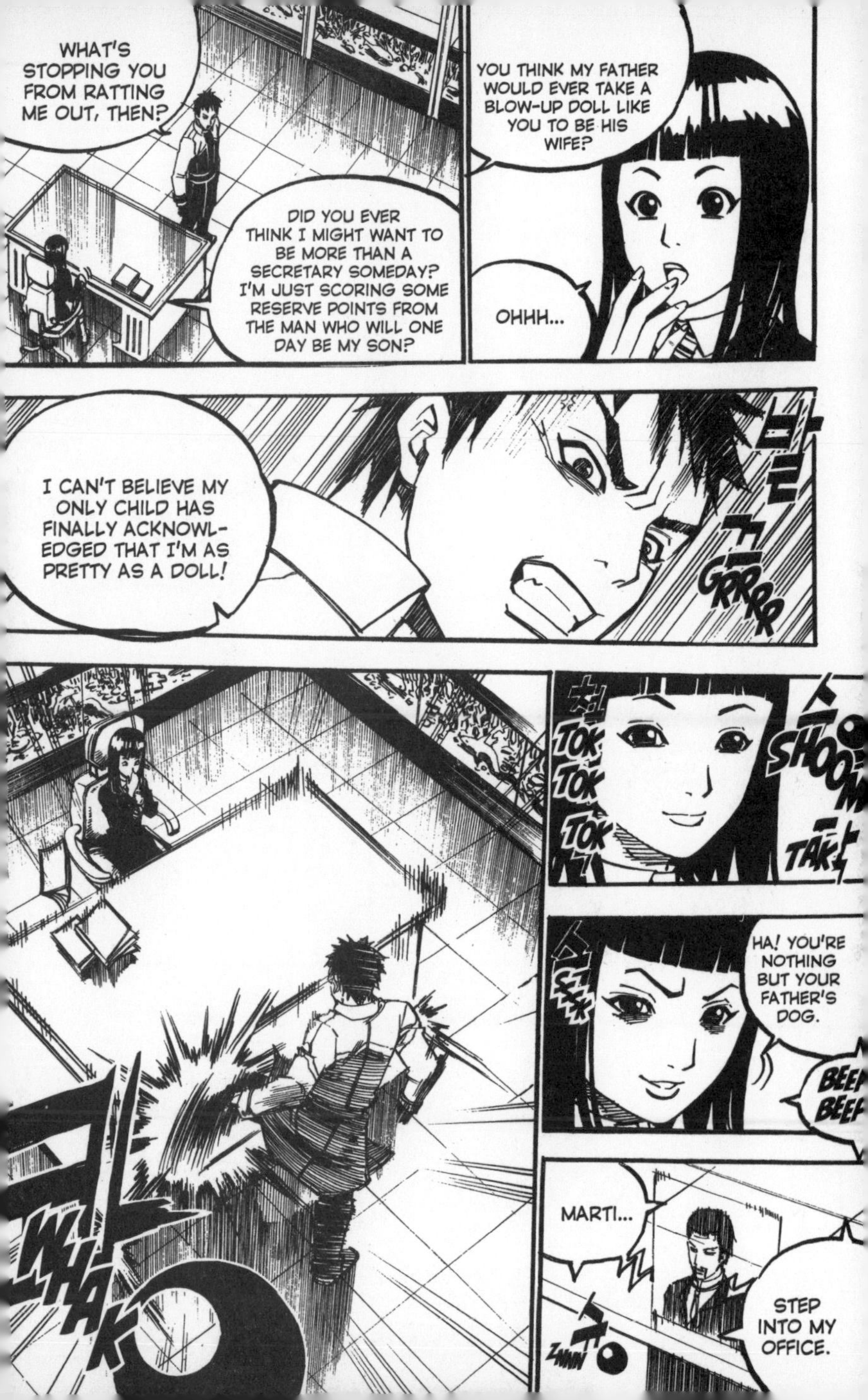
WHAT'S STOPPING YOU FROM RATTING ME OUT, THEN?
DID YOU EVER THINK I MIGHT WANT TO BE MORE THAN A SECRETARY SOMEDAY? I'M JUST SCORING SOME RESERVE POINTS FROM THE MAN WHO WILL ONE DAY BE MY SON?
YOU THINK MY FATHER WOULD EVER TAKE A BLOW-UP DOLL LIKE YOU TO BE HIS WIFE?
OHHH...
I CAN'T BELIEVE MY ONLY CHILD HAS FINALLY ACKNOWL-EDGED THAT I'M AS PRETTY AS A DOLL!
GRRRR
WHAK
TOK TOK TOK
SHOOM
TAK
HA! YOU'RE NOTHING BUT YOUR FATHER'S DOG.
MARTI...
ZNNN
STEP INTO MY OFFICE.

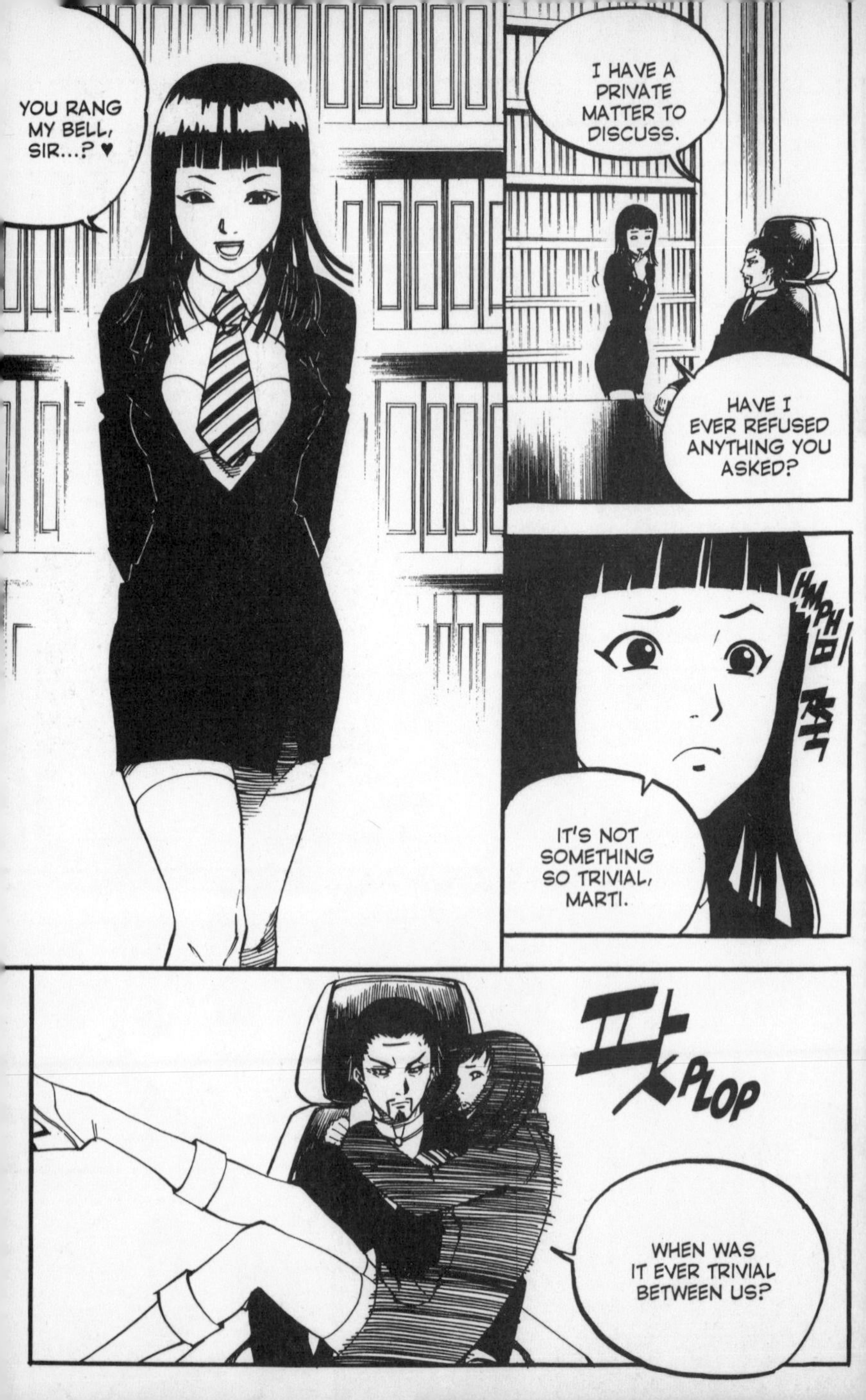
YOU RANG MY BELL, SIR...? ♥
I HAVE A PRIVATE MATTER TO DISCUSS.
HAVE I EVER REFUSED ANYTHING YOU ASKED?
HMPH!
IT'S NOT SOMETHING SO TRIVIAL, MARTI.
PLOP
WHEN WAS IT EVER TRIVIAL BETWEEN US?

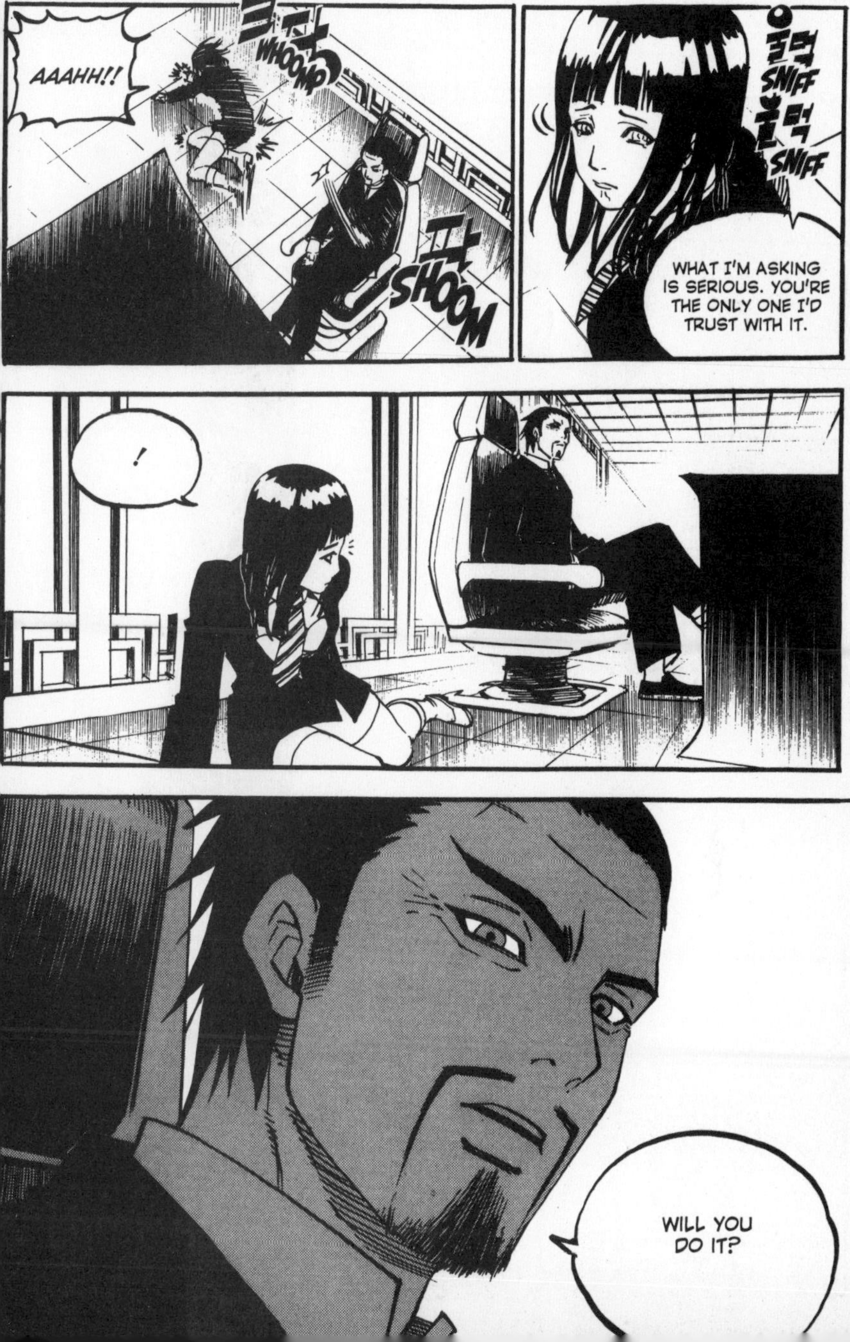

AAAHH!!
WHOOMP
SHOOM
SNIFF
SNIFF
WHAT I'M ASKING IS SERIOUS. YOU'RE THE ONLY ONE I'D TRUST WITH IT.
!
WILL YOU DO IT?

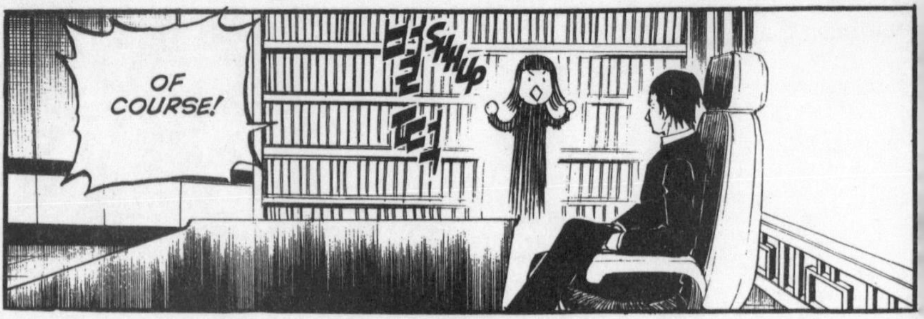
OF COURSE!
벌떡
SHHUP

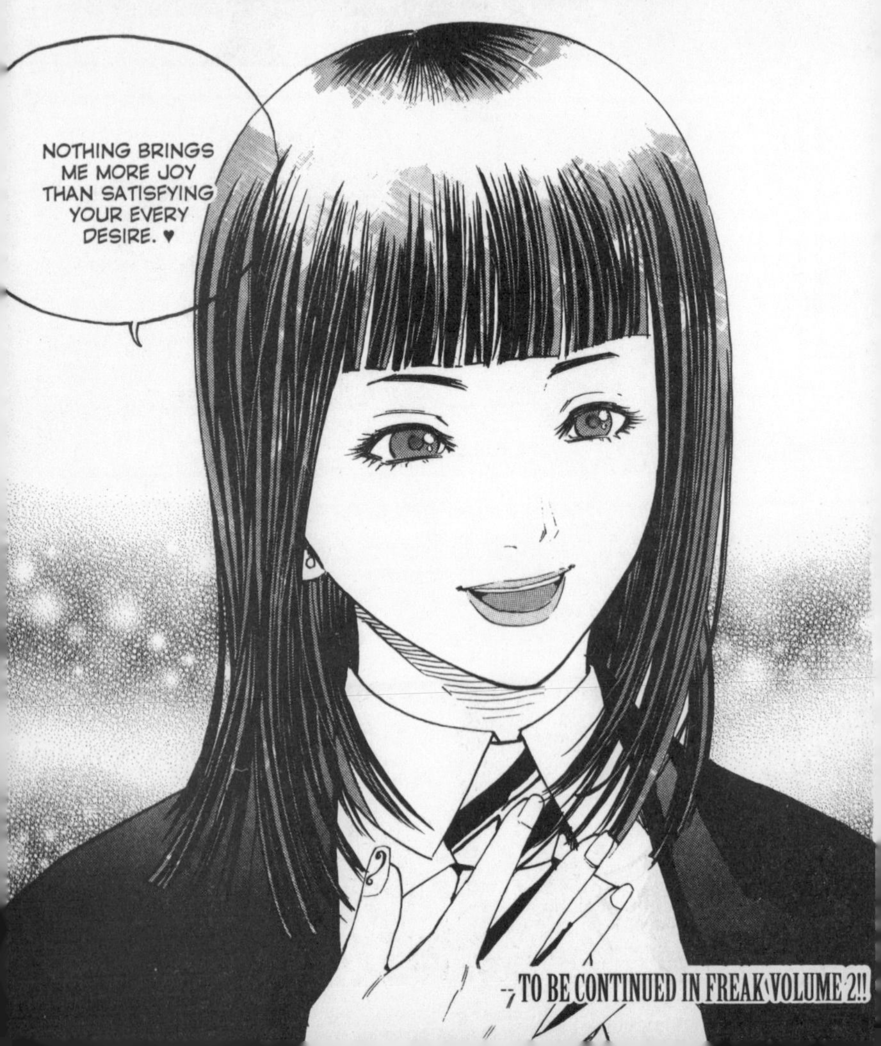
NOTHING BRINGS ME MORE JOY THAN SATISFYING YOUR EVERY DESIRE. ♥
TO BE CONTINUED IN FREAK VOLUME 2!!

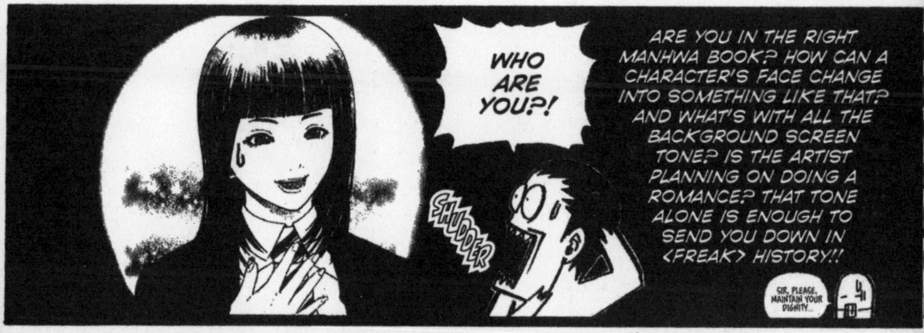
WHO ARE YOU?!
SHUDDER
ARE YOU IN THE RIGHT MANHWA BOOK? HOW CAN A CHARACTER'S FACE CHANGE INTO SOMETHING LIKE THAT? AND WHAT'S WITH ALL THE BACKGROUND SCREEN TONE? IS THE ARTIST PLANNING ON DOING A ROMANCE? THAT TONE ALONE IS ENOUGH TO SEND YOU DOWN IN <FREAK> HISTORY!!
SIR, PLEASE, MAINTAIN YOUR DIGNITY...

BACK TALK...
NO, NO...AFTER WORD?!

IN THIS CHAPTER, CHARACTERS WHO WILL BE IMPORTANT TO THE WHOLE STORY FINALLY MADE THEIR FIRST APPEARANCE: ECLIPTOR/CHROMA AND MARTI. SADLY, THE PRESIDENT DOESN'T HAVE AS LARGE A ROLE. IT'S OBVIOUS I LIKE COLD AND RATIONAL CHARACTERS. MY FAVORITE PASTIME IS DRAWING CYNICAL SMILES...AT FIRST, ECLIPTOR WAS THE EASIEST TO DRAW AND TUBI WAS THE HARDEST, BUT NOW, MAYBE BECAUSE HE'S COME INTO THE NARRATIVE SO LATE...I FOUND MYSELF AT A LOSS ON HOW BEST TO DRAW HIM. THE CHARACTERS GOT ALL MIXED AROUND IN THE STORY. INITIALLY, CHAPTER 1 WAS TO BE ABOUT TUBLERUN, AND CHAPTER 2 WAS TO BE ABOUT ECLIPTOR. THAT CHANGED, OBVIOUSLY, AND I'M REGRETTING THAT THE SECOND MAJOR CHARACTER MADE HIS DEBUT APPEARANCE SO FAR IN. READERS, DO YOU THINK THAT <FREAK> IS MERELY ANOTHER STORY ABOUT DARING THIEVES, SOMETHING LIKE THE GETBACKERS? (THIS IS GETTING DANGEROUSLY CLOSE TO LIBEL.) HONESTLY, I GET UPSET WHENEVER SOMEONE MAKES THAT KIND OF COMPARISON. I PUT THE MIDDLE EPISODE IN THE BOOK TO SHOW THE PERSONALITIES OF ALL THE CHARACTERS AND ESTABLISH THE AMBIENCE OF THEIR LIVES, BUT IT GREW BEYOND MY CONTROL. ROBBERY IS JUST THEIR DAY JOB. ACTUALLY, IN THE BEGINNING, THEY WERE INDUSTRIAL SPIES AND NOT CROOKS FOR HIRE. HOW DID THINGS CHANGE SO MUCH...? "INDUSTRIAL SPY!"...IT HAS A NICE RING TO IT.

OUR PLAN WAS TO INTRODUCE THE SECOND MAJOR CHARACTER AFTER THE FIRST CHAPTER AND TO GO INTO THE MAIN STORY AFTER ONE OR TWO EPISODES. NOW IT'S GOING TO TAKE US THREE BOOKS TO GET THERE.

YIKES, I'M BABBLING. SHOULD I TALK ABOUT THE "SEAL"? A SEAL IS ENCRYPTED DNA INFORMATION INSCRIBED ON THE BODY IN THE FORM OF A TATTOO. YOU CAN PUT THE SEAL ANYWHERE YOU LIKE. IN OUR TIME, IT'S ANALOGOUS TO OUR ID. BY INSCRIBING IT ONTO THE BODY, IT STORES YOUR RECORD OF HEREDITARY DISEASES, BOTH FROM YOUR FAMILY'S PAST AND FOR POTENTIAL FUTURE GENERATIONS. THE MAIN ADVANTAGE OF THIS IS, IF YOU COLLAPSE AND GO TO THE HOSPITAL, THE DOCTORS AND NURSES CAN QUICKLY FIND OUT WHAT MIGHT BE CAUSING YOUR CONDITION WITHOUT COMPLEX TESTING. ALSO, WHEN IT COMES TO WANTED CRIMINALS, THEY WON'T BE ABLE TO ROAM AMONGST DECENT PEOPLE QUITE SO FREELY. IT WOULD BE LIKE IN THE MOVIE 'MINORITY REPORT'. YOU CAN ILLEGALLY ALTER YOUR SEAL TO MASK YOUR MISDEEDS, HOWEVER; FOR INSTANCE, YOU CAN USE AN INTERFERING CREAM THAT WORKS LIKE SUNBLOCK TO PREVENT OUTSIDE READINGS OF THE ENCRYPTION, OR AN INVISIBLE MAN SYSTEM THAT CAN CONFUSE SENSORS. THE REASON WHY I INITIALLY PUT GOGGLES ON TUBLERUN WAS TO MAKE IT BLOCK HIS ENCRYPTION FROM INTRUSIVE DECIPHERING...BUT THEN I THOUGHT OF THE INTERCEPTION CREAM. I'M DIGRESSING AGAIN, BUT PEOPLE OF TUBLERUN'S AGE GET THEIR SEALS SOMEWHERE NEAR ONE OF THEIR EYES. VERNA HAS IT ON HER ARM, AND LOREL...WELL, SOMEWHERE ON HIS BODY. ECLIPTOR'S BEGINS AROUND HIS WAIST AND GOES DOWN HIS RUMP. (SMILES) MARTI FIRST HAD HERS SURROUNDING HER EYES...BUT THEN I SAW A MODEL IN A MAGAZINE WHO HAD DOTS CENTERED RIGHT UNDER HER EYES, AND IT LOOKED AMAZING. THE EDITORS DIDN'T REALLY LIKE THAT AND HAS INSISTED ON IT BEING CHANGED, SO NOW I'M THINKING OF PUTTING IT RIGHT BELOW HER BELLYBUTTON (QUITE SATISFIED).

WELL, ANYWAY...I COUNT CHAPTER 7 AMONG THE TOP 10 WORKS I WANT TO THROW AWAY AND DO OVER AGAIN. THE CHARACTERS CAME OUT BADLY, THEIR PHYSICAL APPEARANCE BEING MORE MUCH POORER THAN USUAL...BUT THE FUTURE'S MORE IMPORTANT THAN THE PAST, RIGHT?

I PROMISE TO WORK HARD, EVEN HARDER THAN BEFORE....

Can you feel the souls of the antiques?
Do you believe?

D id you know that an antique possesses a soul of its own? The Antique Gift shop specializes in such items that charm and captivate the buyers that they are destined to belong to. Guided by a mysterious and charismatic shopkeeper, the enchanted relics lead their new owners on a journey into the alternate cosmic universe to their true destinies. Eerily bittersweet and dolefully melancholy, The Antique Gift shop opens up a portal to a world where torn lovers unite, broken friendships are mended, and regrets are resolved. Can you feel the power of the antiques?

Available at bookstores near you!

The Antique Gift Shop 1~2
Lee Eun

US: $10.95
CAN: $13.95

Available at bookstores near you!

One thousand and one nights 1~2

Han SeungHee · Jeon JinSeok

Totally new Arabian nights where Shahrazad is a guy!

Everyone knows the story of Shahrazad and her wonderful tales in the Arabian Nights. For one thousand and one nights, the stories that she created entertained the mad Sultan and eventually saved her life. In this version, our Shahrazad is a guy who wanted to save his sister from the mad Sultan by disguising himself as a woman. When he puts his life on the line, what kind of strange and wacky stories would he tell? This new twist on one of the greatest classical tales, Arabian Nights, might just keep you awake for another <one thousand and one nights>.

KHAN

Freak vol.1

Story by DongEun Yi
Art by Chung Yu

Translation / WonJae Huh
English Adaptation / Jamie S. Rich
Touch-up and Lettering / Terri Delgado · Marshall Dillon
Graphic Design / EunKyung Kim

ICE Kunion

English Adaptation Editor / HyeYoung Im · J. Torres
Managing Editor / Marshall Dillon
Marketing Manager / Erik Ko
Senior Editor / JuYoun Lee
Editorial Director / MoonJung Kim
Managing Director / Jackie Lee
Publisher and C.E.O. / JaeKook Chun

Freak Vol.1 © 2005 by Yi Dong Eun & Yu Chung
All rights reserved. This translated edition is published by arrangement with Haksan
Publishing Co.,Ltd. in Korea.
English edition Vol.1 © 2006 by ICE Kunion.

Published by ICE Kunion
SIGONGSA 2F Yeil Bldg. 1619-4, Seocho-dong, Seocho-gu, Seoul, 137-878, Korea

ISBN 89-527-4605-8

First printing, August 2006
10 9 8 7 6 5 4 3 2 1
Printed in Canada

www.ICEkunion.com/www.koreanmanhwa.com